Authors & Artists for Young Adults

ISSN 1040-5682

Authors & Artists for Young Adults

VOLUME 40

GALE GROUP

Detroit
New York
San Francisco
London
Boston
Woodbridge, CT

Scot Peacock, *Managing Editor, Literature Product*
Mark W. Scott, *Publisher, Literature Product*

Frank Castronova, *Senior Editor*
Kristen A. Dorsch, Lisa Kumar, Thomas McMahon, Colleen Tavor, *Editors*
Shayla Hawkins, Arlene M. Johnson, Thomas Wiloch, *Associate Editors*
Alana Joli Foster, Jennifer Kilian, Anita Sundaresan, *Assistant Editors*
Anna Marie Dahn, *Administrative Support*
Joshua Kondek, *Technical Training Specialist*

Alan Hedblad, Joyce Nakamura *Managing Editors*
Susan M. Trosky, *Literature Content Coordinator*

Maria Franklin, *Permissions Manager*
Julie Juengling, *Permissions Associate*

Theresa Rocklin, *Manager, Technical Support Systems*
Ryan Cartmill, *Programmer/Analyst*

Mary Beth Trimper, *Manager, Composition and Prepress*
Carolyn A. Roney, *Composition Specialist*

Dorothy Maki, *Manager, Manufacturing*
Stacy L. Melson, *Buyer*

Barbara J. Yarrow, *Manager, Imaging and Media Content*
Randy Bassett, *Imaging Supervisor*
Robert Duncan, Dan Newell *Imaging Specialists*
Pamela A. Reed, *Imaging Coordinator*
Dean Dauphinais, *Senior Editor*
Robyn V. Young, *Project Editor*
Kelly A. Quin, *Image Editor*

Library of Congress Catalog Card Number 89-641100
ISBN 0-7876-4673-3
ISSN 1040-5682

10 9 8 7 6 5 4 3 2 1

Printed in the United States of America

Contents

Introduction

Authors and Artists for Young Adults is a reference series designed to serve the needs of middle school, junior high, and high school students interested in creative artists. Originally inspired by the need to bridge the gap between Gale's *Something about the Author,* created for children, and *Contemporary Authors,* intended for older students and adults, *Authors and Artists for Young Adults* has been expanded to cover not only an international scope of authors, but also a wide variety of other artists.

Although the emphasis of the series remains on the writer for young adults, we recognize that these readers have diverse interests covering a wide range of reading levels. The series therefore contains not only those creative artists who are of high interest to young adults, including cartoonists, photographers, music composers, bestselling authors of adult novels, media directors, producers, and performers, but also literary and artistic figures studied in academic curricula, such as influential novelists, playwrights, poets, and painters. The goal of *Authors and Artists for Young Adults* is to present this great diversity of creative artists in a format that is entertaining, informative, and understandable to the young adult reader.

Entry Format

Each volume of *Authors and Artists for Young Adults* will furnish in-depth coverage of twenty to twenty-five authors and artists. The typical entry consists of:

—A detailed biographical section that includes date of birth, marriage, children, education, and addresses.

—A comprehensive bibliography or filmography including publishers, producers, and years.

—Adaptations into other media forms.

—Works in progress.

—A distinctive essay featuring comments on an artist's life, career, artistic intentions, world views, and controversies.

—References for further reading.

—Extensive illustrations, photographs, movie stills, cartoons, book covers, and other relevant visual material.

A cumulative index to featured authors and artists appears in each volume.

Compilation Methods

The editors of *Authors and Artists for Young Adults* make every effort to secure information directly from the authors and artists through personal correspondence and interviews. Sketches on living authors and artists are sent to the biographee for review prior to publication. Any sketches not personally reviewed by biographees or their representatives are marked with an asterisk (*).

Highlights of Forthcoming Volumes

Among the authors and artists planned for future volumes are:

C. S. Adler	Neil Gaiman	Katherine Anne Porter
Brian Aldiss	Federico Garcia Lorca	Philip Pullman
V. C. Andrews	Maurice Gee	Adam Rapp
Franny Billingsley	Margaret Peterson Haddix	Jay Roach
Pearl S. Buck	Joyce Hansen	John H. Ritter
Ken Burns	Norma Howe	Cindy Sherman
Orson Scott Card	Ji-Li Jiang	M. Night Shyamalan
Carolyn Coman	James Joyce	Lemony Snicket
E. E. Cummings	Susanna Kaysen	Jonathan Swift
Jeffery Deaver	David E. Kelley	Julie Taymor
Annie Dillard	E. L. Konigsburg	Gloria Whelan
Bret Easton Ellis	Cormac McCarthy	Judd Winick

Contact the Editor

We encourage our readers to examine the entire *AAYA* series. Please write and tell us if we can make *AAYA* even more helpful to you. Give your comments and suggestions to the editor:

BY MAIL: The Editor, *Authors and Artists for Young Adults*, 27500 Drake Rd., Farmington Hills, MI 48331-3535.

BY TELEPHONE: (800) 347-GALE

Acknowledgments

Grateful acknowledgment is made to the following publishers, authors, and artists for their kind permission to reproduce copyrighted material.

BERENICE ABBOTT. Abbott, Berenice, illustrator. From a cover of *Berenice Abbott, Designer's Window: Bleecker Street.* Aperture Foundation, 1988. Copyright © 1988 by Aperture Foundation. Back jacket/cover copyright © 1985 by Todd Watts. Reproduced by permission. Abbott, Berenice, photographer. From *Berenice Abbott, Triboro Bridge.* Copyright © 1988 by Aperture Foundation. Photographs copyright © 1988 by Commerce Graphics, Ltd. Reproduced by permission. *Nightview, New York, 1932,* photograph by Berenice Abbott. Commerce Graphics Ltd, Inc. Reproduced by permission. *Pennsylvania Station Interior, New York,* photograph by Berenice Abbott. Berenice Abbott/Commerce Graphics Ltd, Inc. Reproduced by permission. Abbott, Berenice, photograph. © 1983 Todd Watts. Reproduced by permission.

AMELIA ATWATER-RHODES. Dinyer, Eric, illustrator. From a cover of *In the Forests of the Night,* by Amelia Atwater-Rhodes. Dell Laurel Leaf, 1999. Jacket illustration copyright 2000 by Cliff Neilson. Both reproduced by permission. Nielsen, Cliff, illustrator. From a jacket of *Demon In My View,* by Amelia Atwater-Rhodes. Delacorte, 2000. Copyright © 2000 by Amelia Atwater-Rhodes. Jacket illustration © 2000 by Cliff Nielson. Reproduced by permission.

GARY L. BLACKWOOD. Nottingham Castle, engraving from *Life in a Medieval Castle,* by Gary L. Blackwood. Reproduced by permission. Blackwood, Gary L., photograph. Reproduced by permission. Illustration from *Life on the Oregon Trail,* by Gary Blackwood. Courtesy of the Library of Congress.

MARION ZIMMER BRADLEY. Hescox, Richard, illustrator. From a cover of *The Forbidden Tower,* by Marion Zimmer Bradley. DAW, 1977. Copyright © 1977 by Marion Zimmer Bradley. Reproduced by permission. Hescox, Richard. From a jacket in *The Heirs of Hammerfell* by Marion Zimmer Bradley. DAW Books, Inc., 1989. Reproduced by permission. Bralds, Braldt, illustrator. From a cover of *The Mists of Avalon,* by Marion Zimmer Bradley. Ballantine Books, 1982. Reproduced by permission of Ballantine Books, a division of Random House, Inc. Bradley, Marion Zimmer, photograph. © Jerry Bauer. Reproduced by permission.

BRUCE COVILLE. Oberheide, Heide, illustrator. From a cover of *Fortune's Journey* by Bruce Coville. Reproduced by permission. Guay, Rebecca, illustrator. From a cover of *Song of the Wanderer,* by Bruce Coville. Scholastic, 1999. Jacket painting © 1999 by Rebecca Guay. Reproduced by permission. Peters, Lisa, illustrator. From a jacket of *Armageddon Summer,* by Bruce Coville and Jane Yolen. Harcourt Brace & Company. Reproduced by the permission of the publisher. Henderson, D. F., illustrator. From a cover of *The Ghost in the Third Row,* by Bruce Coville. Bantam Books, 1987. Cover illustration D. F. Henderson © 1987. All rights reserved. Reproduced by permission of Bantam Books, a division of Bantam Doubleday Dell Publishing Group, Inc. Coville, Bruce, photograph by Jules Fried. Reproduced by permission of Photography by Jules.

FEDOR DOSTOEVSKY. Grigoryevich, Vasily, illustrator. From a cover of *Crime and Punishment,* by Fedor Dostoevsky. Bantam Books, Inc., 1981. Copyright © 1981 by Bantam Books, Inc. Reproduced by permission. Gaydos, Tim, designer. From a cover of *The Adolescent,* by Fedor Dostoevsky. W.W. Norton, 1981. Copyright © 1971 by Andrew R. MacAndrew. Reproduced by permission. Holbein, Hans, illustrator. From *Christ in the Tome,* used on the cover of *The Idiot* by Fedor Dostoevsky. Translated by Alan Myers. Oxford University Press, 1998. Reproduced by permission. Schell, Maria, with Yul Brynner in a scene from the film *The Brothers Karamazov,* 1958, photograph. The Kobal Collection. Reproduced by permission. Dostoevsky, Fedor, photograph. Ardis Publishers. Reproduced by permission.

W. E. B. DU BOIS. From a cover of *Darkwater: Voices from Within the Veil,* by W. E. B. Du Bois. Dover, 1999. Copyright © 1999 by Dover Publications, Inc. Reproduced by permission. From a jacket of *The Souls of Black*

Folk, by W. E. B. Du Bois. Random House, 1996. Jacket portrait courtesy of the Bettman Archive. Du Bois, W. E. B., photograph courtesy of the Library of Congress.

SHELBY FOOTE. From a cover of *The Civil War: A Narrative, Volume 1: Fort Sumter to Perryville,* written by Shelby Foote. Vintage Books, 1986. Copyright © 1958 by Shelby Foote. Reproduced by permission. From a cover of *The Civil War: A Narrative, Volume 2: Fredericksburg to Meridian,* written by Shelby Foote. Vintage Books, 1986. Copyright © 1963 by Shelby Foote. Reproduced by permission. From a cover of *The Civil War: A Narrative, Volume 3: Red River to Appomattox,* by Shelby Foote. Vintage Books, 1987. Copyright © 1974 By Shelby Foote. Reproduced by permission of Random House, Ltd. Foote, Shelby, photograph. The Bettmann Archive/Newsphotos, Inc.. Reproduced by permission.

JACK GANTOS. Borges, Jose Francisco, illustrator. Book cover from *Desire Lines* by Jack Gantos. © Lion Publishing. Reproduced by permission. Szpura, Beata, illustrator. From a cover of *Heads or Tails: Stories from the Sixth Grade,* written by Jack Gantos. Reproduced by permission. Szpura, Beata, illustrator. From a cover of *Jack's Black Book* by Jack Gantos. Both reproduced by permission of Beata Szpura. Rubel, Nicole, illustrator. From a cover of *Rotten Ralph,* written by Jack Gantos. Reproduced by permission of the illustrator. Gantos, Jack, photograph. Reproduced by permission.

EDWARD GOREY. Gorey, Edward, illustrator. From a cover of *The Wolves of Willoughby Chase,* by Joan Aiken. Yearling Books, 1987. Reproduced by permission of Bantam Doubleday Dell Books for Young Readers. Gorey, Edward, illustrator. From his book *The Gashly Crumb Tinies or, After the Outing.* Harcourt, Brace & Company, 1991. Copyright © renewed 1991 by Edward Gorey. Reproduced by permission. Gorey, Edward, illustrator. From his book *The Haunted Tea-Cozy: A Dispirited and Distasteful Diversion for Christmas.* Harcourt Brace & Company, 1997. Copyright © 1997 by Edward Gorey. Reproduced by permission. Gorey, Edward, photograph by Susan Ragan. AP/Wide World Photos. Reproduced by permission.

TONY HILLERMAN. Grado, Janet illustrator. From a cover of *The Boy Who Made Dragonfly,* a myth retold by Tony Hillerman. University of New Mexico, 1972. Text copyright 1972 by Tony Hillerman. Reproduced by permission. Hillerman, Tony, photograph. AP/Wide World Photos. Reproduced by permission.

NALO HOPKINSON. Altidort, Michel Ange, painter. Book cover illustration, *Mermaid and Butterflies,* by Michel Ange Altidort, from *Whispers from the Cotton Tree Root,* edited by Nalo Hopkinson. Invisible Cities Press, 2000. © 2000 by University of Central Florida Library. Reproduced by permission. Messier, Linda, illustrator. From a cover of *Brown Girl in the Ring,* written by Nalo Hopkinson. Warner Books, 1998. Copyright © 1998 by Nalo Hopkinson. Reproduced by permission. From the cover of *Midnight Robber,* by Nalo Hopkinson. Warner Books, Inc. 2000. Copyright © 2000 by Nalo Hopkinson. Reproduced by permission. Hopkinson, Nalo, photograph by Jon Baturin. Reproduced by permission of Nalo Hopkinson.

PEG KEHRET. Dudash, C. Michael, illustrator. From a cover of *My Brother Made Me Do It,* by Peg Kehret. Minstrel Books, 2000. Reproduced by permission. Dudash, C. Michael, illustrator. From a cover of *The Secret Journey,* by Peg Kehret. Minstrel, 1999. Copyright © 1999 by Peg Kehret. Reproduced by permission. Anderson, Renee, photographer. From a cover of *Small Steps: The Year I Got Polio* by Peg Kehret. Albert Whitman & Company, 1996. Reproduced by permission. Kehret, Peg, photograph. Reproduced by permission of Peg Kehret.

A. C. LEMIEUX. de Groat, Diane. From a cover of *Fruit Flies, Fish & Fortune Cookies* by A. C. LeMieux. Tambourine Books, 1994. Reproduced by permission of Tambourine Books, a division of William Morrow & Co., Inc. Velasquez, Eric, illustrator. From a jacket in *Do Angels Sing the Blues?* by A. C. LeMieux. Jacket art copyright © 1995 by Eric Velasquez. Reproduced by permission of Tambourine Books, a division of William Morrow & Co., Inc. LeMieux, A. C., photograph by Helen Neafsey. Reproduced by courtesy of the Westport News/Helen Neafsey, photographer.

LEONARDO DA VINCI. Leonardo da Vinci, painter. Portrait of the *Mona Lisa,* by The New York Library Collection. Reproduced by permission. Leonardo da Vinci, illustrations. Corbis Corporation. All reproduced by permission. Leonardo da Vinci (self-portrait), illustration. The Kobal Collection. Reproduced by permission.

PETER MATTHIESSEN. Frank, Mary, illustrator. From a cover of *African Silences,* written by Peter Matthiessen. Vintage Books, 1992. Copyright 1991 by Peter Matthiessen. Reproduced by permission of

Berenice Abbott

■ Personal

Born July 17, 1898, in Springfield, OH; died December 9, 1991, in Maine; daughter of Charles E. and Alice (Bunn) Abbott. *Education:* Attended Ohio State University, 1917–18; studied painting and sculpture in New York City, 1918–21, in Paris under Bourdelle and Brancusi, and at Künstschule, Berlin. *Hobbies and other interests:* Travel, playing the concertina.

■ Career

Photographic assistant to Man Ray, Paris, 1923–25; portrait photographer in Paris, 1926–29; portrait and freelance magazine photographer in New York City, 1929–35; Federal Art Project, New York City, photographer, 1935–39. Teacher at New School for Social Research, New York City; lecturer, broadcaster of radio presentations. *Exhibitions:* Abbott's photographs have been exhibited at one–woman shows in Paris, 1926, at the Museum of Modern Art, 1939, 1970, at Art Institute of Chicago, 1951, and at Smithsonian Institution, 1969. She had individual exhibitions or has been the subject of exhibitions at over fifty venues across the United States and Europe. Her work is in the permanent collections of the Museum of Modern Art, New York, NY, the Metropolitan Museum of Art, New York, NY, the Smithsonian Institution, Washington, DC, the Museum of Fine Arts, Boston, MA, the International Museum of Photography, George Eastman House, Rochester, NY, the Art Institute of Chicago, and the Bibliothèque Nationale, Paris, among others.

■ Writings

A Guide to Better Photography, Crown, 1941, revised edition published as *New Guide to Better Photography*, 1953.
The View Camera Made Simple, Ziff–Davis, 1948.
The World of Atget, Horizon Press, 1964.
Photographs, Horizon Press, 1970.

Also the author of numerous articles on photography and photographers in *Popular Photography, Art Front, The Complete Photographer,* and *Art News,* among others. Editor, *Lisette Model,* New York, 1980.

PHOTOGRAPHER

Elizabeth McCausland, *Changing New York,* Dutton, 1939, published as *New York in the Thirties,* Dover, 1973, and *Berenice Abbott: Changing New York,* The Museum of the City of New York, 1998.
Henry W. Lanier, *Greenwich Village: Today and Yesterday,* Harper, 1949.

Evans G. Valens, *Magnet* (juvenile), World Publishing, 1964.

Valens, *Motion* (juvenile), World Publishing, 1965.

Chenoweth Hall, *A Portrait of Maine*, Macmillan, 1968.

Valens, *The Attractive Universe: Gravity and the Shape of Space* (juvenile), World Publishing, 1969.

(With others) Margaretta K. Mitchell, *Recollections: Ten Women of Photography*, Viking Press (New York City), 1979.

(And author of commentary) Hank O'Neal, *Berenice Abbott, American Photographer*, introduction by John Canaday, McGraw–Hill (New York City), 1982.

Berenice Abbott, the '20s and the '30s: A Traveling Exhibition, Smithsonian Institution Press (Washington, DC), 1982.

Nancy Tousley, *The Berenice Abbott Portfolios*, Glenbow Museum (Calgary, Canada), 1982.

Berenice Abbott, with an essay by Julia Van Haaften, Aperture Foundation (New York City), 1988.

Berenice Abbott, Photographer: A Modern Vision: A Selection of Photographs and Essays, edited with an introduction by Julia Van Haaften, New York Public Library (New York City), 1989.

(Editor, with Virginia M. Dortch, and others) *Peggy Guggenheim and Her Friends*, Berenice (Milan), 1994.

Bonnie Yochelson, *Berenice Abbott at Work: The Making of Changing New York*, New Press, Museum of the City of New York (New York City), 1997.

The aerial photograph *Nightview, New York, 1932* was one of a number of Abbott's works that glorified the Manhattan skyline.

■ Sidelights

"At a time when 'career women' were not only unconventional but controversial," wrote G. Aimee Ergas in *Artists: From Michelangelo to Maya Lin*, "[Berenice Abbott] established herself as one of the nation's most gifted photographers." Her work in portraiture, chronicling the residents of Paris in the 1920s, in cityscape, detailing the many facets of New York City during the 1930s, and exploring the realms of science in the 1950s and 1960s have earned her accolades and a special place in the canon of American photographers. Additionally, her work as a teacher of photography introduced a new generation to her theories on photography. Her championing of the French photographer Eugene Atget was a lifelong quest, leading to the groundbreaking publication of *The World of Atget* in 1964. In her photography, Abbott was a proponent of realism and the documentary approach, a style reflected in her last major project—recording the views along Route 1 from Maine to Florida. Her recognition came late, in part because of her tireless campaign to save and preserve the work of Atget, with whose work she had become familiar as a young student in Paris. So dedicated was Abbott to promoting Atget's legacy that she allowed some of her own work to go relatively unnoticed until after she had assured Atget his proper place in the history of photography. Abbott is now recognized as one of the foremost photographers of the twentieth century and is credited with influencing the development of photography by shifting its early emphasis on pictorialism or "artiness" to an appreciation for realism.

Abbott was born in Springfield, Ohio, on July 17, 1898, to Alice and Charles E. Abbott. Shortly after her birth, the couple divorced and Abbott's three older siblings went to live with their father while Abbott stayed with her mother. This split remained permanent throughout Abbott's life: she had little contact with either her siblings or her father. Raised an only child under circumstances which Abbott herself later described as unhappy, she found a certain self–reliance at an early age. Part of the unhappiness she experienced was in no little part due to the repressive view of contemporary society regarding a woman's role in the world. At a time when women were only just gaining the vote and when their proper place was deemed to be in the home, a rebellious spirit such as Abbott's would certainly run up against the wall of conservative social mores. Independent and somewhat defiant, Abbott showed her true spirit early on by changing her given name from Bernice to Berenice—she thought it sounded better with an extra vowel. The example of her parents' divorce as well as the strictures that marriage usually imposed upon women of the time may have led to her decision never to marry.

Entering Ohio State University, Abbott planned on a career in journalism, but quickly became disenchanted with academic life. In 1918 she visited a former classmate, Sue Jenkins, in New York. Jenkins and her future husband, Jimmy Light, were both involved in productions at the Provincetown Playhouse and introduced the eager Abbott to the delights of bohemian culture in New York's Greenwich Village. Life in the Village was to Abbott's liking. Initially she sought to continue in her goal of becoming a journalist, enrolling in Columbia University for that purpose. But after only a week, she once again decided the real world was where she needed to be. As she later noted to Margaretta K. Mitchell in *Recollections: Ten Women of Photography,* Columbia University "seemed like a hell of a sausage factory." This was the end of her dreams of becoming a journalist.

Influenced by the arty life in Greenwich Village, Abbott took part in theater productions and became interested in art and sculpting. In New York she met some of the major art figures of the day, including the critic Malcolm Cowley, the poet Djuna Barnes, the painter Marcel Duchamp, and the photographer Man Ray. Both Ray and Duchamp, well–known Dadaists, had just come from France, and Duchamp became one of Abbott's first clients when he commissioned her to cast a chess set in the small apartment/studio she had set up. But art did not pay the bills. For over three years Abbott worked at a series of temporary jobs such as waiting tables and modeling. In New York she found her artistic self, but increasingly after the World War I the art scene was shifting its base to Paris. In 1921, Abbott bought a one–way ticket to that new world of art.

The Paris Years and Atget

Abbott hit Paris, like so many other American artists flocking to the city of light, with little money but lots of hope. By this time she was determined

A tribute to the architecture of the late nineteenth century, Abbott's 1934 *Pennsylvania Station Interior, New York* serves as a record of a space that would be drastically altered later in the century.

to become a sculptor. "I thought I may as well be poor there as here," she later commented in *Recollections.* In Paris, she studied under Antoine Bourdelle at the Academie de la Grande Chaumiere, again taking a series of menial jobs to pay her way. After two years of struggling in Paris, Abbott went to Berlin to further her sculpting studies at the Künstschule for almost one year. En route back to Paris in 1924, she left a recently completed stone sculpture on the platform of the Cologne station in order not to miss her train. This symbolic act put an end to her dreams of a life in sculpture.

Once back in Paris, she resumed contact with the large group of artist friends she had become acquainted with there. These included many of the luminaries of twentieth–century art and thought, including Jean Cocteau, Janet Flanner, André Gide, the young Ernest Hemingway, James Joyce, Sylvia Beach, Max Ernst, Leo Stein and his sister, Gertrude, Edna St. Vincent Millay, and the famously wealthy American heiress and patroness of the arts, Peggy

Guggenheim. She also resumed her friendship with Duchamp and Ray, and it was Ray who ultimately got the young American expatriate into photography.

Ray, in need of an apprentice in the darkroom, was willing to take on someone completely unfamiliar with photography so that he could train the person properly. Abbott took him up on this and proved a quick study, learning not only the technical requirements of the darkroom, but also the finer points of shooting pictures herself. Soon she found herself in demand among many of her friends as a portrait photographer. In 1925, while at Man Ray's studio still learning her art, Abbott first came into contact with the work of Eugene Atget.

Born in 1857, Atget had spent decades photographing scenes of old Paris with a standard box camera on a tripod using 180 x 240–mm glass negatives. His collection numbered about 10,000 separate scenes of the city, making it one of the most thorough archives ever assembled of any city. Atget looked upon himself as a documenter of real life rather than an art photographer. He eschewed the soft–focus look then all the vogue in favor of a starkly realistic look, selling his urban views to painters and museums alike. By 1920 he had sold much of his work to the French government, and had, ironically, become the pet cause of Dadaists and Surrealists like Man Ray, who saw a metaphorical clarity in Atget's later work. What they took for a naive approach to the real world was, in fact, Atget's own realistic signature, and this appealed greatly to Abbott. His unmanipulated, non–arty technique spoke to her and influenced her own work. From that point on, she saw herself as following somewhat in Atget's path.

Abbott's first one–woman show was held at the gallery Le Sacer du Princeps in Paris in 1926. It was made up mostly of portraits of many of the avant garde artists she knew at the time, including Cocteau, Joyce, and Gide, and it was indeed portraiture that occupied most of her Paris years. Setting up a studio on the Left Bank, she attracted a clientele ranging from the bohemian to the aristocratic. In an interview with *Art in America*, Abbott revealed the factors that contributed to her success as a portrait photographer. "Each person was extremely important to me," she said. "I wasn't trying to make a still life of them, but a person. It's kind of an exchange between people—it has to be—and I enjoyed it." Perhaps her best–known portrait of the time, *James Joyce*, shows the Irish writer in a characteristically dreamy mood, staring myopically off into the middle distance, a fedora stuck at a jaunty angle upon his head. She was known for allowing the

personality of her subjects to come through. "The portraits she made during the 1920s comprise a catalog of the artistic and intellectual life of that time," according to Julia Van Haaften in her *Berenice Abbott*. "Their straightforward artistry masks their great subtlety; Abbott permitted each personality to project outward to the viewer." Noting that these portraits were mainly done in the studio where the photographer could feasibly manipulate all sorts of effects, Van Haaften observed that Abbott avoided such manipulations, preferring to allow "realism to guide her style."

A second show followed, part of a group exhibition at the First Salon of Independent Photographers, which also included works by Ray as well as André Kertesz. Throughout this time, Abbott also kept up her acquaintanceship with Atget; the only existing photo of him was made by Abbott shortly before his death in 1927. Upon his death, Abbot acquired about 8,000 prints and an additional 1,500 glass–plate negatives of that master of French realist photography.

By the time Abbott left Paris, she was firmly in control of her own style of photography, one that critics claimed carried over into her later work and shaped her realistic style. As Abbott noted in *Art in America*, her idea of the "realistic image" referred to the early style of photography which expected photographs to imitate paintings, emphasizing simulation. Holding this to be inevitable and unfortunate, Abbott believed that the view formed by a camera's lens should be the final "reality" presented to the public, making the rearrangement and distortion of what the camera sees unnecessary. The photographer must rely on his or her own instincts. "A photographer," Abbott maintained, "explores and discovers and reacts to the world he lives in. There's also the matter of discernment—the way you interpret things, see things and relate them; the way you bring your subjects together. . . . That to me is the art of photography."

Back to New York

Abbott paid a return visit to New York in 1929, intending to remain only a few weeks. However, she decided to stay in this vital, energetic city which had changed so much in the eight years of her absence. Setting up a portrait studio, she managed to reserve a day each week for photographing the changing sights of Manhattan and the other boroughs of New York City, just as Atget had done for Paris. She took the Atget approach: a detached but meticulously accurate and methodical framing of

Photographed in 1937 while Abbott was in the employ of the Works Projects Administration during the height of the Great Depression, *Triboro Bridge, East 125th Street Approach* **offers a unique view of this complex that spans the East River.**

each shot. Initially she used a small camera to make sketches of the locations she was interested in; then she followed these up with regular shoots using an 8 x 10–inch view camera, which became her standard equipment, though it somewhat restricted her access to certain difficult–to–reach views. She spent much of the next decade in this project, hauling around her camera to view the city at day and night, from the docks to the neighborhoods, and from construction sites to vacant warehouses. That many of these sites disappeared during the 1930s, torn down to make way for skyscrapers, makes Abbott's photographic record even more valuable. Additionally during these years, she arranged sales and printings of Atget's work, leading to the publication of a volume of his work in 1930.

Unfortunately, Abbott's portrait gallery never gained quite the same repute in New York as it had in Paris, and she was forced to appeal for funding from various institutions, including the City of New York and the Guggenheim Foundation for the project she had come to call "Changing New York." But this was in the middle of the Depression and most of her funding requests were rejected. Meanwhile, Abbott took on photographic commissions for the architectural historian Henry Russell Hitchcock, Jr., that focused both on modern architecture on the Eastern seaboard and architecture from before the Civil War as found primarily in the southeastern United States.

Finally in 1935, after she had gained notice from an exhibition of some of her early New York photos at the Museum of Modern Art and at the newly opened Museum of the City of New York, Abbott was funded by the Works Progress Administration at $35 per week to continue with her photography project of New York in transition. She carried on with the work for four more years, until funding ran out and she had to abandon the project. At the same time, beginning in 1935, Abbott began teaching photography at the New School for Social Research in New York, and would remain there for the next two decades.

Dutton published her *Changing New York* in 1939. As Abbott wrote in the book, "To make the portrait of a city is a life work and no one portrait suffices, because the city is always changing. Everything in the city is properly part of the story—its physical body of brick, stone, steel, glass, wood, its lifeblood of living, breathing men and women." Abbott's most lauded work, *Changing New York*, has a text by Elizabeth McCausland, Abbott's long–time companion whom she met at her first solo exhibition in 1934. Commenting on Abbott's style as well as on the photographs in *Changing New York*, a writer for the *New York Times Book Review* noted that "the value of [this series of photographs on New York City in the early 1930s] lies in its 'straight photography.'" Reviewing a 1998 museum exhibit of photos from this collection, Chuck Myers commented in the *Knight–Ridder/Tribune News Service*, "Between 1935 to 1939, Abbott shot 305 black–and–white images of Gotham, producing a rich body of work that has long since become one of the greatest single visual chronicles of a major American city." Myers further observed, "Abbott shot the Big Apple from just about every conceivable angle, in a crisp documentary style. Often, her pictures present the city as a mirror of the modern age, with towering buildings, expansive bridges and elevated public rail system." In addition to the architectural sites, there are also human venues: a butcher in front of his shop, a line of movie–goers waiting for the coming attraction, street vendors, and bustling commuters thronging the city boulevards.

Writing in the magazine *America* of *Changing New York*, Paul Mariani called Abbott's photographs a "superb collection" with "timeless images of a New York there and not there today." One notable exception to the landmarks of New York is the pointed exclusion of the Empire State Building in the collection; Abbott rejected such clichés. Vivian Gornick, commenting in the *Los Angeles Times* on Abbott's classic work, declared, "It is this, the excitement of a live moment of social change as witnessed by a responsive artist, that characterizes 'Changing New York.' . . . The whole of it is photographed in a hard, clear, unshadowed light of modernist interpretation that now, 60 years later, induces a kind of yearning for the uncluttered calm of that harsh time." Gornick concluded that Abbott's work "is like an archaeological dig. . . . New York is like a photograph out of its own past . . . during some legendary time not so long ago."

A Lens Focused on Science

After the publication of *Changing New York*, Abbott turned to other work. In 1941 she published her *Guide to Better Photography*. As a writer for *Gay and Lesbian Biography* pointed out, this guide was "[l]ess instructional than ideological." Abbott, as always the standard bearer for realism, wrote in her *Guide*: "Technic for technic's sake is like art for art's sake—a phrase of artistic isolationism, a creative escapism. . . . In short the something done by photography is communication." In *Berenice Abbott: Photographer* Van Haaften called Abbott's *Guide* "an eloquent and powerful document of the best photography of the period, providing great insight into an empathetic spirit that Abbott was able to

Designer's Window, Bleeker Street was photographed in 1947, the same year Abbott opened her House of Photography in New York City to promote innovation in the photographic arts.

liberate deep within herself." Abbott further commented in her *Guide:* "As I see straight photography, it means using the medium itself, not as painting or theater. . . . All subject matter is open to interpretation, [and] requires the imaginative and intelligent objectivity of the person behind the camera."

Abbott's concern for such communication and her desire to include all subject matter led her into the next phase of her creative life: the illustration and explication of science through photography. Ahead of her time, Abbott spent much of the next two decades perfecting her techniques—such as photographing electricity—as well as developing equipment to the service of science. From 1947 to 1958 she ran the House of Photography in New York, a firm established to sell her photographic inventions. However, this business was a failure and her approaches were largely rebuffed by the scientific community, contemptuous of the need for anything more than simple line drawings to illustrate their work. Then came the Russian advances in space and the launch of *Sputnik* in 1957. In the wake of this, the United States poured money into the sciences and Abbott was invited to take part in the Physical Science Study Committee sponsored by the Massachusetts Institute of Technology. Set on revamping the science curriculum in American high schools, this group was eager to use photographs by Abbott in new physics books. With characteristic commitment, Abbott threw herself into the project, patenting even more new photographic equipment able to shoot such phenomena as magnetism, light refraction, and wave action. Some of her best illustrations were used in high school science books of the time such as *Magnet, The Attractive Universe,* and *Motion.*

If you enjoy the works of Berenice Abbott, you might want to check out the following:

The documentary–style photographs of Eugene Atget, whose work Abbott championed throughout her life.
The Depression–era work of Walker Evans, a pioneer in documentary photography.
The photography of Man Ray, whose Paris studio served as a training ground for Abbott in the 1920s.

In 1956, Abbott bought a house in Maine, and it was there she spent much of her time in the last decades of her life. In 1964, she published her long–

contemplated *The World of Atget;* in 1968, *A Portrait of Maine* appeared, a collection of photos of her newly adopted state. Honored with solo and retrospective exhibitions throughout the world, Abbott also won several honorary degrees, including one from the New School for Social Research where she had for so long taught. Suffering from congestive heart failure, she died in Monson, Maine, in 1991 at the age of ninety–three. As a contributor for *Contemporary Photographers* noted, "Berenice Abbott claims her rightful place as one of the greatest of American photographers. . . . The value of her contribution to the medium should be based not only on the enormous concepts she herself developed and photographed but should also include her defense and advancement of the medium itself which can be summed up in her appreciation of Atget's work." Ergas concluded, "[Abbott] became something of a legend in her own time, honored as a pioneer woman artist who conquered a male–dominated field. . . . But perhaps most importantly, students of the medium recognized the talent and artistry behind Abbott's work, among which reside some of the prize gems of the twentieth–century photography."

■ Biographical and Critical Sources

BOOKS

Abbott, Berenice, *Berenice Abbott, the 20s and the 30s: A Traveling Exhibition,* Smithsonian Institution Press, 1982.
Abbott, Berenice, *A Guide to Better Photography,* Crown, 1941.
Atelier Man Ray: Berenice Abbott, Jacques–André Boiffard, Bill Brandt, Lee Miller: 1920–1935, Le Centre (Paris), 1982.
Contemporary Photographers, 3rd edition, St. James Press, 1996.
Ergas, G. Aimee, "Berenice Abbott," *Artists: From Michelangelo to Maya Lin,* Volume 1, Gale, 1995, pp. 1–7.
Gay and Lesbian Biography, St. James Press, 1997.
Mitchell, Margaretta K., *Recollections: Ten Women of Photography,* Viking, 1979.
O'Neal, Hank, and Berenice Abbott, *Berenice Abbott, American Photographer,* introduction by John Canaday, McGraw–Hill, 1982.
Tousley, Nancy, *The Berenice Abbott Portfolios,* Glenbow Museum, 1982.
Van Haaften, Julia, and Berenice Abbot, *Berenice Abbott, Photographer: A Modern Vision: A Selection of Photographs and Essays,* New York Public Library, 1989.

Van Haaften, Julia, and Berenice Abbot, *Berenice Abbott*, Aperture Foundation, 1988.

Yochelson, Bonnie, *Berenice Abbott at Work: The Making of Changing New York*, New Press, Museum of the City of New York, 1997.

PERIODICALS

America, May 9, 1998, Paul Mariani, review of *Berenice Abbott: Changing New York*, pp. 21–22.

Art in America, November–December, interview with Berenice Abbott, 1976.

Knight–Ridder/Tribune News Service, November 11, 1998, Chuck Myers, "Berenice Abbott's Photographic Chronicle of the 1930s New York at D.C. Museum," p. K2293.

Los Angeles Times, December 7, 1997, Vivian Gornick, "Bright Lights, Big City; 'Berenice Abbott: Changing New York'."

Modern Photography, September, 1976.

Nation, April 29, 1939.

New Republic, May 17, 1939.

New York Times Book Review, April 16, 1939, review of *Changing New York*; September 28, 1941.

Popular Photographer, September, 1938; May, 1939; February, 1940.

Springfield Republican, April 9, 1939; July 6, 1941.

USA Today Magazine, May, 1998, p. 70.

■ Obituaries

PERIODICALS

Times (London), December 14, 1991, p. 16.*

—*Sketch by J. Sydney Jones*

Amelia Atwater-Rhodes

■ Personal

Born April 16, 1984, in Silver Spring, MD; daughter of William (a public–policy consultant in econometrics) and Susan (a school viceprincipal).

■ Addresses

Home—Concord, MA. *Office*—c/o Kathleen Dunn, Random House, kdunn@randomhouse.com.

■ Career

Author and student.

■ Awards, Honors

American Library Association (ALA), Quick Picks for Reluctant Young Readers citation, 2001, for *Demon in My View.*

■ Writings

In the Forests of the Night, Delacorte, 1999.
Demon in My View, Delacorte, 2000.

■ Work in Progress

Further novels in her vampire cycle.

■ Sidelights

Move over, Anne Rice; hold your hat, Christopher Pike. Amelia Atwater–Rhodes has proved herself a publishing phenomenon: At age fifteen, she found herself a literary celebrity after the publication of her vampire novel *In the Forests of the Night* in 1999. A resident of Concord, Massachusetts, she shares literary fame with a host of big guns from the American literary canon who were also once residents in that town, including Henry David Thoreau, Ralph Waldo Emerson, Nathaniel Hawthorne, and Louisa May Alcott, yet she shares a similarity only with Alcott. Alcott also penned a novel as a teenager, but had to wait for adult fame to get her first book published. No such hardships attach to Atwater–Rhodes, who penned her first novel at age thirteen and then landed a publishing contract for it on her fourteenth birthday. Other early writers come to mind: Anne Frank, who began writing her diaries at thirteen, and S. E. Hinton, who wrote *The Outsiders* at sixteen.

The novelty of Atwater–Rhodes's youth attracted a great deal of media attention, as did her serious devotion to the practice of witchcraft. Reviewers gave her debut book guarded praise, complimenting, in

IN THE
FORESTS
OF THE
NIGHT

Amelia Atwater-Rhodes

Atwater–Rhodes' debut novel, published while its author was still attending high school English classes, depicts a 300–year–old vampire who is forced to combat her archrival in order to survive.

particular, its darkly atmospheric prose style. With publication of her second novel, *Demon in My View,* at age sixteen, however, the Atwater–Rhodes phenomenon appeared to have turned into a one–person publishing industry: two further books were quickly contracted and, with her shelves full of twenty–four more completed novels of witchcraft and vampirism and another couple of dozen percolating inside her computer, it seems the youthful novelist runs no risk of being discounted as a one–trick pony. But notoriety, if not fame, has not gone to the teenager's head. "Her mother still makes her do the dishes," commented Susan Carpenter in the

Los Angeles Times, writing about a plethora of teen writers making it in publishing. "Her teachers don't cut her any slack on homework." And Atwater–Rhodes herself is somewhat low–key about her precocious success: "I'm still a high school teen," she told Carpenter.

Forms Early Love for the Supernatural

Atwater–Rhodes was born in Silver Spring, Maryland, on April 16, 1984. Her family subsequently moved to Concord, Massachusetts, where she attended Peabody Middle School and Concord Carlisle High School. Her mother, Susan, serves as a viceprincipal at Acton–Boxborough High School, while her father, William, is an econometrician employed as a public–policy consultant. While both parents acknowledged being horror fiction fans, loving in particular the novels of Anne Rice, Atwater–Rhodes particularly credits her mother with whetting her appetite for the genre. "My mother was a great influence on me, disturbing my mind," she told *USA Today* writer Katy Kelly. "She pretty much raised me on Stephen King and Dracula and aliens. She'd say, 'Just keep in mind: it's fiction. You're not supposed to take an ax to your neighbor. You're not to bite your friend.'"

The urge to create seized Atwater–Rhodes early. As a writer for *People Weekly* noted, at age three she was making up elaborate stories about a stuffed animal of hers named Meow Stripe, who ruled the upside–down world of Catland. The drawings she made to accompany her stories were odd enough to prompt one of her teachers into thinking she had a learning disability. From there, she became interested in dragons, then in science fiction. When she was in the second grade, Atwater–Rhodes crafted a sci–fi novel, subsequently lost when she forgot her password. By age nine, she had discovered Christopher Pike's *The Last Vampire,* a book that served as an inspiration for her own efforts. As she told William Plummer and Tom Duffy for *People Weekly,* "I really liked the way [Pike] portrayed the character's voice. I tried to mimic it."

Another key influence entered her life in 1996 when she came across a book on Wicca during a family trip to Salem. Atwater–Rhodes embraced its teachings and, with several middle–school friends, formed a "Candlelight Circle" and began practicing Wiccan rites and spell–casting rituals. Her group of fellow Wiccans felt themselves at one point to be outsiders. They became tight–knit during middle school, when, according to Atwater–Rhodes in an interview with the *New Yorker*'s Melanie Thernstrom, "people have to form groups to defend themselves. No one would come near our lunch table." But Atwater–Rhodes was quick to point out that Wiccans are not your everyday form of witch. "It's a pagan sort of Earth worship religion," she told *USA Today*. "Technically, it's witchcraft, but people tend to think negatively when you say that word. A lot of things that I've learned from Wicca get put into my books." And as Atwater–Rhodes explained to Thernstrom, "witchcraft is a natural ability . . . a knack for something like some people have good balance. . . . A lot of times we describe things as supernatural just because we can't explain them." Yet Wicca is only one of many of Atwater–Rhodes's interests. She also plays the piano and keyboard, composes songs and poetry, sings, fences, and collects shells and minerals. Haunting the by-ways of the local mall is not high on her list of to-dos. "Wandering around the mall and giggling at magazines doesn't interest me," she told Plummer and Duffy. "I detest shoes."

Lands Book Contract at Age Fourteen

Atwater–Rhodes began writing in earnest after completing fifth grade in 1995. She found time after school, in the middle of the night, or whenever inspiration struck. Sometimes she would write sixty pages at a sitting, and while composing her first novel, she balanced a tiger Beanie Baby on her head and took inspiration from the singer Alanis Morisette's "Jagged Little Pill" album, listening to several tracks over and over. Two years later, she completed *In the Forests of the Night*, the story of a 300–year–old vampire named Risika who was once a teenager in colonial Concord. This human persona, Rachel Weatere, was born in 1684, but after centuries as an Undead, Risika has become adjusted to her status, and as Holly Koelling noted in a *Booklist* review, she "has grown distant from the mortal world. Humans are prey, needed solely for nourishment." Risika sleeps by day and goes hunting in New York City by night, seeking fresh blood. But one night, returning home, she discovers a black rose on her pillow just as she did centuries before, on the eve of her own changeover from human to vampire. She knows this is a sign, a challenge, from her archenemy, the powerful vampire Aubrey, who long ago helped arrange her transformation and who she believes murdered her human brother. Risika goes into action, deciding to confront her old enemy.

With completion of the novel, Atwater–Rhodes's sister Rachel mentioned the book to her tenth–grade English teacher, Tom Hart, who had previously worked as an editor and literary agent. Hart was impressed enough by what he read to send it on to Delacorte Press, a division of Random House. While celebrating her fourteenth birthday, Atwater–Rhodes received a phone call from Hart telling her that Delacorte had accepted the novel for publication. "Amy almost fell out of her chair," her mother told Plummer and Duffy for *People Weekly*. "She had huge eyes like she was in a cartoon." But a contract was only the beginning of a long and complicated revision process that took this debut novel through a dozen drafts before publication. "Once I got over the initial 'I hate my editor'," Atwater–Rhodes told Matt Peiken of the *Houston Chronicle*, "most of [the editing process] made sense." The young novelist also relied on her built–in support group, her Wiccan friends who looked for mistakes in consistency and characterization.

Reviews of *In the Forests of the Night* were generally favorable, with some reservations. A reviewer for *Publishers Weekly* praised Atwater–Rhodes for being "skillful at building atmosphere, insightful in creating characters and imaginative in varying and expanding upon vampire lore," although the same writer also found evidence of "easy, adolescent cynicism." *Booklist*'s Koelling criticized the novel's story as "derivative" and "meandering," but went on to comment that Atwater–Rhodes's "use of language is surprisingly mature and polished for a 13–year–old writer." Koelling concluded, "Both the book's subject and the age of the author will ensure its popularity, especially with middle–schoolers, and it may encourage other young writers to pursue the craft." Kendra Nan Skellen, reviewing the novel in *School Library Journal*, felt that *In the Forests of the Night* "is well written and very descriptive, and has in–depth character development. . . . This first novel by an author with great ability and promise is sure to be popular."

Thernstrom summed up the critical response to the rather startling first novel from a very young writer in the *New Yorker*: "Amelia has an uncanny understanding of the kind of narrative that makes for a successful potboiler: she's skilled at creating characters the reader easily and instantly bonds with, and she's resourceful when it comes to putting them in jeopardy. . . . No one in the world of young–adult publishing has managed to come up with an analogy to Amelia: other early–teenage writers simply don't write coherent multiple–character, time–weaving, metafictional novels."

Demon in My View

But Atwater–Rhodes was too busy working on her novels to bother reading reviews. "Horror keeps my interest," she said in a *Seventeen* interview. "I want to know what's happening to the characters. It's not like when you read a romance and know the main characters will eventually get together." Thus Atwater–Rhodes stuck to her favorite topic for her second novel, *Demon in My View*. Like her first, it draws upon an elaborate genealogy of vampires and related supernatural beings that Atwater–Rhodes had created as background for her characters. By 1999, she had completed some twenty–four novels and claimed to have another two dozen or so uncompleted stories in her computer. "I don't outline," she said of her writing process in the *New Yorker* interview. "I don't draft. . . It's really something that comes to me, not something I've learned." She added, "Sometimes even I get freaked out by my

books." As Thernstrom noted, "It will require a dizzying number of books to straighten . . . out" the histories of her elaborate character genealogy, some 260 and growing. "Unless Amelia manages to achieve the immortality of her characters, her imagination has already extended beyond her own life span."

Demon in My View is a sequel to the first novel, this time focusing on Jessica, a high school student who had a walk–on part in the previous novel. Jessica Ashley Allodola, who writes under the pen name of Ash Night, has just published her first novel, a vampire tale titled *Tiger, Tiger*. At school she is an outsider, something of a misfit, but when writing she goes into a dreamlike state, describing a world of vampires and witches with vivid and detailed accuracy. Jessica marvels at the way her fertile imagination works; what she doesn't realize is that these doings are, in fact, real. The characters she has spread across the pages of her book take great umbrage at Jessica's cheek. As a reviewer for *Publishers Weekly* put it, the vampires "aren't too happy that she's spilled their secrets and wittingly alerted vampire–hunting witches to the location of their undead village, New Mayhem." To reek vengeance, Aubrey, the nemesis of *In the Forests of the Night,* appears at Jessica's high school disguised as a new student, Alex. But Aubrey, attracted to Jessica's aura, is torn between a desire for revenge and the wish to turn her into a vampire like himself. Jessica, too, finds herself attracted to Aubrey. Meanwhile, the plot thickens with the arrival of another student, actually a witch of the Smoke Clan, Caryn, who has arrived to protect Jessica from the vampires.

DEMON IN MY VIEW

Amelia Atwater-Rhodes
author of
IN THE FORESTS OF THE NIGHT

In her 2000 novel, Atwater–Rhodes weaves a tale in which her novel's teen heroine—a published author—confronts a real–life vampire in the form of handsome school newcomer Aubrey.

"The clash between the witches and the vampires and the truth of Jessica's birth take the plot down many twisting and suspenseful paths," according to Jane Halsall, writing in *School Library Journal.* Though Halsall felt there were "too many subplots and minor characters," the reviewer also thought that the book "comes alive when it focuses on the relationship between Jessica and Alex/Aubrey," two characters who are "finely drawn and believable." A reviewer for *Publishers Weekly* found the writing sometimes "pat," but also commented that "fantastic fights will keep readers turning pages quickly." This same writer concluded: "Atwater–Rhodes exercises impressive control over the complex lineages she has imagined, and she comes up with creative solutions to advance her story. Readers will drain this book in one big gulp."

However, not all reviewers were ready with praise for this second novel. Ellen Creager of the *Detroit Free Press* wrote that Atwater–Rhodes's second novel "is nowhere near as polished as the first" with its "compelling plot" and "immediacy." Creager felt that *Demon in My View* "is a bit too close to [the television series] 'Buffy the Vampire Slayer' for comfort" and also "a bit sloppy around the edges as it barrels along." Halsall, writing in *School Library Journal,* concurred in this opinion, noting that the second novel "is not as tightly plotted or generally as well written as . . . [the] first."

If you enjoy the works of Amelia Atwater–Rhodes, you might want to check out the following books and films:

Annette Curtis Klause, *Blood and Chocolate,* 1997.
Anne Rice, *Interview with the Vampire,* 1976.
Chelsea Quinn Yarbro, *The Saint–Germain Chronicles,* 1983.
Bram Stoker's Dracula, a film starring Anthony Hopkins and Winona Ryder, directed by Francis Ford Coppola, 1992.

But whether the critics agree or not, Atwater–Rhodes's books have already found intense popularity with young readers. Whereas YA books normally sell only in four–digit editions, *In the Forests of the Night* went back to press repeatedly resulting in over 50,000 copies in print only a few months after publication. Such popularity has its residual effects. For an adolescent who once banded with other young girls for protection in middle school, Atwater–Rhodes has become a center of attention. Following publication of her first novel, her school principal referred to her as the next Anne Rice in a school assembly, and as the author recalled for *People Weekly,* "I was shocked when he called me up. Afterwards, everyone wanted me to sign their yearbooks." "A lot of kids at school deemed me weird and insane," she told *Teen People* reporter Kellie Vaughan. "Now everybody wants to be my friend." But for Atwater–Rhodes, there is life after writing. She told Thernstrom that she could not imagine being a full–time writer because, as she put it, "I need to get away from it." In the same article, Atwater–Rhodes's mother noted that her daughter had other interests in addition to writing: "Amy's a doer, a collector, a person with a million interests. . . . She sews, she fences, is deep into the Internet, animals, ecology. I guess I would be surprised if in twenty years all she's doing is writing." As for the

author's father, he has more immediate plans: "What I'm concerned about is that she does her homework," he told Thernstrom.

Atwater–Rhodes has plans to attend college even as she continues her writing career, filling out the lineage of her Smoke Clan Witch Line. In her interview with Vaughan of *Teen People,* she offered a clear–eyed assessment of her creative strengths at age fourteen: "As a teen, I bring a different perspective to writing. I can offer immediate emotions, experiences and insight that adult writers often have to reach back and find in order to write about them." And as she told Peiken, she is also getting used to celebrity. "At first, it was a little weird and unnerving to think lots of people would be reading my book, but now I like having fans." Her advice to other would–be writers? "Write what you feel like writing," she told Sittenfeld.

■ Biographical and Critical Sources

PERIODICALS

Booklist, June 1, 1999, Holly Koelling, review of *In the Forests of the Night,* p. 1812.
Book Report, November–December, 1999, p. 65.
Detroit Free Press, July 16, 2000, Ellen Creager, "15–year–Old Is on a Roll with Her Second Novel," p. 5E.
Entertainment Weekly, March 26, 1999, p. 80.
Houston Chronicle, July 29, 1999, Matt Peiken, "Characters Speak to Author," p. 6.
Literary Cavalcade, October, 1999, p. 37.
Los Angeles Times, July 30, 2000, Susan Carpenter, "Teen Authors' Novel Approach," p. E2.
New Yorker, October 18–25, 1999, Melanie Thernstrom, "The Craft," pp. 136, 138, 140–42.
People Weekly, August 9, 1999, William Plummer and Tom Duffy, "Author Rising," pp. 103–04.
Publishers Weekly, May 24, 1999, review of *In the Forests of the Night,* p. 80; April 24, 2000, review of *Demon in My View,* p. 92.
School Library Journal, July, 1999, Kendra Nan Skellen, review of *In the Forests of the Night,* p. 92; May 1, 2000, Jane Halsall, review of *Demon in My View,* p. 166.
Seventeen, June, 1999, Curtis Sittenfeld, "Freshman Debut."
Teen People, February, 1999, Kellie Vaughan, interview with Amelia Atwater–Rhodes.
USA Today, May 6, 1999, Katy Kelly, "A Writer Grave beyond Her Years," p. 1D.*

—Sketch by J. Sydney Jones

Gary L. Blackwood

■ Personal

Born October 23, 1945, in Meadville, PA; son of Roy W. and Susie (Stallsmith) Blackwood; married Jean Lantzy, October 3, 1977; children: Gareth, Giles, Tegan. *Education:* Grove City College, B.A., 1967. *Hobbies and other interests:* Music, outdoor pursuits.

■ Addresses

Home—6031 CR 105, Carthage, MO 64836. *E-mail*—gblackwood@hotmail.com.

■ Career

Writer of fiction and nonfiction books, playwright, and writing teacher. Missouri Southern State College, teacher of play writing, 1989–93, 1997—; Trinidad State Junior College, teacher of writing–for–publication course, 1995. *Military service:* U.S. Army, Sergeant, E–5, 1968–70.

■ Member

Society of Children's Book Writers and Illustrators.

■ Awards, Honors

American Library Association (ALA) Recommended List for Reluctant Readers, Fields Book Club, and Silver Burdett Library selection, all for *Wild Timothy;* Friends of American Writers Best YA Novel, 1989, for *The Dying Sun;* Macmillan/McGraw Hill Science Program selection, 1991, for *Beyond the Door;* Best Book for Young Adults and Notable Book citation, ALA, 1998 and 1999, *Smithsonian* Notable Children's Book, *School Library Journal* Best Books list, 1998, *Voice of Youth Advocates* Books in the Middle Outstanding Title, 1998, and National Council on Social Studies/Children's Book Council Notable Children's Trade Book in the Field of Social Studies, 1999, all for *The Shakespeare Stealer;* *Smithsonian* Notable Children's Books, 1999, for *Moonshine.* Blackwood's plays have also won awards, including the Ozark Creative Writers Conference first prize for *Attack of the Mushroom People,* and Missouri Scriptworks first prize, as well as the Ferndale Rep Play Competition, for *Dark Horse.*

■ Writings

NOVELS

The Lion and the Unicorn (adult historical), Eagle Books, 1983.
Wild Timothy, Atheneum, 1987.
The Dying Sun, Atheneum, 1989.

Beyond the Door, Atheneum, 1991.
Time Masters, EPB Publishers, 1995.
The Shakespeare Stealer, Dutton, 1998.
Moonshine, Cavendish, 1999.
Shakespeare's Scribe, Dutton, 2000.

NONFICTION

Rough Riding Reformer: Theodore Roosevelt, Benchmark, 1997.
Life on the Oregon Trail, Lucent, 1999.
Life in a Medieval Castle, Lucent, 1999.
The Bad Guys (five–book juvenile series), Benchmark, 2001.

"SECRETS OF THE UNEXPLAINED" SERIES

Alien Astronauts, Benchmark, 1999.
Extraordinary Events and Oddball Occurrences, Benchmark, 1999.
Fateful Forebodings, Benchmark, 1999.
Long–Ago Lives, Benchmark, 1999.
Paranormal Powers, Benchmark, 1999.
Spooky Specters, Benchmark, 1999.

Also has written stage plays, including *Come on in, the Water's over Your Head, Attack of the Mushroom People, Thoreau, Futures, Dark Horse,* and *Morning Star;* contributor to anthologies, including *Short Circuits: Thirteen Short Stories from Outstanding Writers for Young Adults,* edited by Donald R. Gallo, Delacorte, 1992; also contributor to periodicals, including *Wild West.*

■ Sidelights

Gary L. Blackwood turns the familiar "write what you know" dictum on its head: having never traveled to England, and surely having never experienced the highs and lows of sixteenth–century English life, he has produced two successful volumes recounting the adventures of Widge, an Elizabethan boy in Shakespearean England. His highly popular *The Shakespeare Stealer* and its sequel, *Shakespeare's Scribe,* both prove that young readers do care about events more distant than last week's game or tomorrow's party. Additionally, Blackwood, a playwright as well as novelist, has penned juvenile novels in genres as diverse as outdoor survival to science fiction, as well as realistic fiction set during the Great Depression. His interests have also led him to nonfiction, in which he has produced books

about famous Americans, such as Teddy Roosevelt the Rough Rider, or American history, as in his *Life on the Oregon Trail,* as well as more speculative discussions of the paranormal and inexplicable events in his six–book series, *Secrets of the Unexplained.*

"I grew up in the country outside the small town of Cochranton, in Northwestern Pennsylvania," Blackwood told *Authors and Artists for Young Adults (AAYA).* "My love of books was either instilled in me very early on by my parents, or else carried over from a previous life. While I was still young enough to be sleeping in a crib, I struck a deal with my mother: I'd give up sucking my thumb if she bought me a series of Gene Autry comics I'd seen advertised on the back of a cereal box." Blackwood attended one of the last remaining one–room schoolhouses in the state of Pennsylvania. "Our school library consisted only of a single set of bookshelves," Blackwood told *AAYA,* "but it did contain a full set of the Dr. Doolittle books. I had a competition going with one of my classmates to see who could read the entire series first. I don't recall who won, but it was probably me; I've always been the sort to pursue things relentlessly and single–mindedly. It's a good thing too, or I probably never would have realized my dreams of becoming a published writer."

Growing up without a phone or television, Blackwood focused on the written and spoken word for his entertainment. In fact he had two main passions as a young boy, the outdoors, and reading. Reading about the outdoors was pure gravy. Sometimes he also combined these interests by walking the three miles into town, buying some Classics Comics, and then reading them on the walk back home. Some of his favorite stories and books as a young reader were *The Prince and the Pauper, The Prisoner of Zenda, Ivanhoe,* and *Under Two Flags.*

In high school, Blackwood discovered another driving interest, the theater. "I had leading roles in my junior and senior plays," Blackwood told *AAYA,* "did some acting in college, then did musicals in community theater. Then Uncle Sam drafted me, but I continued to perform in plays—and began writing some of my own—during my two year stay in the army." Actually Blackwood started writing before he went into the military. He penned a "cliché–ridden western" when he was thirteen, and a science–fiction novel set on Venus when he was fifteen. Then, at age sixteen he got his first encouraging rejection from an editor; at nineteen he sold his first story. But it took another twenty–one years for Blackwood to sell his first novel.

Inspired by his love of history, Blackwood researched the way of life pioneer families often endured during a wagon train's trip westward for the 1999 nonfiction work, *Life on the Oregon Trail.*

Early Fiction

While Blackwood published his first adult fiction, the historical novel, *The Lion and the Unicorn,* in 1983, it was not until 1987 that his first YA novel, *Wild Timothy,* appeared. This story blended his twin love of adventure stories and the outdoors. While on a camping trip with his father in the Adirondack Mountains, thirteen–year–old Timothy Martin, pudgy and nerdy and never physically tested, gets lost and then has to use his wits to survive without food, tools, or shelter. It does not help that Timothy's father has put it into the boy's head that he is incompetent, but this adventure lets Timothy know that he has real courage and ability within. Barbara Chatton, writing in *School Library Journal,* called this debut YA novel a "suspenseful and philosophical survival story," while Mary K. Chelton, reviewing the same title in *Voice of Youth Advocates,* thought it was "engrossing." Chelton concluded that *Wild Timothy* is a "good booktalk title for young adolescents." And though Roger Sutton, writing in

Bulletin of the Center for Children's Books found the writing to be "bland," he also noted that "the details of building shelter, finding food, and handling various dangers have built–in appeal." *Wild Timothy* was an ALA Recommended Book for Reluctant Readers.

From the extreme reality of a survivalist tale, Blackwood turned his hand to a science–fiction novel set in a twenty–first–century ice age. In *The Dying Sun,* the sun has cooled, and the expanding polar ice caps have forced people to move toward the equator. As life becomes more and more crowded and dangerous in the warm South of Matamoras, where Mexicans have begun to rebel against the number of settlers from the United States, two young boys— James and Robert—decide to leave their crime–ridden locale and head to a more primitive existence in chilly Missouri where James's parents live on a farm. There they all get ready for the brutal winter. Disillusioned with the North, Robert decides to head back home while James stays on with his own family, wiser for his experience. Jack Forman, writing in *School Library Journal*, felt that setting of this coming–of–age novel was "imaginatively drawn and feasible," but concluded that the story was "colorless and reflective in tone," and lacking "the fire that would melt the ice in James's narration."

More science fiction is served up in *Beyond the Door*, in which technology–loving Scott Shaffer, still reeling from his father's desertion, steps through a study room door and finds himself in a primitive alternate world, the pre–industrial world of Gale'tin. At first Scott attempts to bring technology to these people until another visitor from his school makes Scott "confront the evils of uncontrolled intellect," according to Margaret A. Chang in *School Library Journal,* and makes him also think twice about the balance between technological progress and the environment. "Danger and action combine," noted a reviewer for *Bulletin of the Center for Children's Books* in a review of *Beyond the Door.* Carolyn Phelan, reviewing the title in *Booklist,* concluded, "readers looking for an adventure will find this worth reading."

Time Masters, a juvenile novel, followed in 1995, but it was not until three years later, in 1998, when Blackwood finally found a publisher for a book that he had worked on over the course of several decades.

Elizabethan Entanglements

The Shakespeare Stealer was published in 1998, but the idea for the story came to Blackwood in the late 1960s, from an item he found in the newspaper. "It

In *Life in a Medieval Castle,* Blackwood allows readers to share the everyday experiences of the kings and queens, princesses, knights, and even serving boys who lived surrounded by the massive stone walls of castles and fortresses throughout Great Britain and Europe.

informed me that, in the sixteenth century, an English doctor named Timothy Bright had invented an early system of shorthand," Blackwood told *AAYA*. "I knew something of that time period already, from studying Shakespeare in college. The elements of shorthand and Shakespeare melded in my mind, and expanded to become my first novel, which I called *An Art of Short, Swift, and Secret Stealing.*"

Blackwood never found a publisher for the book, so he gave up on it for a number of years. But looking back on this first effort of novel-writing, Blackwood decided to rewrite it "as a book for kids." "For a long time," Blackwood stated, "it looked as if the new improved version of the book, now called *The Shakespeare Stealer,* would be consigned to oblivion like its predecessor. Most of the editors who saw it liked it a lot, but didn't feel it would sell well. . . . After being turned down sixteen times over a period of seven years, the book finally found a home at Dutton."

The Shakespeare Stealer concerns Widge, a fourteen-year-old boy who has spent his life in a Yorkshire orphanage. Soon after the story opens Widge is apprenticed to Dr. Bright, a minister who teaches Widge his system of "charactery," or shorthand, for the purpose of stealing other ministers' sermons. But before long, Bright sells his young apprentice for the sum of tens pounds to Simon Bass, a London theatrical manager. Bass plans to use the boy's skills to have him steal Shakespeare's new play, *The Tragedy of Hamlet, Prince of Denmark,* so that Bass's own theater can produce it without having to pay royalties.

Widge has not gotten very far with his copy when he is discovered hiding in a balcony by the Globe players; thinking fast, he pretends to be stage-struck, and is so convincing that the group take him on as an acting apprentice. At first Widge thinks he will use his new position to steal the Globe's own copy of the play, but the "brave new world of friendship, fun, and backstage intrigue," in the words of a *Kirkus Reviews* critic, make him question his unethical quest. Instead, Widge practices lines, learns the arts of stagecraft and sword fighting, and works to evade Bass's brutal henchmen. Jennifer M. Brabander, writing in *Horn Book,* pointed out that "like *Hamlet,* Blackwood's story focuses on its protagonist's doubt and deliberation about his interrupted quest." By the end of the story, Widge, in the typical pants part of the day, plays Ophelia for the Queen.

Critics were nearly uniformly charmed by Blackwood's tale. Deborah Stevens, in her review in *Bulletin of the Center for Children's Books,* noted that

"there's a pleasing air of high adventure to Widge's escapades that is enhanced by Blackwood's careful but never dry use of period and theatrical detail." Brabander, in *Horn Book,* credited Blackwood with "set[ting] the stage for future reading and play-going" for its young readers. The *Kirkus Reviews* critic called the book a "delightful and heartwarming romp through Elizabethan England," and Phelan, writing in *Booklist,* commented that "this historical novel makes an exciting introduction to the period and to Shakespearean theater."

A *Publishers Weekly* reviewer, however, complained that the story was marred by "[a] myriad of anachronisms," including Widge's reference to London's square city blocks, to having his supper warmed on a stove, and to the recovery of an injured man in a hospital—all apparently imprecise. But the reviewer did admire Blackwood's "lively depictions of Elizabethan stagecraft and street life." Writing in *Book Report,* Dorothy Lilly felt that the story is "full of intrigue and adventure." Sally Margolis, who reviewed the book for the *School Library Journal,* noted that this "is a fast-moving historical novel that introduces an important era with casual familiarity," and further commented that "Blackwood puts a young boy in a sink-or-swim predicament in alien territory where he discovers his own strength." Winner of many awards, including an ALA Best Book for Young Adults citation, *The Shakespeare Stealer* was ripe for a sequel.

"All writing should have a purpose; I guess the purpose of my work is to offer readers a chance to learn about and experience things beyond the bounds of the ordinary."

—Gary L. Blackwood

Readers did not have long to wait. The character of Widge was reprised in the year 2000 sequel, *Shakespeare's Scribe,* in which an outbreak of the Black Plague in London closes the Globe Theater and sends the troupe on the road, traveling from town to town in order to survive. When Shakespeare breaks his arm in a brawl, he desperately needs Widge and his talent for charactery to be able to finish his play for the queen. But not even this rare privilege can make Widge feel better after having been ousted from roles by a talented new apprentice with the troupe. Into all this comes a person who claims to know secrets of Widge's past, secrets that may take him away from the theater and back to his real family.

Reviewers were equally enthusiastic about this second adventure of young Widge. Nancy Menaldi–Scanlan, writing in *School Library Journal,* observed, "As with his earlier title, Blackwood has created a vivid portrait of Elizabethan England via wonderful period details, along with plenty of references to the plays and life." Menaldi–Scanlan further commented on the "well developed" characters, the "realistic" dialogue, and "humorous" plays on words. *Booklist'*s Phelan wrote that "Blackwood sweeps readers along in a fast–paced tale convincingly set in Elizabethan England." Phelan also pointed to the "[r]ich language and descriptions of places."

Blackwood told *AAYA* that he pored over "dozens of tomes about Elizabethan theater and lifestyles" for *Shakespeare's Scribe,* as well as "books about 17th century speech and sword fighting. . . . But of course I wrote the book not for Shakespeare experts but for kids, who generally care less about accuracy than they do about reading a ripping yarn. So I tried my utmost best to provide *Shakespeare's Scribe* with exciting situations, unexpected plot twists, real–seeming characters, and a good deal of humor—in short, the very elements I relished in books when I was their age."

Beyond Shakespeare

Blackwood, who teaches writing at Missouri Southern State College, lives with his wife and daughter in the country near Carthage, Missouri. In addition to his popular Elizabethan adventure tales, he has also penned a juvenile novel about the Great Depression, *Moonshine.* This book tells the story of young Thad McCune, who grows up dirt poor in the Missouri Ozarks and makes extra money for his family—his waitress mother and himself—by running illegal liquor, or moonshine, for a one–armed veteran of World War I. A tourist befriends Thad and becomes something of a father figure for him. A reviewer for the *Bulletin of the Center for Children's Books* called *Moonshine* a "[w]ell–crafted historical novel" with an "[e]ngaging protagonist." The same reviewer concluded, "Readers will appreciate the novel's quiet humor and consistent clarity, and its thoughtful depiction of the ways we grow up." Writing in *Booklist,* Linda Perkins commented, "The story jumps off to a quick start, and despite exploration of several side issues, the pace never slackens." A contributor for *Smithsonian* called it "another masterful offering from the author of *The Shakespeare Stealer.*"

Besides his well–received fiction, Blackwood has also authored many nonfiction titles, including both history and more speculative matters. Reviewing his *Life on the Oregon Trail,* Laura Glaser noted in *School Library Journal* that it was a "thorough and appealing account. . . . Well organized and extremely informative." More popular nonfiction is served up in Blackwood's six–part series, *Secrets of the Unexplained,* a series that "offers kids front–row seats at some fascinating phenomena," according to *Booklist'*s Ilene Cooper. Reviewing Blackwood's *Alien Astronauts* and other titles in the series, Ann G. Brouse, writing in *School Library Journal,* called the writing and presentation in these books "balanced," and further noted that the volumes "have large, full–color photographs and illustrations with information–packed captions."

If you enjoy the works of Gary L. Blackwood, you might want to check out the following books:

John Marsden, *The Dead of Night,* 1997.
Harry Mazer, *The Wild Kid,* 1998.
Pamela Melnikoff, *Plots and Players: The Lopez Conspiracy,* 1989.

From Elizabethan England to UFOs, Blackwood continues to follow a personal dictum of writing about "what I'd like to know," as he told *AAYA,* rather than what he already knows. "That's why my books are almost always set, not in familiar territory, but in Terra Incognito—the distant past, the future, some parallel universe, a time or place or situation in which readers are never likely to find themselves. All writing should have a purpose; I guess the purpose of my work is to offer readers a chance to learn about and experience things beyond the bounds of the ordinary."

■ Biographical and Critical Sources

PERIODICALS

ALAN Review, winter, 2001, Lori Atkins–Goodson, review of *Shakespeare's Scribe,* p. 36.

Booklist, February 1, 1991, Carolyn Phelan, review of *Beyond the Door*, p. 1175; June 1, 1998, Carolyn Phelan, review of *The Shakespeare Stealer*, p. 1763; September 1, 1999, Linda Perkins, review of *Moonshine*, p. 131; March 1, 2000, Ilene Cooper, review of *Extraordinary Events and Oddball Occurrences*, p. 1237; September 1, 2000, Carolyn Phelan, review of *Shakespeare's Scribe*, p. 112.

Book Report, March–April, 1999, Dorothy Lilly, review of *The Shakespeare Stealer*, p. 56; January–February, 2000.

Bulletin of the Center for Children's Books, September, 1987, Roger Sutton, review of *Wild Timothy*, p. 3; March, 1991, review of *Beyond the Door*, p. 135; July–August, 1998, Deborah Stevenson, review of *The Shakespeare Stealer*, p. 483; November, 1999, review of *Moonshine*.

English Journal, November–December, 1989, p. 77.

Horn Book, July–August, 1989, p. 485; May–June, 1998, Jennifer M. Brabander, review of *The Shakespeare Stealer*, p. 353.

Kirkus Reviews, April 15, 1998, review of *The Shakespeare Stealer*, p. 576.

Publishers Weekly, June 1, 1998, review of *The Shakespeare Stealer*, p. 63; June 26, 2000, p. 77; August 8, 2000, p. 97.

School Library Journal, October, 1987, Barbara Chatton, review of *Wild Timothy*, p. 137; May, 1989, Jack Forman, review of *The Dying Sun*, p. 124; March, 1991, Margaret A. Chang, review of *Beyond the Door*, p. 192; June, 1998, Sally Margolis, review of *The Shakespeare Stealer*, p. 140; March, 1999, Ann G. Brouse, review of *Alien Astronauts*, et al, pp. 216–17; August, 1999, Laura Glaser, review of *Life on the Oregon Trail*, p. 166; October, 1999, p. 144; September, 2000, Nancy Menaldi–Scanlan, review of *Shakespeare's Scribe*, p. 225.

Smithsonian, November, 1999, review of *Moonshine*.

Voice of Youth Advocates, October, 1987, Mary K. Chelton, review of *Wild Timothy*, p. 231.

Wilson Library Bulletin, January, 1990, p. 99; March, 1990.

—Sketch by J. Sydney Jones

Marion Zimmer Bradley

Personal

Born June 3, 1930, in Albany, NY; died of a heart attack, September 25, 1999, in Berkeley, CA; daughter of Leslie (a carpenter) and Evelyn (a historian; maiden name, Conklin) Zimmer; married Robert A. Bradley, October, 1949 (divorced, 1963); married Walter Henry Breen (a numismatist), June, 1964 (divorced); children: (first marriage) David Stephen Robert; (second marriage) Patrick Russell Donald, Moira Evelyn Dorothy. *Education:* Attended New York State College for Teachers (now State University of New York at Albany), 1946–48; Hardin–Simmons College, B.A., 1964; additional study at University of California, Berkeley.

Career

Writer, editor, and musician.

Award, Honors

Hugo Award nomination, 1963; Nebula Award nominations, 1964 and 1978; Invisible Little Man Award, 1977; Leigh Brackett Memorial Sense of Wonder Award, 1978, for *The Forbidden Tower;* Locus Award for best fantasy novel, 1984, for *The Mists of Avalon.*

Writings

SCIENCE FICTION AND FANTASY

The Door through Space (bound with *Rendezvous on Lost Planet* by A. Bertram Chandler), Ace Books, 1961.

Seven from the Stars (bound with *Worlds of the Imperium* by Keith Laumer), Ace Books, 1962.

The Colors of Space, Monarch, 1963, revised edition, illustrated by Barbi Johnson, Donning (Norfolk, VA), 1983, illustrated by Lee Moyer, 1988.

Falcons of Narabedla [and] *The Dark Intruder and Other Stories,* Ace Books, 1964.

The Brass Dragon (bound with *Ipomoea* by John Rackham), Ace Books, 1969.

(With brother, Paul Edwin Zimmer) *Hunters of the Red Moon,* DAW Books, 1973.

The Parting of Arwen (short story), T–K Graphics, 1974.

The Endless Voyage, Ace Books, 1975, expanded edition published as *Endless Universe,* 1979.

The Ruins of Isis, illustrated by Polly and Kelly Freas, Donning (Norfolk, VA), 1978.

(With P. E. Zimmer) *The Survivors,* DAW Books, 1979.

The House between the Worlds, Doubleday, 1980, revised edition, Del Rey, 1981.

Survey Ship, illustrated by Steve Fabian, Ace Books, 1980.

The Mists of Avalon, Knopf, 1982.

The Web of Darkness, illustrated by V. M. Wyman and C. Lee Healy, Donning (Norfolk, VA), 1983.

Web of Light, illustrated by C. Lee Healy, Donning (Norfolk, VA), 1983.

(Editor and contributor) *Greyhaven: An Anthology of Fantasy*, DAW Books, 1983.

Night's Daughter, Ballantine, 1985.

(With Vonda McIntyre) *Lythande* (anthology), DAW Books, 1986.

The Fall of Atlantis (includes *Web of Light* and *Web of Darkness*), Baen Books, 1987.

The Firebrand, Simon & Schuster, 1987.

Warrior Woman, DAW Books, 1988.

(With Andre Norton and Julian May) *The Black Trillium*, Doubleday, 1990.

Witch Hill, Tor Books, 1990.

The Forest House, Viking, 1994.

(With Elisabeth Waters) *Lady of the Trillium*, Bantam, 1995.

(With Andre Norton and Mercedes Lackey) *Tiger Burning Bright*, Morrow, 1995.

(With Rosemary Edghill) *Ghostlight*, Tor Books, 1995.

(With Rosemary Edghill) *Witchlight*, Tor Books, 1996

(With Holly Lisle) *Glenraven*, Baen Books, 1996.

The Lady of Avalon, Viking, 1997.

(With Rosemary Edghill) *Gravelight*, Tor Books, 1997.

Gratitude of Kings (novella), Roc, 1997.

(With Rosemary Edghill) *Heartlight*, Tor Books, 1998.

(With Holly Lisle) *Glenraven 2: In the Rift*, Baen Books, 1998.

Priestess of Avalon, HarperCollins, 2000.

"DARKOVER" SCIENCE FICTION SERIES

The Sword of Aldones [and] *The Planet Savers*, Ace Books, 1962, *The Sword of Aldones*, published separately with introduction by Richard A. Lupoff, Gregg Press (Boston), 1977, *The Planet Savers*, published separately with introduction by Bradley, Gregg Press, 1979, both volumes reprinted and bound together as *Planet Savers: The Sword of Aldones*, Ace Books, 1984.

The Bloody Sun, Ace Books, 1964, revised edition, 1979, with introduction by Bradley, Gregg Press, 1979.

Star of Danger, Ace Books, 1965, with introduction by Bradley, Gregg Press, 1979.

The Winds of Darkover (bound with *The Anything Tree* by John Rackham), Ace Books, 1970, with introduction by Bradley, Gregg Press, 1979.

The World Wreckers, Ace Books, 1971, with introduction by Bradley, Gregg Press, 1979.

Darkover Landfall, DAW Books, 1972, with introduction by Theodore Sturgeon, Gregg Press, 1978.

The Spell Sword, DAW Books, 1974, with introduction by Bradley, Gregg Press, 1979.

The Heritage of Hastur, DAW Books, 1975, with introduction by Susan Wood, Gregg Press, 1977.

The Shattered Chain, DAW Books, 1976, with introduction by Bradley, Gregg Press, 1979.

The Forbidden Tower, DAW Books, 1977, with introduction by Bradley, Gregg Press, 1979.

Stormqueen!, DAW Books, 1978, with introduction by Bradley, Gregg Press, 1979.

(Editor and contributor) *Legends of Hastur and Cassilda*, Thendara House Publications (Berkeley, CA), 1979.

(Editor and contributor) *Tales of the Free Amazons*, Thendara House Publications (Berkeley, CA), 1980.

Two to Conquer, DAW Books, 1980.

(Editor and contributor) *The Keeper's Price and Other Stories*, DAW Books, 1980.

Sharra's Exile, DAW Books, 1981.

Children of Hastur (includes *The Heritage of Hastur* and *Sharra's Exile*), Doubleday, 1981.

Hawkmistress!, DAW Books, 1982.

(Editor and contributor) *Sword of Chaos*, DAW Books, 1982.

Thendara House, DAW Books, 1983.

Oath of the Renunciates (includes *The Shattered Chain* and *Thendara House*), Doubleday, 1983.

City of Sorcery, DAW Books, 1984.

(Editor, contributor, and author of introduction) *Free Amazons of Darkover: An Anthology*, DAW Books, 1985.

(Editor and contributor) *Red Sun of Darkover*, DAW Books, 1987.

(Editor and contributor) *The Other Side of the Mirror and Other Darkover Stories*, DAW Books, 1987.

(Editor and contributor) *Four Moons of Darkover*, DAW Books, 1988.

The Heirs of Hammerfell, DAW Books, 1989.

(Editor) *Domains of Darkover*, DAW Books, 1990.

(Editor) *Renunciates of Darkover*, DAW Books, 1991.

(Editor) *Leroni of Darkover*, DAW Books, 1991.

(Editor) *Towers of Darkover*, DAW Books, 1993.

(With Mercedes Lackey) *Rediscovery: A Novel of Darkover*, DAW Books, 1993.

Marion Zimmer Bradley's Darkover (short stories), DAW Books, 1993.

(With Adrienne Martine–Barnes) *Exile's Song*, DAW Books, 1996.

"Darkover" novels left unfinished at the time of Bradley's death were: *Reluctant King, Thunderlord,* and *Clingfire Trilogy.*

GOTHIC FICTION

(Under pseudonym Miriam Gardner) *The Strange Woman*, Monarch, 1962.

Castle Terror, Lancer (New York City), 1965.

Souvenir of Monique, Ace Books, 1967.

Bluebeard's Daughter, Lancer (New York City), 1968.

Dark Satanic, Berkley Publishing, 1972.

Drums of Darkness: An Astrological Gothic Novel, Ballantine, 1976.

The Inheritor, Tor Books, 1984.

NOVELS

(Under pseudonym Lee Chapman) *I Am a Lesbian,* Monarch, 1962.

(Under pseudonym Morgan Ives) *Spare Her Heaven,* Monarch, 1963.

(Under pseudonym Miriam Gardner) *My Sister, My Love,* Monarch, 1963.

(Under pseudonym Miriam Gardner) *Twilight Lovers,* Monarch, 1964.

(Under pseudonym Morgan Ives) *Knives of Desire,* Cornith (San Diego, CA), 1966.

(Under pseudonym John Dexter) *No Adam for Eve,* Cornith (San Diego, CA), 1966.

The Catch Trap, Ballantine, 1979.

CRITICISM

Men, Halflings, and Hero Worship, T–K Graphics, 1973.

The Necessity for Beauty: Robert W. Chamber and the Romantic Tradition, T–K Graphics, 1974.

The Jewel of Arwen, T–K Graphics, 1974.

OTHER

Songs from Rivendell, privately printed, 1959.

A Complete, Cumulative Checklist of Lesbian, Variant, and Homosexual Fiction, privately printed, 1960.

(Translator) Lope de Vega, *El Villano en su Rincon,* privately printed, 1971.

In the Steps of the Master (teleplay novelization), Tempo Books, 1973.

Can Ellen Be Saved? (teleplay novelization), Tempo Books, 1975.

(With Alfred Bester and Norman Spinrad) *Experiment Perilous: Three Essays in Science Fiction,* Algol Press, 1976.

The Ballad of Hastur and Cassilda (poem), Thendara House Publications (Berkeley, CA), 1978.

(Editor) *Sword and Sorceress* (annual anthology), Volumes 1–19, DAW Books, 1984–2002.

The Best of Marion Zimmer Bradley, edited by Martin H. Greenberg, Academy Chicago (Chicago, IL), 1986, revised edition published as *Jamie and Other Stories: The Best of Marion Zimmer Bradley,* 1991.

Contributor, sometimes under name Elfrida Rivers and other pseudonyms, to anthologies and periodicals, including *Essays Lovecraftian,* edited by Darrell Schweitzer, T–K Graphics, 1976, *Magazine of Fantasy and Science Fiction, Amazing Stories,* and *Venture.* Editor of *Marion Zimmer Bradley's Fantasy Magazine,* 1988–99. Bradley also published works under the pseudonym Valerie Graves.

■ **Adaptations**

The Mists of Avalon was filmed for television by TNT, 2001. Further volumes in the "Darkover" series have been written by Adrienne Martine–Barnes.

■ **Sidelights**

At the time of her death in 1999, Marion Zimmer Bradley was among the most popular writers of her generation. Author of one of the best–loved series in science fiction and fantasy, her "Darkover" novels have not only inspired their own fan magazines, known as "fanzines," but also a series of story collections in which other authors set their tales in Bradley's universe. In addition, as the creator of the bestselling *The Mists of Avalon,* and its prequels, *The Forest House* and *Lady of Avalon,* Bradley became one of the genre's most widely known writers. Her re-telling of the Arthurian legend from the female point of view has brought her insightful examinations of human psychology and her skill in plot and characterization to the attention of an appreciative new audience, including young adults. As Sister Avila Lamb stated in *Kliatt Young Adult Paperback Book Guide,* "The name of Marion Zimmer Bradley is a guarantee of excellence. Creative imagination, strong, fleshed–out characters, compelling style, an uncanny ability to make all totally credible combine to involve readers from the first pages, never releasing them until long after the last page." And as a contributor for *St. James Guide to Young Adult Writers* noted, "As long as inheritance is both desirable and frightful, and adolescence is a terrifying time of crisis and loss of control, the work of Marion Zimmer Bradley will have appeal for young adults."

Bradley grew up in Albany, New York, and focused on reading and schoolwork to escape family troubles. She excelled in school and once recalled that, while it wasn't popular for girls to show their smarts, "I thought most of the time that having brains was just fine, and I built my life on it, since I

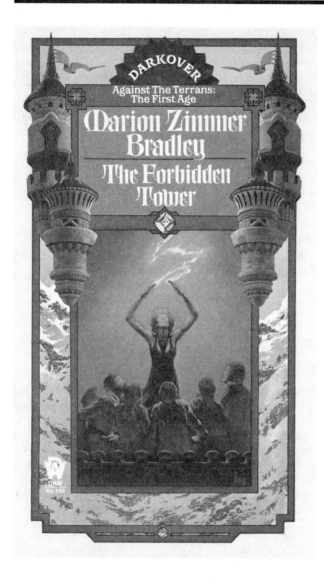

The escapades of four adventurers united in their defiance of their planet's oppressive guardianship by a group of fanatics is the focus of this 1977 work from Bradley's popular "Darkover" series.

was stuck with it anyhow." Her academic achievements earned her a National Merit Scholarship, and at age sixteen Bradley graduated from high school. "I went to college and, almost at the same time, discovered pulp science fiction," she once said. "I think I can honestly say this was the turning point of my life."

Bradley had always harbored a desire to write; "I'm told that I started dictating poems to my mother before I could print," she related in Daryl Lane, William Vernon, and David Carson's *The Sound of Wonder.* But when the author entered college, she

wasn't sure which direction her ambition would take her. Bradley soon discovered the world of science–fiction fandom, however, with its conventions, newsletters, and amateur magazines, or "fanzines." As she recalled in *The Sound of Wonder* interview: "When I discovered the new pulp magazines—*Astounding, Thrilling Wonder Stories,* that sort of thing—and I saw the fan magazines in the back . . . it made me realize that there were other people who liked this sort of thing. All of a sudden, I realized that not only did I want to write for a living but that I wanted to write science fiction and fantasy." Through fandom the author saw her first story published—at age nineteen—and although she married young and was soon a mother, she continued writing while raising her children.

By the early 1960s, Bradley had published her first novels and was well on her way to establishing herself as a prominent figure in the genre. Although at that time science fiction was still dominated by male writers and editors, Bradley encountered no problems with discrimination. "I never knew an editor who cared whether I was a man or a woman or one of Aldous Huxley's fifty million apes as long as I could tell a good story," she recalled to Rosemary Herbert in *Publishers Weekly.* Bradley's first full–fledged Darkover works, *The Sword of Aldones* and *The Planet Savers,* appeared in a 1962 Ace double edition. By 1970 Bradley had written three more novels set on the forgotten Terran settlement of Darkover, and the series was gaining popularity among science fiction fans.

The "Darkover" Novels

Bradley explained in *The Sound of Wonder* her rationale for returning to Darkover for material: "I realized that I'd had to cut out so much [from the first book] that what I had cut out would make a sizable new book." Because she was also busy caring for her husband and children, including two toddlers, using a familiar setting was easier than working out the details for an entirely new world. "I figured that since people would read lots of books about Tarzan, Perry Mason, or Nero Wolfe . . . that people evidently liked reading about stories with the same background; it was easier to write about [Darkover] than to invent a whole new universe for each book."

Despite her frequent trips to the Darkover universe, Bradley made it a point to keep the novels independent from each other. "I had a feeling, and other writers told me, rather cynically, that the life of a paperback book was about five or six months," Bradley stated in *The Sound of Wonder.* "I realized that it was not safe to assume that anyone who read any of my books had ever read a previous book or would ever read another book by me. So I work[ed] very hard to make each book stand on its own feet and not assume any knowledge of previous books." This strategy—and the intelligent, challenging novels that resulted from it—was rewarded with the loyalty and appreciation of readers; by the time Bradley thought people "must be getting tired of it," the series was well established and Bradley's fans demanded more novels of Darkover. As Margaret Miles asserted in *Voice of Youth Advocates*, Bradley's "tremendously popular network of writings" about Darkover "has long been notable for holding something for almost every taste."

Consisting of over thirty books and spanning centuries of the world's history, Bradley's Darkover novels are less a "series" with a specific order than a network of individual stories linked by a common setting. Rediscovered after centuries of neglect by Earth's Terran Empire, the planet Darkover has now developed an independent society and a science based on powers of the mind. Darkover fascinates so many readers because it is a world of many contradictions; not only do the psychic abilities of the natives contrast with the traditional science of the Empire, but a basically repressive, male–dominated society coexists—however uneasily—with groups such as the Free Amazons, independent bands of women that govern themselves. The variety of internal and external conflicts produced by the collision of the Terran and Darkovan societies has provided Bradley with a wide range of story lines, told from the point of view of different people from different eras.

The constant culture clash on Darkover is one of the foremost conflicts in the series; the Empire is dependent on advanced technology—symbolized by the long–range blasters carried by the Terran Spaceforce—while the realms of Darkover have made a Compact that outlaws weapons that can kill from a distance. As a result, "the Darkover novels test various attitudes about the importance of technology," Rosemarie Arbur claimed in *Twentieth–Century Science Fiction Writers*, "and more important, they study the very nature of human intimacy." The critic explained that by contrasting Darkover's technologically "backward" yet fiercely independent people with the bureaucratic Empire of the Terrans, "Bradley sets up a conflict to which there is no 'correct' resolution." The author never settles the issue herself; as she commented in *The Sound of Wonder*, "There are different universes for different mental sets. . . . The idea of leaving open options and choices for everybody so they can find the kind of life–style that suits them best instead of assuming that everybody has to belong to the same life–style

[is] something that I felt very strongly about when I was a kid and I feel even more strongly about now than when I was fifteen." As a consequence, Bradley presents multiple viewpoints and "allows her readers almost complete freedom to decide which of the technologies, or which combination of the two, is the more humanely practical solution," Arbur concluded.

In *The Sword of Aldones*, for instance, a man of mixed Terran–Darkovan ancestry is called back to Darkover from self–imposed exile to oppose a renegade's illegal use of a destructive supernatural force known as "Sharra." Scarred by a previous encounter with Sharra's power, Lew Alton must use his Darkovan heritage in the service of a society that has never fully accepted him. "The most classically alienated of all Bradley heroes," as Laura Murphy described him in the *Dictionary of Literary Biography*, Alton "is a metaphor for the uneasy union between the two cultures." In contrast to Alton, who remains outside both cultures, Terran Andrew Carr of *The Spell Sword* and *The Forbidden Tower* chooses Darkovan society over that of the Empire. Other books have followed the earlier exploits of Lew Alton, the friendship between a Terran boy and a youthful Kennard Alton (Lew's father), and a Terran scientist's efforts to cure a Darkovan plague; still others trace the long history of the planet prior to its discovery by the Empire, from the colony's founding to the forming of the Compact.

In *Exile's Song* and *The Shadow Matrix*, the focus is on Margaret Alton and her return to Darkover after two decades of absence. She knows very little of her birth world and her return is at first met with a series of obstacles: the death of her academic mentor, a bevy of ridiculous marriage proposals, and a bad case of readjustment sickness from the recovery of her telepathic "laran" powers. Finally, reunited with her father she finds her place in Darkovan society. Reviewing *Exile's Song*, the 1996 addition to the Darkover series, in *Booklist*, Roland Green commented that the book was "an almost unalloyed pleasure from beginning to end and one of the few recent Darkover novels that someone unfamiliar with the series can pick up and get into immediately." In *The Shadow Matrix*, Margaret Alton learns to control her gifts, including the shadow matrix of the title, and she and her lover, Mikhail, are trying to overcome parental objections to their marriage. *Booklist*'s Green dubbed it a "high–class addition" to the Darkover saga, noting that the whole plot has a "certain melodramatic, even operatic, quality, but the pacing is brisk" and Bradley keeps the reader "turning pages." Green concluded that the Darkover saga "remains a monumental achievement" despite some signs of age.

Despite the disparity in subjects, one theme in particular provides a foundation for the Darkover novels, Susan M. Shwartz observed in *The Feminine Eye: Science Fiction and the Women Who Write It:* "For every gain, there is a risk; choice involves a testing of will and courage." Unlike some fantasy worlds where struggles are easily or simply decided, "on Darkover any attempt at change or progress carries with it the need for pain–filled choice," Shwartz commented. While Bradley provides her characters with ample avenues of action "in the Darkover books, alternatives are predicated upon two things . . . sincere choice and a willingness to pay the price choice demands." For example, Shwartz continued, "in *The Shattered Chain,* the payment for

taking an oath is the payment for all such choices: pain, with a potential for achievement. In Bradley's other books, too, the price of choice is of great importance."

The Shattered Chain is one of Bradley's most renowned Darkover novels and, as Arbur described it in her study *Marion Zimmer Bradley,* the novel "is one of the most thorough and sensitive science–fiction explorations of the variety of options available to a self–actualizing woman." The novel begins as a traditional quest when Lady Rohana, a noblewoman of the ruling class, enlists the aid of a tribe of Free Amazons to rescue a kidnapped kinswoman from a settlement where women are chained to show that they are possessions. But while the rescue is eventually successful, it is only the beginning of a series of conflicts. Rohana's experiences force her to reevaluate her life, and both the daughter of the woman she rescues and a Terran agent who studies the Amazons find themselves examining the limits of their own situations. "In terms of its structure, plot, characterization, and context within the series," Shwartz argued, *The Shattered Chain* "is about all the choices of all women on Darkover and, through them, of all people, male and female, Darkovan and Terran."

The last title in the series published in Bradley's lifetime, *Traitor's Sun,* was a collaborative effort with Adrienne Martine–Barnes. Here a wide range of characters that populate the planet of Darkover take the stage when Senator Hermes–Gabriel Aldaran returns home to Darkover to prevent the destruction of his beloved world by the Expansionists of the Terran Federation. A reviewer for *Publishers Weekly* observed that "fans of the series . . . should be satisfied with the happy glow engendered by spending time with familiar characters and their warm, humanistic values."

Avalon and Beyond

Murphy stated in the *Dictionary of Literary Biography* that Bradley emphasizes two main themes in her Darkover works: "The first is the reconciliation of conflicting or opposing forces—whether such forces are represented by different cultures or by different facets of a single personality. The second," the critic continued, "closely related to the first, is alienation or exile from a dominant group." While these ideas are featured in Bradley's Darkover series, they also appear in the author's first mainstream best seller, *The Mists of Avalon.* "Colorfully detailed as a medieval tapestry, *The Mists of Avalon* . . . is probably the most ambitious retelling of the Arthurian legend in

Bradley's well–regarded 1982 novel presents the legend of King Arthur from the point of view of the female characters in his life, including Arthur's mother, Igraine; his half–sister, Morgaine; and his wife, Gwenhwyfar.

the twentieth century," Charlotte Spivack maintained in *Merlin's Daughters: Contemporary Women Writers of Fantasy.* The critic added that this novel "is much more than a retelling. . . . [It] is a profound revisioning. Imaginatively conceived, intricately structured, and richly peopled, it offers a brilliant reinterpretation of the traditional material from the point of view of the major female characters," such as Arthur's mother Igraine; the Lady of the Lake, Viviane; Arthur's half–sister, the enchantress Morgaine; and Arthur's wife, Gwenhwyfar.

In addition, Bradley presents the eventual downfall of Arthur's reign as the result of broken promises to the religious leaders of Avalon. While Arthur gained his crown with the aid of Viviane and the Goddess she represents, the influence of Christian priests and Gwenhwyfar led him to forsake his oath. Thus not only does Bradley present Arthur's story from a different viewpoint, she roots it "in the religious struggle between matriarchal worship of the goddess and the patriarchal institution of Christianity, between what [the author] calls 'the cauldron and the cross,'" wrote Spivack. Despite critical praise for Bradley's fresh approach to Arthurian legend, *Washington Post* contributor Maude McDaniel finds *The Mists of Avalon* too motionless in its treatment of the Arthurian legend: "It all seems strangely static," the critic observed, "set pieces the reader watches rather than enters. Aside from a couple of lackluster jousts, everything is intrigue, jealousy and personal relationships, so that finally we are left with more bawling than brawling."

Maureen Quilligan, however, believed that Bradley's emphasis on Morgaine and the other female characters is both effective and appropriate; as she wrote in the *New York Times Book Review,* by "looking at the Arthurian legend from the other side, as in one of Morgaine's magic weavings, we see all the interconnecting threads, not merely the artful pattern. . . . *The Mists of Avalon* rewrites Arthur's story so that we realize it has always also been the story of his sister, the Fairy Queen." By presenting another side, the critic added, "this, the untold Arthurian story, is no less tragic, but it has gained a mythic coherence; reading it is a deeply moving and at times uncanny experience." "In short," concluded Beverly Deweese in a *Science Fiction Review* article, "Bradley's Arthurian world is intriguingly different. Undoubtedly, the brisk pace, the careful research and the provocative concept will attract and please many readers. . . . [But] overall, *Mists of Avalon* is one of the best and most ambitious of the Arthurian novels, and it should not be missed."

Bradley employs similar themes and approaches in reworking another classic tale: *The Firebrand,* the story of the fall of ancient Troy and of Kassandra,

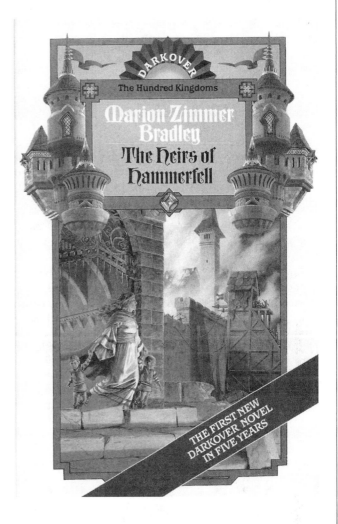

One of the later installments in her "Darkover" series, Bradley's 1989 novel introduces readers to young twins endowed with magical powers and impelled by their unique destiny: to free their people from exile.

royal daughter of Troy and onetime priestess and Amazon. As the author remarked in an interview with *Publishers Weekly*'s Lisa See, in the story of Troy she saw another instance of male culture overtaking and obscuring female contributions: "During the Dorian invasion, when iron won out over bronze, the female cult died," Bradley explained. "The Minoan and Mycenaean cultures were dead overnight. But you could also look at [that period of history] and say, here were two cultures that should have been ruled by female twins—Helen and Klytemnestra. And what do you know? When they married Menelaus and Agamemnon, the men took over their cities. I just want to look at what history was really like before the women–haters got hold of it. I want to look at these people like any other people, as though no one had ever written about them before." The result of Bradley's reconstruction, as *New York Times Book Review* contributor Mary Lefkowitz described it, is that Kassandra "becomes active, even aggressive; she determines the course of history, despite the efforts of her father, her brothers and other brutal male warriors to keep her in her place." "The dust of the war fairly rises off the page," noted a *Publishers Weekly* reviewer, "as Bradley animates this rich history and vivifies the conflicts between a culture that reveres the strength of women and one that makes them mere consorts of powerful men."

Bradley returns to ancient Britain with *The Forest House,* the story of the love between the erstwhile British priestess Eilan and the Roman officer Gaius Marcellius. The pair conceive a child before their respective families separate them, and Eilan in particular is caught between her feelings for Gaius, her position in the Forest House as High Priestess of the Great Goddess, and her problems with the competing influences of the Druids. After the two lovers are killed, Eilan's mentor takes their son Gawen to "Afallon." "With the sure touch of one at ease in sketching out mystic travels. . . " explained a critic for *Kirkus Reviews,* "Bradley writes with an unhurried pace and uncluttered staging." "History and legend collide," declared Carolyn Cushman in *Locus,* "and though history dominates, by the end the mythic elements grow to hint satisfactorily at the Arthurian wonder to come."

The 1997 novel *Lady of Avalon* creates a link between *The Forest House* and *The Mists of Avalon,* in a three–part fantasy set in Roman Britain that spans four centuries and deals with the priestesses and ladies of Avalon. Here Bradley traces the High Priestess of Avalori as well as the Sacrificed King through several cycles of reincarnation. Beginning with the orphaned Gawen, whose mother was killed in *The Forest House,* the novel follows him as he is initiated as Pendragon, and then on through time as Avalon is transported to a magic realm whose descendants form the destiny of Britannia. "A pillar of the fantasy field," wrote a critic for *Publishers Weekly,* "Bradley here combines the romance, rich historical detail, magical dazzlements, grand adventure and feminist sentiments into the kind of novel her fans have been yearning for." Writing in *Booklist,* Patricia Monaghan noted that "Bradley's women are, as usual, strong and vibrant, but never before has she so effectively depicted the heroic male." A further installment in the Avalon cycle is *Priestess of Avalon,* published after Bradley's death.

Despite this emphasis on female viewpoints in *The Firebrand* and her other fiction, Bradley is not a "feminist" writer. "Though her interest in women's

rights is strong," elaborated Murphy, "her works do not reduce to mere polemic." Arbur similarly stated in her study that Bradley "refuses to allow her works to wander into politics unless true concerns of realistic characters bring them there. Her emphasis is on character, not political themes." "Bradley's writing openly with increasing sureness of the human psyche and the human being rendered whole prompted Theodore Sturgeon to call the former [science fiction] fan 'one of the Big ones' currently writing science fiction," Arbur related in *Twentieth–Century Science–Fiction Writers.* "That she has extended her range" beyond science fiction and into "mainstream" fiction, the critic concluded, "suggests that Sturgeon's phrase applies no longer only to the science–fiction writer Marion Zimmer Bradley continues to be, for she has transcended categories."

Although Bradley's reputation spread beyond the science–fiction and fantasy community, she never abandoned the genre. She enjoyed it and appreciated both the new people and the new ideas she encountered through it. As she explained in *The Sound of Wonder,* "One thing that distinguishes the science fiction and fantasy fans [is that] they are thinking very seriously about the meaning of human life. Science fiction deals with the technological society in which we find ourselves and its various ramifications," the author continued. "Fantasy goes even deeper because it forces us to confront, you might say, the archetypal images in our own unconscious." She added that the science fiction and fantasy genre opens people's minds: "I think imagination is the one great thing that distinguishes us from the beasts, and science fiction is a very valuable corrective to modern education because it makes people think and it forces them to stretch their imaginations." Besides, she remarked in the introduction to *The Best of Marion Zimmer Bradley,* "I cannot imagine that the content of mainstream novels . . . can possibly compete with a fiction whose sole raison d'etre is to think about the future of the human race."

Although she had diabetes and suffered two strokes, Bradley continued working from her office in Berkeley, California, up until the end of her life, turning out new novels in the "Darkover" series and in the Avalon books. There, with the assistance of a cousin, Bradley dealt with the business end of being a writer: responding to mail, producing booklets of writing tips, editing original anthologies that introduce the work of new writers—in addition to working on original fiction. Much of her later work was done in collaboration with other well–known writers in the field. Her *Black Trillium,* for example, was written with Andre Norton and Julian May and deals with three heroines who undertake a quest, each according to her abilities. A sequel to that, *Lady of the Trillium,* was produced with Elisabeth Waters. *Booklist*'s Green, in a review of *Lady of the Trillium,* felt that "Bradley turns out a thoroughly satisfying yarn that brings to a fine conclusion a project that might have been a disaster in lesser hands."

If you enjoy the works of Marion Zimmer Bradley, you might want to check out the following books:

C. J. Cherryh, *Angel with the Sword,* 1985.
Bernard Cornwell, *Excalibur,* 1998.
Sharon Gree, *Silver Princess, Golden Knight,* 1993.
Anne McCaffrey, *The Rowan,* 1990.

On September 21, 1999, Bradley suffered a massive heart attack. Hospitalized at the Alta Bates Hospital in Berkeley, California, she passed away four days later. Whether working in science fiction, fantasy, gothics, nonfiction, or editing and inspiring the work of others, Bradley will be remembered for her works and for her vision, one that transported readers from the wonders of Darkover to the mysteries of Avalon and back.

■ **Biographical and Critical Sources**

BOOKS

Alpers, H. J., editor, *Marion Zimmer Bradley's Darkover,* Corian, 1983.
Arbur, Rosemarie, *Leigh Brackett, Marion Zimmer Bradley, Anne McCaffrey: A Primary and Secondary Bibliography,* G. K. Hall, 1982.
Arbur, Rosemarie, *Marion Zimmer Bradley,* Starmont House, 1985.
Arbur, Rosemarie, "Marion Zimmer Bradley," *Twentieth–Century Science Fiction Writers,* 2nd edition, St. James Press, 1986, pp. 75–77.
Bradley, Marion Zimmer, introduction to *The Best of Marion Zimmer Bradley,* edited by Martin H. Greenberg, DAW Books, 1988.
Bradley, Marion Zimmer, *Contemporary Authors Autobiography Series,* Volume 10, Gale, 1989, pp. 19–28.

Breen, Walter, *The Gemini Problem: A Study of Darkover,* T–K Graphics, 1975.
Breen, Walter, *The Darkover Concordance: A Reader's Guide,* Pennyfarthing Press, 1979.
The Darkover Cookbook, Friends of Darkover, 1977, revised edition, 1979.
Lane, Daryl, William Vernon, and David Carson, editors, *The Sound of Wonder: Interviews from "The Science Fiction Radio Show,"* Volume 2, Oryx, 1985, pp. 111–32.
Murphy, Laura, "Marion Zimmer Bradley," *Dictionary of Literary Biography,* Volume 8: *Twentieth–Century American Science Fiction Writers,* Gale, 1981, pp. 77–80.
Paxson, Diana, *Costume and Clothing as a Cultural Index on Darkover,* Friends of Darkover, 1977, revised edition, 1981.
Roberson, Jennifer, *Return to Avalon,* DAW Books, 1996.
St. James Guide to Young Adult Writers, 2nd edition, edited by Tom Pendergast and Sara Pendergast, St. James Press, 1999.
Shwartz, Susan M., "Marion Zimmer Bradley's Ethic of Freedom," *The Feminine Eye: Science Fiction and the Women Who Write It,* edited by Tom Staicar, Ungar, 1982, pp. 73–88.
Spivack, Charlotte, *Merlin's Daughters: Contemporary Women Writers of Fantasy,* Greenwood Press, 1987.
Wise, S., *The Darkover Dilemma: Problems of the Darkover Series,* T–K Graphics, 1976.

PERIODICALS

Algol, winter, 1977/1978.
Booklist, February 15, 1993, p. 1011; January 15, 1994, p. 875; March 15, 1995, p. 1313; September 1, 1995, p. 37; June 1, 1996, Roland Green, review of *Exile's Song,* p. 1681; September 1, 1996, p. 60; April 1, 1997, Patricia Monaghan, review of *Lady of Avalon,* p. 1268; July, 1997, Roland Green, review of *The Shadow Matrix,* p. 1773; September 1, 1998, p. 73; September 15, 1998, p. 213; January 1, 1999, p. 781.
Entertainment Weekly, May 20, 1994, p. 57.
Fantasy Review of Fantasy and Science Fiction, April, 1984.
Journal of Popular Culture, summer, 1993, pp. 67–80.
Kirkus Reviews, February 1, 1994, review of *The Forest House,* pp. 81–82.
Kliatt, November, 1983, Sister Avila Lamb, review of *Thendara House,* p. 1.
Library Journal, December, 1990, p. 167; December 15, 1991, p. 117; March 15, 1992, p. 129; June 15, 1992, p. 106; March 15, 1993, p. 111; May 15, 1993,

p. 100; June 15, 1993, p. 104; March 15, 1994, p. 104; June 15, 1994, p. 99; May 15, 1995, p. 99; May 15, 1997, p. 105; September 15, 1997, p. 106.

Locus, April, 1994, Carolyn Cushman, review of *The Forest House,* p. 29.

Los Angeles Times Book Review, February 3, 1983.

Mythlore, spring, 1984.

New York Times Book Review, January 30, 1983, Maureen Quilligan, "Arthur's Sister's Story," pp. 11, 30; November 29, 1987, Mary Lefkowitz, review of *The Firebrand,* p. 27.

Publishers Weekly, May 23, 1986, Rosemary Herbert, "The Author's Vision," pp. 42–45; September 11, 1987, review of *The Firebrand,* p. 79; October 30, 1987, Lisa See, "PW Interviews: Marion Zimmer Bradley," pp. 49–50; March 15, 1993, p. 74; February 28, 1994, p. 72; February 27, 1995, p. 91; May 19, 1997, review of *Lady of Avalon,* p. 71; February 23, 1998, p. 56; August 31, 1998, p. 53; December 14, 1998, review of *Traitor's Sun,* p. 61.

San Francisco Examiner, February 27, 1983.

Science Fiction Review, summer, 1983, Beverly Deweese, review of *The Mists of Avalon,* pp. 20–21.

Voice of Youth Advocates, June, 1990, Margaret Miles, review of *The Heirs of Hammerfell,* p. 113.

Washington Post, January 28, 1983, Maude McDaniel, review of *The Mists of Avalon.*

West Coast Review of Books, number 5, 1986.

■ **Obituaries**

PERIODICALS

Los Angeles Times, September 30, 1999, p. A24.
New York Times, September 29, 1999, p. A25.
Washington Post, October 3, 1999, p. C6.*

Bruce Coville

■ Personal

Born May 16, 1950, in Syracuse, NY; son of Arthur J. (a sales engineer) and Jean (an executive secretary; maiden name, Chase) Coville; married Katherine Dietz (an illustrator), October 11, 1969; children: Orion Sean, Cara Joy. *Education:* Attended Duke University and State University of New York at Binghamton; State University of New York at Oswego, B.A., 1974. *Politics:* "Eclectic." *Religion:* Unitarian.

■ Addresses

Agent—Ashley Grayson, 1342 18th Street, San Pedro, CA 90732.

■ Career

Author and playwright. Wetzel Road Elementary, Liverpool, NY, teacher, 1974–81. Co–host and co–producer of *Upstage,* a cable program promoting local theater, 1983. Has also worked as a camp counselor, grave digger, assembly line worker, and toy maker.

■ Member

Society of Children's Book Writers and Illustrators.

■ Awards, Honors

California Young Reader Medal, 1996–97, for *Jennifer Murdley's Toad;* Knickerbocker Award, New York State Library Association, 1997, for entire body of work; over a dozen Children's Choice awards from various states, including Arizona, Hawaii, Maryland, Maryland, and Nevada.

■ Writings

PICTURE BOOKS

The Foolish Giant, illustrated by wife, Katherine Coville, Lippincott, 1978.
Sarah's Unicorn, illustrated by K. Coville, Lippincott, 1979.
Sarah and the Dragon, illustrated by Beth Peck, Harper, 1984.
My Grandfather's House, illustrated by Henri Sorensen, BridgeWater, 1996.

JUVENILE FICTION

Spirits and Spells, Dell, 1983.
The Eyes of the Tarot, Bantam, 1983.

Waiting Spirits, Bantam, 1984.

Amulet of Doom, Dell, 1985.

The Brave Little Toaster Storybook, Doubleday, 1987.

Murder in Orbit, Scholastic, 1987.

Monster of the Year, Pocket, 1989.

Goblins in the Castle, Pocket, 1992.

The Dragonslayers, Pocket, 1994.

Oddly Enough (short stories), illustrated by Michael Hussar, Harcourt, 1994.

The World's Worst Fairy Godmother, illustrated by K. Coville, Pocket, 1996.

The Lapsnatcher, illustrated by Marissa Moss, Bridge-Water, 1997.

I Was a Sixth–Grade Alien, illustrated by Tony Sansevero, Pocket, 1999.

Odder than Ever (short stories), Harcourt, 1999.

The Attack of the Two–Inch Teacher, illustrated by T. Sansevero, Pocket, 1999.

I Lost My Grandfather's Brain, illustrated by T. Sansevero, Pocket, 1999.

Peanut Butter Lover Boy, illustrated by T. Sansevero, Pocket, 2000.

The Prince of Butterflies, illustrated by John Clapp, Harcourt, 2000.

Zombies of the Science Fair, illustrated by T. Sansevero, Pocket, 2000.

YOUNG ADULT NOVELS

Space Station ICE III, Archway, 1985.

Fortune's Journey, BridgeWater, 1995.

(With Jane Yolen) *Armageddon Summer,* Harcourt, 1998.

"CHAMBER OF HORROR" SERIES; YOUNG ADULT NOVELS

Bruce Coville's Chamber of Horror: Amulet of Doom, Archway, 1983.

Bruce Coville's Chamber of Horror: Spirits and Spells, Archway, 1983.

Bruce Coville's Chamber of Horror: The Eyes of the Tarot, Archway, 1984.

Bruce Coville's Chamber of Horror: Waiting Spirits, Archway, 1985.

"A. I. GANG" SERIES

Operation Sherlock, NAL, 1986.

Robot Trouble, NAL, 1986.

Forever Begins Tomorrow, NAL, 1986.

"CAMP HAUNTED HILLS" SERIES

How I Survived My Summer Vacation, Pocket, 1988.

Some of My Best Friends Are Monsters, Pocket, 1989.

The Dinosaur That Followed Me Home, illustrated by John Pierard, Pocket, 1990.

"MY TEACHER" SERIES

My Teacher Is an Alien, Pocket, 1989.

My Teacher Fried My Brains, Pocket, 1991.

My Teacher Glows in the Dark, Pocket, 1991.

My Teacher Flunked the Planet, Pocket, 1992.

"MAGIC SHOP" SERIES

The Monster's Ring, Knopf, 1982.

Jeremy Thatcher, Dragon Hatcher, illustrated by Gary A. Lippincott, Harcourt, 1991.

Jennifer Murdley's Toad, illustrated by G. A. Lippincott, Harcourt, 1992.

The Skull of Truth, illustrated by G. A. Lippincott, Harcourt, 1997.

"NINA TANLEVEN" SERIES

The Ghost in the Third Row, Bantam, 1987.

The Ghost Wore Gray, Bantam, 1988.

Ghost in the Big Brass Bed, Bantam, 1991.

"SPACE BRAT" SERIES; CHAPTER BOOKS

Space Brat, illustrated by K. Coville, Pocket, 1992.

Blork's Evil Twin, illustrated by K. Coville, Pocket, 1993.

The Wrath of Squat, illustrated by K. Coville, Pocket, 1994.

Planet of the Dips, illustrated by K. Coville, Pocket, 1995.

The Saber–toothed Poodnoobie, illustrated by K. Coville, Pocket, 1997.

"ALIEN ADVENTURES" SERIES

Aliens Ate My Homework, illustrated by K. Coville, Pocket, 1993.

I Left My Sneakers in Dimension X, illustrated by K. Coville, Pocket, 1994.

The Search for Snout, illustrated by K. Coville, Pocket, 1995.

Aliens Stole My Body, illustrated by K. Coville, Pocket, 1998.

"UNICORN CHRONICLES" SERIES

Into the Land of the Unicorns, Scholastic, 1994.
The Song of the Wanderer, Scholastic, 1999.

COMPILER AND EDITOR

Bruce Coville's Book of Monsters, Scholastic, 1993.
Bruce Coville's Book of Aliens, Scholastic, 1994.
Bruce Coville's Book of Ghosts, illustrated by J. Pierard, Scholastic, 1994.
Bruce Coville's Book of Nightmares, Scholastic, 1995.
Bruce Coville's Book of Spine Tinglers, Scholastic, 1996.
Bruce Coville's Book of Magic, Scholastic, 1996.
Bruce Coville's Book of Monsters II, illustrated by J. Pierard, Scholastic, 1996.
Bruce Coville's Book of Aliens II, Scholastic, 1996.
Bruce Coville's Book of Ghosts II, illustrated by J. Pierard, Scholastic, 1997.
Bruce Coville's Book of Nightmares II, illustrated by J. Pierard, Scholastic, 1997.
Bruce Coville's Book of Spine Tinglers II, Scholastic, 1997.
Bruce Coville's Book of Magic II, Scholastic, 1997.

RETELLER; PICTURE BOOKS

William Shakespeare, *William Shakespeare's The Tempest,* illustrated by Ruth Sanderson, Bantam, 1993.
William Shakespeare, *William Shakespeare's A Midsummer Night's Dream,* illustrated by Dennis Nolan, Dial, 1996.
William Shakespeare, *William Shakespeare's Macbeth,* illustrated by Gary Kelley, Dial, 1997.
William Shakespeare, *William Shakespeare's Romeo and Juliet,* illustrated by D. Nolan, Dial, 1999.

OTHER

(Author of book and lyrics) *The Dragon Slayers,* music by Angela Peterson, first produced at Syracuse Musical Theater, 1981.
(Author of book and lyrics) *Out of the Blue,* music by A. Peterson, first produced at Syracuse Musical Theater, 1982.
(Author of book and lyrics with Barbara Russell) *It's Midnight: Do You Know Where Your Toys Are?,* music by A. Peterson, first produced at Syracuse Musical Theater, 1983.
(With others) *Seniority Travel Directory,* Schueler Communications, 1986.
(With others) *The Sophisticated Leisure Travel Directory,* Schueler Communications, 1986.

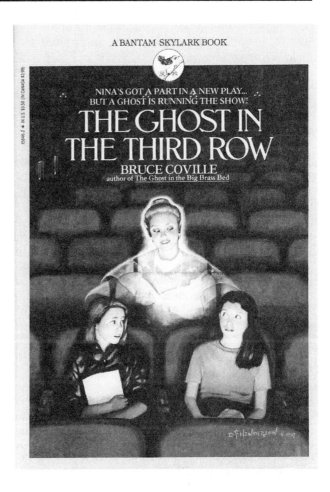

In his 1987 novel, the first of three books featuring feisty protagonist Nina Tanleven, Coville mixes myth with modernity as Nina's latest acting stint is upstaged by the antics of a mysterious spectre.

(Compiler and editor) *The Unicorn Treasury,* illustrated by Tim Hildebrandt, Doubleday, 1987.
The Dark Abyss (adult novel), Bantam, 1989.
Prehistoric People (nonfiction), illustrated by Michael McDermott, Doubleday, 1990.
(Compiler and editor) *Herds of Thunder, Manes of Gold: A Collection of Horse Stories and Poems,* illustrated by Ted Lewin, Doubleday, 1991.
(Compiler) *A Glory of Unicorns,* illustrated by Alix Berenzy, Scholastic, 1998.

Contributor to anthologies, including *Dragons and Dreams,* 1986, and *Read On! Two,* Books 4 and 6, 1987. Contributor to *Harper's Bookletter, Sesame Street Parent's Newsletter, Cricket,* and *Wilson Library Bulletin.* Associate editor, *Syracuse Business* and *Syracuse Magazine,* both 1982–83; editor and columnist, *Seniority,* 1983–84. Author, under pseudonym Robyn Tallis, of two books in the "Planet Builder" series, *Night of Two New Moons*, 1985, and *Mountain of Stolen Dreams*, 1988.

■ Adaptations

The Monster's Ring (cassette), Recorded Books, 1992; *The Ghost Wore Gray* (cassette), Recorded Books, 1993; *Jennifer Murdley's Toad* (cassette), Listening Library, 1996; *Jeremy Thatcher, Dragon Hatcher* (cassette), Listening Library, 1996; *Aliens Ate My Homework* (cassette), Listening Library, 1998; *Into the Land of the Unicorns: The Unicorn Chronicles Book I* (cassette), Listening Library, 1998; *The Skull of Truth* (cassette), Listening Library, 1998; *My Teacher Is an Alien* (cassette), Listening Library, 1998.

■ Work in Progress

Half Human, for Scholastic; *Twelfth Night*, the fifth of in the Shakespeare retellings series, for Dial; *The Ghost Saw Red*, for Bantam; *The Last Hunt*, the third volume of the "Unicorn Chronicles" series, for Scholastic; *The Wizard's Boy* and *In the Land of Always October*, both for Harcourt.

■ Sidelights

Bruce Coville is well known as a writer of juvenile fiction and the author of children's best–sellers such as *Jeremy Thatcher, Dragon Hatcher*. His novels draw heavily on mythic creatures, such as unicorns and dragons, as well as on science–fiction traditions, such as aliens and space stations, often with a humorous twist. He has also contributed to and edited volumes of short stories and completed several musical plays for younger audiences. Coville cherishes memories of his childhood, and once noted that his early surroundings nurtured his vivid imagination: "I was raised in Phoenix, a small town in central New York. Actually, I lived well outside the town, around the corner from my grandparents' dairy farm, which was the site of my happiest childhood times. I still have fond memories of the huge barns with their mows and lofts, mysterious relics, and jostling cattle. It was a wonderful place for a child to grow up. In addition to the farm, there was a swamp behind the house, and a rambling wood beyond that, both of which were conducive to all

Drama, history, and adventure combine in Coville's 1995 novel about a teen actress who travels the Oregon Trail in search of fame and fortune and discovers romance along the way.

kinds of imaginative games." It was during this period that Coville began to develop the heightened sensibility usually possessed by writers of fantasy.

Coville's father, not bookish himself, was instrumental in exposing the young Bruce to the delightful world of literature. Coville once recounted: "Despite this wonderful setting, much of what went on at that time went on in my head, when I was reading, or thinking and dreaming about what I had read. I was an absolute bookaholic. My father had something to do with this." Coville went on to explain: "He was a traveling salesman, a gruff but loving man, who never displayed an overwhelming interest in books. But if anyone was to ask me what was the best thing he ever did for me I could reply without hesitation that he read me *Tom Swift in the*

City of Gold. Why he happened to read this to me I was never quite certain, but it changed my life. One night after supper he took me into the living room, had me sit in his lap, and opened a thick, ugly brown book (this was the *original* Tom Swift) and proceeded to open a whole new world for me. I was enthralled, listened raptly, waited anxiously for the next night and the next, resented an intrusion, and reread the book several times later on my own. It was the only book I can ever remember him reading to me, but it changed my life. I was hooked on books."

An Early Interest in Writing

Coville may have loved books, but like many other authors, the realization that he wanted to be a writer came very abruptly. He once recalled: "I think it was sixth grade when I first realized that writing was something that I could do, and wanted to do very much. As it happened, I had spent most of that year making life miserable for my teacher by steadfastly failing to respond to the many creative devices she had to stimulate us to write. Then one day she simply (finally!) just let us write—told us that we had a certain amount of time to produce a short story of substance. Freed from writing topics imposed from without, I cut loose, and over several days found that I loved what I was doing. This may not be the first time that I knew I wanted to write, but it's the time that I remember." In addition to writing, Coville himself went on to be a teacher. He held a full–time position at Wetzel Road Elementary School, in Liverpool, New York, for seven years starting in 1974.

However, writing was always to be Coville's first love. He was introduced to the possibilities of writing for children by the woman who would later become his mother–in–law. He once explained that she "gave me a copy of *Winnie the Pooh* to read, and I suddenly knew that what I really wanted to write was children's books—to give to other children the joy that I got from books when I was young. This is the key to what I write now. I try with greater or lesser success, to make my stories the kinds of things that I would have enjoyed myself when I was young; to write the books I wanted to read, but never found. My writing works best when I remember the bookish child who adored reading and gear the work toward him. It falters when I forget him."

As he developed into an experienced writer, Coville worked in different genres. He created musical plays such as *The Dragon Slayers,* first produced at Syracuse Musical Theater. He contributed to anthologies of fantasy stories, such as *Dragons and Dreams.* But it was in the area of picture books, beginning with the publication of *The Foolish Giant* in 1978, that Coville made a significant mark. Illustrated by his wife, Katherine, that first tale for younger readers tells of a mild, clumsy giant who has difficulty being accepted by the ordinary people of his village until he saves them from an evil wizard. In the years since that first book, Coville has published numerous other tales for children, culminating in the appearance of several of his works on children's best–seller lists.

Many of Coville's books are jam–packed with the trappings of traditional mythic imagery: supernatural spirits, tarot cards, unicorns, prehistoric monsters, and futuristic creatures at the outer edge of the universe. He once noted that "myth is very important to me. My picture books have firm roots in basic mythic patterns. Hopefully, the patterns do not intrude, but provide a structure and depth that enhances my work." Coville often combines imaginary creatures with present–day people to create a tale of mystery or adventure. In *The Ghost in the Third Row,* for instance, Nina discovers an actual ghost haunting the theater where she is acting in a murder drama. Nina returns with her friend Chris in *The Ghost Wore Gray,* where the two try to discover the story behind the spirit of a Confederate soldier who appears in a New York hotel. "Despite the fantasy element of a ghost, this is a mystery," notes *School Library Journal* contributor Carolyn Caywood, who adds that the tale "evokes real feeling."

Baby Dragons, Magic Toads, and Shakespeare

Some of Coville's most popular books have been those that involve Mr. Elive's Magic Shop. In the first, *Jeremy Thatcher, Dragon Hatcher,* young Jeremy escapes his tormenter Mary Lou only to find himself in a strange shop where he buys an unusual egg. When the egg hatches a baby dragon—that no one else but Mary Lou can see—Jeremy finds himself in the midst of adventure. "The book is filled with scenes that will bring laughter and near tears to readers," notes Kenneth E. Kowen in *School Library Journal.* Reviewer Kathleen Redmond writes in *Voice of Youth Advocates* that the story is a good combination of real and fantasy worlds and "is right on target." Coville returns to the magic shop in *Jennifer Murdley's Toad,* where Jennifer purchases a lonely toad hatched from a witch's mouth. In aiding her pet, Bufo, who seeks his lost love, Jennifer herself is turned into a toad and learns to appreciate her inner strengths. *School Library Journal* contributor Margaret C. Howell praises Coville's theme as "particularly well handled," adding that "the story moves well, with realistic characterizations."

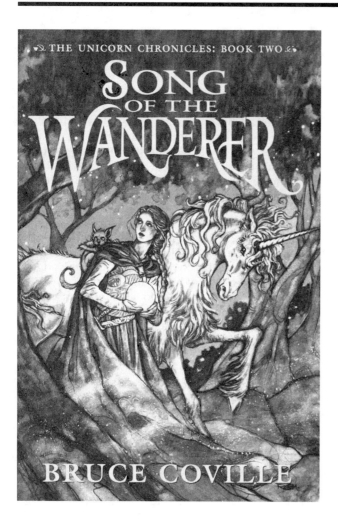

One of several books featuring unicorn lore, Coville's 1999 sequel to *Into the Land of the Unicorns* finds Cara on her way back to earth to save her grandmother, resisting at the same time the destructive magic of a fanatic ancestor determined to destroy all unicorns.

Coville believes that a knowledge of mythic patterns and imagery can facilitate children's growth and social understanding. He once argued: "This 'making sense' is a process that generally takes a lifetime and yet, sadly, it is all too often never even begun. To utilize myth as a guide in this quest one must be familiar with its patterns and structures, a familiarity that is best gained from reading or hearing myth and its reconstructions from earliest childhood on." Coville thinks that the literature he himself writes plays a part in exposing young people to the mythological realm. "I do not expect," he once explained, "a child to read my picture books and suddenly discover the secret of the universe. I do hope that something from my works will tuck itself

away in the child's mind, ready to present itself as a piece of a puzzle on some future day when he or she is busy constructing a view of the world that will provide at least a modicum of hope and dignity."

Beyond his grounding in classic fantasy, Coville has filled many of his books with a zany, pungent humor aimed squarely at his young audience. In reviewing *Planet of the Dips, School Library Journal* critic Anne Connor referred to the book as "literary junk food" appealing to "beginning readers with a passion for weird words, stupid jokes and odd behavior." For his part, Coville defends the outrageous extremes of such stories. "There are those who want to keep children's books 'tasteful,' and ten–year–old boys are not tasteful," he once said. "One of the reasons we have this problem of reluctant readers, especially among boys, is that we're not writing to who and what we are. If you write a book that's a brilliant character study and is wonderfully tasteful and no kid ever reads it, you've failed. . . . There's another problem, where you publish to only the lowest common denominator, where you start with that and don't go anywhere else. If you do that, you've failed, too. To me, there's a sweet spot in between, where you start with boisterous energy that will engage, and then you take the reader somewhere else."

Coville acknowledges that he has a particular knack for fast–paced comedic storytelling, a talent borne out by the success of his four books in the "My Teacher" series, each of which sold over one million copies. But he also diversified into other types of books during the 1990s, including a series of retellings of Shakespeare's classic plays. Coville found the task of adapting *The Tempest, A Midsummer Night's Dream, Macbeth,* and other works a satisfying challenge. "I've learned little ways to squeeze in more and more of the language, but keep it accessible," he once commented. "Both my editor and I are aware of the hutzpah of what we are doing. We want to be respectful of the source and of the audience. We work really hard on these books." Reviewing *William Shakespeare's Romeo and Juliet* in *Booklist,* Michael Cart calls the picture book "an accessible and entertaining introduction to one of Shakespeare's most popular works." Describing the text for *William Shakespeare's Macbeth* as being "true to the dark, brooding spirit of the play," *Booklist* contributor Hazel Rochman predicted that Coville's "dramatic narrative will keep [middle graders] reading."

Expanding further, Coville published several novels for young adults during the 1990s as well. *Fortune's Journey* combined action and romance in its tale of a resourceful teenage actress leading a theater troupe across the West during the Gold Rush era. The book received mixed reviews, with some critics praising the work strongly and others faulting the author for less–than–believable characters. "Part of it was, people complained that it was warped by a kind of contemporary mindset taking on these historical characters," Coville once recalled. "But I'd done the research, and I knew there was a lot more that young women were doing back then than people now think." *Armageddon Summer* follows the story of two teenagers caught up in a religious cult with their parents. Co–written with author Jane Yolen, the novel received more consistently favorable reviews. Writing in *Booklist*, Roger Leslie praised Coville and Yolen for "explor[ing] their rich, thought–provoking theme with the perfect balance of gripping adventure and understated pathos, leavened by a dollop of humor."

If you enjoy the works of Bruce Coville, you might want to check out the following books:

Lynne Reid Banks, *The Indian in the Cupboard*, 1980.
Debra Doyle and James D. MacDonald, *Groogleman*, 1996.
Margaret Peterson Haddix, *Leaving Fishers*, 1997.
Patricia C. Wrede, *Dealing with Dragons*, 1990.

Coville has remained committed to educating as well as entertaining young people. As he once explained: "This may seem like a long–term goal and a minimal result for the work involved, but I am, after all, a teacher. This has always been our lot. We deal with a child for a year, pour our hearts and souls into his development, and then send him on his way with the scant hope that somehow, someday, some little of what we have tried to do may present itself to him when it is needed. . . . But this is idle speculation. The first and foremost job in writing is to tell a whacking good story. You just have to hope it might mean something before you're done."

Personal motivation and social idealism both fuel Coville's commitment to children's literature. "There are two reasons that people go into writing for children," he once stated. "It's either to heal a wounded childhood, or to celebrate a happy one. It's about nine to one (in favor of) the healing to the happy. But I had a happy childhood, and I love children's books. They're delicious . . . the writing is better, the stories are more interesting. I do it out of a sense of joy and excitement. But it's also a political choice. I feel that one of the ways I can have real impact is working for kids."

■ **Biographical and Critical Sources**

PERIODICALS

Booklist, November 15, 1994, p. 593; September 1, 1996, p. 133; November 1, 1997, Hazel Rochman, review of *William Shakespeare's Macbeth*, p. 464; August, 1998, Roger Leslie, review of *Armageddon Summer*, p. 272; December 1, 1999, Michael Cart, review of *William Shakespeare's Romeo and Juliet*, p. 700.

Bulletin of the Center for Children's Books, February, 1991, p. 133; July, 1992, p. 292; July, 1996, p. 385; January, 1998, p. 117.

Kirkus Reviews, June 15, 1994, p. 842.

Locus, November, 1991, p. 53; April, 1992, p. 45; July, 1992, p. 48.

Publishers Weekly, July 27, 1992, p. 63.

School Library Journal, December, 1984, p. 100; February, 1988, p. 72; December, 1989, p. 98; September, 1990, p. 239; January, 1992, p. 108; September, 1988, Carolyn Caywood, review of *The Ghost Wore Gray*, p. 183; May, 1991, Kenneth E. Kowen, review of *Jeremy Thatcher, Dragon Hatcher*, p.91; September, 1992, Margaret C. Howell, review of *Jennifer Murdley's Toad*, p. 250; December, 1995, Anne Connor, review of *Planet of the Dips*, p. 79.

Voice of Youth Advocates, October, 1989, p. 221; June, 1991, Kathleen Redmond, review of *Jeremy Thatcher, Dragon Hatcher*, p. 106; February, 1996, p. 369

Times Educational Supplement, November 20, 1987, p. 30.

ONLINE

Bruce Coville's Web site, http://www.brucecoville.com (March 13, 2001).*

Fedor Dostoevsky

■ Personal

Born Fedor Mikhailovich Dostoevsky, October 30, 1821, in Moscow, Russia; died after suffering a hemorrhage in his throat, January 29, 1881, in St. Petersburg, Russia; buried in the Alexander Nevsky Monastery in Leningrad; name also transliterated as Feodor, Fyodor; also Mikhaylovich; also Dostoyevsky, Dostoievsky, Dostoevskii, Dostoevsky, Dostoiewsky, Dostoiefski, Dostoievski, Dostoyevskiiy, Dostoieffski; son of Mikhail Andreevich (a physician) and Maria Fedorovna (Nechaeva) Dostoevsky; married Maria Dmitrievna Konstant Isaeva (died April 15, 1864); married Anna Grigorevna Snitkina (a stenographer), February 15, 1867; children: (second marriage) Sonia, Lyubov, Fyodor, Alexey. *Education:* Military Engineering School, St. Petersburg, 1837–43. *Religion:* Russian Orthodox.

■ Career

Novelist, journalist, and short–story writer. Member of the Petrashevsky Circle (a radical group of socialist thinkers), 1847–49; political prisoner at a prison labor camp in Tobolsk, Russia, 1850–54; *Vremya* (journal), Russia, co–owner and editor, 1861–63;

Epokha (journal; title means "Epoch"), Russia, co–owner and editor, 1864–65; *Grazhdanin* (journal; title means "The Citizen"), Russia, editor and columnist, 1871–74; *Dnevnik pisatelya* (monthly journal), Russia, owner, author, and publisher, 1876–77, 1881. Public Speaker. *Military service:* Russian Army, 1843–44, served in engineering; rank of lieutenant; and 1854–59, served in Semipalatinsk; became lieutenant.

■ Writings

(Translator) Honore de Balzac, *Eugenie Grandet,* [Russia], 1844.

Bednye lyudi (title means "Poor Folk"), [Russia], 1846.

Dvoinik (translation published as *The Double*), [Russia], 1846.

Roman v devyati pis'makh (title means "A Novel in Nine Letters"), [Russia], 1847.

Chuzhaya zhena i muzh pod krovat'yu (title means "Another Man's Wife and a Husband under the Bed"), [Russia], 1848.

Elka i svad'ba (title means "A Christmas Party and a Wedding"), [Russia], 1848.

Netochka Nezvanova, [Russia], 1849, translated by Jane Kentish as *Netochka Nezvanova,* Viking, 1986.

Dyadyushkin son (novella; title means "Uncle's Dream"), [Russia], 1859.

Selo Stepanchikovo (novella; title means "The Friend of the Family"), [Russia], 1859.

Zapiski iz mertvogo doma (title means "The House of the Dead"), [Russia], 1860–62.

Unizhennye i oskorblennye (translations published as *The Insulted and Injured* and *Injury and Insult*), [Russia], 1861.

Prestuplenie i nakazanie, [Russia], 1866, translated by Jessie Coulson as *Crime and Punishment*, edited by George Gibian, [New York], 1964.

Igrok (novella; title means "The Gambler"), [Russia], 1867.

Idiot, [Russia], 1868, translated as *The Idiot*, 1887.

Vechnyi muzh (novella; title means "The Eternal Husband"), [Russia], 1870.

Besy, (title means "The Devils" translation published as *The Possessed*), [Russia], 1872.

Dnevnik pisatelya (title means "The Diary of a Writer"; essays and short stories), [Russia], 1873–77; translated by Kenneth Lantz as *A Writer's Diary,*, Northwestern University Press, 1993.

Podrostok (title means "A Raw Youth" or "The Adolescent"), [Russia], 1875, translated by Richard Freeborn as *An Accidental Family*, with introduction and notes, Oxford University Press, 1994.

Brat'ya Karamazovy, [Russia], 1880, translated by Constance Garnett as *The Brothers Karamazov*, edited by Ralph Matlaw, Norton (New York City), 1976.

The Notebooks for "Crime and Punishment," translated by Edward Wasiolek, University of Chicago Press, 1967.

The Notebooks for "The Idiot," edited by E. Wasiolek, translated by Katharine Strelsky, University of Chicago Press, 1967.

The Notebooks for "The Possessed," edited by E. Wasiolek, translated by Victor Terras, University of Chicago Press, 1968.

The Notebooks for "A Raw Youth," translated by V. Terras, University of Chicago Press, 1969.

The Notebooks for "The Brothers Karamazov," translated by E. Wasiolek, University of Chicago Press, 1971.

COLLECTIONS

Novels, translated by Constance Garnett, Macmillan (New York City), 1912.

Polnoe sobranie khudozhestvennykh proizvedenii; Dnevnik pisatelya; stat'i, thirteen volumes, edited by B. Tomashevskii and K. Khalabaev, [Russia], 1926–30.

Pis'ma, four volumes, edited by A. S. Dolinin, [Russia], volumes 1–3, 1928–34, volume 4, 1959.

The Short Novels of Dostoevsky, translated by C. Garnett, Dial (New York City), 1945.

The Short Stories of Dostoevsky, edited by William Phillips, translated by C. Garnett, Dial (New York City), 1946.

Dostoevsky's Occasional Writings, translated and edited by David Magarshack, Random House (New York City), 1963.

The Unpublished Dostoevsky, Diaries and Notebooks, 1860–1881, three volumes, University of Michigan Press (Ann Arbor), 1973–76.

OTHER

Complete Letters, five volumes, translated by David A. Lowe, Ardis, 1989–91.

Also author of short stories, including "Mr. Prokharchin," 1846; "Khozyaika" (translation published as "The Landlady"), 1847; "Belye nochi" (title means "White Nights"), 1848; "Polzunkov," 1848; "Slaboe serdtse" (title means "A Faint Heart"), 1848; "Chestnyi vor" (title means "An Honest Thief"), 1848; "Skvernyi anekdot" (title means "A Vile Anecdote"), 1861; "Zapiski iz podpol'ya" (translation published as "Notes from Underground"), 1864; "Neobyknovennoe sobytie, ili passazh v passazhe" (title means "The Crocodile, or Mauled in the Mall"), 1865; "Bobok," 1873; "Krotkaya" (title means "A Gentle Creature" or "The Meek One"), 1876; and "Son Smeshnogo cheloveka" (title means "The Dream of a Ridiculous Man"), 1877.

■ Sidelights

Russian writer Fedor Dostoevsky represents many things to many people. There is Dostoevsky the existentialist, Dostoevsky the psychologist, Dostoevsky the arch conservative who foretold the repression and tyranny of the Soviet state, Dostoevsky the Orthodox Christian. His novels and short stories plumb the depths of human experience, exposing frailties, asking searching questions, and during his lifetime perplexing, with each succeeding book, those who thought they knew him. Novels such as *Crime and Punishment*, *The Idiot*, *Notes from the Underground*, *The Possessed* (also known as *The Devils*), and *The Brothers Karamazov* have all passed into the canon of world literature. However, as William J. Leatherbarrow noted in his critical study *Fedor Dostoevsky*, "Dostoevsky appears to be in no danger of becoming a 'classic,' a literary fossil respected for his historical achievement but of limited relevance to modern thought." Leatherbarrow further commented, "His works speak directly and with urgency in the present age, and have contributed greatly to the shape and psychology of modern fiction." The eminent critic George Steiner also noted this degree in which Dostoevsky still lives in his writing. "Dostoevsky has penetrated more deeply than Tolstoy into the fabric of contemporary thought," Steiner wrote. Dostoevsky's novels, according to Leatherbarrow, "which tend toward plurality and discord in both their technique and the image they project of modern man, correspond so perfectly to the complex nature of modern life as to engage the interest of all readers, no matter how diverse their outlooks. The twentieth century has done everything possible to confirm the accuracy of Dostoevsky's chaotic vision."

And chaos there is in Dostoevsky. The axe murder of a female pawnbroker sets off a strangled chain of events and an interior monologue of startling prescience; a radical and a nihilist involve the innocent in their schemes for a brave new world; four brothers explore realms of guilt over the death of their father; a truly Jesus–like figure is all but destroyed by the modern world. These are only some of the bleak plots around which Dostoevsky built his amazing novels. "Dostoevsky was," according to D. A. Traversi writing in *The Criterion*, "the master of all explorers of physical and spiritual disorder, and . . . his findings expose an erring adventure in human experience—the experiment, ultimately, of replacing the true balance of living by the despotic activity of the independent mind." The critic Georg Lukacs called Dostoevsky "a writer of world eminence" whose works "illuminated all the deepest questions of [his] age, sooner, more deeply, and more widely than in average life itself." Lukacs went on to declare that Dostoevsky's works "have become even more topical and more fresh as time goes on." The great irony of Dostoevsky's life is perhaps that his thought fits better into the modern age to which he in part gave birth, than in his own epoch, a tyrannical, pre–industrial state tottering into the twentieth century and ripe for revolution, yet fearful of change.

Considered among the greatest works of fiction ever written, Dostoevsky's 1866 novel concerns a young man whose successful commission of the perfect crime is later undone by a fervent desire for spiritual redemption.

A Raw Youth

Dostoevsky was born on October 30, 1821, in Moscow, the second of seven children. The date of his birth foreshadowed the many interpretations Dostoevsky the writer would later receive. By the Old Style, or Julian calendar, the date is October 30, but by the time of the Russian Revolution in 1917 the Old Style was left behind for the Gregorian calendar which places his date of birth on November 11, 1821. Despite what date is assigned to his birth, Dostoevsky was brought up in what amounted to a

lower middle class household, though his father, Mikhail Andreevich, a retired army surgeon and a doctor for the Marinsky Hospital for the poor at the time of his son's birth, was accorded noble status. A stern and strict father, Mikhail Andreevich was balanced by his wife, Maria Fedorovna, daughter of a merchant family and sensitive, frail, and understanding. Dostoevsky's older brother, Mikhail, was his closest friend through youth and on into adulthood: the two learned of books together while young, and later collaborated on literary journals. The Dostoevsky family was, as many observers have noted, an insular, self–contained one, relying on one another for close friendships rather than looking elsewhere. Educated at home for his first twelve years, Dostoevsky's early learning focused on Orthodox religious training and mathematics, and he took long walks for physical activity. Unlike such contemporaries as Leo Tolstoy and Ivan Turgenev, Dostoevsky did not enjoy the cultural privileges of the aristocracy and acutely felt the absence of such an upbringing all his life.

In 1833, both Dostoevsky and his older brother began outside education in Moscow, boarding at a private school where the young Dostoevsky never really fit in with the other pupils. Though he had now escaped the stern discipline of his father, he was still under the thumb of peer pressure. Books became a refuge for him, and he began to read the works of the great writers of the European tradition, including the adventures of Sir Walter Scott and the fantasies of E. T. A. Hoffmann in addition to the work of the Russian, Alexander Pushkin, who died in 1837, the same year as Dostoevsky's mother. Shortly after her death, Dostoevsky set out for St. Petersburg with brother Mikhail. Their father had determined that a career in the military was the fate for both and they sat for entrance exams to the St. Petersburg Academy of Military Engineering. Passing these tests, Dostoevsky was more on his own than he had ever been, for his brother failed to gain entrance. The two began a long correspondence which would last until Mikhail's death in 1864, but Dostoevsky was largely without friends at first at the Academy. "Sensitive, sickly, withdrawn, and emotionally volatile," he was "singularly unpromising material for a military life," according to Leatherbarrow. The one shining light of his years in the academy was the education in the humanities it provided. Pupils were educated in the great works of the Russian tradition, including Pushkin, Mikhail Lermontov, and Nikolay Gogol, as well as Europeans such as William Shakespeare, Johann Wolfgang von Goethe, Victor Hugo, George Sand, and, above all, Friedrich Schiller, whose works he grew to know by heart, and Honore de Balzac, whose work he would later translate. During the summer months Dostoevsky stayed with his father, who had bought an estate in the country, and during the latter part of his stay at the Military Academy he also made the acquaintance of an older poet, Ivan Shidlovsky, who encouraged the young student's reading and interest in literature.

In 1839, Dostoevsky's father died; some biographers and critics have contended that he was murdered. Sigmund Freud later made much of the supposed murder, claiming that, as a result of the death, Dostoevsky most probably suffered the first of his epileptic fits and was burdened by guilt for possibly wishing the old tyrant dead. There is little evidence to prove such a murder at the hands of the elder Dostoevsky's serfs, yet it is probable that his father's death did affect Dostoevsky. In 1843, he graduated from the Military Academy and served one year in the army. Yet he had no desire to remain in the military or in engineering. By now his first love was literature, and he determined to become a full–time writer.

Early Works

Partly as an exercise in translation and partly as a course of study in the composition of a novel, Dostoevsky translated and published Balzac's *Eugenie Grandet*, in 1844. It was his first published work. From here, the journeyman writer decided to try his own hand at a novel, eschewing the gothic romanticism of Schiller, Scott, and Pushkin and turning instead to the real world and the tradition of Balzac for inspiration. By 1846 he had produced his first novel, *Poor Folk*, a naturalistic tale about a poor civil servant and a humiliated girl written in the form of an epistolary novel. Makar Devushkin is a poor copying clerk who exchanges letters with the impoverished Varvara Dobrosyolova, who has been procured for a wealthy man whom she, in the end, marries. As such, Varvara is the first of a long line of "fallen women" about whom Dostoevsky would write. This first novel looked not just at the material effects of poverty but also, for the first time, at the psychological ones as well, going far beyond the inspiration of Gogol, who had also written about a poor copying clerk in his tale "The Overcoat."

This first novel was passed on via a friend to the poet Nikolay Nekrasov, who in turn took it to the influential critic Vissarion Belinsky. This powerful man declared that a new genius had arisen in Russian letters, and Dostoevsky's career was seemingly made. Sudden fame came to the writer—who was only twenty–five at the time of publication of *Poor Folk*. Even in America the novel gained popularity in the nineteenth century, dubbed as it was a "simple, intensely pathetic story" and "one of the gems of literature" by a reviewer for *Nation*. However, such fame proved fleeting, as Dostoevsky managed, with his poorly developed social skills and arrogance, to alienate those who had at first lionized him. Publishing further stories and novels, such as *The Double* and *White Nights*, Dostoevsky lost his champion Belinsky who faulted the writer for his concentration on psychological states rather than social issues. In *The Double*, his second novel, Dostoevsky creates a study of schizophrenia boldly narrated through the voice of one of the main character's split selves. Though critics since the time of writing have come to see *The Double* as one of Dostoevsky's most significant early works and one far in advance of its time, contemporary critics, including Belinsky, disliked the novel. In *White Nights,* Dostoevsky depicts the mentality of a dreamer via a nameless narrator who walks the streets of St. Petersburg as a substitute for human connections. Saving a young woman, Natasenka, from a drunkard, he becomes entangled with her in a mysterious, dream–like attachment through the white nights of early summer. Short stories, including "Mister Prokarchin" and "The Landlady," only served to complete the rift between Belinsky and his young protégé. By 1847, Dostoevsky was on the outs with

OXFORD WORLD'S CLASSICS

FYODOR DOSTOEVSKY
THE IDIOT

A new translation by Alan Myers

A portrait of Russia under the final decades of Tsarist rule, Dostoevskys 1868 novel introduces the Christ–like Prince Myshkin, whose innocence, idealism, and quest for truth in a materialistic and spiritually empty society ultimately causes his downfall.

the established writing community. By this time, however, he was also already involved in other activities that would change his life forever.

In 1847, Dostoevsky began to participate in the Petrashevsky Circle, which was one of many such groups during the repressive régime of Tsar Nicholas I that met to discuss matters of social utopianism. Far from being a radical, Dostoevsky was drawn to such secret meetings in part because of his strong disapproval of serfdom. By 1849, he had withdrawn from the Petrashevsky Circle but was still taking part in a more moderate group which discussed mostly literary matters. Now he came under the influence of Nikolay Speshnev, a romantic intellectual recently returned from abroad who manipulated this new group into more revolutionary topics. On April 23, 1849, Dostoevsky and the other members of the Petrashevsky Circle were arrested and sent to the infamous Peter and Paul Fortress to await trial on charges of subversion. At his trial, he and other members were found guilty and sentenced to death. The execution was scheduled to take place on December 22, but at the very last moment the death sentences were commuted by imperial decree. This had been the Tsar's intention all along; it was his way of teaching the condemned men a lesson, and it did. Dostoevsky was sentenced to four years in a Siberian prison and an indeterminate number of years in the military to follow. Dostoevsky's career as a writer had seemingly come to an abrupt end.

To Siberia and Back Again

Dostoevsky was sent to the Omsk penal colony in Siberia where he suffered severe deprivations but also came into contact with what he now saw as the real Russian people—those not influenced by European ideas. The four years he spent in the labor camp also brought him into contact with the criminal mind, a fact that would greatly influence much of his later work, for at the heart of each of his major novels is a murder. It was in Omsk that he probably had the first of his epileptic fits, a condition that would plague him for the rest of his life. Released from the penal colony in 1854, he was sent as a private in the army to Semipalatinsk in Siberia. With his relative freedom he took up writing again as well as reading; he had his brother send the philosophical works of Immanuel Kant and Georg Wilhelm Friedrich Hegel, and also read from the *Koran.* It was during this time that he fell in love with a married woman, Maria Dmitrievna Isaeva, a highly strung, emotional person who also suffered from tuberculosis. Though they were a torment to one another, the two married in 1857, about the time that Dostoevsky earned the right to once again publish. Several stories had been published in journals in St. Petersburg by December of 1859 when Dostoevsky, along with his new wife, were allowed to return to that city.

Dostoevsky's long exile in Siberia had turned him into a reactionary and an enemy of radicalism, but the Russia he returned to was a changed one, moderated by the death of Nicholas I and the succession of his son, Alexander II, who ultimately freed the serfs in 1861. There was also a new sense of materialism and reform in the air, yet Dostoevsky was devoted to Christian beliefs and had a strong fear of political change. In the common Russian people, Dostoevsky saw the purest essence of Christianity in action, unaltered by Western influences and the new materialism. Back in St. Petersburg, Dostoevsky and his brother founded the journal *Vremya* ("Time"), in which he published three of his own works, including *The House of the Dead,* the precursor to the twentieth-century genre of prison camp literature, describing his years in Siberia. Told from the point of view of Alexander Petrovich Goryanchikov, the novel relates the prison experiences of this former French tutor who was sentenced to ten years hard labor for the murder of his wife. In the end, Goryanchikov has learned the true meaning of freedom, in much the same way Dostoevsky had.

Dostoevsky's literary journal was closed down by the government after it published a questionable article, and then he and his brother started a new magazine, *Epokha* ("Epoch"), in 1864. Much of the 1860s was spent in western Europe. In 1862, he traveled with a young woman, Appolinara Suslova, with whom he was having an affair. He made subsequent trips, drawn by his newfound love of gambling and by a need to stay one step ahead of his creditors. Meanwhile he managed to publish in *Epokha* his *Notes from the Underground,* considered by many to be among his finest works and the first major work of the second phase of Dostoevsky's writing career. In this short, first-person novel, existential and psychological matters—always a part of his writing—now supercede the social realism of his earlier works. The nameless narrator, the Underground Man, incisively attacks positions held by liberals and radicals alike, such as the possibility of designing a utopian society or the rejection of individual choice over the good of the community. Divided into two parts, the first segment, narrated from a sort of cave inhabited by the Underground Man for four decades, is an extended diatribe on society. The second part of the novel explains events leading up to the man's self-imposed exile, culminating in his fleeting relationship with the prostitute Liza, who makes him wonder if it is better to pursue simple animal happiness or a higher life of suffering. "By all standards *Notes from the Under-ground* is one of the strangest and most urgent works of modern fiction," wrote Leatherbarrow, and most critics concur in this judgment. Though the novel was in part intended to advocate Christianity as a means by which individual freedom could be reached, the Underground Man in the end remains unredeemed, partly because Dostoevsky was unable to publish a large tract of the tale. The state censor refused to allow Gospel messages to come from the mouth of this profane hero who comes across as coarse and petty as well as cowardly. But Dostoevsky did accomplish the introduction of a totally new type of protagonist into literature, the antihero who is both bitter and frustrated.

Dostoevsky had his own share of frustration, bitterness, and suffering in these years, with the deaths of his estranged wife in 1864 and of his beloved brother later that year, the closing of his journal, and the refusal by his long-time mistress of his offer of marriage. And there was also the gambling which, along with the new burden of helping to support his brother's family, created a financial pressure that forced him to write rapidly and often. For the rest of his creative life, Dostoevsky was rushing to meet deadlines. Returning abroad in 1865, he found himself short of money and sold first serial publication rights to his next novel, *Crime and Punishment,* to the magazine *Russian Herald.* However, he already owed another novel to a different publisher who would have rights to free publication of his works if he failed to deliver on time. Thus, with *Crime and Punishment* taking longer than projected, Dostoevsky decided to do the impossible: he hired a stenographer and transcribed *The Gambler* in just under four weeks to satisfy the one publisher in between writing the final portions of *Crime and Punishment* for the other. The stunt paid off not only financially; Dostoevsky subsequently married the stenographer, Anna Grigorevna Snitkina, who helped to put the chaotic writer's financial life on an even keel and who built a family of four with Dostoevsky.

Crime and Punishment

One of Dostoevsky's greatest novels, *Crime and Punishment* explores the theme of individual redemption by suffering. Set in St. Petersburg in the middle of the nineteenth century, *Crime and Punishment* features an impoverished young law student, Rodion Raskolnikov, who ruminates committing a perfect crime. Raskolnikov's very name—derived from the Russian for "schism" or "split"—becomes part of the symbolic apparatus of the novel, for this student is intended to represent spiritual nihilism. He kills an old pawnbroker and her sister with an ax and steals the jewelry from their flat in part to help out his own family but also to rid the world of the pawnbroker, whom Raskolnikov sees as an odious person. Summoned by the police, he thinks all is over, but they only want to question him about money he owes to his landlady. He falls ill after this, only to discover that a neighbor has been arrested for the murder. Tortured by guilt, Raskolnikov talks with the examining magistrate, Porfiry Petrovitch, about the case, hypothesizing that a man of superior intelligence might be justified in committing such a crime, one that an ordinary person would not be allowed to get away with. Such "superman" theories predate those of the philosopher Friedrich Nietzche by over a decade.

Raskolnikov fears that he has put the detective on his trail, but is distracted for a time by the death of his friend, Marmeladov, and the changing fortunes of his sister whom he was partly protecting with his crime. He forms a relationship with Sonia, the daughter of his dead friend and a pious young girl who had once taken to prostitution to save her family. Tortured by guilt, and confessing his sins to Sonia, Raskolnikov finally admits his crime to the police and is sent to Siberia where, it seems, he ultimately finds peace and salvation through Christianity. He has finally come to learn that he cannot simply guide his life through reason and intellect alone. Convinced of his own superiority at first, through the course of the novel Raskolnikov slowly learns that free will is, in fact, limited and that happiness is achieved through suffering rather than through reasoning.

Dostoevsky's novel became a sensation as it was serialized, and was considered a popular and critical success. Upon its English publication in the 1880s, the British and American press also extolled its virtues. Calling Dostoevsky "one of the most remarkable modern writers," a reviewer for *Athenaeum* went on to describe *Crime and Punishment* as "one of the most moving of modern novels" and "the best and fullest explanation of Nihilism in existence." A contributor for *Spectator* felt the novel was Dostoevsky's "finest work," one whose keynote is "suffering and sacrifice." The same reviewer further noted that "[t]o be understood, it must be studied. . . . None but a Russian and a genius could draw such a character as Rodion Raskolnikov." The famed Scottish novelist and essayist Robert Louis Stevenson noted in a letter to John Addington Symonds in 1886 that *Crime and Punishment* "is easily the greatest book I have read in ten years," while the American writer and critic, William Dean Howells wrote in *Harper's* that in this novel "the author studies the effect of murder in the assassin, who is brought to confession and repentance by a hapless creature whom poverty has forced to a life of

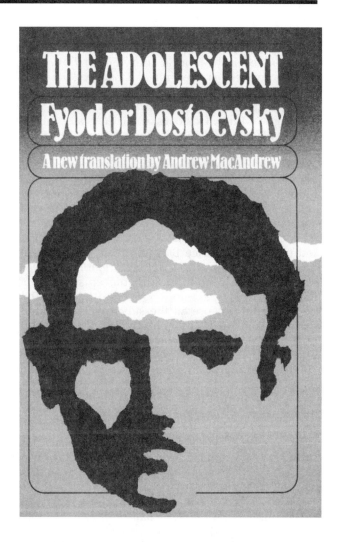

In his 1875 novel, Dostoevsky deals with a young man's coming of age as he idealistically searches for spiritual guidance in a society torn between the conservative values of old Russia and the nihilism of the coming modern age.

shame." Howells felt that although *Crime and Punishment* depicts "a lurid chapter of human life," there is also "the light of truth . . . in it. . . . It is the reverse of a pessimistic book." "Dostoevsky's characters retain the saving element of manhood," commented a contributor to *Literary World*, "and their author never makes the error of depicting them as beasts." The same critic went on to say that it is "a book that gains in power by a second or a third reading, that takes hold upon the memory and leaves it peopled with new shapes . . . pulsating with the universal longings that cry from the depths for the comprehension and sympathy of a common humanity."

Over the years the repute of *Crime and Punishment* continued to grow. The English critic J. Middleton Murry noted in his critical study *Fyodor Dostoevsky*, that the novel "is the first of Dostoevsky's great books," and that it "is the first in which he dared really to state the doubt which tortured him." According to Murry, Dostoevsky finally dealt with the nature of true evil in this book, especially in the character of Svidrigailov, once the evil employer and would–be seducer of Raskolnikov's sister, Dounia, and a complex character in his own right who ultimately kills himself out of ennui. "Before *Crime and Punishment* Dostoevsky is a novelist in the old and familiar sense," Murry wrote. "With *Crime and Punishment* he leaves the material world, never to return to it." Maurice Baring, in his *Landmarks in Russian Literature*, called *Crime and Punishment* "Dostoevsky's 'Macbeth'." Noting the episode when Raskolnikov kneels before Sonia and tells her that he is kneeling before all the suffering of mankind, Baring commented, "[t]hat is what Dostoevsky does himself in this and his books." Baring further noted, however, that in none of Dostoevsky's other books "is the suffering of all mankind conjured up before us in more living colours, and in none of them is his act of homage in kneeling before it more impressive." Writing in *Partisan Review*, Philip Rahv noted that "Dostoevsky is the first novelist to have fully accepted and dramatized the principle of uncertainty or indeterminacy in the presentation of character." Rahv went on to call *Crime and Punishment* a "masterpiece."

Serial publication of *Crime and Punishment* gained Dostoevsky widespread popular acclaim and placed him once again at the top of the literary class in Russia. However, it gained little financially for the ever–pressed novelist, and after its publication Dostoevsky left for Europe once again.

The Idiot and *The Possessed*

Dostoevsky and his new wife, Anna Grigorevna, remained in Europe for four years, living variously in Geneva, Florence, Vienna, Prague, and lastly Dresden. These were creative years for Dostoevsky, with publication of *The Idiot, The Eternal Husband,* and *The Possessed* in 1871 when he returned to St. Petersburg. In Geneva, partly inspired by a Hans Holbein painting he had seen, Dostoevsky resolved to write a novel about a wholly good and beautiful man and to do so in a psychologically convincing manner. As usual, Dostoevsky was beset by money problems during the writing of *The Idiot*, problems in large part brought on by his addiction to gambling. As a strong antidote to this gambling sickness, Dostoevsky threw himself into the writing,

finishing one hundred pages in twenty–three days. The couple also lost their first–born daughter, Sonia, during this time, another psychological burden that crept into the writing.

The hero of *The Idiot* is Prince Myshkin, a kind of modern Christ, who returns to St. Petersburg after four years in Europe where he was being treated for epilepsy. Attempting to do good, the Prince is thought to be an idiot by those around him, and ultimately his very goodness brings disaster to the female protagonist of the novel, Natasya Fillipovna, one of Dostoevsky's strongest female characters, yet another fallen woman, seduced in youth and badly used by the world. Unlike Sonia in *Crime and Punishment*, however, Natasya does not believe in forgiveness—she wants to get even. Throughout the novel she is both attracted and repelled by Myshkin as well as by Parfen Rogozhin, who represents the life of passion and nihilism where the Prince is the symbol of light and serenity. Finally, Natasya, agreeing to marry Myshkin, decides to run away with Rogozhin instead. Frantic, the Prince searches for his missing bride only to find that Rogozhin has killed her at his apartment. The police take Rogozhin away, and the Prince, deeply upset, returns to his Swiss sanitarium a broken man. That the Prince's goodness should lead to the destruction of himself and those around him is one more example of Dostoevsky's major theme: redemption only through suffering. Do not look for any earthly utopia, he seems to say; distrust materialism. Only through pain do we attain Christian redemption.

A mixture of Don Quixote as well as Christ, Myshkin has become one of Dostoevsky's most beloved characters, and Natasya, in a role reminiscent of Mary Magdalene, gave the book and literature one of the most fascinating female characters of all time. Though it was not well received in its day, the novel is now seen by some as one of Dostoevsky's foremost works. Writing in *Reference Guide to World Literature*, Arnold McMillin noted that "[o]f all Dostoevsky's great novels, *The Idiot* was written with the greatest difficulty, and yet it contains some of the author's boldest and most cherished ideas as well as an intriguing plot and a plethora of fascinating characters." In McMillin's eyes the book is "a flawed masterpiece," but one still "rich in psychology, moral and social ideas, high drama," and one that "possesses some of the most memorable characters in all of Dostoevsky's oeuvre." Leatherbarrow called *The Idiot* "the most obviously contrived" of all Dostoevsky's great works, and "a complex allegory." According to Murray Krieger in *The Tragic Vision*, "*The Idiot* is a novel of the desperate struggle for personal human dignity in a world that finds endless ways of depriving man of it." And Malcolm Jones, in his *Dostoyevsky: The Novel of Discord*, felt

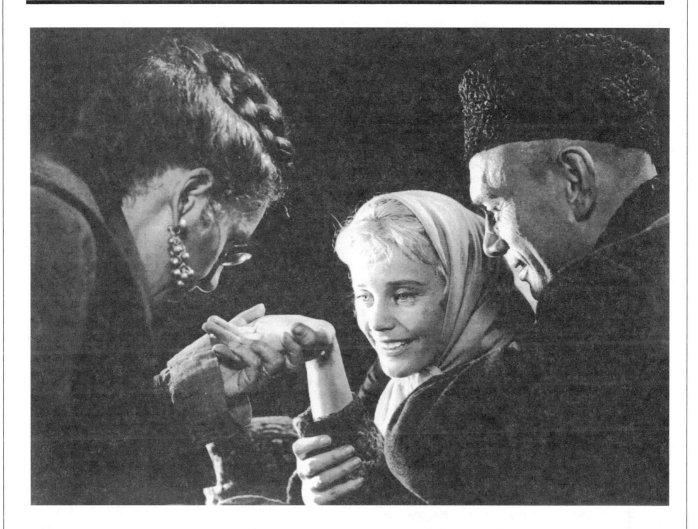

Maria Schell (center) and Yul Brynner (right) star in the 1958 film adaptation of *The Brothers Karamazov*, **Dostoevsky's powerful novel about guilt and redemption.**

that *"The Idiot* shows how men now consume each other spiritually." Comparing the novel to a "voyage of discovery" with "its storms, its shipwrecks, and its ports of call," Jones went on to conclude that *"The Idiot* presents some of the most important [ideas] on Dostoevsky's pilgrimage as a novelist."

Dostoevsky's next novel, *The Eternal Husband*, helped keep the wolf from the door and has had many admirers over the years, including the American writer Henry Miller, who favored it above all Dostoevsky's other novels. Leatherbarrow called it "technically perhaps the most accomplished of Dostoevsky's works." However, it was a slight work and the next major novel was *The Possessed* or *The Devils* as it is alternately titled, serialized once Dostoevsky returned to Russia. This book earned Dostoevsky the lasting enmity of the liberals and radi-

cals in that country, for it represents the height of his reaction against revolution and socialism. One of the great political novels in any language, *The Possessed* is based on and partly inspired by the murder of a young revolutionary by his own comrades at the behest of the radical leader, Sergey Nechaev.

At the center of Dostoevsky's novel is Nikolay Stavrogin, a nihilist of the first order, a man seemingly without a moral center. He, along with like–minded thinker Pyotr Stepanovitch Verkhovensky, manage to sow destruction, mayhem, and murder among the members of a sleepy provincial town. Pyotr is the son of an aging liberal dandy, Stepan Verkhovensky, a buffoon–like caricature of the writer Turgenev, and Nikolay is the son of Varvara Stavrogin, with whom the elder Verkhovensky has been carrying on an affair for years. Stepan has, in fact, educated her son, Nikolay, and when he and his own son return from a trip abroad with Western ideas and morality, this quiet corner of Orthodox Russia is changed drastically. Pyotr ultimately is responsible for the death of Shatov, a local member of their political cell who has transformed himself from budding socialist to Orthodox Slavophile and wants to leave the group. Meanwhile, Stavrogin stands apart from these doings but is responsible for his own nihilistic actions which seemingly have no other motivation than wanton destruction. Having learned and discarded all philosophies from liberalism to populism, he is now empty, and more evil than Pyotr who at least acts out of his cynical beliefs. In one of the most prescient of passages, Dostoevsky has Pyotr declare that when the revolution comes, "Cicero will have his tongue cut out, Copernicus will have his eyes put out, Shakespeare will be stoned," and all in the name of "equality."

A profoundly conservative and Christian work, *The Possessed* is not necessarily a reactionary work, for Dostoevsky does not defend the monarchy, aristocracy, or censorship. Instead he suggests that Orthodox Christianity, not revolution, is the proper path to follow in a challenge to the state. Yet at the time, his critics took the book as a direct rejection of liberalism. "No other novel by Dostoevsky provoked as much controversy as *The Possessed*," wrote Marc Slonim in an afterword to a 1962 English edition of the novel. "Any attempt to look at *The Possessed* dispassionately and to appraise it objectively was thwarted by political passion: the rightists were enthusiastic about it, and the leftists rejected it uncompromisingly." Jones has noted that "the novel tells of a period of breakdown and transition in Russian life which extends to every level of provincial society." Thus the chaos and disorder the novel depicts is a realistic portrayal of Russia at the time. "The breakdown is not just social," Jones further observed, "it is personal too." For Jones "Stavrogin is the Romantic hero reduced to impotence." The renowned critic Irving Howe, in his *Politics and the Novel*, commented on the strangely comic tone of the novel: "*The Possessed* is drenched in buffoonery." Howe went on to write, "This itself is a major reason for the atmosphere of violent negation which hangs over the book." Howe believed that such buffoonery was appropriate for the novel "because the characters are mainly pretenders," and concluded that "Dostoevsky is the greatest of all ideological novelists." Slonim also pointed out that "as a foreboding of all the distortions of the Russian revolution [*The Possessed*] is frightening in its insight and accuracy. For this alone *The Possessed* would still be an important novel today." But for Slonim, the importance of the book transcends mere historical prescience: "*The Possessed* is not only a novel about revolution, crime, atheism, religion, strong men, underground men, and the Russian past and present. It is . . . one of the most captivating and thrilling tales of modern literature."

The Brothers Karamazov

In 1873, Dostoevsky took over editorship of the conservative magazine, *Grazhdanin* ("Citizen"), where he published a regular column, "The Diary of a Writer." In 1874, he spent two days in prison for violation of the censorship laws and soon thereafter left *Grazhdanin* to work on his novel *A Raw Youth*, published in 1875. This novel was disliked by both liberals and conservatives, though it had been intended as an appeasement to liberal opinion. Thereafter he devoted attentions to publishing a one–man journal, *The Diary of a Writer*, which gave him the opportunity to publish his short stories, essays, and sketches. Though the magazine proved both popular and financially rewarding, Dostoevsky was soon moving on to work on what would be his final novel, *The Brothers Karamazov*. Here once again he focuses on his favorite themes: the craving for faith, the nature and origin of evil and the construct of freedom and free will. Inspired not only by the theological philosophy of a new friend, Vladimir Solovev, but also by the death of his son, Alexey, from inherited epilepsy, the novel deals extensively with paternal and filial guilt.

Fyodor Karamazov is both a profligate and a strict, even vicious father. He has three sons by different wives: the oldest, Dmitri, then Ivan and Alexey. There is also a fourth son, Smerdyakov, an epileptic who has been adopted by Karamazov's servant, Grigory, who also has been charged with the care of the other three sons. Dmitri is a wild, passionate man; Ivan attended college and has become an impoverished and bitter professor and writer, and Alexey, good–natured and likable, has entered a monastery where he studies under a respected elder, Father Zosima. Smerdyakov, the illegitimate son, is malicious and seeks revenge for his lowly station. Dmitri and his father compete for the affections of the scheming Grushenka while Ivan, an artistic cousin to Raskolnikov in *Crime and Punishment*, preaches to his half brother that "if God does not exist, then all is permitted." Ivan also shares with his brother Alexey the now famous parable, *The Grand Inquisitor*, in which God returns to earth in human form during the Spanish Inquisition and is arrested for the heresy of advocating freedom. This parable indeed explores the conflict between intellect and faith. When Fyodor Karamazov is murdered, evidence at first leads to the arrest of Dmitri, though in fact it is Smerdyakov who has killed the old man, a fact Ivan learns when visiting his half–

brother in the hospital where he is recovering an epileptic seizure. Ivan also learns that Smerdyakov killed their father because of what he, Ivan, has said about it being best for everyone if the old man were dead. That night Ivan, his mind coming unhinged, dreams the devil comes to visit him and he is neither terrifying nor grand, but a quite petty demon. Smerdyakov also hangs himself that night. At his brother's trial, Ivan tells of Smerdyakov's confession, but it is evident that he is now mentally unstable, and when another witness lies, Dmitri is convicted and sent to Siberia, accompanied by Alexey, who has left the monastery, and Grushenka, Dmitri's amoral mistress.

Often called Dostoevsky's greatest, most powerful novel, *The Brothers Karamazov* is surely his tightest in construction, spanning three days of action, and situated mainly in one well–described locale. Jones wrote that *Karamazov* "is the most carefully and consciously planned and structured of all Dostoevsky's novels." The nature of fatherhood is the major theme in the book, though with Ivan's parable of *The Grand Inquisitor* and his visitation from the devil, important questions about God and Christianity are also brought forward. As Leatherbarrow noted, this novel is "a work distilled from ideas and projects that had occupied the author for much of his life." Commenting on the characters, Leatherbarrow felt that the "three brothers are clearly intended to be viewed, in at least one light, as a collective symbol of man." But ultimately, as with most of Dostoevsky's work, the novel is about redemption. Leatherbarrow concluded that though the "ingratiating, slippery, sly lackey," Smerdyakov, offends against the "collective man" as represented in the three brothers, this in turn allows them to "take the first steps along the road that leads first to Calvary, but ultimately to the promise of salvation." One of Dostoevsky's biographers, Geir Kjetsaa, also keys on this theme of salvation: "In *The Brothers Karamazov* Dostoevsky demonstrates how evil becomes the starting point for the growth of good. He shows us life not merely as decay but also as resurrection."

Reception of the novel at the time was quite good and even brought about the reprint of many of Dostoevsky's earlier titles. For the first time, things were looking up financially for the writer who was planning a sequel to *Karamazov*. A speech Dostoevsky delivered at the Pushkin ceremonies in 1880 further increased the author's renown. But a mere three months after publication of his last novel, Dostoevsky died of a lung hemorrhage. He was fifty–nine, and at his funeral thirty thousand citizens of St. Petersburg took to the streets to mourn his passing. A hearse was not used; instead students

and fellow writers carried the coffin over two miles to the cemetery of Alexander Nevsky Monastery where he was buried on February 1, 1881.

If you enjoy the works of Fedor Mikhailovich Dostoevsky, you might want to check out the following books:

The writings of Honore de Balzac, whose work Dostoevsky admired.
The narrative verse and novels of Alexander Pushkin, who served as a literary influence for Dostoevsky.
The works of German poet and playwright Friedrich Schiller.
The novels of Leo Tolstoy, a contemporary of Dostoevsky's.

In the more than a century since his death, Dostoevsky's importance and fame as a writer has not flagged. Great thinkers and writers, from Sigmund Freud to D. H. Lawrence, have written about this Russian genius. The British writer Arnold Bennett summed up Dostoevsky's importance in his *Books and Persons*: "Nobody, perhaps, ever understood and sympathized with human nature as Dostoevsky did. Indubitably nobody ever with the help of God and good luck ever swooped so high into tragic grandeur. But the man had fearful falls. He could not trust his wings. He is an adorable, a magnificent, and a profoundly sad figure in letters." Jones, in his *Dostoyevsky: The Novel of Discord*, analyzed the author's lasting achievement thusly: "It is because he perceived elements of complexity which still extend our vision that he can still excite and command serious philosophical interest. Like all great imaginative writers, Dostoevsky confronts the reader with wisdom that civilised man cannot afford to forget."

■ **Biographical and Critical Sources**

BOOKS

Amsenga, B. J., Editor, *Miscellanea Slavica: To Honour the Memory of Jan M. Meijer*, Rodopi, 1983.
Bakhtin, M. M., *Problemy tvorchestva Dostoevskogo*, [Moscow], 1929, translation by R. W. Rostel published as *Problems of Dostoevsky's Poetics*, University of Michigan Press (Ann Arbor), 1973.

Baring, Maurice, *Landmarks in Russian Literature,* Methuen, 1960.

Beach, Joseph Warren, *The Twentieth Century Novel: Studies in Technique,* Appleton–Century, 1932.

Belknap, Robert L. *The Structure of "The Brothers Karamazov,"* Mouton, 1967.

Bennett, Arnold, *Books and Persons: Being Comments on a Past Epoch, 1908–1911,* Doran, 1917.

Berdyaev, Nicholas, *Dostoevsky,* Meridian, 1957.

Blackmur, R. P., *Eleven Essays in the European Novel,* Harcourt, Brace, 1964.

Bowers, Fredson, editor, *Lectures on Russian Literature,* Harcourt, Brace, 1981.

Buber, Martin, *Israel and the World: Essays in a Time of Crisis,* Schocken, 1948.

Carr, Edward Hallett, *Dostoevsky (1821–1881): A New Biography,* Allen & Unwin, 1931.

Dolan, Paul J., *Of War and War's Alarms: Fiction and Politics in the Modern World,* Macmillan, 1976.

Dostoevskaya, A. G., *Vospominaniya,* [Moscow], 1925, translation by Beatrice Stillman published as *Reminiscences,* Liveright, 1975.

Erlich, Victor, editor, *Twentieth–Century Russian Literary Criticism,* Yale University Press, 1975.

Fanger, Donald, *Dostoevsky and Romantic Realism, a Study of Dostoevsky in Relation to Balzac, Dickens and Gogol,* Harvard University Press, 1965.

Farrell, James T., *The League of Frightened Philistines and Other Papers,* Vanguard, 1945.

Frank, Joseph, *Dostoevsky: The Seeds of Revolt,* Princeton University Press, 1976.

Frank, Joseph, *Dostoevsky: The Years of Ordeal, 1850–1859,* Princeton University Press, 1983.

Frank, Joseph, *Dostoevsky: The Stir of Liberation, 1860–1865,* Princeton University Press, 1986.

Gidé, André, *Dostoevsky,* New Directions, 1949.

Gissing, George, *Charles Dickens: A Critical Study,* Dodd, Mead, 1904.

Goldstein, David I., *Dostoyevsky and the Jews,* University of Texas Press, 1981.

Guerard, Albert J., *The Triumph of the Novel: Dickens, Dostoevsky, Faulkner,* Oxford University Press, 1976.

Holquist, Michael, *Dostoevsky and the Novel,* Princeton University Press, 1977.

Howe, Irving, *Politics and the Novel,* Horizon Press, 1957.

Huneker, James, *Ivory Apes and Peacocks,* Scribners, 1938.

Jackson, Robert L., *Dostoevsky's Quest for Form,* Yale University Press, 1965.

Jackson, Robert L., editor, *Twentieth–Century Interpretations of "Crime and Punishment,"* Prentice–Hall, 1974.

Jackson, Robert L., *The Art of Dostoevsky,* Princeton University Press, 1981.

Jackson, Robert L., *Dostoevsky: New Perspectives,* Prentice–Hall, 1984.

Jenson, Peter Alberg, and others, editors, *Text and Context: Essays to Honor Nils Ake Nilsson,* Almqvist Wiksell International, 1987.

Jones, Malcolm V., *Dostoevsky: The Novel of Discord,* Barnes & Noble, 1976.

Jones, Malcolm V., and Garth M. Terry, editors, *New Essays on Dostoevsky,* Cambridge University Press, 1983.

Kjetsaa, Geir, *Fyodor Dostoevsky: A Writer's Life,* Viking, 1987.

Jones, Peter, *Philosophy and the Novel,* Clarendon Press, 1975.

Krieger, Murray, "Dostoevsky's 'Idiot': The Curse of Saintliness," in *The Tragic Vision,* Holt, Rinehart, 1960.

Laing, R. D., *Self and Others,* Pantheon, 1969.

Lavrin, Janko, *Dostoevsky: A Study,* Macmillan, 1947.

Leatherbarrow, William J., *Fedor Dostoevsky,* Twayne, 1981.

Lednicki, Waclaw, *Russia, Poland, and the West: Essays in Literary and Cultural History,* Roy Publishers, 1953.

Linner, Sven, *Starets Zosima in "The Brothers Karamazov": A Study in the Mimesis of Virtue,* Almqvist Wiksell, 1975.

Lukacs, Georg, "Dostoevsky," in *Der russische Realismus in der Weltliteratur,* translated by Rene Welleck, [Berlin], 1949.

Magarshack, David, *Dostoevsky,* Secker & Warburg, 1962.

Maugham, W. Somerset, *The Art of Fiction: An Introduction to Ten Novels and Their Authors,* Doubleday, 1955.

McMillin, Arnold, "The Idiot: An Overview," *Reference Guide to World Literature,* 2nd edition, edited by Lesley Henderson, St. James Press, 1995.

Miller, Robin, *Dostoevsky and "The Idiot,"* Harvard University Press, 1981.

Mirsky, D. S., *A History of Russian Literature,* Knopf, 1949.

Mochul'skii, K. D., *Dostoevskii, zhizn' i tvorchestvo,* [Paris], 1927, translation by Michael Minihan published as *Dostoevsky, His Life and Work,* Princeton University Press, 1967.

Murry, J. Middleton, *Fyodor Dostoevsky: A Critical Study,* Martin Secker, 1916.

Nineteenth–Century Literature Criticism, Gale, Volume 2, 1982, Volume 7, 1984, Volume 21, 1989, Volume 33, 1992, Volume 43, 1994.

O'Connor, Frank, *The Mirror in the Roadway,* Knopf, 1956.

O'Toole, L. Michael, *Structure, Style, and Interpretation in the Russian Short Story,* Yale University Press, 1982.

Passage, Charles E., *Dostoevski the Adapter: A Study in Dostoevski's Use of the Tales of Hoffmann,* University of North Carolina Press, 1954.

Peace, Richard, *Dostoyevsky: An Examination of the Major Novels,* Cambridge University Press, 1971.

Poggioli, Renato, *The Kafka Problem,* Octagon, 1963.

Priestly, J. B., *Literature and Western Man,* Heinemann, 1960.

Pritchett, V. S., *In My Good Books,* Kennikat Press, 1970.

Proust, Marcel, *Marcel Proust on Art and Literature: 1896–1919,* Meridian, 1958.

Rahv, Philip, *Literature and the Sixth Sense,* Houghton Mifflin, 1969.

Reeve, F. D., *The Russian Novel,* McGraw–Hill, 1966.

Rowe, William Woodin, *Dostoevsky: Child and Man in His Works,* New York University Press, 1968.

Rozanov, Vasily, *Dostoevsky and the Legend of the Grand Inquisitor,* Cornell University Press, 1972.

Seduro, Vladimir, *Dostoevsky in Russian Literary Criticism, 1846–1956,* Columbia University Press, 1957.

Seduro, Vladimir, *Dostoevsky's Image in Russia Today,* Nordland, 1975.

Sewall, Richard, *The Vision of Tragedy,* Yale University Press, 1980.

Short Story Criticism, Gale, Volume 2, 1989, Volume 33, 1999.

Slonim, Marc, *The Epic of Russian Literature,* Oxford University Press, 1950.

Slonim, Marc, *Three Loves of Dostoevsky,* Rinehart, 1955.

Slonim, Marc, "Afterword," Fedor Michaelovich Dostoevsky, *The Possessed,* translated by Andrew R. MacAndrew, Signet.

Steiner, George, *Tolstoy or Dostoevsky: An Essay in the Old Criticism,* Knopf, 1959.

Stevenson, Robert Louis, *The Letters of Robert Louis Stevenson: 1880–1887,* Volume 7, Scribners, 1911, pp. 322–25.

Tate, Allen, *On the Limits of Poetry: Selected Essays 1928–48,* Morrow, 1948.

Terras, Victor, *The Young Dostoevsky (1846–1849),* Mouton, 1969.

Terras, Victor, *A Karamazov Companion: Commentary on the Genesis, Language, and Style of Dostoevsky's Novel,* University of Wisconsin Press, 1981.

Thompson, Diane Oenning, *"The Brothers Karamazov" and the Poetics of Memory,* Cambridge University Press, 1991.

Trace, Arthur, *Furnace of Doubt: Dostoevsky and "The Brothers Karamazov,"* Sherwood Sugden & Company, 1988.

Trilling, Lionel, *Speaking of Literature and Society,* Harcourt, 1980.

Troyat, Henri, *Firebrand: The Life of Dostoevsky,* Roy Publishers, 1946.

Tyler, Parker, *Every Artist His Own Scandal: A Study of Real and Fictive Heroes,* Horizon Press, 1964.

Warner, Rex, *The Cult of Power: Essays,* Lippincott, 1947.

Wasiolek, Edward, editor, *"Crime and Punishment" and the Critics,* Wadsworth, 1961.

Wasiolek, Edward, *Dostoevsky, the Major Fiction,* Harvard University Press, 1964.

Wellek, Rene, editor, *Dostoevsky, a Collection of Critical Essays,* Prentice–Hall, 1962.

Wilson, Colin, *The Outsider,* Houghton, 1956.

Wilson, Edmund, *The Shores of Light: A Literary Chronicle of the Twenties and Thirties,* Farrar, Straus, 1952.

World Literature Criticism, Gale, 1992.

Yarmolinsky, Avrahm, *Dostoevsky: His Life and Art,* S. G. Phillips, 1965.

Zander, L. A., *Dostoevsky,* SCM Press, 1948.

Zweig, Stefan, *Three Masters: Balzac, Dickens, Dostoeffsky,* Viking, 1919.

PERIODICALS

American Imago, April, 1947; spring, 1959.

Athenaeum, January 16, 1886, review of *Crime and Punishment,* pp. 99–100.

Canadian Slavonic Papers, Volume 10, number 1, 1968.

Chimera, winter, 1943.

College English, December, 1955.

Commentary, February, 1987; June, 1992.

Criterion, Volume 16, 1937, D. A. Traversi, "Dostoevsky," pp. 585–602.

Cross–Currents, fall, 1952.

Economist, July 9, 1988.

Explicator, fall, 1981; spring, 1982; fall, 1982.

Harper's, September, 1886, William Dean Howells, review of *Crime and Punishment,* pp. 639–42.

Hudson Review, spring, 1948; summer, 1960.

Journal of Aesthetics and Art Criticism, winter, 1968.

Journal of American Folklore, July–September, 1956.

Journal of Criminal Law and Criminology, November–December, 1937.

Journal of Religions, April, 1956.

Literary World, October 30, 1886, review of *Crime and Punishment,* pp. 364–65.

Literature and Psychology, Volume 22, number 1, 1972.

London Mercury, November, 1927.

Michigan Quarterly Review, fall, 1983.

Minnesota Review, January–April, 1965.

Modern Fiction Studies, autumn, 1958.

Nation, September 6, 1894, review of *Poor Folk,* pp. 181–82.

National Review, May 22, 1987.

New Republic, June 15, 1915; April 27, 1987; December 5, 1988; March 6, 1989; October 12, 1992.

New York Review of Books, January 17, 1991; June 13, 1991.

New York Times Book Review, June 14, 1987; February 21, 1988; June 4, 1989; April 26, 1992; February 27, 1994.

Partisan Review, summer, 1960, Philip Rahv, "Dostoevsky in *Crime and Punishment,*" pp. 393–425.

Psychoanalytic Review, April, 1930.

Russian Literature Triquarterly, fall, 1971.

Russian Review, January, 1951; April, 1971.

Slavic and East European Journal, spring, 1966; spring, 1973.

Slavonic and East European Review, May, 1949.

Soviet Literature, December, 1981.

Spectator, July 10, 1886, "A Russian Novelist," pp. 937–39.

Studies in Short Fiction, fall, 1973.

Texas Studies in Literature and Language, fall, 1972.

Yale Review, December, 1977.*

—Sketch by J. Sydney Jones

W. E. B. Du Bois

■ Personal

Born February 23, 1868, in Great Barrington, MA; immigrated to Ghana, 1960; naturalized Ghanaian citizen, 1963; died August 27, 1963, in Accra, Ghana; buried in Accra; son of Alfred and Mary (Burghardt) Du Bois; married Nina Gomer, 1896 (died, 1950); married Shirley Graham (an author), 1951 (died, 1977); children: Burghardt, Yolande Du Bois Williams. *Education:* Fisk University, B.A., 1888; Harvard University, B.A. (cum laude) 1890, M.A., 1891, Ph.D., 1896; graduate study at University of Berlin, 1892–94. *Politics:* Communist.

■ Career

Wilberforce University, Wilberforce, OH, professor of Greek and Latin, 1894–96; University of Pennsylvania, Philadelphia, assistant instructor in sociology, 1896–97; Atlanta University, Atlanta, GA, professor of history and economics, 1897–1910, professor and chairman of department of sociology, 1934–44; National Association for the Advancement of Colored People (NAACP), New York City, director of publicity and research and editor of *Crisis*, 1910–34, director of special research, 1944–48; Peace Information Center, New York City, director, 1950. Co–founder and general secretary of Niagara Movement, 1905–09. Organizer of the Pan–African Congress, 1919. Vice–chairman of the Council of African Affairs, 1949. American Labor Party candidate for U.S. Senator from New York, 1950.

■ Awards, Honors

Spingarn Medal, NAACP, 1932; elected to the National Institute of Arts and Letters, 1943; Lenin International Peace Prize, 1958; Knight Commander of the Liberian Humane Order of African Redemption conferred by the Liberian Government; Minister Plenipotentiary and Envoy Extraordinary conferred by President Calvin Coolidge; LL.D., Howard University, 1930, and Atlanta University, 1938; Litt. D., Fisk University, 1938; L.H.D., Wilberforce University, 1940; also recipient of honorary degrees from Morgan State College, University of Berlin, and Charles University (Prague).

■ Writings

NOVELS

The Quest of the Silver Fleece, A. C. McClurg, 1911.
Dark Princess: A Romance, Harcourt, 1928.

The Ordeal of Mansart (first novel in trilogy), Mainstream Publishers, 1957.

Mansart Builds a School (second novel in trilogy), Mainstream Publishers, 1959.

Worlds of Color (third novel in trilogy), Mainstream Publishers, 1961.

The Black Flame (trilogy collection; includes *The Ordeal of Mansart, Mansart Builds a School,* and *Worlds of Color*), Kraus Reprint, 1976.

POETRY

Selected Poems, Ghana University Press, c. 1964.

PLAYS

Haiti, included in *Federal Theatre Plays,* edited by Pierre De Rohan, Works Progress Administration, 1938.

Also author of pageants "The Christ of the Andes," "George Washington and Black Folk: A Pageant for the Centenary, 1732–1932," and "The Star of Ethiopia."

EDITOR; PUBLISHED IN CONJUNCTION WITH THE ANNUAL CONFERENCE FOR THE STUDY OF NEGRO PROBLEMS

Mortality among Negroes in Cities, Atlanta University Press, 1896.

Social and Physical Condition of Negroes in Cities, Atlanta University Press, 1897.

Some Efforts of American Negroes for Their Own Social Benefit, Atlanta University Press, 1898.

The Negro in Business, Atlanta University Press, 1899.

A Select Bibliography of the American Negro: For General Readers, Atlanta University Press, 1901.

The Negro Common School, Atlanta University Press, 1901.

The Negro Artisan, Atlanta University Press, 1902.

The Negro Church, Atlanta University Press, 1903.

Some Notes on Negro Crime, Particularly in Georgia, Atlanta University Press, 1904.

A Select Bibliography of the Negro American, Atlanta University Press, 1905.

The Health and Physique of the Negro American, Atlanta University Press, 1906.

Economic Co–operation among Negro Americans, Atlanta University Press, 1907.

The Negro American Family, Atlanta University Press, 1908.

Efforts for Social Betterment among Negro Americans, Atlanta University Press, 1909.

(With Augustus Granville Dill) *The College–bred Negro American,* Atlanta University Press, 1910.

(With Dill) *The Common School and the Negro American,* Atlanta University Press, 1911.

(With Dill) *The Negro American Artisan,* Atlanta University Press, 1912.

(With Dill) *Morals and Manners among Negro Americans,* Atlanta University Press, 1914.

Atlanta University Publications, two volumes, Hippocrene, 1968.

NONFICTION

The Suppression of the African Slave–Trade to the United States of America, 1638–1870, Longmans, Green, 1896.

The Conservation of Races, American Negro Academy, 1897.

The Philadelphia Negro: A Special Study, (bound with *A Special Report on Domestic Service,* by Isobel Eaton), University of Pennsylvania, 1899.

The Souls of Black Folk: Essays and Sketches, A. C. McClurg, 1903.

(With Booker Taliaferro Washington) *The Negro in the South: His Economic Progress in Relation to His Moral and Religious Development* (lectures), G. W. Jacobs, 1907.

John Brown (biography), G. W. Jacobs, 1909, 2nd revised edition, International Publishing, 1974.

The Negro, Holt, 1915.

Darkwater: Voices from within the Veil (semi–autobiographical), Harcourt, 1920.

The Gift of Black Folk: The Negroes in the Making of America, Stratford Co., 1924.

Africa: Its Geography, People, and Products, Haldeman–Julius Publications, 1930.

Africa: Its Place in Modern History, Haldeman–Julius Publications, 1930, reprinted with *Africa: Its Geography, People and Products,* Unipub–Kraus International, 1977.

Black Reconstruction: An Essay toward a History of the Part Which Black Folk Played in the Attempt to Reconstruct Democracy in America, 1860–1880, Harcourt, 1935, published as *Black Reconstruction in America, 1860–1880,* Atheneum, 1969.

Black Folk, Then and Now: An Essay in the History and Sociology of the Negro Race, Holt, 1939.

Dusk of Dawn: An Essay toward an Autobiography of a Race Concept, Harcourt, 1940.

Color and Democracy: Colonies and Peace, Harcourt, 1945.

The World and Africa: An Inquiry into the Part Which Africa Has Played in World History, Viking, 1947, revised edition, 1965.

(Editor) *An Appeal to the World: A Statement on the Denial of Human Rights to Minorities in the Case of Citizens of Negro Descent in the United States of America and an Appeal to the United Nations for Redress,* [New York], 1947.

In Battle for Peace: The Story of My 83rd Birthday (autobiography), Masses Mainstream, 1952.

The Autobiography of W. E. Burghardt Du Bois: A Soliloquy on Viewing My Life from the Last Decade of Its First Century, edited by Herbert Aptheker, International Publishers, 1968.

Black North in 1901: A Social Study, Ayer, 1970.

COLLECTIONS AND CORRESPONDENCE

An ABC of Color: Selections from Over Half a Century of the Writings of W. E. B. Du Bois, Seven Seas Publishers (Berlin), 1963.

Three Negro Classics, edited by John H. Franklin, Avon, 1965.

W. E. B. Du Bois Speaks: Speeches and Addresses, edited by Philip S. Foner, Pathfinder Press, 1970.

The Selected Writings of W. E. B. Du Bois, edited by Walter Wilson, New American Library, 1970.

W. E. B. Du Bois: A Reader, edited by Meyer Weinberg, Harper, 1970.

The Seventh Son: The Thought and Writings of W. E. B. Du Bois, edited by Julius Lester, Random House, 1971.

A W. E. B. Du Bois Reader, edited by Andrew G. Paschal, Macmillan, 1971.

W. E. B. Du Bois: The Crisis Writings, edited by Daniel Walden, Fawcett Publications, 1972.

The Emerging Thought of W. E. B. Du Bois: Essays and Editorials from "The Crisis," edited by Harvey Lee Moon, Simon & Schuster, 1972.

The Correspondence of W. E. B. Du Bois, edited by Aptheker, University of Massachusetts Press, Volume I: *1877–1934,* 1973, Volume II: *1934–1944,* 1976, Volume III: *1944–1963,* 1978.

The Education of Black People: Ten Critiques, 1906–1960, edited by Aptheker, University of Massachusetts Press, 1973.

The Writings of W. E. B. Du Bois, edited by Virginia Hamilton, Crowell, 1975.

Book Reviews, edited by Aptheker, KTO Press, 1977.

Prayers for Dark People, edited by Aptheker, University of Massachusetts Press, 1980.

(And editor) *Writings in Periodicals,* UNIPUB–Kraus International, 1985.

Creative Writings by W. E. B. Du Bois: A Pageant, Poems, Short Stories and Playlets, UNIPUB–Kraus International, 1985.

Pamphlets and Leaflets by W. E. B. Du Bois, UNIPUB–Kraus International, 1985.

Against Racism: Unpublished Essays, Papers, Addresses, 1887–1961, edited by Aptheker, University of Massachusetts Press, 1985.

W. E. B. Du Bois on Sociology and the Black Community, edited by Dan S. Greene and Edwin D. Driver, University of Chicago Press, 1987.

W. E. B. Writings, Library of America, 1987.

W. E. B. Du Bois: A Reader, Holt (New York City), 1995.

The Oxford W. E. B. Du Bois Reader, Oxford University Press (New York City), 1996.

The Selected Speeches of W. E. B. Du Bois, Modern Library (New York City), 1996.

OTHER

Columnist for newspapers, including *Chicago Defender, Pittsburgh Courier, New York Amsterdam News,* and *San Francisco Chronicle.* Contributor to numerous periodicals, including *Atlantic Monthly* and *World's Work.* Founder and editor of numerous periodicals, including *Moon,* 1905–06, *Horizon,* 1908–10, *Brownies' Book,* 1920–21, and *Phylon Quarterly,* 1940. Editor–in–chief of *Encyclopedia of the Negro,* 1933–46. Director of *Encyclopedia Africana.* Some of Du Bois's books have been published in French and Russian.

■ Sidelights

"[T]he problem of the Twentieth Century is the problem of the color line," wrote W. E. B. Du Bois in *The Souls of Black Folk,* arguably the best, if not most famous, of all the works of this remarkable scholar, intellectual, journalist, activist, educator, historian, and novelist. Hard to pigeonhole, Du Bois spanned a century of American life which also saw the birth of the modern civil rights movement. His own development in part mirrored that movement: from believing in the integration of black people into American society Du Bois gradually adopted a separatist, Pan–African viewpoint that saw African Americans developing a separate culture and ethos within but also "outside" American society.

As the editor of *Crisis,* the official publication of the National Association for the Advancement of Colored People (NAACP) for a quarter of a century, Du Bois wielded immense political and social power with American blacks, reaching hundreds of thousands of readers and writing scathing denunciations of racial discrimination and racially motivated crimes. Du Bois became, through his writings and teachings, a major force in American society and a major definer of African American causes. Both a prophet and at times a pariah of these causes, he battled with both word and deed. In 1905, he helped form the Niagara Movement, the first African American protest movement of the new century; five years later he became the only black founding member of the NAACP. As much a maker of history as a writer of it, Du Bois pioneered the use of sociological and historical methods in the study of black history. Writing in genres as disparate as history, sociology, autobiography, journalism, and fiction, Du Bois almost single–handedly created an intellectual approach to the history of blacks in America. His series of fourteen essays gathered in *The Souls of Black Folk* is "perhaps the most influential work on blacks in America since *Uncle Tom's Cabin,*" according to Arnold Rampersad in *The Art and Imagination of W. E. B. Du Bois.* Other influential nonfiction works include *The Philadelphia Negro,* the first systematic approach to the study of blacks in America, *The Gift of Black Folks,* a survey of black contributions to civilization, *Black Reconstruction,* a revisionist view of blacks during the post–Civil War years, and *Black Folk, Then and Now,* a historical overview of blacks in both Africa and America. In the field of fiction, Du Bois also published five novels. *The Quest of the Silver Fleece, Dark Princess,* and *The Black Flame* comprise a trilogy built around the activities of a black man who works as a teacher and educator to serve his race. Written late in its author's life, this trilogy is somewhat autobiographical. Additionally, Du Bois wrote two full autobiographies.

"The problem of the Twentieth Century is the problem of the color line."

—*W. E. B. Du Bois*

In his later life, Du Bois grew increasingly frustrated with attempts to change society in America, and ultimately left the country to settle in Ghana, giving up his citizenship. He had long since been displaced as a major voice of black America, and at his death in 1963, on the very eve of the huge March on Washington in which Martin Luther King, Jr., would give his famous "I have a dream" speech, there were many young people among the 250,000 crowded around the Reflecting Pool at the nation's capital who had never heard of Du Bois. Yet it was in part due to his groundbreaking work that such a march was feasible, even imaginable. He was, as David

Levering Lewis pointed out in *W. E. B. Du Bois: Biography of a Race, 1868–1919,* "the paramount custodian of the intellect that so many impoverished, deprived, intimidated, and desperately striving African–Americans had either never developed or found it imperative to conceal." Lewis further observed, "His chosen weapons were grand ideas propelled by uncompromising language." Du Bois was quite simply, in the words of Lewis, "The premier architect of the civil rights movement in the United States."

A New England Childhood

Born William Edward Burghardt Du Bois on February 23, 1868, in Great Barrington, Massachusetts, Du Bois was the only child of Alfred and Mary Silvina (Burghardt) Du Bois. His father was of French and African descent, and his mother also was of mixed ancestry, both Dutch and African. Du Bois's father, a barber, deserted the family shortly after William's birth, and Mary and her son went to live with her parents on a farm until the death of her father, Othello Burghardt, in 1872. Thereafter, they moved to the village of Great Barrington where Mary worked as a domestic servant. Life in this New England town was mostly pleasant for the fifty or so black families among the total population of 5,000. Often the only black child in his Sunday school or pubic school classes, Du Bois excelled in most subjects.

When a paralytic stroke left his mother with limited mobility in one leg and arm, Du Bois pitched in to help out with jobs after school: shoveling coal and delivering papers among others. In high school, Du Bois edited the school paper, *The Howler,* and was encouraged by his principal to take college preparatory classes. At age fifteen, the precocious Du Bois was already the Great Barrington correspondent for the *Springfield Republican* and wrote on the local black community for the black newspaper, the *New York Globe.* Graduating from high school the only black in his class, he delivered the valedictory address on the abolitionist Wendell Phillips. His hopes for entering Harvard University, however, came to nothing because of lack of funds and of adequate preparation. Instead, with the help of his local church and family members, he enrolled at all–black Fisk University in Nashville, Tennessee. Just before he was scheduled to arrive on campus, his mother, long an inspiration for the young Du Bois, died.

That autumn, Du Bois traveled south to Nashville where he would enter Fisk with a sophomore standing. Coming from a state that boasted relative racial equality, Du Bois was shocked at the racism of the South. He was, however, delighted with his teachers and began writing in earnest and also learned the art of public speaking. That first Octo-

W.E.B.
DU BOIS

THE
SOULS OF
BLACK
FOLK

INTRODUCTION
BY HERB BOYD

A classic work penned while its author taught economics and history at Atlanta University, Du Bois's 1903 collection of essays and sketches proclaimed the leading problem of the coming century to be "the color line."

Santayana in philosophy, Frank Taussig in economics, and Albert Bushnell Hart in history. Unlike his time at Fisk, Du Bois did not mix much in student life. He was not accepted to the glee club and he took this as a racial rebuke. Neither did he submit work to be published at Harvard; he kept largely to himself in the almost–white atmosphere of one of America's oldest and most respected institutions of higher education. Instead, he formed connections among Boston's black community, participating in church activities and amateur theatricals. During these years, he did make friends with Josephine Ruffin, one of the founders of the National Association of Negro Women and the publisher of the black weekly, the *Courant*, in whose pages many of Du Bois's early essays were published. His work with Hart and James more than compensated for his isolation; in later life he credited James with being—along with his mother—one of the greatest influences in his life. He often visited James's house, and it was this renowned philosopher who ultimately convinced the young scholar to move away from philosophy to the study of history and social problems.

Once again called upon to give the commencement speech when he graduated cum laude in philosophy, he spoke on Jefferson Davis, earning praise in the prestigious *Nation* for his presentation. Accepted at Harvard for graduate study in political science and history, he was the Henry Bromfield Rogers Fellow from 1890 to 1892, earning a master's degree. Following this, he studied in Europe for two years. Enrolling at the University of Berlin, he came under the sway of Max Weber in sociology. He also studied under Gustav Schmoller, Adolf Wagner, and Heinrich von Treistschke, traveling across the European continent during his breaks. For the first time in his life, Du Bois felt totally free from the stigma of race. The two years he spent out of his native country were a calm before the storm.

Returning Home

Coming back to the United States in 1894, Du Bois felt as if he was once again set into the middle of a racial maelstrom. A cosmopolitan with patrician looks, dress, and demeanor, Du Bois was just one more colored person back in America. The only work he could find was at an African Methodist school in Ohio, Wilberforce University, where he taught Latin and Greek and worked on his dissertation for Harvard. He earned his doctorate the following year from Harvard, the first African American to do so, and his dissertation, *The Suppression of the African Slave–Trade to the United States of America, 1638–1807*, was published as the first volume in

ber at Fisk, in 1885, Du Bois contracted typhoid fever and nearly died. Recovering, he took over editorship of the *Fisk Herald*, the school newspaper, and studied German, Greek, Latin, classical literature, ethics, and philosophy, as well as chemistry and physics. During the summers while at Fisk, Du Bois taught school in a poor, rural, black hamlet in Tennessee. Here he witnessed firsthand the bravery of blacks in the face of extreme poverty, and was introduced to the world of black folk music. Graduating with honors from Fisk in 1888, he gave an oration on Bismarck, and the next fall was finally admitted to Harvard University with the partial help of a Price–Greenleaf grant.

Entering as a junior, Du Bois studied at Harvard under such luminaries as William James and George

Harvard's Historical Monograph series. As Murray Arndt noted in *Dictionary of Literary Biography,* the published book "was a solid accomplishment, well received in periodical reviews." This work led directly to his appointment as assistant instructor in sociology at the University of Pennsylvania, where he was commissioned to write a study of the blacks of Philadelphia. The same year his dissertation was published, he married Nina Gomer, a student at Wilberforce, and the couple set up house in a rented room in an impoverished area of Philadelphia where Du Bois would carry out 5,000 interviews for his study of the black population of that city.

The book resulting from that study, *The Philadelphia Negro: A Social Study,* was published in 1899 and set new standards for such studies, relying on the collection and collation of economic and sociological data. Du Bois intended to dispel myths about blacks by such scrupulous attention to detail as statistics about their occupations, daily life patterns, and organizations. That book was, according to Addison Gayle, Jr., also writing in the *Dictionary of Literary Biography,* "the first systematic study of a large number of blacks in any major city in America." Du Bois, at the time much under the sway of Booker T. Washington and Washington's reliance on self–help for black advancement and vocation training as a key to black progress, concluded his book with a strong bit of advice: "Simply because the ancestors of the present inhabitants of America went out of their way barbarously to mistreat and enslave [blacks] . . . gives those blacks no right to ask that the civilization and morality of the land be seriously menaced for their benefit . . . a nation may rightly demand even of a people it has consciously and intentionally wronged, every effort and sacrifice possible on their parts towards making themselves fit members of the community within a reasonable length of time." In other words, as Gayle put it, "upon the shoulders of the victim, [Du Bois] placed much of the blame for poverty, crime, and lack of progress."

The irony was, however, that Du Bois himself, though unsympathetic at the time to cries of unfair treatment and a paragon of hard work and diligence, was the victim of racial discrimination. Despite all his efforts at the University of Pennsylvania, he failed to earn a regular appointment once his study was concluded, simply because he was black. He was forced to take a position instead at another all–black college, Atlanta University, as a professor of economics and history. In Atlanta he transferred the research methodology he had developed at Philadelphia determined to explicate the American black so that there could be no misunderstanding between the races. Such statistical, sociological truths about his race would ultimately set blacks free, he naively assumed. To that end, he instituted the annual Atlanta Conference for the Study of Negro Problems, editing subsequent conference proceedings. As long as he was at Atlanta University, such proceedings were an ongoing project. Thus by 1900, Du Bois was a conscientious scholar and advocate for his people, relying on the tools of social science to fight bigotry and racism.

The Making of a Radical and *The Souls of Black Folk*

All this changed, however, with the case of an illiterate black, Sam Hose, who was accused of raping and murdering a white woman. Du Bois, investigating the case, found that Hose was acting in self–defense, but before he could publish his findings the man suffered the usual white justice of the time: he was lynched by a mob and his fingers set on display at a grocery shop. As Du Bois later wrote in *The Autobiography of W. E. B. Du Bois,* "Two considerations thereafter broke in upon my work and eventually disrupted it: first, one could not be a calm, cool, and detached scientist, while Negroes were lynched, murdered and starved; and secondly, there was no such definite demand for scientific work of the sort I was doing." Scholarship was not what was needed in support of the cause, Du Bois decided.

Attending the Pan–African Conference in London in 1900, Du Bois made his famous comment that the color line was the major problem in the twentieth century. He also became increasingly friendly with black radicals such as the publisher and firebrand William Monroe Trotter, who rejected the accommodating policies of Booker T. Washington and that black leader's acceptance of the separate–but–equal stance of the white majority. With his next work, *The Souls of Black Folk,* Du Bois descended "dramatically from the ivory tower of cool factual collection in the arena of passion, propaganda, and effective confrontation," according to Arndt. "[T]he scientific statistician turns ardent activist." Called "among the great primal texts of black American literature" by Geoff Sadler in *Reference Guide to American Literature, The Souls of Black Folk* is a collection of fourteen essays that attempts to lift the veil from racial prejudice and shows what it meant to be black at the turn of the twentieth century. Du Bois blended history, memoir, sociology, biography, and fiction, stretching the essay form for his dramatic purpose. Rampersad wrote of this seminal work: "[A]ll of Afro–American literature of a creative nature has proceeded from Du Bois's comprehensive statement on the nature of the people in *The Souls of Black Folk.*"

All essays in the volume address the question of the color line; it is Du Bois's major contention that blacks are shut out of the white–dominated world by what seems to be an impenetrable veil of both prejudice and discrimination. Some of the essays, such as "Of Our Spiritual Strivings," lay out the history of America's black people and the eternal duality blacks experience, identifying both as Americans and Negroes. Other essays, like "Of the Meaning of Progress," deal with his days as a teacher in the Tennessee hills, or with the tragic effects of poverty as in "Of the Quest for the Golden Fleece." But perhaps the most famous and influential of all the essays was "Of Booker T. Washington and Others," in which he took to task the influential black educator's assimilationist theories. "Mr. Washington's programme practically accepts the alleged inferiority of the Negro races," wrote Du Bois, going on to accuse the administrator of the Tuskegee Institute of preaching "a gospel of Work and Money," calling on blacks to give up the struggle for civil rights, education, and political power in return for a place in society.

The Souls of Black Folk was a controversial book in its day. Houston A. Baker, Jr., explained in his *Black Literature in America* that white Americans were not "ready to respond favorably to Du Bois's scrupulously accurate portrayal of the hypocrisy, hostility, and brutality of white America toward black America." Many blacks were also shocked by the book, especially by Du Bois's denunciation of the conciliatory policy of Washington and his followers, who argued for the gradual development of the Negro race through vocational training. Du Bois declared: "So far as Mr. Washington apologizes for injustice, North or South, does not rightly value the privilege and duty of voting, belittles the emasculating effects of caste distinctions, and opposes the higher training and ambition of our brighter minds—so far as he, the South, or the Nation, does this—we must unceasingly and firmly oppose him. By every civilized and peaceful method we must strive for the rights which the world accords to men." In retrospect, many scholars have pointed to *The Souls of Black Folk* as a prophetic work. Harold W. Cruse and Carolyn Gipson noted in the *New York Review of Books* that "nowhere else was Du Bois's description of the Negro's experience in American Society to be given more succinct expression. . . . *Souls* is probably his greatest achievement as a writer. Indeed, his reputation may largely rest on this remarkable document, which had a profound effect on the minds of black people."

The NAACP and *Crisis*

A few years after *The Souls of Black Folk* was published, Du Bois banded with other black leaders and began the Niagara Movement, which sought to abolish all distinctions based on race. Although this movement disintegrated, it served as the forerunner of the NAACP. Du Bois helped to establish the NAACP, and in 1910 left his position at Atlanta University to work as its director of publicity and research for many years. As the editor of *Crisis*, a journal put out by the NAACP, he became a well–known spokesman for the black cause. For almost a quarter of a century, Du Bois edited the magazine, raising its circulation from a first printing of 1,000 to a circulation one hundred times that number by 1919. For many of these years, *Crisis* was the most important black magazine in America, featuring articles by Du Bois and others protesting lynchings, the Southern caste system, and other racial outrages; cheering the achievements of blacks in America and discussing around the world; reviewing works; urging voter registration; socialism, economic cooperation among blacks, civil disobedience, and Pan–Africanism; and generally stimulating pride of African American culture. Arndt called *Crisis* "a magazine that ranks among the most important organs of protest ever published in the United States," and divided Du Bois's editorship into three phases: the politically progressive early years, a more militant middle period that rejected political solutions in favor of such international policies as Pan–Africanism and socialism, and the final years in which Du Bois preached boycotts, separatism, and political and social segregation. This last phase was, ultimately, too much for the NAACP and its leaders, including Walter White, whose stated aim was integration of the races, and in 1934, Du Bois and the NAACP parted ways, with Du Bois returning to Atlanta University.

During the over two decades he edited *Crisis*, Du Bois was at the very center of the color problem in America. His widely disseminated views were wide–ranging and not always consistent. In 1917, for example, with U.S. troops committed to the European war, Du Bois penned a controversial article in *Crisis* urging blacks to close ranks with white Americans and join in the war effort. After the war, Du Bois traveled to Europe to examine the treatment of black soldiers at the front and wrote a scathing report of the racism inside the military in an edition of *Crisis* which the U.S. Post Office was very slow to deliver, but which garnered some of the largest readership the magazine ever had. A leading proponent of Pan–Africanism—the liaisoning of blacks on an international level—he reported on movements both at home and abroad. His dispute with Washington did not end with that man's death; in Washington's 1915 obituary Du Bois again denounced Washington's conciliatory policies. And when the Universal Negro Improvement Association, under the leadership of Marcus Garvey, openly espoused segregationist policies and criticized the

DOVER · THRIFT · EDITIONS

DARKWATER:

VOICES FROM WITHIN THE VEIL

W. E. B. DU BOIS

This work proclaims its author's social and political ideals through essays, poetry, and sketches originally published in national periodicals in the first decade of the twentieth century.

NAACP for its integrationist position, Du Bois was initially on Garvey's side. By 1923, however, he found Garvey and his movement to be a threat to black progress and was not hesitant to denounce the man in the pages of *Crisis*. Likewise, Du Bois was of two minds about the Harlem Renaissance, praising its outpouring of creativity, but often severely attacking the anti–political artistic freedom demanded by such writers as Langston Hughes and Claude McKay.

During these years at *Crisis*, Du Bois also wrote a great deal outside of the pages of his magazine. In 1909, he published what he thought was his best book, *John Brown*, a biography of the Kansas

abolitionist. In 1911, he brought out his first novel, *The Quest of the Silver Fleece*, the story of a young black man who, during Reconstruction, travels north after gaining an education and there becomes politicized. Thereafter, he returns to the South to fight for his people. In 1915 came *The Negro*, a history of black Americans; *The Gift of Black Folk* appeared in 1924 and detailed black contributions worldwide. His second novel, *Dark Princess*, was published four years later, and deals with a young black man who is so embittered by racial conditions in America that he flees his country for Europe and there becomes involved in an anti–colonial plot to overthrow white domination. Arndt called both these early novels "strangely gentle and genteel," and further commented that they were "characterized by a sentimentalization of black beauty and an idealization of international movements." After reading *Dark Princess*, a reviewer for the *Springfield Republican* observed: "The truth is, of course, that Du Bois is not a novelist at all, and that the book judged as a novel has only the slightest merit. As a document, as a program, as an exhortation, it has its interest and value."

Du Bois' "*Crisis*" period ended with the publication of his important *Black Reconstruction*, a revisionist, Marxist interpretation that argued that blacks played a hitherto unacknowledged and vital role in the Reconstruction era. Arndt, writing of this book in *Dictionary of Literary Biography*, declared that Du Bois was "not so much interested in facts as he was in truth," and went on to comment that Du Bois was essentially a "redresser, determined to set straight a record of black experience that had been grossly distorted by ignorant white historians or those with vested interest."

A Lion in Winter

At age sixty–six, when most men think of retiring, Du Bois left the NAACP and his editorship of *Crisis* to return to academia at Atlanta University's sociology department, determined to resume his role of dispassionate scholar. He continued publishing, writing columns in newspapers and magazines and released *Black Folk, Then and Now*, which further elucidated black history. H. J. Seligmann found the book impressive in the *Saturday Review of Literature*: "No one can leave it without a deepened sense of the part the Negro peoples have played and must play in world history." An even higher compliment was paid by Barrett Williams, reviewing for the *Boston Transcript*: "Professor Du Bois has overlooked one of the strongest arguments against racial inferiority, namely, this book itself. In it, a man of color has proved himself, in the complex and exacting field of scholarship, the full equal of his white colleagues."

Also during this time, Du Bois wrote the first of two complete biographies, *Dusk at Dawn*, and was busy with *Phylon*, a scholarly publication he established in 1940 at Atlanta University and of which he was the editor. Additionally, he organized a grand scheme of study of the black race by a score of colleges. Never one to take the easy or the quiet path, he also managed to step on toes and egos at Atlanta University, and by 1944 he retired from the university and miraculously was brought back to the NAACP in charge of special research. He continued his heavy involvement with Pan–Africanism, attending conferences around the world, and became known as the "father of Pan–Africanism." In 1945, he published *Color and Democracy: Colonies and Peace*, which presented a case against imperialism. "This book by Dr. Du Bois is a small volume of 143 pages," critic H. A. Overstreet observed in the *Saturday Review of Literature*, "but it contains enough dynamite to blow up the whole vicious system whereby we have comforted our white souls and lined the pockets of generations of free–booting capitalists." *The World and Africa*, published two years later, contained a further indictment of the treatment of colonials in an epic history of Africa's role in world history. Du Bois "does not seek exaggeration of Africa's role, but he insists the role must not be forgotten," Saul Carson remarked in the *New York Times*. "And his insistence is firm. It is persuasive, eloquent, moving. Considering the magnitude of the provocation, it is well–tempered, even gentle."

Once again, however, Walter White, head of the NAACP, and Du Bois butted heads over policies, and their conflicts finally came to a head when Du Bois championed Progressive Party candidate Henry Wallace over Democrat Harry Truman in the 1948 presidential election. For the second time, Du Bois found himself on the outside of the NAACP, an organization he had helped to found.

Thereafter, Du Bois became, according to Arndt, "a prophet without power." He ran for the U.S. Senate in 1950 as a civil rights and peace candidate, but never stood a real chance of election. Increasingly, he became involved with communist causes, a stance sure to bring him trouble in McCarthyite America of the early 1950s. He became vice–chairman of the Council on African Affairs, an organization that was led by the singer and activist Paul Robeson, later designated as subversive by the attorney general. In 1950, he also became chairman of the Peace Information Center, an organization formed to disseminate information against the spread of nuclear weapons. In 1951, Du Bois and four other members of the Peace Information Center were tried in federal court as unregistered agents of a foreign power, but were found not guilty. Nonetheless, this was a frightening situation for Du Bois, already eighty–three years of age. That same year, he married long–time friend Shirley Lola Graham; his first wife had died the year before.

In his final years, Du Bois became more committed to the cause of Communism, even to the extent of publicly mourning the passing of Soviet dictator Josef Stalin. He published over a hundred articles in the leftist journal *National Guardian* between 1948 and 1961. The U.S. State Department insured that he would not spread his message abroad by refusing to issue him a passport until he declared he was not a Communist Party member. This Du Bois refused to do. He turned to fiction as an outlet, for he had largely been forgotten by the political movement he had been so instrumental in starting. In 1957, he published the first part of the "Black Flame" trilogy, *The Ordeal of Mansart*. The second novel, *Mansart Builds a School,* came out two years later, followed by *Worlds of Color* in 1961. Mansart, not unlike Du Bois himself, aimed to serve his race as a teacher. Not terribly gifted intellectually, Mansart is a man of honor, and through him Du Bois manages to relate the major events of black history in America, from Reconstruction onward. Capitalism is taken to task in these novels, while the cooperative life of socialism is extolled.

In 1958, Du Bois's passport was restored by a U.S. Supreme Court decision, and he traveled extensively throughout Eastern Europe and Asia, receiving honorary degrees and accolades from Prague to Moscow and Peking. In 1958, he was awarded the International Lenin Prize and in 1961, Ghana's first president, Kwame Nkruma, invited Du Bois to come to his country to work on the *Encyclopedia Africana*. The ninety–three–year–old Du Bois accepted the offer, and the same year applied for and received membership in the Communist Party. He explained in his autobiography how he reached this decision: "I have studied socialism and communism long and carefully in lands where they are practiced and in conversation with their adherents, and with wide reading. I now state my conclusion frankly and clearly: I believe in communism. . . . I believe that all men should be employed according to their ability and that wealth and services should be distributed according to need. Once I thought that these ends could be attained under capitalism, means of production privately owned, and used in accord with free individual initiative. After earnest observation I now believe that private ownership of capital and free enterprise are leading the world to disaster."

Du Bois left America forever in October of 1961. While in Ghana he worked on the *Encyclopedia*, as well as on his second memoir, *The Autobiography of*

W. E. B. Du Bois. In 1963, he renounced his U.S. citizenship and became a citizen of Ghana on February 23 of that same year. From half a world away, Du Bois, who had long outlived his two children and first wife, watched carefully as the leaders of the black movement in the United States prepared their March on Washington, but he did not live to see it. He died on the eve of the demonstration, on August 27, 1963, and was buried in a state funeral outside of Accra, Ghana.

If you enjoy the works of W. E. B. Du Bois, you might want to check out the following books:

Frederick Douglass, *The Life and Times of Frederick Douglass, Written by Himself,* 1881.

William James, *The Will to Believe, and Other Essays in Popular Philosophy,* 1897.

Martin Luther King, Jr., *Letter from Birmingham Jail,* 1963.

Booker T. Washington, *Up from Slavery: An Autobiography,* 1901.

Du Bois was a controversial figure in his lifetime, and though by the time of his death he had been cast aside and partly forgotten by the movement he helped found, his reputation has grown since that time. A new generation of black leaders has taken on the questions Du Bois raised, free of the taint of Communism which his critics leveled at him in his last years. His legacy lives on, not only in creating a black intelligentsia, but also in inculcating a pride in blacks for their culture and a sense of history for their African roots. Du Bois blended academic rigor and political activism to an extent never before seen in America, either black or white. The author of twenty works of nonfiction, five novels, a volume of poetry and a play, in addition to hundreds of newspaper and magazine articles, Du Bois was a tireless promoter of his people. In his best works, such as *The Souls of Black Folk,* Du Bois established himself firmly as one of the major interpreters of American history and culture. The critic Irving Howe noted in *Celebrations and Attacks: Thirty Years of Literary and Cultural Commentary,* that Du Bois was the "first American Negro in the twentieth century to gain national recognition as intellectual, tribune, and agitator." Howe went on to characterize Du Bois as "[p]rickly, gifted, endlessly articulate."

"In its transcendence of place, time, and, ultimately, even of race, [Du Bois's] fabulous life encompassed large and lasting meanings," wrote his biographer, Lewis. "Always controversial," Lewis further observed, "he espoused racial and political beliefs of such variety and seeming contradiction as to often bewilder and alienate as many of his countrymen and women, black and white, as he inspired and converted. Nearing the end, Du Bois himself conceded mischievously that he would have been hailed with approval if he had died at fifty." Summing up in *Dictionary of Literary Biography,* Arndt wrote: "W. E. B. Du Bois was, in almost every sense of the word, a great man—his vision was large, his dreams great, his influence extraordinary." And in a discussion of the revival of interest in Du Bois, Cruse and Gipson wrote: "In so far as he grasped the basic dilemma of Western blacks as being a people with 'two souls, two thoughts, two unreconciled strivings,' Du Bois's attitudes have been vindicated. He was, as we can now see, one of those unique men whose ideas are destined to be reviled and then revived, and then, no doubt, reviled again, haunting the popular mind long after his death." Writing in *Nation,* Kevin Brown put Du Bois's long life "spanning Reconstruction, *Plessy v. Ferguson,* two World Wars, *Brown v. Board of Education,* and now the civil rights movement," into perspective: Du Bois was "the literal embodiment of the nineteenth century's collision with the twentieth."

■ Biographical and Critical Sources

BOOKS

Baker, Houston A., Jr., *Black Literature in America,* McGraw, 1971.

Bell, Bernard W., Emily Grosholz, and James B. Stewart, *The Critique of Custom: W. E. B. Du Bois and Philosophical Questions,* Routledge (New York City), 1996.

Black Writers, Gale, Volume 1, 1989, Volume 3, 1999.

Bone, Robert A., *The Negro Novel in America,* Yale University Press, revised edition, 1965.

Byerman, Keith Eldon, *Seizing the Word: History, Art, and Self in the Work of W. E. B. Du Bois,* University of Georgia Press (Athens), 1994.

Concise Dictionary of American Literary Biography: Realism, Naturalism, and Local Color, 1865–1917, Gale, 1988.

Contemporary Literary Criticism, Gale, Volume 1, 1973, Volume 2, 1974, Volume 13, 1980, Volume 64, 1991, Volume 96, 1997.

Dictionary of Literary Biography, Gale, Volume 47: *American Historians, 1866–1912,* 1986, Volume 50: *Afro–American Writers before the Harlem Renaissance,* 1986, Volume 91: *American Magazine Journalists, 1900–1960,* 1990.

Du Bois, Shirley Graham, *His Day Is Marching On: A Memoir of W. E. B. Du Bois,* Lippincott, 1971.

Du Bois, W. E. B., *The Philadelphia Negro,* University of Pennsylvania, 1899.

Du Bois, W. E. B., *The Souls of Black Folk,* A. C. McClurg, 1903.

Du Bois, W. E. B., *The Autobiography of W. E. B. Du Bois: A Soliloquy on Viewing My Life from the Last Decade of Its First Century,* International Publishers, 1968.

Hawkins, Hugh, editor, *Booker T. Washington and His Critics: Black Leadership in Crisis,* Heath, 1974.

Horne, Gerald, and Mary Young, editors, *W. E. B. Du Bois: An Encyclopedia,* Greenwood, 2001.

Howe, Irving, "W. E. B. Du Bois: Glory and Shame," *Celebrations and Attacks: Thirty Years of Literary and Cultural Commentary,* Horizon Press, 1979, pp. 170–179.

Katz, Michael B., and Thomas J. Sugrue, *W. E. B. Du Bois, Race, and the City: The Philadelphia Negro and Its Legacy,* University of Pennsylvania Press, 1998.

Lewis, David Levering, *W. E. B. Du Bois: Biography of a Race, 1868–1919,* Holt, 1993.

Lewis, David Levering, *W. E. B. Du Bois: The Fight for Equality and the American Century, 1919–1963,* Holt, 2000.

Logan, Rayford W., editor, *W. E. B. Du Bois: A Profile,* Hill & Wang, 1971.

Moss, Nathaniel, *W. E. B. Du Bois: Civil Rights Leader,* Chelsea Juniors (New York City), 1996.

Pobi–Asamani, Kwadwo, *W. E. B. Du Bois: His Contribution to Pan–Africanism,* Borgo Press (San Bernardino, CA), 1994.

Rampersad, Arnold, *Art and Imagination of W. E. B. Du Bois,* Harvard University Press, 1976.

Reed, Adolph L., *Fabianism and the Color Line: W. E. B. Du Bois and American Political Thought in Black and White,* Oxford University Press (New York City), 1997.

Rudwick, Elliott M., *W. E. B. Du Bois: Propagandist of the Negro Protest,* Atheneum, 1968.

Sadler, Geoff, "Souls of Black Folk: Overview," *Reference Guide to American Literature,* 3rd edition, edited by Jim Kamp, St. James Press, 1994.

Sterne, Emma Gelders, *His Was the Voice: The Life of W. E. B. Du Bois,* Crowell–Collier, 1971.

Wintz, Cary D., *African–American Political Thought,* M. E. Sharpe (Armonk, NY), 1996.

Zamir, Shamoon, *Dark Voices: W. E. B. Du Bois and American Thought, 1888–1903,* University of Chicago Press, 1995.

PERIODICALS

American Visions, February–March, 1994, p. 24.

Black Literature Forum, summer, 1990, pp. 299–313.

Boston Transcript, June 24, 1939, Barrett Williams, review of *Black Folk, Then and Now.*

CLA Journal, June, 1990, pp. 415–427.

Ebony, August, 1972; August, 1975; November, 1994, p. 102.

Forbes, December 5, 1994, p. 84.

German Quarterly, spring, 1997, pp. 123–135.

Jet, November 14, 1994, p. 20.

Los Angeles Times Book Review, January 25, 1987.

Massachusetts Review, summer, 1994, pp. 249–282.

Nation, December 11, 2000, Kevin Brown, "After the Renaissance," pp. 52, 54–56.

New Republic, February 26, 1972; August 4, 1994, p. 28.

Newsweek, August 23, 1971.

New York Review of Books, November 30, 1972, Harold W. Cruse and Carolyn Gipson.

New York Times, March 9, 1947, Saul Carson, review of *The World and Africa;* October 24, 1979.

New York Times Book Review, September 29, 1985.

Phylon, December, 1973, pp. 358–367.

Saturday Review of Literature, July 29, 1939, H. J. Seligmann, review of *Black Folk, Then and Now;* June 23, 1945, H. A. Overstreet, review of *Color and Democracy.*

Springfield Republican, May 28, 1928, review of *Dark Princess.**

—*Sketch by J. Sydney Jones*

Shelby Foote

■ Personal

Born November 17, 1916, Greenville, MS; son of Shelby Dade (a business executive) and Lillian (Rosenstock) Foote; married Gwyn Rainer, September 6, 1956; children: Margaret Shelby, Huger Lee. *Education:* Attended University of North Carolina, 1935–37.

■ Addresses

Home and office—542 East Parkway S., Memphis, TN 38104.

■ Career

Novelist, historian, and playwright. Novelist–in–residence, University of Virginia, Charlottesville, 1963; Arena Stage, Washington, DC, playwright–in–residence, 1963–64; Hollins College, Roanoke, VA, writer–in–residence, 1968. Judge for the National Book Award in history, 1979. *Military service:* U.S. Army, artillery, 1940–44; became captain. U.S. Marine Corps, 1944–45.

■ Member

American Academy of Arts and Letters, Society of American Historians, Fellowship of Southern Writers.

■ Awards, Honors

Guggenheim fellowships, 1955, 1956, 1957, 1958, 1959, and 1960; Ford Foundation grant, 1963; Fletcher Pratt Award, 1964, for *The Civil War: A Narrative*; named distinguished alumnus, University of North Carolina, 1974; Dos Passos Prize for Literature, 1988; Charles Frankel Award, 1992; St. Louis Literary Award, 1992; Nevins–Freeman Award, 1992. Received honorary D.Litt degrees from University of the South, 1981, Southwestern University, 1982, University of South Carolina, 1991, University of North Carolina, 1992, Millsaps University, 1992, and Notre Dame University, 1994, Loyola College and the College of William and Mary, both 1999.

■ Writings

NOVELS

Tournament, Dial (New York City), 1949.
Follow Me Down, Dial, 1950.

Love in a Dry Season, Dial, 1951.

Shiloh, Dial, 1952.

Jordan County: A Landscape in Narrative, Dial, 1954.

Three Novels (contains *Follow Me Down, Love in a Dry Season*, and *Jordan County: A Landscape in Narrative*), Dial, 1964.

September September, Random House, 1978.

(Editor) *Chickamauga, and Other Civil War Stories* (short stories), Dell, 1993.

Child by Fever, Random House, 1995.

Ride Out, Modern Library, 1996.

Also author of play, *Jordan County: A Landscape in the Round*, produced in Washington, DC, 1964. Author of introduction to *The Red Badge of Courage*, Random House, 1998, *Anton Chekhov: Early Short Stories 1883–1888*, Modern Library, 1998, and *Anton Chekhov: Later Short Stories 1888–1903*, Modern Library, 1999.

NONFICTION

The Civil War: A Narrative, Random House, Volume 1: *Fort Sumter to Perryville*, 1958, Volume 2: *Fredericksburg to Meridian*, 1963, Volume 3: *Red River to Appomattox*, 1974.

A Novelist's View of History, Dial, 1981.

Stars in Their Courses: The Gettysburg Campaign, Random House, 1994.

The Beleaguered City: The Vicksburg Campaign, December 1862–July 1863 (originally published in Volume 2 of *The Civil War: A Narrative*), Modern Library (New York City), 1995.

The Correspondence of Shelby Foote and Walker Percy, edited by Jay Tolson, Norton, 1997.

■ **Adaptations**

September September was adapted as the television movie, *Memphis*, starring Cybill Shepherd.

■ **Sidelights**

"I think of myself as a novelist who wrote a three-volume history of the Civil War," writer Shelby Foote told an interviewer for *Paris Review*. "I don't think it's a novel, but I certainly think it's by a novelist. The novels are not novels written by a historian." This elemental fact defines Foote as a writer: starting out as a novelist who plumbed the depths of the South in books such as *Tournament,*

Follow Me Down, Love in a Dry Season, and *Jordan County: A Landscape in Narrative,* he dissected a particular mythical region much as did his fellow Mississippian, William Faulkner, in his tales set in the fictional Yoknapatawpha County. Recounting much of the history of Mississippi's Delta region in these novels, Foote assembled a cast of characters, from hardscrabble farmers to well-to-do planter families, in order to profile the region where he had grown up and which had formed him. Even with his fourth novel, *Shiloh,* which follows that epic Civil War battle, Foote includes characters that make appearances in his "Jordan County" cycle of novels. Then came a quarter century hiatus from novels, during which time Foote wrote his massive, million-word, three-volume narrative history of the U.S. Civil War, a project initially planned to last a couple of years. On the other end of that undertaking, Foote once again returned to novel writing with his 1978 *September September,* set in Memphis in 1957 during an era of racial tensions. Though he was long considered a novelist and writer of note by the critical establishment, Foote became something of a mini-celebrity as a commentator on Ken Burns's *The Civil War,* which was broadcast on the Public Broadcasting Service in 1990. Thereafter, he was viewed as a Civil War guru as well as an embodiment of the Old South's eloquence and acerbity.

Born in Greenville, Mississippi, on November 17, 1916, Shelby Dade Foote, Jr., was the only child of a family that had been, on both sides, prominent in the late nineteenth and early twentieth centuries in the Mississippi Delta. However, by the time of Foote's birth, the family wealth and plantations had largely been lost, either on the gambling table or, shortly to come, in the Depression. As Foote told John Carr in *Conversations with Shelby Foote,* "Though [my grandfathers] were both extremely rich in their lifetimes, they barely had the money at their deaths to pay for the shovel that buried them." There was little time for mourning after lost wealth, however, Shelby Sr. had a living to make in corporate America, and this eventually took the family from Mississippi to Florida and on to Alabama where he served as a supervisor for regional operations of Armour Meats.

Foote's father died not long after this move, victim of a fluke medical procedure resulting in septicemia. The widow took her five-year-old son back to Greenville, which would be his home for the next thirty years. There, Foote grew up "a latchkey kid before there were any latchkey kids," as he noted in his *Paris Review* interview. "Cast on my own, I began to read very early and with great pleasure. I read pretty good stuff in addition to terrible stuff. The most illuminating thing that ever happened to me in those early days was winning as a Sunday-school prize a copy of *David Copperfield*." Reading Charles Dickens' classic work was a revelation for the young Foote, whose earlier reading efforts had included *Tom Swift* and the Tarzan books. When Foote finished that book he realized, as he noted in *Paris Review*, "that I'd been in the presence of something realer than real. I knew David better than I knew myself or anyone else. The way Dickens told that story caught me right then and there." Eventually, Foote wanted to do what Dickens had done, to make "a world that's somehow better in focus than real life, which goes rushing past you." By high school, this dream had coalesced in Foote's editing of the school paper, *The Pica,* which won the national championship for the best high school newspaper in the United States.

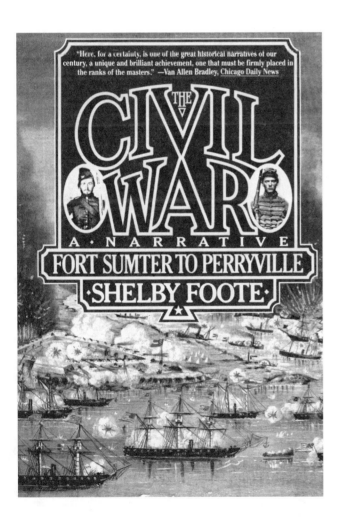

First in a series of three volumes, Foote's 1958 work began as a concise, one–volume history of the War between the States but evolved into an extensively researched study of military tactics.

As a young boy, Foote also fell under the influence of a local lawyer and sometime poet, William Alexander Percy, one of whose much younger cousins, the novelist Walker Percy, became a lifelong friend and an influence on Foote's life. At the older Percy's house, Foote met literary luminaries such as Sherwood Anderson and Langston Hughes. Foote began a wider reading that encompassed the novels of James Joyce, Marcel Proust, Thomas Mann, and most importantly, William Faulkner.

Entering the University of North Carolina in 1935, Foote widened his literary interests, but found the college setting too confining and conservative for his tastes. He contributed short stories and reviews to the college periodical, *Carolina Magazine,* but was otherwise underwhelmed with academic life. In 1937, fed up with classes which he seldom attended and seeing that war was brewing in Europe, he returned to Greenville where he worked for a time on the *Delta Star* and began his first novel, *Tournament,* a semi–biographical, fictionalized account of his grandfather. Three years in the writing, *Tournament* was initially turned down by Knopf. Then came the war years.

Joining the Mississippi National Guard, Foote eventually became a captain in the artillery dispatched to Northern Ireland to prepare for the D–Day invasions. However his individualistic personality earned him a court martial and discharge for defending one of his men against a superior officer. After working for a time with the Associated Press in New York, Foote joined the U.S. Marines, and at war's end, he was in California, preparing for the invasion of Japan. After the war, Foote returned to Greenville with his Irish wife, whom he had met while on duty in Northern Ireland. He got back to his writing desk full of enthusiasm.

Early Success

Foote set about reworking his first novel and also writing short stories. The first of these, "Flood Burial," about a Confederate major who dies during a Mississippi flood and cannot be buried, was immediately taken by *Saturday Evening Post.* Amazed at his instant success, Foote decided to follow it up with another short story that would be twice as long and perhaps earn him twice as much money from the *Post.* "Ride Out," later collected in *Jordan County,* was forty–four pages in length and did indeed earn Foote $1,500, twice the amount of his first tale. "I was pleased with that, God knows," Foote recalled in his *Paris Review* interview. "But I got to thinking, It's not supposed to happen like this; this is not the way you learn how to be a writer." Working on the same principle, Foote next wrote a sixty–six–page short story that later formed the basis of his novel, *Love in a Dry Season,* and that was immediately rejected by the same magazine. "I was sort of relieved," Foote noted. "I had a strong feeling that it was not supposed to go on like that."

Foote returned to novel writing and produced his Civil War tale, *Shiloh,* an experimental novel told through the monologues of seven Northern and Southern soldiers during the two days of the 1862 battle. An encouraging rejection from Dial Press led to their publishing his first novel, *Tournament.* In that book, Foote chronicles the transformation of successful plantation owner Hugh Bart to a destitute gambler who loses all. While Bart's loss of the plantation, Solitaire, serves as the focus of the novel, Foote also explores the origins of the plantation and of the history behind it through the character of Isaac Jameson, an early settler in the Delta region. "*Tournament* is not essentially a novel about history," according to Thomas H. Landess writing in *Mississippi Quarterly,* "but is concerned with the struggle for survival and supremacy, an archetypal role of the male in society." Foote uses history, as Landess pointed out, as the background and "matrix" for the story of a transitional period in the South, from an agrarian to business economy. Thus "the narrative marks the true beginnings of a saga of the region which [Foote] continues in succeeding works."

The immediately succeeding work was *Follow Me Down,* "perhaps Foote's most powerful work of fiction," according to Landess. Also set on the plantation Solitaire, introduced in his first novel, *Follow Me Down* tells the story of a tenant farmer, middle–aged Luther Eustis, and the teenage girl, Beulah, whom he seduces and ultimately kills. Divided into three sections, the book is largely told in monologue format. The first and third section are narrated by the accounts of witnesses to both the crime and the ensuing court case, while the middle section is told from the point of view of both Eustis and Beulah. This change of focus and point of view allows the reader to get a multi–layered perspective of the tragedy, to slowly discover that the God–fearing Eustis was responding to what he took for the voice of God (or the devil) when he strangled his lover. Beulah's tale of being sold in prostitution at an early age takes the story one level deeper. Landess felt that Foote's "consistent emphasis on the origins of Luther Eustis—his family history and its associations with the plantation Solitaire—point both to a past of moral certitude and to a future of increasing decadence."

With *Love in a Dry Season,* Foote takes this decadence one step further, to the Delta in the decades between 1920 and the World War II. Here is a South "scarred and enfeebled by the legacy of the Civil War," according to Paul S. Bodine in *Contemporary Popular Writers.* Bodine went on to note that the four principal characters—Major Malcolm Barcroft, Harley Drew, and Amy and Jeff Carruthers—"represent the amoral and diminished quality of the new South." Anderson Clark, writing in *Contemporary Novelists,* called *Love in a Dry Season* a "tour de force in which the author links two separate stories centered on the subject of money." Landess commented, "as the title suggests, the novel is about love, or rather its absence," and further observed that the "temper of this novel is similar to that of Fitzgerald's best work, and is an excellent example of Foote's virtuosity as a novelist."

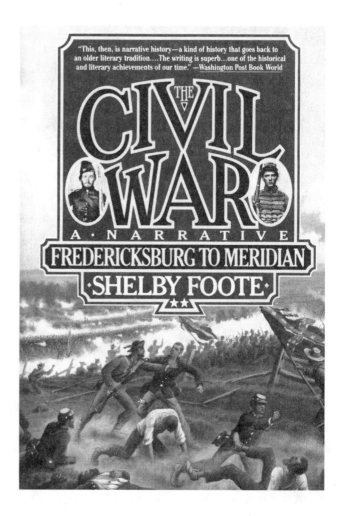

Covering the strategies employed by both Union and Confederate leaders during the battles fought from late 1862 to 1864, Foote's 1963 volume joined the others in the trilogy in earning praise for its unbiased approach.

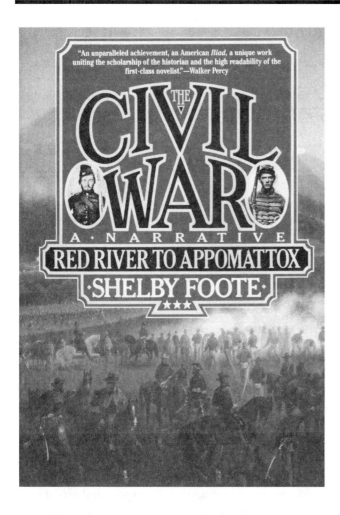

"An unparalleled achievement, an American *Iliad*, a unique work uniting the scholarship of the historian and the high readability of the first-class novelist."—Walker Percy

THE CIVIL WAR
A·NARRATIVE
RED RIVER TO APPOMATTOX
·SHELBY FOOTE·

The final battles of the Civil War are covered in Foote's 1974 work, the long-awaited closing chapter of his epic narrative about America's bloodiest war.

Finally, in 1952, Foote's novel *Shiloh* was published. The Civil War, which loomed in the background of all his novels to date, takes front and center stage in this historical novel in which Foote employs a cast of Union and Confederate soldiers to provide a view of that crucial Civil War battle in Tennessee. Often compared to Stephen Crane's *Red Badge of Courage*, Foote's *Shiloh* takes a graphic look at modern warfare, focusing much of its attention on the actions of Nathan Bedford Forrest, one of the leading participants in the battle. Published on the ninetieth anniversary of the battle, *Shiloh* "is unique as a twentieth-century chronicle of war," according to Landess, and one that "pushes that pushes the action of the novel toward the level of pure epic."

A collection of stories and short novels, *Jordan County* followed, but already Foote was deeply en-tangled in a novel, *Two Gates to the City*, that he had been planning for a decade. This new novel would be big in the largest sense—a history of the Delta and the South in the first half of the twentieth century. Work on this bogged down, however; parts of it were incorporated in *Jordan County*, but Foote struggled on until, on the strength of *Shiloh*, an editor at Random House suggested he undertake work on a short history of the Civil War. Foote agreed and started the research, only to quickly discover that the work would be anything but short.

The Civil War: A Narrative

Originally envisioned as a one-volume work, Foote's effort grew into what has been called a "monumental" project that took some twenty years to complete. In the *New York Times Book Review*, Nash K. Burger explained: "Shelby Foote was asked by a New York publisher to write a short, one-volume history of that conflict. Foote agreed. It seemed a nice change of pace before his next novel. Now, 20 years later, the project is completed: Three volumes . . . , 2,934 pages, a million and a half words." Burger followed his account of the writing of *The Civil War: A Narrative* with this assessment: "It is a remarkable achievement, prodigiously researched, vigorous, detailed, absorbing."

Using Guggenheim fellowships to partly finance the writing of the first volume, Foote completed *Fort Sumter to Perryville*, a 400,000-word account, in 1958. The second volume appeared in 1963, *Fredericksburg to Meridian*. Work on the third volume, *Red River to Appomattox*, was slowed down as Foote spent time in Washington, D.C., as writer-in-residence for the Arena Theater, and as he grew increasingly disenchanted with the segregationist policies of leaders from the South. It took him as long to write the third volume, which finally appeared in 1974, as it had to write both earlier volumes of the set. Focusing largely on battles, Foote's history does not lack for character or humor. As Helen White and Redding S. Sugg, Jr., noted in *Virginia Quarterly*, "Although epic in magnitude, seriousness, and scope and tragic impact, the book conveys much of the human quality of events through humor." The same critics also commented, "*The Civil War* exemplifies, preeminently, the 'sense of place' in its economical, functional use of concrete details, the sensory effects that anchor the narrative, the human story, to the 'world's body'."

Other reviewers voiced similar praise. *Newsweek*'s Peter S. Prescott stated that "the result [of Foote's labor] is not only monumental in size, but a truly impressive achievement." He reported that "Foote the novelist cares less for generalizations about dialectics, men and motives than for creating 'the illusion that the observer is not so much reading a book as sharing an experience.'" According to M. E. Bradford in *National Review,* in this endeavor the author has succeeded: "There is, of course, a majesty inherent in the subject [of the Civil War]. . . . [And] the credit for recovering such majesty to the attention of our skeptical and unheroic age will hereafter belong . . . to Mr. Foote."

Foote's account of the war is strictly a military one, detailing the battles, men, and leaders on both sides of the conflict. "The War itself . . . is indeed Foote's subject," Bradford remarked. "The *war,* the *fighting*—and not its economic, intellectual, or political causes." Lance Morrow echoed this summation in a *Time* review: "[Foote's] attention is focused on the fighting itself—fortification, tactics, the strange chemistries of leadership, the workings in the generals' minds. Foote moves armies and great quantities of military information with a lively efficiency."

Critics note that though such military histories concerning the Civil War are not uncommon, Foote's is one of the most comprehensive, covering as it does the Union and Confederate armies in both the eastern and western theaters of the war. Moreover, they express admiration for the author's balanced and objective view of the conflict. C. Vann Woodward of the *New York Review of Books* contended that "in spite of his Mississippi origins, Foote . . . attempts to keep an even hand in giving North and South their due measure of praise and blame." Burger added that although Foote's chronicle begins and ends with reports on the activities of Jefferson Davis, this "is not indicative of any bias in favor of the South or its leader. . . . The complete work," the critic continued, "is a monumental, even-handed account of this country's tragic, fratricidal conflict." Foote himself, in *Paris Review,* commented on this approach. "I've been complimented for an absence of bias; I've had people tell me that if they didn't already know, they couldn't tell whether I was a Northerner or a Southerner, but you can't help noticing that my heart beats a little faster when the Confederacy is out in front." Expanding on this, Foote also noted that if he had been alive during the Civil War, he would have fought for the South. "What's more," he added, "I would fight for the Confederacy today if the circumstances were similar. There's a great deal of misunderstanding about the Confederacy, the Confederate flag, the whole thing." Foote pointed to the idea of states rights which the Confederacy was defending as being one of the positive elements of that fight.

In discussing Foote's concentration on the war itself and "therefore the persons who made, died in, or survived that conflict," Bradford asserted that it is not "an exaggeration to speak of the total effect produced by this emphasis as epic." Prescott concluded: "To read Foote's chronicle is an awesome and moving experience. History and literature are rarely so thoroughly combined as here; one finishes [the last] volume convinced that no one need undertake this particular enterprise again." James M. Cox, writing in *Southern Review,* called Foote's immense history "a great work of literature, surely one of the great works written in this or any other country—a work to rank with that of Thucydides, Clarendon, Gibbon, or Henry Adams. . . . To read this great narrative is to love the nation too."

While researching his epic history, Foote relied heavily on the one hundred twenty-eight volumes of *The War of Rebellion: A Compilation of the Official Records of the Union and Confederate Armies.* Critics have complained not about Foote's accuracy and depth of research, but that his books lack documentation. There are no notes, so the reader has difficulty pursuing avenues of research opened up by Foote's writing. But no one doubts the quality of the writing or the effort put into the vast project. But Foote emphasizes with his subtitle that his is a narrative history, one meant both to inform and entertain. James I. Robertson, Jr., writing in *Civil War History,* neatly summed up the importance of *The Civil War* and of Foote's contribution: "He has provided a superb view of the forest rather than the usual and tiring look at a few trees; and he has done so in a writing style both fluid and appealing."

Antebellum Foote

There was literary life for Foote after his monumental Civil War history. He soon published his first novel in over two decades, *September September.* Set in Memphis in 1957, the novel features a thriller format—the kidnapping of a young black boy—to illuminate the integration of Central High in Little Rock, Arkansas. Three whites kidnap the young boy in an attempt to extract a large ransom from his wealthy family. "Foote skillfully presents a black bourgeois family dealing with this trauma," according to P. Campbell in *Twentieth-Century Romance and Historical Writers.* Foote combines particulars of the time to give the feel of 1950s America. The book was later turned into a television movie.

If you enjoy the works of Shelby Foote, you might want to check out the following books and films:

William Faulkner, *The Sound and the Fury,* 1929.
Don Robertson, *By Antietam Creek,* 1960.
Michael Shaara, *The Killer Angels,* 1974.
The Civil War, a documentary by filmmaker Ken Burns, based on Foote's three–volume history, 1990.

Throughout the 1980s, Foote continued work on his big novel, as well as on small projects, albeit in virtual obscurity. Then in the early 1990s Foote became something of a national celebrity for his on–camera commentary in Ken Burns's PBS documentary, *The Civil War,* which originally aired in 1990. Since that time, interest in Foote's life and work has increased markedly. Suddenly, his literary reputation was reborn, his books came back into print, and he became a much–sought–after speaker. In 1971, a critic such as Landess could declare, "Taken as a whole the work of Shelby Foote is an achievement of importance, and one which has been shamefully neglected by the literary establishment." Today only the first part of that judgment would hold true. In 1997, his correspondence with the novelist Walker Percy was published, adding to the stature of both men. Foote, while consoled by such notoriety, has not let it got to his head. At heart, he is still a novelist plying a writer's craft. "There's no better feeling in the world," he noted in his *Paris Review* interview, "than to lay your head on the pillow at night looking forward to getting up in the morning and returning to the desk. That's real happiness."

■ Biographical and Critical Sources

BOOKS

Bodine, Paul S. "Shelby Foote: An Overview," *Contemporary Popular Writers,* edited by Dave Mote, St. James Press, 1997.
Campbell, P., *Twentieth–Century Romance and Historical Writers,* 3rd edition, edited by Aruna Vasudevan, St. James Press, 1994.
Carter, William C., editor, *Conversations with Shelby Foote,* University Press of Mississippi, 1989.

Clark, Anderson, "Shelby Foote: An Overview," *Contemporary Novelists,* 6th edition, edited by Susan Windisch Brown, St. James Press, 1996.
Phillips, Robert L., Jr., *Shelby Foote: Novelist and Historian,* University Press of Mississippi, 1992.
Tolson, Jay, *Pilgrim in the Ruins,* Simon & Schuster, 1989.
White, Helen, and Redding S. Sugg, Jr., *Shelby Foote,* Twayne Publishers, 1982.

PERIODICALS

American Heritage, July–August, 1991.
Atlantic Monthly, May, 1952; December, 1963.
Book Week, December 15, 1963.
Chicago Sunday Tribune, November 16, 1958.
Christian Century, November 12, 1997, p. 1048.
Christian Science Monitor, December 4, 1963.
Civil War History, June, 1975, James I. Robertson, Jr., review of *The Civil War,* pp. 172–75.
Commonweal, January 9, 1959.
Mississippi Quarterly, fall, 1971, Thomas H. Landess, "Southern History and Manhood: Major Themes in the Works of Shelby Foote," pp. 321–47.
National Review, February 14, 1975, M. E. Bradford, review of *The Civil War.*
New Republic, September 8, 1997, pp. 41–46.
Newsweek, December 2, 1974, Peter S. Prescott, review of *The Civil War;* January 30, 1978.
New York Herald Tribune Book Review, July 16, 1950; October 21, 1951; April 6, 1952; May 2, 1954; November 23, 1958.
New York Review of Books, March 6, 1975, C. Vann Woodward, review of *The Civil War.*
New York Times, September 25, 1949; September 23, 1951; April 6, 1952; April 25, 1954; November 16, 1958; December 1, 1996.
New York Times Book Review, December 1, 1963; December 15, 1974, Nash K. Burger, review of *The Civil War;* March 5, 1978.
Paris Review, summer, 1999, "Shelby Foote: The Art of Fiction CLVIII," pp. 48–91.
Publishers Weekly, October 14, 1996, p. 75.
San Francisco Chronicle, November 28, 1958.
Saturday Review, November 19, 1949; June 5, 1954; December 13, 1958.
Southern Review, spring, 1985, James M. Cox, "Shelby Foote's Civil War," pp. 329–350.
Time, July 3, 1950; January 27, 1975, Lance Morrow, review of *The Civil War.*
Virginia Quarterly, spring, 1979, Helen White and Redding S. Sugg, Jr., "Shelby Foote's 'Iliad'," pp. 234–250.

—Sketch by J. Sydney Jones

Jack Gantos

ciate professor of creative writing and literature, 1992–96. Visiting professor at Brown University, 1986, University of New Mexico, 1993–95, and Vermont College, 1996. Frequent speaker at schools, libraries, and educational conferences, and facilitator of writing workshops.

■ Personal

Born John Bryan Gantos, Jr., July 2, 1951, in Mount Pleasant, PA; son of John (a construction superintendent) and Elizabeth (maiden name, Weaver) Gantos, a banker; married Anne A. Lower (an art dealer), November 11, 1989; children: Mabel Grace. *Education:* Emerson College, B.F.A., 1976, M.A., 1984.

■ Member

National Council of Teachers of English, Society of Children's Book Writers and Illustrators, Writer's Guild.

■ Addresses

Home—45 Concord Sq., #1, Boston, MA 02118. *Office*—Emerson College, Division of Writing, Literature, and Publishing, 1001 Beacon St., Boston, MA 02116. *Agent*—Fran Leibowitz, Writers House, 21 West 26th St., New York, NY 10010.

■ Awards, Honors

Best Books for Young Readers citation, American Library Association (ALA), 1976–93, for the "Rotten Ralph" series; Children's Book Showcase Award, 1977, for *Rotten Ralph;* Alumni award, Emerson College, 1979, for Outstanding Achievement in Creative Writing; Massachusetts Council for the Arts Awards finalist, 1983, 1988; Gold Key Honor Society Award, 1985, for Creative Excellence; National Endowment for the Arts grant and fellowship, 1987; Quarterly West Novella Award, 1989, for *X–Rays;* Children's Choice citation, International Reading Association, 1990, for *Rotten Ralph's Show and Tell;* Batavia Educational Foundation grant, 1991; West Springfield Arts Council grant, 1991; Parents' Choice

■ Career

Author and educator. Emerson College, Boston, MA, part–time writing instructor, 1978–80, adjunct instructor, 1980–86, assistant professor, 1986–92, asso-

citation, 1994, for *Not So Rotten Ralph*; "One Hundred Books to Read and Share" selection, New York Public Library, and ALA Book Links selection, both 1994, both for *Heads or Tails*; Best Books of 1995 citation, *Bulletin of the Center for Children's Literature*, for *Jack's New Power*; New York Public Library Books for the Teen Age, 1997, and Arizona and Maine Reader's Choice Awards, 1998, all for *Jack's Black Book*; Parents Choice Silver Award, 1999, and Dorothy Canfield Fisher Master List citation (Vermont), both for *Jack on the Tracks*; Great Stone Face Award, Children's Librarians of New Hampshire, National Book Award finalist for Young People's Literature, ALA Notable Children's Book, NCSS and CBC Notable Children's Trade Book in the Field of Social Studies, *School Library Journal* Best Book of the Year, *Riverbank Review* Children's Book of Distinction, New York Public Library "One Hundred Titles for Reading and Sharing," all 1999, Iowa Teen Award, Iowa Educational Media Association, Flicker Tale Children's Book Award nomination, North Dakota Library Association, Sasquatch Award nomination, all 2000, all for *Joey Pigza Swallowed the Key*; Newbery Honor Book award, ALA Notable Children's Book citation, *Booklist* Editor's Choice selection, ALA Book Links Lasting Connections citation, and Parents Choice Gold Award, all 2001, all for *Joey Pigza Loses Control*. Gantos has also received other regional and child-selected awards.

Joey Pigza Swallowed the Key also received state reading award nominations from Georgia, New Hampshire, Maine, Arizona, Texas, Pennsylvania, Iowa, New Mexico, Michigan, Florida, Washington, California, and the Northwest Territories.

■ Writings

"ROTTEN RALPH" PICTURE BOOK SERIES; ILLUSTRATED BY NICOLE RUBEL

Rotten Ralph, Houghton Mifflin (Boston), 1976.
Worse than Rotten, Ralph, Houghton Mifflin (Boston), 1978.
Rotten Ralph's Rotten Christmas, Houghton Mifflin (Boston), 1984.
Rotten Ralph's Trick or Treat!, Houghton Mifflin (Boston), 1986.
Rotten Ralph's Show and Tell, Houghton Mifflin (Boston), 1989.
Happy Birthday Rotten Ralph, Houghton Mifflin (Boston), 1990.
Not So Rotten Ralph, Houghton Mifflin (Boston), 1994.

Rotten Ralph's Rotten Romance, Houghton Mifflin (Boston), 1997.
The Christmas Spirit Attacks Rotten Ralph, HarperCollins (New York City), 1998.
Rotten Ralph's Halloween Howl, HarperCollins (New York City), 1998
Back to School for Rotten Ralph, HarperCollins (New York City), 1998.
Wedding Bells for Rotten Ralph, HarperCollins (New York City), 1999.
Rotten Ralph's Thanksgiving Wish, Farrar, Strauss & Giroux (New York City), 1999.
Rotten Ralph Helps Out, Farrar, Strauss & Giroux (New York City), 2001.
Rotten Ralph Plays Fair, Farrar, Strauss & Giroux (New York City), 2002.

The "Rotten Ralph" books have been translated into other languages, including Hebrew and Japanese.

PICTURE BOOKS; ILLUSTRATED BY NICOLE RUBEL

Sleepy Ronald, Houghton Mifflin (Boston), 1976.
Fair-Weather Friends, Houghton Mifflin (Boston), 1977.
Aunt Bernice, Houghton Mifflin (Boston), 1978.
The Perfect Pal, Houghton Mifflin (Boston), 1979.
(With Nicole Rubel) *Greedy Greeny*, Doubleday (New York City), 1979.
Swampy Alligator, Simon & Schuster (New York City), 1980.
The Werewolf Family, Houghton Mifflin (Boston), 1980.
Willy's Raiders, Parents Magazine Press (New York City), 1981.
Red's Fib, Jim Henson Associates, 1985.

"JACK HENRY" SERIES; AUTOBIOGRAPHICAL FICTION FOR MIDDLE-GRADE READERS

Heads or Tails: Stories from the Sixth Grade, Farrar, Strauss & Giroux (New York City),, 1994.
Jack's New Power: Stories from a Caribbean Year, Farrar, Strauss & Giroux (New York City), 1995.
Jack's Black Book, Farrar, Strauss & Giroux (New York City), 1997.
Jack on the Tracks: Four Seasons of Fifth Grade, Farrar, Strauss & Giroux (New York City), 1999.

OTHER

Zip Six (adult novel), Bridge Works (Bridgehampton, NY), 1996.
Desire Lines (young adult novel), Farrar, Strauss & Giroux (New York City), 1997.

Joey Pigza Swallowed the Key (middle–grade fiction), Farrar, Strauss & Giroux (New York City), 1998.

Joey Pigza Loses Control, (middle–grade fiction), Farrar, Straus (New York City), 2000.

Hole in My Life, (young adult autobiography), Farrar, Strauss & Giroux (New York City), 2001.

Also author of novella *X–15's.* Contributor of short story "Cradle Hold" to *No Easy Answers: Short Stories about Teenagers Making Tough Choices,* edited by Donald R. Gallo, Delacorte (New York City), 1997, short story "The Penny Tree" for *Storyworks* magazine, October, 1999, and short story "Muzak for Prozac" to *On the Fringe,* edited by Gallo, 2001.

■ Adaptations

Joey Pigza Swallowed the Key, read by the author, was released on audio cassette by Listening Library in 1999; *Joey Pigza Loses Control,* read by the author, was released on audio cassette by Listening Library in 2000; *Heads or Tails* has also been released on audio cassette. The "Rotten Ralph" books have been adapted for television. Two Rotten Ralph animated specials were produced and broadcast on the Disney Channel; in addition, Italtoons and the British Broadcasting Company produced a series based on the character for broadcast in the European, Asian, and South American markets; Fox Family Channel was scheduled to broadcast the programs in the United States. *Joey Pigza Swallowed the Key* was adapted for a television film by Showtime, to be aired in 2002.

■ Work in Progress

Living in the Library, a young adult novel and *Brasilia,* an adult novel. both for Farrar, Strauss & Giroux.

■ Sidelights

A popular and prolific author of books for readers ranging from the early primary grades through high school, as well as for adults, John Gantos, Jr.—better known as Jack Gantos—is considered by many critics and readers to be both a gifted humorist and an insightful observer of childhood feelings and behavior. Gantos has written witty cautionary tales, middle–grade fiction that presents bittersweet reflections on the pains and pleasures of growing up, and young adult fiction that deals frankly with serious themes. However, he is perhaps best known as the creator of Rotten Ralph, a large, anthropomorphic, red cat whose devilish, mostly unrepentant behavior is always forgiven by his owner, Sarah, a patient and loving little girl. Gantos has collaborated on the multi–volume series of picture books featuring the rascally feline with illustrator Nicole Rubel; Rubel's bright colors and bold designs are generally thought to complement the author's brisk, droll prose style well and have contributed to the huge popularity of the character.

Gantos is also well known for creating the "Jack Henry" books, autobiographical fiction that describes the experiences of the author's alter ego as a fifth–, sixth–, and seventh–grader. Other popular books by Gantos include *Joey Pigza Swallowed the Key* and *Joey Pigza Loses Control* (a 2001 Newbery Honor book), both stories about a boy with Attention Deficit Disorder (ADD), and *Desire Lines,* a young adult novel about how a teenage boy outs two lesbian classmates in order to save his own reputation. Throughout his works, Gantos has addressed issues that are meaningful to young people, such as the nature of friendship, dealing with jealousy and loneliness, being forgiven and accepted, the importance of playing fair and doing the right thing, and learning how to fit into the often baffling world of adults. Although some of the author's works are considered by some critics to be exaggerated, irreverent, unsubtle and containing elements described as gross or unsettling, many reviewers have noted the positive values in his books, as well as their outrageous humor and underlying poignancy. Gantos is generally regarded as a talented, imaginative writer who understands children and what appeals to them.

Youthful Creativity

Born in Mount Pleasant, Pennsylvania, Gantos is the eldest son of John Gantos, Sr., a construction superintendent and salesman of Lebanese Catholic descent, and Elizabeth Weaver Gantos, a bank employee and Lutheran who came from Mount Pleasant. Gantos is one of four children; he has an older sister, Karen, and two younger brothers, Alex and Eric. As a first grader, Gantos was in the Bluebird reading group, which he later discovered was for slow readers. He began expressing his creativity at an early age. Gantos recalled that his favorite game as a small boy was to pretend that his clothes were on fire and then to roll down a hill to save himself. When he was in the second grade, Gantos

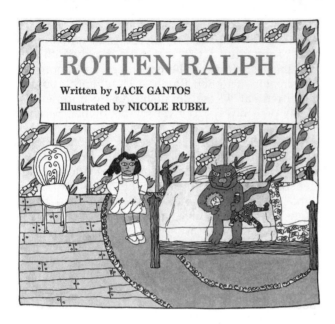

A troublesome feline and his long–suffering young owner pair up for their fictional debut in this humorous 1976 picture book, which brought Gantos his first taste of fame.

received his first diary. He once remarked, "I had an older sister who was very smart. She was in fifth grade and I liked to do everything that she did.... One day my mother came home from work and gave her a diary.... When I saw that diary, I wanted one, too. My mother said I was too young to have a diary but I didn't think so. I pitched a fit. I howled and sobbed. 'I want a diary,' I cried. 'I want a diary.' She finally gave me one. 'But you better write in it every day,' she said." Gantos did as his mother requested. He recalled, "I wrote the date, the weather, and what I ate for breakfast, lunch, and dinner. Food was the most important thing in the world to me and so I wrote about it all the time." Gantos also collected what he now calls "a lot of junk"—shells, rocks, stamps, pennies, bottle caps, baseball cards, butterflies, and "lots more good stuff."

As a second grader, Gantos moved with his family from Pennsylvania to Barbados, where his father believed he could find more work. Young Jack was able to move all of his collections by putting them into his diaries—gluing, pasting, and even drilling holes in the books. The move to Barbados prompted a change in Jack's journal entries. He said, "I began to write about all the stuff that was in my diary. I wrote about where I caught my bugs. I wrote about the stamps I collected. I wrote stories about the pho-

tographs I had saved. And I became a lot more excited about keeping a diary because so much of what I wrote about had personal meaning to me. To this day I still put lots of junk in my notebooks and write about it. The junk and stuff has become the details in much of my writing." While in Barbados, Gantos attended British schools that emphasized the importance of reading and writing; he claims that by fifth grade he had managed to learn ninety percent of what he needed as an adult. When the family moved from Barbados to south Florida, Gantos found that his new classmates were less interested in their studies and that his teachers generally acted more like disciplinarians than instructors. Consequently, he retreated to an abandoned bookmobile and read. Gantos began collecting anecdotes—many of which he overheard standing outside the teacher's lounge—in the sixth grade. In addition, he began writing down his own thoughts and feelings. Gantos once recalled, "Most of the stories were from real life. I saw a plane crash and wrote about it. My father rescued a drowning husband and wife in the ocean. He was heroic, and I wrote about it. Once my sister accidentally started a grease fire in the kitchen. The whole house almost burned down but my mom was only thankful that we were safe. She wasn't even angry, and I wrote about how she loved us. I wrote many more stories from my life." Many of these stories were later to provide the inspiration for the author's "Jack Henry" series.

In junior high, Gantos went to a school that had once been a state prison. Once again, he spent most of his time reading outside of the classroom. Gantos decided to become a professional writer when he was in high school. He told an interviewer from *Amazon.com*, "[M]y diary and journal writing background gave me a lot of confidence that writing was something I had loved all my life." After graduating from high school, Gantos left Florida to attend Emerson College in Boston. While at Emerson, Gantos met art student Nicole Rubel; the pair became friends and decided to work together on picture books for children. Gantos wrote in *Fifth Book of Junior Authors and Illustrators*, "She had illustrated a book without words and when I saw it I asked for permission to write the story. We started that way." The author once acknowledged, "I made a lot of mistakes. I thought children's books had to be sweet, warm, and gentle." After Gantos received his first rejection letters, he became frustrated. "Then," he recalled, "I remembered what one of my teachers had told me. She said, 'Write about what you know.' I was sitting at my desk and I looked down at the floor and saw my lousy, grumpy, hissing creep of a cat that loved to scratch my ankles, throw fur around the house, and shred the clothes in my closet." His cat became Rotten Ralph, and a new antihero was born. Gantos's first book, *Rotten Ralph*, was published in 1976, the year that he received his B.F.A. in creative writing from Emerson College and decided to become a freelance writer. Gantos once remembered, "It was a great day when I saw that first published book. All the hard work had paid off."

Rotten Ralph

In *Rotten Ralph* the title character indulges in bad behavior at home, such as crashing his bike into the dining room table; sawing the tree limb that supports the swing of his owner, Sarah; and wearing Father's slippers. Sarah's family takes him to the circus, but Ralph misbehaves so badly that he is left there as punishment. While in the circus, Ralph becomes unhappy as a performer, and he runs away. He is found, ill and underfed, by Sarah, who welcomes him back home. It appears that Ralph has learned his lesson and will become less rotten, but Gantos gives indications that Ralph will revert back to his impish self. Writing in *Language Arts*, Ruth M. Stein called *Rotten Ralph* a "successful first book by both author and illustrator." Although Zena Sutherland of *Bulletin of the Center for Children's Books* noted, "There's some humor in the situation, but it seems overworked," *Washington Post Book World* critic Brigitte Weeks called *Rotten Ralph* "a moral tale" that children will "highly appreciate" for seeing a cat in trouble instead of a child.

In subsequent volumes of the series, Ralph continues to be naughty and to get away with it. He ruins Christmas, Thanksgiving, Halloween, Valentine's Day, show and tell, birthday parties, and even a wedding. In *Not So Rotten Ralph,* Sarah—who, at her most exasperated, simply chastises Ralph mildly—takes him to Mr. Fred's Feline Finishing School, where he is hypnotized into good behavior; however, Sarah misses the old, mischievous Ralph, and successfully lures him back into his natural state. In all of the books in the series, Sarah always gives Ralph her unconditional love, no matter how many stunts he pulls.

Critics have noted that Ralph, with his tricks, ploys, and demands for attention, is very much like a child, and that children are attracted to his gleeful overindulgence. In addition, reviewers have acknowledged that Ralph is popular with children because he ultimately gets away with his crimes and is still accepted by Sarah. In their *Wilson Library Bulletin* review of *Rotten Ralph's Rotten Christmas,* Donnarae MacCann and Olga Richard stated, "Rotten Ralph may be satirizing the arrested develop-

ment of the spoiled child, but the character of Sarah serves as a wry comment upon overindulgent parents." Writing in the *Horn Book* about *Rotten Ralph's Rotten Romance,* Elizabeth S. Watson said, "It's no wonder kids love Ralph—what a perfect vicarious way to get back at all those well–meaning adults who make you go to parties where everyone else seems to be having a great time." Assessing the same title in *Booklist*, Stephanie Zvirin commented that this work, like all of the books in the series, "allows children the vicarious thrill of being unabashedly naughty. But at the same time it provides assurance that even in the face of bad behavior they'll still be loved—something worth talking about."

Not all observers, though, are fond of Rotten Ralph. For example, a reviewer in *Children's Book Review*

What are the torments and triumphs of a twelve-year-old?

Jack Henry has been on the go for most of his twelve years, and his efforts to fit in at yet another new school are recorded diary–style in Gantos's semi–autobiographical 1994 book.

Service called *Worse than Rotten, Ralph* a "do–it–y-ourself guide to mayhem which can be summed up in a few phrases—ridiculous, garish, and makes no sense," while *School Library Journal* critic Mary B. Nickerson added, "The unrelieved, gratuitous may-hem is, depending on one's age, either boring or threatening." However, most reviewers find Ralph's adventures both amusing and appealing and extol Gantos's slyly written texts and Rubel's psychedelic line drawings. In his review of *Back to School for Rot-ten Ralph* in *Booklist*, Michael Cart called Ralph "a cat so rambunctiously rotten that you've just gotta love him," while a reviewer for *Horn Book* added, "Gantos's skillful examination of the child's world is once again evident as the author probes a com-mon negative emotion and suggests, but never preaches, a positive outcome."

In addition to their works about Rotten Ralph, Gan-tos and Rubel have collaborated on several other picture books, including *Sleepy Ronald, Aunt Bernice, Greedy Greeny,* and *The Werewolf Family.* While writ-ing his picture books in collaboration with Rubel, Gantos began working part–time at Emerson Col-lege as a writing instructor. After receiving his mas-ter's degree in creative writing from Emerson, Gan-tos became an associate professor of creative writing and literature there. He married art dealer Anne A. Lower in 1989; the couple have a daughter, Mabel Grace. In 1993, Gantos became graduate coordina-tor for the M.A. degree in creative and professional writing at Emerson and also built the M.A./M.F.A. degree concentration in children's book writing and literature.

Autobiographical Novels

In 1994, Gantos produced the first of his "Jack Henry" books, *Heads or Tails: Stories from the Sixth Grade.* In this collection of autobiographical and semi–autobiographical vignettes, Jack, who has lived in nine houses and has gone to five schools because of his dad's desire to find a better job by moving from place to place, is living in southern Florida. The text, which is written in diary form, is accompanied by samples of Jack's handwriting and photocopied items such as a mouse skin and a squashed bug. Jack gets into situations with family, friends, and neighbors and at school. He fights with his know–it–all sister, attends the funeral of his ma-ternal grandfather, sees his dog eaten by an alliga-tor, and generally tries to do the right thing but lands in trouble. However, Jack bounces back, and in the process performs what Michael Cart called in *School Library Journal* "acts of unself–conscious kindness." Cart continued, "Jack's a survivor, an 'everyboy' whose world may be wacko but whose

What happens when you flunk an IQ test?

Likeable narrator Jack Henry returns as the focus of Gantos' award–winning 1997 novel, this time to begin a fiction–writing career that romanticizes his experiences with dead dogs, shop class, and a regrettable trip to the tattoo parlor.

heart and spirit are eminently sane and generous." In his conclusion, Cart called *Heads or Tails* a "memorable book" and Gantos a "terrific writer with a wonderfully wry sensibility, a real talent for turning artful phrases, and a gift for creating memo-rable characters." A *Publishers Weekly* reviewer com-mented that the author "makes an auspicious foray into new ground" and concluded that a "bittersweet resonance filters the humor in these stories and lin-gers most welcomely."

In the second volume of the series, *Jack's New Power: Stories from a Caribbean Year,* Jack and his family have moved from Florida to Barbados. Among his other adventures, Jack makes new friends, thinks his parents are lost at sea, gets his heart broken, sees his dad rescue a drowning couple who turn out to be English royalty, loses his birthday money to a shady friend of his father's, and searches for a lost boy who turns up dead. He also thinks that he has gained the power to make things happen and, in the process of trying to be a man, conquers his fear of horses. As in the first volume, Gantos presents readers with both laughable moments and serious thoughts. Writing in *Booklist*, Susan Dove Lempke said that "the eight stories here convey with sharp humor Jack's uncomfortable yet exhilarating early adolescence." The critic concluded that readers will "anxiously await the next installment of Jack's life." Elizabeth S. Watson added in *Horn Book* that, as in the first book in the collection, "the

first–person narrative authentically reproduces the language and observations of twelve–year–olds. Quirky and funny with some good advice subtly inserted."

In *Jack's Black Book* Jack is back in Florida after the end of his seventh–grade year. Deciding that he wants to be a serious writer, Jack buys a black book in which to write a novel. His junior high, a former detention center, is a magnet school for training in shop; consequently, the pressure is on him to do well in this subject. Jack makes a dog coffin for his class project, and then has to dig out his dead dog in order to pass seventh grade. When he tries to make a summer business by writing postcards for hire, Jack loses out when a client, a prisoner out on furlough, doesn't like his work and tosses Jack's typewriter into the ocean. Hanging out with his next–door neighbor, juvenile delinquent Gary Pagoda, Jack gets a tattoo of his dead dog on his big toe. He decides to give up his schemes to concentrate on just being himself. A critic for *Kirkus Reviews* noted that Gantos "trots out one disgusting and dangerous event after another to give his morose protagonist material for jokes." The critic added, "With a mean–spirited reliance on shock and cheap laughs, the book gets some tacked–on introspection at the end." Writing in *Horn Book*, a reviewer noted, "There's enough descriptive disaster, some good solid writing, and a bizarre plot that even reluctant adults can't help but appreciate."

Gantos is also the author of *Jack on the Tracks: Four Seasons of Fifth Grade*, a prequel to the other volumes in the "Jack Henry" series. In this book, Jack bonds with his father when he eats a seventy–two ounce steak, accidentally kills his cat, writes a gross story that appalls his teacher, is locked out of the house naked for putting a live roach in his sister's mouth, and hides from what he thinks are two escaped convicts (actually two of his friends) by lying in a shallow hole along the railroad tracks as a train passes overhead. Jack also wonders why he cries all the time, tries to exercise more self–control, and resolves to do the adult thing rather than the childish one. Writing in *Booklist*, Susan Dove Lempke stated, "[Gantos's] books about Jack Henry ... succeed precisely because they present a hilarious, exquisitely painful, and utterly on–target depiction of the life of an adolescent and preadolescent boy."

Gantos became a full professor at Emerson College in 1995. The next year he went to Vermont College, where he became a core faculty member, designed the M.F.A. program, and taught a class on writing for children before returning to Emerson, then retired from full–time teaching. He has also been a visiting professor at other universities. Gantos pro-

Addressing the problems faced by homosexual teens, Gantos published this 1997 novel which follows sixteen–year–old Walker and his efforts to gain the popularity of his fellow high school students by exposing a lesbian relationship between two of his classmates.

duced *Zip Six*, an adult novel, in 1996. In this work, a drug dealer meets an Elvis impersonator in prison, becomes his manager on the prison circuit, and is betrayed by him on the outside. In 1997 Gantos published *Desire Lines*, a young adult novel about sixteen–year–old Walker, a loner who lives in Fort Lauderdale, Florida, and spends much of his time alone on a golf course. Walker has been spying on two classmates, Karen and Jennifer, who have been making love at a duck pond on the course. When an anonymous teenage preacher comes to the school trying to enlist students for the hate group headed by his father, a minister building a church in town, the boy tries to entice Walker, who refuses to participate. The boy then tries to blackmail Walker by accusing him of being gay. In order to prove his masculinity, Walker forms an alliance with three tough classmates in a gang they call the Box. When Box members desecrate the new church and Walker is caught, the boys in the Box turn on him and pressure him to identify gays at their school. Walker outs Karen and Jennifer to save himself. When Karen confronts him at school, she asks Walker if he was the person who identified her and her lover, but he refuses to admit the truth. At the duck pond, Walker watches while Karen shoots Jennifer, then herself, in a suicide pact. Jennifer dies, but Karen survives to come back to school, where she again confronts Walker. Walker learns that the Box ratted him out. However, he still refuses to acknowledge his act to Karen. At the end of the novel, Walker is left alone with his guilt. A critic noted in *Publishers Weekly*, "Gantos projects an unsettling image of cowardice and survival of the toughest.... The author reduces the players of this drama to near–stereotypes whose 'desire lines' (chosen paths) are not all that different; in doing so he transmits a one–sided (and pessimistic) view of humanity." A critic in *Kirkus Reviews* stated that Gantos "is explicit when demonstrating how a climate of fear and suspicion can be concocted in a community, and how insecure young people—gay, straight—can be tormented by it."

In 1998 Gantos published what would become one of his most critically acclaimed works: *Joey Pigza Swallowed the Key*. In this book, which is directed at middle graders, Joey, a boy in the early primary grades, has attention deficit disorder (ADD) and hyperactivity. He inadvertently does things like swallowing his house key, cutting off his fingernail in a pencil sharpener, and slicing off the tip of his classmate's nose while running with a pair of scissors. Sent to a special education center for six weeks, he is given regulated medication and learns how to manage his behavior. Joey feels strong and hopeful when his treatment is completed. At the end of the story, he returns to his old school, where he is allowed to sit and read in the Big Quiet Chair.

Throughout the book, which is narrated by Joey with flashes of humor, readers learn that he has been emotionally abused by his grandmother, who, like Joey, is hyperactive. *Horn Book* critic Jennifer M. Brabandee noted that Joey's "own brand of goodness has an unaffected charm and an uncloying sweetness. Joey is always explaining to people that he's a good kid; readers of this compelling tragicomedy will know almost from the start that Joey's not just a good kid—he's a great kid." Susan Dove Lempke added in *Booklist*, "Most teachers and students know at least one child with attention deficit hyperactivity disorder (ADHD), and this book will surely help them become more understanding, even as they enjoy Gantos's fresh writing style and tart sense of humor." Writing in *School Library Journal*, Shawn Brommer commented, "from the powerful opening lines and fast–moving plot to the thoughtful inner dialogue and satisfying conclusions, readers will cheer for Joey, and for the champion in each of us."

Gantos chronicled more of Joey's adventures in *Joey Pigza Loses Control*, which was named a Newbery Honor Book in 2001. In this novel, Joey is sent to spend the summer with his father, an alcoholic struggling with recovery. At first Joey and his dad share some good times, until his father decides that Joey is too reliant on his medication and flushes the drugs down the toilet. Although he wants to please his father, Joey slowly loses control as the positive effects of the medication fade. At the same time, his dad's behavior begins to deteriorate, and he grows increasingly dependent on alcohol. A *Publishers Weekly* reviewer noted that this book, "like its predecessor . . . mixes humor, pain, fear, and courage with deceptive ease." *School Library Journal* contributor LaTronica Starr remarked that for Gantos's hero, "the ride home isn't smooth, but it is hopeful and loving." Writing in *Booklist*, Lempke found that the author's "skillful pacing, sly humor, and in–depth characterization make [*Joey Pigza Loses Control*] a truly memorable read."

If you enjoy the works of Jack Gantos, you might want to check out the following books:

C. S. Adler, *Kiss the Clown*, 1986.
Sherry Bunin, *Dear Great American Writers School*, 1995.
Jan Alford, *I Can't Believe I Have to Do This*, 1997.
Francesca Lia Block, *Baby Be–Bop*, 1995.

A frequent speaker at schools, libraries, conferences, and festivals, Gantos has also been the facilitator of writing workshops on children's literature for students and teachers. Regarding his literary career, Gantos once said, "I write for children because they are sincere and authentic in their reactions. I write for adults because I am an adult and I need to write about subjects, dreams, and characters outside the limited scope of the children's genre. I enjoy my work as much as possible. I read good books and I want to write good books." Gantos once recalled that he was passing by the window of a book store where copies of Rotten Ralph were on display: "Several children were chanting 'Rotten Ralph ... Rotten Ralph ... Rotten Ralph ...' over and over. For a writer to receive such sincere attention is rare. They are a good audience and deserve good books."

■ Biographical and Critical Sources

BOOKS

Children's Literature Review, Volume 18, Gale, 1989, pp. 140–43.
Fifth Book of Junior Authors and Illustrators, edited by Sally Holmes Holtze, H.W. Wilson, 1983, pp. 123–24.

PERIODICALS

ALAN Review, winter, 2001, Gail P. Gregg, "Jack Gantos: On Domestic Craziness and Big–Hearted Kids," pp. 25–28.
Booklist, October 1, 1976, Betsy Hearne, review of *Sleepy Ronald,* p. 251; October 15, 1979, Denise M. Wilms, review of *Greedy Greeny,* p. 351; December 1, 1995, Susan Dove Lempke, review of *Jack's New Power,* p. 616; November 15, 1996, Stephanie Zvirin, review of *Rotten Ralph's Rotten Romance,* p. 593; August, 1998, Michael Cart, review of *Back to School for Rotten Ralph,* p. 201; December 15, 1998, S. D. Lempke, review of *Joey Pigza Swallowed the Key,* p. 752; June 1, 1999, Ilene Cooper, review of *Wedding Bells for Rotten Ralph;* September 1, 1999, S. D. Lempke, review of *Jack on the Tracks,* p. 132; September 1, 2001, S. D. Lempke, review of *Joey Pigza Loses Control,* p. 114.
Bulletin of the Center for Children's Books, July, 1976, Zena Sutherland, review of *Rotten Ralph,* p. 174.
Children's Book Review Service, November, 1978, review of *Worse than Rotten, Ralph,* p. 22; December, 1980, review of *The Werewolf Family,* p. 24.
Emergency Librarian, November 1, 1997.

Horn Book Magazine, November–December, 1984, Ann A. Flowers, review of *Rotten Ralph's Rotten Christmas,* p. 740; March–April, 1996, Elizabeth S. Watson, review of *Jack's New Power,* p. 231; November–December, 1996, E. S. Watson, review of *Rotten Ralph's Rotten Romance,* p. 723; January, 1998, review of *Jack's Black Book,* p. 70; September, 1998, review of *Back to School for Rotten Ralph,* p. 598; November–December, 1998, Jennifer M. Brabandee, review of *Joey Pigza Swallowed the Key,* pp. 729–30; September, 2000, review of *Joey Pigza Loses Control,* p. 567.
Kirkus Reviews, August 15, 1976, review of *Sleepy Ronald,* p. 903; February 15, 1978, review of *Aunt Bernice,* pp. 173–74; February 1, 1980, review of *Greedy Greeny,* pp. 120–21; October 1, 1980, review of *The Werewolf Family,* p. 1293; February 15, 1997, review of *Desire Lines;* August 1, 1997, review of *Jack's Black Book,* p. 1221.
Language Arts, May, 1977, Ruth M. Stein, review of *Rotten Ralph,* p. 582.
New York Times Book Review, November 19, 2000, Linnea Lannon, "Wired," p. 20.
Publishers Weekly, February 6, 1978, review of *Aunt Bernice,* p. 101; August 22, 1988, review of *Rotten Ralph's Trick or Treat,* p. 95; June 6, 1994, review of *Heads or Tails,* p. 66; February 24, 1997, review of *Desire Lines,* p. 92; August 14, 2000, review of *Joey Pigza Loses Control,* p. 356; November 6, 2000, "Best Children's Books 2000," p. 43.
School Library Journal, October, 1976, Allene Stuart Phy, review of *Sleepy Ronald,* p. 97; October, 1978, Mary B. Nickerson, review of *Worse than Rotten, Ralph,* p. 132; October, 1980, Patricia Homer, review of *The Werewolf Family,* p. 134; October, 1986, John Peters, review of *Rotten Ralph's Trick or Treat,* p. 160; June, 1994, Michael Cart, review of *Heads or Tails,* p. 128; November, 1995, p. 119; December, 1998, Shawn Brommer, review of *Joey Pigza Swallowed the Key,* p. 124; September, 2000, LaTronica Starr, review of *Joey Pigza Loses Control,* p. 228; February, 2001, Barbara Wysocki, review of *Joey Pigza Loses Control,* p. 68; April, 2001, Jack Gantos, "Smart, Sensitive, and out of Control," pp. 63–64.
Teaching Pre–K—8, March, 1996.
Washington Post Book World, June 13, 1976, Brigitte Weeks, review of *Rotten Ralph,* p. 112.
Wilson Library Bulletin, February, 1985, Donnarae MacCann and Olga Richard, review of *Rotten Ralph's Rotten Christmas,* p. 404.

ONLINE

"Amazon.com Talks to Jack Gantos," http://www.amazon.com/ (April 28, 2000).

—*Sketch by Gerard J. Senick*

Edward Gorey

■ Personal

Born February 22, 1925, in Chicago, IL; died April 15, 2000, in Cape Cod, MA; son of Edward Leo (a newspaperman) and Helen (maiden name, Garvey) Gorey. *Education:* Harvard University, A.B., 1950; attended Art Institute of Chicago. *Hobbies and other interests:* Cats, movies, opera, concerts, country cooking, ballet, book collecting.

■ Career

Writer, illustrator, and designer. Employed in art department of Doubleday & Co., Inc., New York City, 1953–60. Gorey's illustrations have been shown in museums and galleries, including Graham Gallery, New York City, and Yale University Library, both 1974. *Military service:* U.S. Army, 1943–46.

■ Awards, Honors

Best Illustrated Book of the Year award, *New York Times,* 1966, for *The Monster Dens,* 1969, for illustrations of Edward Lear's *The Dong with the Luminous Nose,* and 1971, for illustrations of Florence Parry Heide's *The Shrinking of Treehorn; The Shrinking of Treehorn* was included in the Graphic Arts Fifty Books Exhibit and Children's Books Show and earned an ALA Notable Book citation, both 1971, and was named best picture book at Bologna Children's Book Fair, 1977; Children's Book Showcase selection, 1972, for *Lions and Lobsters and Foxes and Frogs, The Shrinking of Treehorn, Sam and Emma,* and *Red Riding Hoods;* Antoinette Perry ("Tony") Award, 1978, for costume design of the Broadway revival "Dracula"; Parents Choice Award for Illustration, 1982, for *The Dwindling Party.*

■ Writings

SELF—ILLUSTRATED

The Unstrung Harp; or, Mr. Earbrass Writes a Novel (also see below), Duell, Sloan & Pearce/Little, Brown, 1953.

The Listing Attic (also see below), Duell, Sloan & Pearce/Little, Brown, 1954.

The Doubtful Guest (also see below), Doubleday, 1957, reprinted, Dodd, 1978.

The Object Lesson (also see below), Doubleday, 1958.

(Compiler) *The Haunted Looking Glass: Ghost Stories,* Looking Glass Library, 1959, reprinted as *Edward Gorey's Haunted Looking Glass: Ghost Stories,* Crown, 1984.

The Bug Book (also see below), Epstein & Carroll, 1960, reprinted, Adama Books, 1987.

The Fatal Lozenge (also see below), Obolensky, 1960; published in England as *The Gorey Alphabet*, Constable, 1960.

The Hapless Child (also see below), Obolensky, 1961, reprinted, Dodd, 1980.

(Under pseudonym Ogdred Weary) *The Curious Sofa* (also see below), Obolensky, 1961, reprinted, Dodd, 1980 Harcourt, 1997.

(Under pseudonym Ogdred Weary) *The Beastly Baby*, Fantod Press, 1962.

The Willowdale Handcar; or, The Return of the Black Doll (also see below), Bobbs–Merrill, 1962, reprinted, Dodd, 1979.

The Gashlycrumb Tinies (also see below), Simon & Schuster, 1962, reprinted, Beaufort Books (New York City), 1986.

The Vinegar Works (includes *The Gashlycrumb Tinies*, *The Insect God*, and *The West Wing*; also see below), Simon & Schuster, 1963.

The Wuggly Ump (also see below), Lippincott, 1963, reprinted, Adama Books, 1986.

15 Two: or, The Nursery Frieze, Fantod Press, 1964.

The Sinking Spell (also see below), Obolensky, 1964.

The Remembered Visit: A Story Taken from Life (also see below), Simon & Schuster, 1965.

The Inanimate Tragedy, Fantod Press, 1966.

The Gilded Bat, Simon & Schuster, 1966.

(Under pseudonym Eduard Blutig) *The Evil Garden*, Fantod Press, 1966.

(Under pseudonym Mrs. Regera Dowdy) *The Pious Infant*, Fantod Press, 1966.

The Utter Zoo Alphabet, Dutton, 1967.

(With Victoria Chess) *Fletcher and Zenobia*, Meredith Corp., 1967.

The Other Statue, Simon & Schuster, 1968.

The Blue Aspic, Meredith Corp., 1968.

The Epiplectic Bicycle, Dodd, 1968.

The Secrets, Simon & Schuster, 1968.

The Deranged Cousins: or, Whatever, Fantod Press, 1969.

The Iron Tonic: or, A Winter Afternoon in Lonely Valley, Albondonaci Press, 1969, Harcourt, 2000.

(Under pseudonym Raddory Gewe) *The Eleventh Episode*, Fantod Press, 1969.

(With Peter F. Neumeyer) *Donald and the . . .*, Young Scott Books, 1969, reprinted, Borgo, 1988.

(With Neumeyer) *Donald Has a Difficulty*, Fantod Press, 1970.

(With Neumeyer) *Why We Have Day and Night*, Young Scott Books, 1970, reprinted, Borgo, 1989.

The Osbick Bird, Fantod Press, 1970.

The Chinese Obelisks: Fourth Alphabet, Fantod Press, 1970.

The Sopping Thursday, Gotham Book Mart, 1970, reprinted, Borgo Press, 1988.

(With Chess) *Fletcher and Zenobia Save the Circus*, Dodd, 1971.

The Disrespectful Summons, Fantod Press, 1971.

(Translator) Alphonse Allais, *Story for Sara: What Happened to a Little Girl*, Albondocani Press, 1971.

(Under pseudonym Edward Pig) *The Untitled Book*, Fantod Press, 1971.

The Awdrey–Gore Legacy, Dodd, 1972, reprinted, Beaufort Books (New York City), 1988.

Leaves from a Mislaid Album, Gotham Book Mart, 1972.

The Abandoned Sock, Fantod Press, 1972.

Amphigorey (includes *The Unstrung Harp, The Listing Attic, The Doubtful Guest, The Object–Lesson, The Bug Book, The Fatal Lozenge, The Hapless Child, The Curious Sofa, The Willowdale Handcar, The Gashlycrumb Tinies, The Insect God, The West Wing, The Wuggly Ump, The Sinking Spell,* and *The Remembered Visit*), Putnam, 1972.

The Lavender Leotard: or, Going a Lot to the New York City Ballet, Gotham Book Mart, 1973.

A Limerick, Salt–Works Press, 1973.

Category: Fifty Drawings, Gotham Book Mart, 1973, reprinted as *Cat E Gory*, Adama Books, 1986.

The Lost Lions, Fantod Press, 1973.

The Glorious Nosebleed: Fifth Alphabet, Dodd, 1974.

The Listing Attic [and] *The Unstrung Harp*, Abelard Schumann, 1975.

Amphigorey Too (anthology), Putnam, 1975.

L'Heure bleue, Fantod Press, 1975.

The Broken Spoke, Dodd, 1976.

Gorey x 3: Drawings by Edward Gorey, Addison–Wesley, 1976.

The Loathsome Couple, Dodd, 1977.

The Fantod Words, ten volumes, Diogenes, 1978.

Gorey Endings: A Calendar for 1978, Workman, 1978.

The Green Beads, Albondocani Press, 1978.

(With Larry Evans) *Gorey Games*, Troubadour Printing, 1979.

Dracula: A Toy Theatre, Scribner, 1979.

Gorey Posters, Abrams, 1979.

Dancing Cats and Neglected Murderesses, Workman, 1980.

Le Melange Funeste, Gotham Book Mart, 1981.

The Dwindling Party, Random House, 1982.

The Water Flowers, Congdon & Weed, 1982.

Gorey Cats: Paper Dolls, Troubadour Press, 1982.

(With Howard Moss) *Instant Lives*, Avon, 1982.

The Prune People, Albondocani Press, 1983.

(Under pseudonym E. D. Ward) *A Mercurial Bear*, Gotham Book Mart, 1983.

The Eclectic Abecedarium, Bromer, 1983.

Amphigorey Also (anthology), Congdon & Weed, 1983.

The Tunnel Calamity, Putnam, 1984.

Les Echanges Malandreux, Metacom, 1985.

The Insect God, Beaufort Books, 1986.

The Raging Tide: or, The Black Doll's Imbroglio, Beaufort Books (New York City), 1987.

The Fraught Settee, Fantod Press, 1990.

Figbash Acrobate, Fantod Press, 1994.

The Retrieved Locket, Fantod Press, 1994.

The Fantod Pack, Gotham Book Mart, 1995.

The Unknown Vegetable, Fantod Press, 1995.

The Haunted Tea Cosy: A Dispirited and Distasteful Diversion for Christmas, Harcourt, 1998.

The Headless Bust: A Melancholy Meditation on the False Millennium, Harcourt, 1999.

ILLUSTRATOR OF WORKS BY JOHN BELLAIRS

The Mansion in the Mist, frontispiece by Gorey, Dial Books for Young Readers, 1992.

The House with a Clock in Its Walls, Puffin Books, 1993.

The Ghost in the Mirror, completed by Brad Strickland, frontispiece by Gorey, Dial Books for Young Readers, 1993.

The Vengeance of the Witch–finder, completed by Strickland, frontispiece by Gorey, Dial Books for Young Readers, 1993.

ILLUSTRATOR OF OTHER WORKS

Joan Aiken, *The Wolves of Willoughby Chase,* frontispiece by Gorey, Yearling Books, 1987.

John Ciardi, *You Know Who,* Wordsong (Honesdale, PA), 1991.

John Ciardi, *The Monster Den, or, Look What Happened at My House and to It,* Wordsong (Honesdale, PA), 1991.

Ennis Rees, *More of Brer Rabbit's Tricks,* Hopscotch Books, 1989.

Ennis Rees, *Brer Rabbit and His Tricks,* Hyperion Paperbacks for Children, 1994.

Beatrice Schenk de Regniers, *Red Riding Hood,* retold in verse, Aladdin Books, 1990.

Brad Strickland, *The Bell, the Book, and the Spellbinder,* frontispiece by Gorey, Dial Books for Young Readers, 1997.

Also illustrator of over fifty books, including Edward Lear's *The Jumblies* and *The Dong with the Luminous Nose,* Young Scott Books, 1968–69, Florence Parry Heide's *The Shrinking of Treehorn,* Holiday House, 1971, and T. S. Eliot's *Old Possum's Book of Practical Cats,* Harcourt, 1982; also illustrator of title

sequence animation for PBS's *Mystery* television series, and of numerous book jackets, posters, and magazines. Designer of sets for productions of *Les Ballets Trockadero de Monte Carlo,* 1977, and of sets and costumes for the musical *Dracula,* and adaptation *Gorey's Stories,* both 1978. Contributor of cartoons to periodicals, including *New York Times, Sports Illustrated,* and *Esquire.*

OTHER

The Black Doll (filmscript), Gotham Book Mart, 1973.

Gorey's Stories (musical revue), produced in New York, 1978.

More Gorey Stories (musical revue), produced at Barnstable, MA, 1981.

Lost Shoelaces (musical revue), produced at Woods Hole, MA, 1985.

Tinned Lettuce, or The New Musical (musical revue), music by David Aldrich, first produced in New York by New York University's Tisch School of the Arts, April, 1985.

Useful Urns (musical revue), produced at Provincetown, MA, 1990.

Stuffed Elephants (musical revue), produced at Woods Hole, MA, 1990.

Flapping Ankles (musical revue), produced at Provincetown, MA, 1991.

The Betrayed Confidence: Seven Series of Dogear Wryde Postcards, Parnassus Imprints, 1992.

Amphigorey: The Musical, music by Peter Golub, produced at American Music Theater Festival, Philadelphia, PA, 1992.

The Gorey Details (musical revue), music by Peter Matz, produced at Century Center for the Performing Arts, New York, 2000.

Author of the plays *Blithering Christmas* and *Chinese Gossip.* Also published works under the pseudonyms Drew Dogyear, Wardore Edgy, Roy Grewdead, Redway Grode, O. Mude, and Dreary Wodear Wryde.

■ Adaptations

The Vinegar Works, comprised of *The Gashlycrumb Tinies, The Insect God,* and *The West Wing,* was adapted for the theatre and produced in London in 1989. Many of Gorey's works have also been adapted for audiocassette.

■ Sidelights

"To look at an Edward Gorey drawing is to cross into a turn–of–the–century twilight zone," wrote Michael Dirda in a *Smithsonian* review of *The World*

Gorey's 1962 contribution to alphabetology was *The Gashlycrumb Tinies, or, After the Outing,* complete with his macabre artistry.

of Edward Gorey," a faded black–and–gray realm where bats—or possibly umbrellas—swoop above the shrubbery, buildings appear as attractive and sturdily built as the House of Usher, and everything feels autumnal, crepuscular, rain–swept and more than a little menacing." Amy Hanson, writing in *Biblio,* further delineated that strange world "which teems with unknown creatures: sinister mustachioed gentlemen and elegant women in a place out of time, the Roaring Twenties crossed with Edwardian London, and an ominous, stretching landscape awash with urns, alligators, and unfortunate children meeting even more unfortunate ends." Hanson went on to observe, "Gorey's images do not go lightly into the realms of forgotten memory. They stick, and they stick well." That sticking power comes, not a little, from Gorey's "vivid words and images," according to Hanson, "executed primarily

in black–and–white cross–hatched pen–and–ink drawings" which are "often combined with convoluted, rhyming text . . . providing post–modern fairy tales for the boomer generation."

Gorey, who died in 2000, was a prolific illustrator, writer, and set designer, with over one hundred books to his credit, mostly small in design, published by his own independent press and sometimes collected in omnibus volumes published by larger houses. His works have often, and somewhat mistakenly, been called children's books, and indeed he did publish some dozen or more titles specifically for or about kids, classic books such as *The Doubtful Guest, The Wuggly Ump, The Lavender Leotard,* and *The Dwindling Party,* as well as providing illustrations for picture books with texts by others, such as the "Treehorn" books of Florence P. Heide and the nonsense verse of Edward Lear. "But are Gorey's . . . books actually for children?" pondered a contributor for *St. James Guide to Children's Writers.* That reviewer noted that while Gorey's works fall into the general categories of children's picture books—alphabet books like *The Gashlycrumb Tinies* and animal stories such as *The Bug Book,* for example—"they are hardly the stuff of the typical toddler's . . . book." Children are not necessarily lovable and cuddly in Gorey–land, nor are they safe. But in aggregate, the books appeal to a wide age range, according to the same contributor: "Absurdist texts, sinister situations, child–eating monsters and child–throwing parents, strange–sounding words (some of the limericks are all in French)—just the sort of thing to shock, thrill, and amuse many a child." Writing a posthumous tribute to Gorey in the *New York Review of Books,* Alison Lurie noted, "In many of these books, children especially are at risk: they fall victim to natural disasters, are carried off by giant birds, or eaten by comic monsters like the Wuggly Ump. . . . Yet somehow the overall effect is not tragic but comic." Lurie dubbed Gorey–land "a kind of parallel Gothic universe, full of haunted mansions, strange topiary, and equally haunted and strange human beings." Whether child–safe or not, this landscape fascinated readers of all ages throughout the half century in which Gorey worked.

The Heir to Hoffmann and Lear

Douglas Street noted in *Dictionary of Literary Biography* that Gorey was the twentieth–century "heir apparent to the great tradition of Heinrich Hoffman and Edward Lear—two of the nineteenth century's most esteemed practitioners of nonsense literature for children." Born in Chicago in 1925, Gorey was the son of a journalist; his parents were split religiously—one Catholic and the other Episcopalian—and young Gorey was brought up Catholic. Drawing came to him at an early age and was encouraged by both his parents. "My first drawings came at the age of one–and–a–half," Gorey told Scott Baldauf in an interview for the *Christian Science Monitor,* "and I hasten to add that they showed no talent whatever. They looked rather like irregular sausages. . . . Looking back, it's all a mystery. . . . I just drifted into this." Gorey had little formal training in art, absorbing styles from the books he loved to read as a child, Victor Hugo's *Les Misérables* and Lewis Carroll's *Alice's Adventures in Wonderland* among them.

"Somewhere along the line," Gorey once told Sally Lodge in a *Publishers Weekly* interview, "I was obviously very taken with Victorian illustration, though I think it is more for the feel of it, the formal texture of those wooden engravings and what not. I seem to have wandered into it somehow. And it's the subject matter too, I'd say. I really prefer Victorian literature to modern literature on the whole. I think Victorian literature is the period I've done the most reading in. Jane Austen is one of my favorite writers." An only child, Gorey was the best show in town within the Gorey household. The author–illustrator told Lodge, "I think I might have been better off if my parents hadn't paid so much attention to me. I tend to use children in my books, not symbolically really, but it's much easier to do all this overdone pathos business with children."

Graduating from high school, Gorey served in the army from 1944 to 1946, then entered Harvard University where he graduated four years later with a degree in French. Working as an illustrator on various projects, Gorey joined the art department of Doubleday and Company publishers in 1953. There he was responsible for the typography and cover design of many of the Anchor Book series, doing covers for books by Joseph Conrad, C. P. Snow, and Henry James, among others. In 1953, Gorey also published his first illustrated tale, *The Unstrung Harp,* which already had the trenchant wit and scratchy line that would so define his work. The horrors of the literary life are depicted in this deft debut, following the misadventures of Mr. Earbrass, resident of the mythical Hobbies Odd, a fine little burgh in the vicinity of Collapsed Pudding in Mortshire. Reviewing this volume in *Atlantic,* Phoebe–Lou Adams called Gorey's illustrations "inexplicably sinister," exactly the thing that endeared them to early devotees. This initial volume "propelled [Gorey] onto the highly idiosyncratic path," according to Hanson, and was followed up in 1954 by *The Listing Attic* and then in 1957 by one of his most popular works, *The Doubtful Guest.*

Typical of all his work, *The Doubtful Guest* is hard to categorize. Usually noted as his first children's book, it attracts many adult readers as well. "A lot of my books I intended as much for children as for adults," Gorey told Lodge, "but no one would ever publish them as children's books." In *The Doubtful Guest,* his archetypal British upper–crust Edwardian household, decked out in smoking jackets and high collars or tiny–tot sailor suits, are suddenly stuck with an unusual guest: a cross between a penguin and an anteater, also clothed in Gorey signature items: a flowing scarf and high–top sneakers. This critter sticks around and sticks around, much like an unwanted child, in fact. "It came seventeen years ago—and to this day / It has shown no intention of going away," Gorey concluded his anti–child, tongue–in–cheek paean. "Gorey seems to have created both a child metaphor—for the character is quite childlike," noted Street in *Dictionary of Literary Biography,* "and a symbolic representation of himself, the young author garbed in fur coat and sneakers." This humorous look at children increased Gorey's cult status in the 1950s.

In 1953, Gorey also published *The Object Lesson,* a book that delivers "sophisticated nonsense," according to Street, and two years later he came out with *The Bug Book,* which was a bit of a departure from his usual style, done in reds, blues, and yellows instead of his usual black and white. In this parable, three groups of bugs eventually triumph over the intrusions of a newcomer, a black bug who is not part of any of the groups. They eventually drop a stone on him and squash him flat. Elizabeth Janeway, reviewing this title in the *New York Times Book Review,* called it "a brightly illustrated children's story whose moral is that violence pays." In *The Wuggly Ump,* three playmates are eaten by the strange creature of the title, while *The Hapless Child*

In addition to writing, illustrating, and designing sets and costumes for the stage, Gorey created a number of individual works of art, among which was the cover illustration for Joan Aiken's popular 1987 novel.

starts out like a simple Victorian story of a lost little girl. Charlotte Sophia runs away from her miserable boarding school after her father has disappeared in Africa and her mother has died. She is then kidnapped and forced to work in a poorly lit basement, going almost blind in the process. When the father at last returns to look for his little Charlotte, he accidentally runs her down in his car.

George R. Bodmer, writing in *Children's Literature Association Quarterly,* called this denial of a happy ending in Gorey an "explosion of expectations." Bodmer further commented, "His macabre approach and gloomy pictures . . . make it clear that while Gorey is using the appearance of children's books he is actually satirizing the genre." Bodmer noted also Gorey's use of the alphabet in what he called "anti–alphabet" books: *The Utter Zoo, The Chinese Obelisks, The Glorious Nosebleed,* and most notorious of all, *The Gashlycrumb Tinies,* which chronicles the deaths of twenty–six children, all in rhyming order: "A is for AMY who fell down the stairs / B is for BASIL assaulted by bears." "[T]his is no book for children," Bodmer declared. "Rather, it is a revenge against those who would take the alphabet book seriously, a sarcastic rebellion against a view of childhood that is sunny, idyllic, and instructive." Comparing Gorey to Dr. Seuss, Bodmer noted that they were equally prolific, though Gorey "made the decision earlier in his career to switch to a purely adult audience."

"Gorey would make W. C. Fields sound like Father of the Year," declared D. Keith Mano in *People Weekly.* "Gorey children are swallowed by huge cats or carried off by large bugs. In his work the infant mortality rate is higher than it was in 1556." But Gorey himself was not necessarily pro– or anti–kid. "I don't really feel about children much at all," Gorey once told an interviewer for *Something about the Author.* "I don't know any children as children; I never have. It's obviously more awful for something to happen to a tiny little figure than to somebody full–grown. Nothing serious should be deduced about my attitude towards children from what I put them through. But I don't tend to think of my work as being as strange as everybody else does. Every now and then somebody completely baffles me by telling me that *The Curious Sofa* is their seven–year–old child's favorite story, and I think, What? Obviously children have no idea what it's about, but that doesn't bother them. Of course it never bothered me that I never understood a great many things. A lot of my favorite stuff, I don't really know what it's about."

Originally gracing the pages of the *New Yorker* **magazine, Gorey's 1997 offering,** *The Haunted Tea–Cosy,* **lived up to its subtitle as** *A Dispirited and Distasteful Diversion for Christmas.*

For Children of All Ages

Between *The Wuggly Ump* and Gorey's next nominal children's book, *The Osbick Bird,* there were sixteen other titles and seven years. By this time, Gorey had left full–time employment at Doubleday to work on his own books. He published books under his own name as well as under many pseudonyms, several of which were anagrams of Edward Gorey: Ogdred Weary, author of *The Curious Sofa* and *The Beastly Baby;* Mrs. Regera Dowdy, author of *The Pious Infant* and translator of *The Evil Garden* by another Gorey anagram, Eduard Blutig. During the late 1960s and early 1970s, Gorey also did some of

"his most distinctive work," according to Street, illustrating the work of other authors, including Peter F. Neumeyer and the poems of Edward Lear.

Much wider prominence came to Gorey with omnibus publication of his works in 1972's *Amphigorey, Amphigorey Too* in 1975, and 1983's *Amphigorey Also.* In the first volume, fifteen of Gorey's early tales were collected, works both for adults and children. Janeway, reviewing *Amphigorey* in the *New York Times Book Review,* commented, "Gorey's messages to the reader, then, are conveyed by his style, by the content of text and not–always–consonant content of drawings, but most of all by the tension with which these elements attract and repel each other." Janeway concluded, "So this is really a retrospective exhibition. I love it. I hope you do too." Reviewing *Amphigorey, Also,* Adams noted in *Atlantic,* "Devotees of Mr. Gorey's subtle, macabre little comedies will rejoice to find seventeen of them in one big book."

Gorey also indulged one of his favorite pastimes, attending the New York City Ballet under the leadership of George Balanchine, in one of his books aimed at children, *The Lavender Leotard,* in which he traced the half–century–long attachment to ballet in two diminutive relatives. Street, writing of this book in *Dictionary of Literary Biography,* observed, "[Gorey] has given the child reader an accessible yet lighthearted introduction to a normally remote (for many youths) area of the dance." The book is somewhat autobiographical in content, as Gorey himself did not miss an evening at the ballet from 1957 until the death of Balanchine, attending performances in his fur coat and tennis shoes, like a character out of one of his own books.

"I'd been going to ballet as such since I was about twelve," Gorey told the interviewer for *Something about the Author.* "I had seen a few Balanchine ballets, but I hadn't liked them very much because I'd grown up on entirely other things. But all my friends were great devotees of the New York City Ballet, and when I first moved to New York, in the winter of 1953, I got dragged off to see the performances. I got hooked fairly quickly and I began going to every performance, since that was easier than trying to decide which nine out of ten I was going to. It really wasn't so much ballet; it was George Balanchine. I felt he was the ballet equivalent of Mozart, at least, and I couldn't get enough of him and his company. When he died, though I heard for a while afterward that they were still dancing as well as before, somehow the whole meaning began dropping out of it for me."

Gorey ventured further into the theater with the set designs for the 1977 revival of *Dracula,* for which he was awarded a Tony. Many of his own written works have been adapted for musical revues, as well, such as *Gorey Stories, Tinned Lettuce,* and *Amphigorey,* and Gorey often collaborated on stage and set designs for these productions. In 1986, Gorey left New York for the peace of Cape Cod, working in somewhat seclusion and accompanied only by his resident cats. However, his production of bizarre and absurdist picture books came to a halt for a time.

In the 1990s, Gorey once again began producing his picture books. *The Haunted Tea Cosy: A Dispirited and Distasteful Diversion for Christmas,* appeared in 1998.

In it, Gorey offered up an alternate version of Charles Dickens's *A Christmas Carol,* focusing on one Edmund Gravel, a reclusive sort who is visited by the specters of Christmas as he prepares to take tea one Christmas Eve. These specters represent in Gorey's topsy–turvy universe the ghosts of Christmas That Never Was, That Isn't, and That Never Will Be. So moved by these visitations is Gravel that he decides to throw a party for the whole town. "As always," noted Brad Hooper in a *Booklist* review, "Gorey's illustrations are the real draw." Hooper further commented, "[Gorey's] human figures and weird creatures, at once stilted and animated, amuse and titillate us." A reviewer for *Publishers Weekly* called the same title "easily the most bizarre of the holiday books" and "an antic retelling" of Dickens's classic tale. The same reviewer concluded that "it's all a grand antidote to fruitcake, inspirational uplift and Christmas cheer." "You'll find less of a moral in Gorey's short, pictorial version of the Dickens classic than in the original," wrote Scott Medintz in a *Money* magazine review, "but just as much wicked fun."

The commotion over the millennium caused Gorey to put pen to paper for his last book, 1999's *The Headless Bust: A Melancholy Meditation on the False Millennium.* Gorey reprised Edmund Gravel from *The Haunted Tea Cosy* for this tale of the millennial New Year's Day. Gravel and his companion, the six–legged Bahhumbug, are whisked away by an oversized insect to a remote provincial town where they witness several odd occurrences that may augur things to come. "The last page leaves the pair quizzically contemplating millennium's end," noted Ray Olson in a *Booklist* review. Olson also observed that it was fitting that the turn of the century be celebrated through the pen of Gorey, whose specialty was the fin de siecle of the previous century. "The Victorian world was about to shatter," noted Olson and it is exactly that feeling which "infest[s] Gorey's fey—that is doomed, daft, and forbidding as well as campy—little books." Olson concluded, "Delicious."

Indeed, "Delicious" might well sum up the reaction of fans to the entirety of Gorey's output. A reviewer for *Publishers Weekly* called him "the master of the mock–macabre," and others have also commented on this "mock–macabre" nature. "Like the famed film director Alfred Hitchcock," Baldauf wrote in the *Christian Science Monitor,* "Gorey creates tension by suggesting violence, rather than showing it. Inanimate legs jut out from underneath shrubs or out of doorways, and the only hint that something awful has happened comes in a wry footnote." Street noted that Gorey was the twentieth century's "unclassifiable, most unorthodox children's writer and illustrator." But Gorey himself had a much simpler formula for what he did, classifiable or not: "I don't set out to be funny," Gorey told Baldauf. "Obviously, if I find myself giggling about something, I'll keep it in."

If you enjoy the works of Edward Gorey, you might want to check out the following books:

Lewis Carroll, *The Hunting of the Snark: An Agony in Eight Fits*, 1876.

Edward Lear, *Nonsense Songs, Stories, Botany, and Alphabets*, 1871.

Lemony Snicket's "A Series of Unfortunate Events" series of novels, 1999—.

Gorey, who never married, died of a heart attack in Yarmouth, Massachusetts, on April 15, 2000, leaving behind "more than 100 morbidly funny books," according to a contributor for *Time International*. His intensely busy crosshatched illustrations and scratchy calligraphy are instantly recognizable worldwide and still the debate goes on whether he created children's books or merely books that looked like they were for children. "But to readers of any age," wrote *Newsweek*'s David Gates, in a remembrance of the author–illustrator, "[Gorey's] sedulously uninstructive ironies and pointedly unpunished cruelties offered only this comfort: that someone else could know the scary and the strange, and make it, literally, funny as hell."

■ Biographical and Critical Sources

BOOKS

Children's Literature Review, Volume 36, Gale, 1995.

Conversations with Writers, Volume 1, Gale, 1977.

Gorey, Edward, *The Doubtful Guest,* Doubleday, 1957.

Gorey, Edward, *The Gashlycrumb Tinies,* Simon & Schuster, 1962.

Gorey, Edward, *The Betrayed Confidence: Seven Series of Dogear Wryde Postcards,* Parnassus Imprints, 1992.

Ross, Clifford, and Karen Wilkin, *The World of Edward Gorey,* Harry N. Abrams, 1996.

St. James Guide to Children's Writers, 5th edition, edited by Sara Pendergast and Tom Pendergast, St. James Press, 1999.

Street, Douglas, "Edward Gorey," *Dictionary of Literary Biography,* Volume 61: *American Writers for Children since 1960: Poets, Illustrators, and Nonfiction Authors,* Gale 1987, pp. 99–107.

Toledano, Henry, *Goreyography: A Diverse Compendium of and Price Guide to the Works of Edward Gorey,* contributions by Jim Weiland and Malcolm Whyte, Word Play Publishers, 1996.

PERIODICALS

Atlantic, January, 1983, Phoebe–Lou Adams, review of *Amphigorey Also,* p. 103; November, 1983, p. 149; June, 1999, P. Adams, review of *The Unstrung Harp,* p. 137; November, 1999, p. 125.

Biblio, January, 1998, Amy Hanson, "Edward Gorey's Fiendish Fables and Bizarre Allegories," p. 16.

Booklist, October 1, 1998, Brad Hooper, review of *The Haunted Tea Cosy,* p. 276; September 1, 1999, Ray Olson, review of *The Headless Bust,* p. 4.

Children's Literature Association Quarterly, fall, 1989, George R. Bodmer, "The Post–Modern Alphabet," pp. 114–117.

Christian Science Monitor, April 21, 1994, p. 10; October 31, 1996, Scott Baldauf, "Edward Gorey: Portrait of the Artist in Chilling Color," p. 10.

Commentary, January, 1973.

Commonweal, August 14, 1992, p. 28.

Dance Magazine, July, 2000, pp. 12–14.

Detroit Free Press, October 29, 1982.

Detroit News, November 15, 1983.

Esquire, June, 1974.

Guardian, December 18, 1995, p. T9.

Horizon, November, 1977.

Money, December, 1998, Scott Medintz, review of *The Haunted Tea Cosy,* p. 171.

New Republic, November 26, 1966.

Newsweek, August 26, 1963; October 30, 1972; October 31, 1977; May 1, 2000, David Gates, "E Is for Edward, Whose Works Were So Strange," p. 72.

New Yorker, December 26, 1959.

New York Review of Books, May 25, 2000, Alison Lurie, "On Edward Gorey (1925–2000)," p. 20.

New York Times, May 1, 1985; April 22, 1994, p. B1; October 16, 2000, p. B1.

New York Times Book Review, October 29, 1972, Elizabeth Janeway, review of *Amphigorey,* pp. 6–7, 30; November 6, 1983; September 1, 1996, p. 17.

People Weekly, July 3, 1978, D. Keith Mano, "Edward Gorey Inhabits an Odd World of Tiny Drawings, Fussy Cats, and 'Doomed Enterprises'," pp. 10–72, 74.

Publishers Weekly, November 26, 1982, Sally Lodge, "An Interview with Edward Gorey," pp. 6–7; September 14, 1998, review of *The Haunted Tea Cosy,* p. 50; September 6, 1999, "October Publications," p. 84; October 9, 2000, p. 76.

Saturday Review, January 6, 1979.

Smithsonian, June, 1997, Michael Dirda, review of *The World of Edward Gorey,* p. 150.

Time International, May 1, 2000, "Milestones," p. 13.

Variety, October 23, 2000, p. 59.

Washington Post, October 8, 1991, p. C1.

■ Obituaries

PERIODICALS

Horn Book, September–October, 2000, p. 541.
Los Angeles Times, April 18, 2000, p. A9.
New York Times, April 16, 2000, p. 52.
Times (London), April 18, 2000, p. 25.
U.S. News and World Reports, May 1, 2000, p. 14.
Washington Post, April 17, 2000, p. B6.*

—Sketch by J. Sydney Jones

Tony Hillerman

■ Personal

Born May 27, 1925; son of August Alfred (a farmer) and Lucy (maiden name, Grove) Hillerman; married Marie Unzner, August 16, 1948; children: Anne, Janet, Anthony, Monica, Stephen, Daniel. Education: Attended Oklahoma State University, 1943; University of Oklahoma, B.A., 1946; University of New Mexico, M.A., 1966. *Politics:* Democrat. *Religion:* Roman Catholic. *Hobbies and other interests:* Trout fishing.

■ Career

Borger News Herald, Borger, TX, reporter, 1948; *Morning Press–Constitution,* Lawton, OK, city editor, 1948–50; United Press International, Oklahoma City, OK, political reporter, 1950–52, Santa Fe, NM, bureau manager, 1952–54; *New Mexican,* Santa Fe, NM, political reporter and executive editor, 1954–63; University of New Mexico, Albuquerque, associate professor, 1965–66, professor, 1966–85, professor emeritus of journalism, 1985—, chairman of department, 1966–73, assistant to the president, 1975–80; writer. *Military service:* U.S. Army, 1943–45; received Silver Star, Bronze Star, and Purple Heart.

■ Member

International Crime Writers Association, Mystery Writers of America (president, 1988), Albuquerque Press Club, Sigma Delta Chi, Phi Kappa Phi.

■ Awards, Honors

Edgar Allan Poe Award, Mystery Writers of America, 1974, for *Dance Hall of the Dead;* Golden Spur award, Western Writers of America, 1987; Special Friend of Dineh award, Navajo Tribal Council, 1987; National Media Award, American Anthropological Association, 1990; Public Services Award, Department of the Interior, 1990; Arrell Gibson Lifetime Award, Oklahoma Center for the Book, 1991; Grandmaster Award, Mystery Writers of America, 1991; Ambassador award, Center for the Indian, 1992; Grand Prix de Littérature Policière; inducted into the Oklahoma Hall of Fame, 1997; D.Litt., University of New Mexico, 1990, and Arizona State University, 1991.

■ Writings

MYSTERY NOVELS

The Blessing Way, Harper (New York City), 1970.
The Fly on the Wall, Harper (New York City), 1971.

Dance Hall of the Dead, Harper (New York City), 1973.

Listening Woman, Harper (New York City), 1978.

People of Darkness, Harper (New York City), 1980.

The Dark Wind, Harper (New York City), 1982.

The Ghostway, Harper (New York City), 1984.

Skinwalkers, Harper (New York City), 1986.

A Thief of Time, Harper (New York City), 1988.

Talking God, Harper (New York City), 1989.

Coyote Waits, Harper (New York City), 1990.

Sacred Clowns, HarperCollins (New York City), 1993.

The Fallen Man, HarperCollins (New York City), 1996.

The First Eagle, HarperCollins (New York City), 1998.

Hunting Badger, HarperCollins (New York City), 1999.

COLLECTIONS

The Joe Leaphorn Mysteries, Harper (New York City), 1989.

The Jim Chee Mysteries, Harper (New York City), 1992.

Leaphorn and Chee: Three Classic Mysteries Featuring Lt. Joe Leaphorn and Officer Jim Chee, Harper (New York City), 1992.

OTHER

The Boy Who Made Dragonfly: A Zuni Myth (juvenile), Harper (New York City), 1972.

The Great Taos Bank Robbery and Other Indian Country Affairs, University of New Mexico Press (Albuquerque), 1980.

(Editor) *The Spell of New Mexico,* University of New Mexico Press (Albuquerque), 1984.

Indian Country: America's Sacred Land, illustrated with photographs by Bela Kalman, Northland Press (Flagstaff, AZ), 1987.

(Author of foreword) Erna Fergusson, *Dancing Gods: Indian Ceremonials of New Mexico and Arizona,* University of New Mexico Press (Albuquerque), 1988.

Hillerman Country: A Journey through the Southwest with Tony Hillerman, illustrated with photographs by Barney Hillerman, HarperCollins (New York City), 1991.

(With Ernie Bulow) *Talking Mysteries: A Conversation with Tony Hillerman,* University of New Mexico Press (Albuquerque), 1991.

(Editor) *Best of the West: An Anthology of Classic Writing from the American West,* HarperCollins (New York City), 1991.

(Author of foreword) Bulow, *Navajo Taboos,* Buffalo Medicine Books, 1991.

(Author of introduction) Howard Beyan, editor, *Robbers, Rogues, and Ruffians: True Tales of the Wild West,* Clear Light (New York City), 1991.

New Mexico, Rio Grande, and Other Essays, illustrated with photographs by David Muench and Robert Reynolds, Graphic Arts Center, 1992.

(Editor) *The Mysterious West,* HarperCollins (New York City), 1994.

Finding Moon, HarperCollins (New York City), 1995.

(Editor with Rosemary Herbert) *The Oxford Book of American Detective Stories,* Oxford University Press (New York City), 1996.

(Editor) *The Best American Mystery Stories of the Century,* Houghton (Boston, MA), 2000.

Also contributor to periodicals, including *New Mexico Quarterly, National Geographic,* and *Reader's Digest.*

■ **Adaptations**

Many of Hillerman's mysteries have been recorded on audiocassette.

■ **Sidelights**

Tony Hillerman "created the American Indian policier," according to critic Herbert Mitgang in the *New York Times.* Hillerman also "breaks out of the detective genre," as Daniel K. Muhlestein noted in the *Dictionary of Literary Biography.* "He is a writer of police procedurals who is less concerned with the identity of his villains than with their motivation." Muhlestein further commented, "Most mystery writers begin with plot. Hillerman begins with setting." Setting, for Hillerman, is nine times out of ten the sprawling, arid, high plateau of the Southwest: the Four Corners region of Arizona, Utah, Colorado, and New Mexico that comprises Navajo country. Into this vast empty space, Hillerman sets his two protagonists, Jim Chee and Joe Leaphorn, detectives with the Navajo Tribal Police who solve crimes using the most modern police methods as well as the most traditional of Navajo beliefs: a sense of *hozro,* or harmony. Hillerman has written a dozen–plus Leaphorn–Chee mysteries, books that have garnered him awards ranging from the Mystery Writers of America to the Navajo Tribal Council's commendation to France's esteemed Grand Prix de Littérature Policière.

Hillerman's interest in the U.S. Southwest is evident in both his popular mystery series and nonfiction works which explore the natural wonders of the region. A student of southwestern history and culture, Hillerman often draws his themes from the conflict between modern society and traditional Native American values and customs. The complex nature of this struggle is perhaps most evident in the author's works featuring Leaphorn and Chee, whose contrasting views about heritage and crime–fighting form an interesting backdrop to their criminal investigations. The intricate nature of Hillerman's plots, combined with detailed descriptions of people, places, and exotic rituals, has helped make his novels—from the first in the series, 1970's *The Blessing Way*, to the 1999 *Hunting Badger*—popular with readers and critics alike. Hillerman's novels, are, as so many critics have observed, much more than mere police procedurals. His use of character and setting have pushed them beyond the bounds of the detective genre, a fact supported by their large sales.

"When I met the Navajos I now so often write about, I recognized kindred spirits. Country boys. More of us. Folks among whom I felt at ease."

—Tony Hillerman

A Country Boy

Hillerman is no stranger to the world he portrays in his novels and nonfiction. Born on May 27, 1925, the youngest of three children of August Alfred and Lucy Grove Hillerman, Hillerman grew up in rural Oklahoma. His parents farmed and ran a local store. He loved reading and books as a youth, and in those days before television and without even enough money for batteries for the radio, Hillerman also formed an early love for oral storytelling. He would listen to the men who gathered at his parents' store to tell stories and tall tales, and learned pacing, timing, and the importance of detail. Hillerman's youth was spent, as Muhlestein noted, "poor in money but rich in the tools of a future writer."

Hillerman also learned, according to Muhlestein, "what it meant to be an outsider," attending a boarding school for Potawatomie Indian girls. Doubly removed because of both race and gender, Hillerman internalized this feeling of being an outsider, but also formed a deep and abiding respect for Indian ways and culture. It was a lesson that he would

carry with him into adulthood. As important as that message was, he learned another, about class differences in the United States. As a youngster, he always looked at himself as a country boy, not a city boy, one who got his haircuts at home, not at a barber shop. If the world were divided into urban and rural, he would opt for the latter.

After graduating from high school, Hillerman enrolled at Oklahoma State University, but then joined the army to fight in World War II. He took part in the D–Day landings, was wounded in Alsace, and earned a Silver Star, among other decorations. His letters home, later read by a journalist, were so detailed and spirited that the newspaperman convinced the young returning soldier to take up a career in writing. Enrolling in journalism courses, Hillerman also worked part–time to support his education. It was in 1945, while driving a truckload of drilling pipe from Oklahoma to New Mexico, that he first encountered the Navajo and their reservation. The Navajos he first saw were engaged in a curing ceremony called the Enemy Way, during which a young Navajo fresh from service in the war, like Hillerman himself, was cured of the foreign contamination and brought back into harmony with his own people. "When I met the Navajos I now so often write about," Hillerman told Ernie Bulow in *Talking Mysteries,* "I recognized kindred spirits. Country boys. More of us. Folks among whom I felt at ease." In 1948, Hillerman graduated from the journalism program at the University of Oklahoma. He was also married that year to Marie Unzner, and the couple would eventually have one child together, and adopt an additional five children.

From Journalist to Author

Hillerman took several newspaper jobs in and around Oklahoma, Texas, and New Mexico before joining the staff of the Santa Fe *New Mexican* in 1954. He stayed with the paper until 1963, working at the end of his journalism career as its executive editor. But he had a longing to become a novelist and, with the encouragement of his wife, Hillerman left journalism behind to study writing, soon becoming a journalism professor at the University of New Mexico where he remained until 1985. It was while teaching journalism that he wrote his first novel, *The Blessing Way*, in which he introduces Joe Leaphorn, a fiftyish Navajo with the Tribal Police on the reservation. Leaphorn, however, was almost cut out of this manuscript at the urging of Hillerman's agent. Finally, an editor at Harper and Row wrote an enthusiastic critique of the manuscript, encouraging Hillerman to increase Leaphorn's role, and the writer's first major protagonist was born.

In this debut novel, the motive for the murder of a young Navajo is witchcraft in the shape of a Navajo Wolf, akin to a werewolf. According to Geoff Sadler, a contributor for *Contemporary Popular Writers,* this novel "is a tense, exciting adventure that mixes espionage with witchcraft." Hillerman's second novel, *Fly on the Wall,* is a story of political corruption with a journalist serving as the chief investigator. Returning with his third novel to Navajo country, as he has remained with all but one more of his novels, Hillerman next sent his reserved, logical, and partially assimilated detective, Leaphorn, into Zuni country to investigate tribal rites in *The Dance Hall of the Dead.* This second Leaphorn novel earned Hillerman the Edgar Allan Poe Award from the Mystery Writers of America, and begins with the murder of Ernesto Cata, a Zuni boy who is in training for an important ceremonial role in his tribe. Suspicion falls on a Navajo boy, George Bowlegs, but when Bowlegs in turn is murdered, Leaphorn follows leads—and his instinct—until he discovers a white archaeologist has killed the boys to keep them from disclosing that he had been fudging the finds at his excavation site. Hillerman's third Leaphorn novel followed in 1978, *Listening Woman,* in which the Navajo detective has to investigate two homicides and also gets trapped in an underground cavern with terrorists and their hostages. "The novel combines clever plotlines with sharp character insights and a taut, nail–biting payoff," wrote Sadler.

With *People of Darkness,* Hillerman introduces a second major protagonist, Jim Chee, who, like Leaphorn, is a Navajo Tribal officer, but who, unlike Leaphorn, is more traditional, less experienced, younger, and more in flux. One major reason for creating Chee was that Hillerman had sold the television rights for his Leaphorn character; with *People of Darkness,* he knew he needed a different kind of protagonist, someone younger and less sophisticated than Leaphorn. In this story, Chee, a part–time ceremonial singer who is also drawn to the anglo lifestyle and the possibility of a career in the FBI, investigates a burglary at a wealthy white man's house that uncovers a thirty–year–old crime aboard an oil rig. Chee's second adventure, *The Dark Wind,* has the younger Navajo detective chasing criminals involved in a cocaine ring who have killed several Navajos. In *The Ghostway,* Chee is off to Los Angeles in pursuit of two Navajos who are stealing luxury cars. When the thieves return to the reservation, one of them is killed in his uncle's hogan (dwelling). Chee's heritage comes to the fore when he discovers that whoever laid the young man out for burial neglected one of the ceremonies and was thus not really a Navajo. Such a connection with tradition might come in handy in Chee's work, but not in his love life, for it isolates him from his white

Based on a myth of one of the southwestern Native American tribes, Hillermans 1972 book for children finds a young Zuni boy and his sister determined to help their people survive a drought that has destroyed all their crops.

schoolteacher lover who ultimately leaves the reservation. Reviewing *The Ghostway* in *Entertainment Weekly,* a contributor noted that you don't have to be "a regular at Tribal Policeman Jim Chee's pow–wows to dig *The Ghostway,* one of the freshest of Hillerman's whodunits."

Leaphorn and Chee Team Up

After finishing *The Ghostway,* Hillerman bought back the rights to Joe Leaphorn, and in his next novel, *Skinwalkers,* paired the detective with Chee, as he would do in many succeeding titles. The two men act as foils to one another: Leaphorn the older, more mature and methodical detective, and Chee the more quixotic, impulsive loner. The Skinwalkers of the title are Navajo ghosts, and the novel, which starts out with a shotgun attack on Chee, has witchcraft at its very heart. Leaphorn helps the younger detective get to the bottom of this attack and others on the reservation. A Golden Spur Award winner, *Skinwalkers* is a "strong, neatly worked novel with a shocking climax," according to Sadler. Writing in *People Weekly*, Campbell Geeslin noted that Hillerman "packs his novels with compelling details of Navajo life and beautiful descriptive passages about the land and weather." Geeslin concluded, "Chee . . . is a perfect guide through Hillerman's effective, dreamlike world."

Skinwalkers was, according to Michael Neill in *People Weekly*, Hillerman's "commercial breakthrough," selling 40,000 copies in hardcover and 100,000 in paperback. Yet it was his next title, *A Thief of Time*, that secured him a place on the best–seller charts and propelled Hillerman to national attention. Beginning with a murder at an Anasazi historical site, the book features a psychopathic killer and more development of the relationship between Leaphorn and Chee. In this novel, Leaphorn has to cope with his wife's death as well as his own impending retirement. As Hillerman's main recurring characters, Leaphorn and Chee serve a dual function. On one level, the officers act as guides into a world of traditions and customs unfamiliar to most readers; on another level, Hillerman's depiction of Leaphorn and Chee's day–to–day struggles—with bureaucratic red tape, discrimination, and intimate relationships—helps readers understand the difficulty of living in what amounts to two worlds with different, and often contradictory, sets of rules. This culture clash is not always depicted in a negative light, however. In books such as *Listening Woman* and *The Ghostway*, Leaphorn and Chee use both standard police procedures and their special knowledge of tribal customs to solve a wide variety of baffling crimes. In *Listening Woman*, Leaphorn finds clues to a double murder in a group of ritual sand paintings. An oddly performed death ceremony puts Chee on the trail of a missing girl and a killer in *The Ghostway*. Stolen pottery from a "lost" tribe becomes the focus of Leaphorn's investigation into artifact trafficking in *A Thief of Time*, a book that is at once "[c]areful with the facts," and one that "transmutes knowledge into romance," as a contributor to *Time* magazine wrote. Karl G. Fredrikkson and Lilian Fredrikkson called *A Thief of Time* "probably Hillerman's best novel," in *St. James Guide to Crime and Mystery Writers*, and further noted that "History and tradition play integral parts in all Hillerman's novels and especially in this one." The Fredrikksons concluded that the main theme of all Hillerman's work "is the clash between the Navajo Way and the so–called American Way of Life, between tradition and the emptiness of modern society."

As with *Dance Hall of the Dead* and *A Thief of Time*, Hillerman's 1989 *Talking God* deals with anthropology. This time, both Chee and Leaphorn desert the reservation for Washington, D.C., in search of missing Native American artifacts. "The plot," noted Louise Bernikow in a *Cosmopolitan* review, "comes to a crashing finale in the Smithsonian Institute, and the evil that has disturbed the spirits of the Navajo is laid to rest." Bernikow also commented that Hillerman's story "is complicated, emotional, and incredibly suspenseful." In *Coyote Waits*, an officer in the Navajo Tribal Police, Delbert Nez, is gunned down, and Leaphorn and Chee set out to find his killer. It looks as if a Navajo shaman might be responsible for the killing, until other suspects turn up, including a Vietnamese teacher. Behind it all lurks the mythic Navajo character representing chaos, the Coyote of the title. Phoebe–Lou Adams, writing in the *Atlantic*, felt the plot "is a humdinger even by the high Hillerman standard," while a writer for *Entertainment Weekly* dubbed it "sturdy work from an incorruptible craftsman." Reviewing the title in *People Weekly*, Neill concluded, "Hillerman's elevation into the best–seller ranks is a great justice of American popular writing. While his novels are mysteries, they are also exquisite explorations of human nature—with a great backdrop." Reviewing *Coyote Waits*, a contributor for *Publishers Weekly* commented, "Hillerman weaves an understated, powerful tale from strands of ancient Navajo mythology, modern greed and ambition, and above all, the sorrows and delights of characters."

Hillerman's mysteries are "telling commentaries upon American life in the Southwest, for in addition to beautiful nature imagery and remarkably clear and effective glimpses into Native American life, they offer vivid accounts of the difficulties of operating in a multi–ethnic society."

—Jane S. Bakerman

In *Sacred Clowns*, the duo investigate the seemingly unrelated murders of a shop teacher at the mission school and a sacred clown dancer, a Hopi koshare.

In this novel, Chee is increasingly attracted to the Navajo lawyer, Janet Pete, while Leaphorn considers a relationship with a linguistics professor. "Telling his story the Navajo way," wrote a contributor to *Publishers Weekly*, "Hillerman fully develops the background of the cases . . . so that the resolutions . . . ring true with gratifying inevitability." Gene Lyons, writing in *Entertainment Weekly*, noted that even "devoted readers . . . will find *Sacred Clowns* just a bit different from earlier books in the series." Lyons pointed to the essentially "comic" structure and tone of the novel.

Time Passes for Chee and Leaphorn

One interesting aspect of Hillerman's novels is that his protagonists do not stay rooted in time, but rather develop and age before the reader's eyes. Leaphorn retires, yet keeps a hand in police affairs. Chee begins to settle down. The pair took a hiatus in the mid–1990s while Hillerman turned his hand to various other projects, including *The Mysterious West* and another novel set in Vietnam, *Finding Moon*. Then in 1997, the duo returned with *The Fallen Man*. In this novel, mountaineers find a skeleton near the summit of Ship Rock in northwestern New Mexico. The skeleton in question turns out to be that of a member of a local white family who disappeared eleven years earlier. Leaphorn, who remembers the earlier disappearance, comes back into action, though Chee, now a lieutenant, at first bristles at his intrusion. Meantime also the romance between Chee and the ambitious attorney, Janet Pete, whom he is courting, takes twists and turns. "As always," noted a reviewer for *Publishers Weekly*, "Hillerman treats Indian tradition and modern troubles . . . with unsentimental respect, firmly rooting his mystery in the region's distinctive peoples and geography." Sikki Andur, writing in *Entertainment Weekly*, called this thirteenth novel "a scenic ride through a land where police are more worried about cattle rustling than dope dealing," and where "a cop who's been shot doesn't crave revenge—he wants harmony." *Booklist*'s Stephanie Zvirin commented, "As usual, Hillerman masterfully sets the scene, conveying contemporary culture and weaving in intriguing side plots to add depth to character and scene." Zvirin concluded that "with all Hillerman's stories, it's the oblique way" of getting to the end "that pulls [the reader] along."

The First Eagle, published in 1998, features another scientist who comes from outside to the "res," a theme found in several of Hillerman's books. This time it is a missing female biologist who has been tracking the Bubonic plague in the prairie dogs of the Southwest. Leaphorn is hired by the scientist's grandmother to find her; meanwhile Chee is investigating the bludgeon death of a Navajo Police officer at the site where the biologist was last seen. "Hillerman's trademark melding of Navajo tradition and modern culture is captured with crystal clarity in this tale of an ancient scourge's resurgence in today's word," noted a reviewer for *Publishers Weekly*. *Booklist*'s Zvirin felt that "Hillerman's respect and deep affection for his creations and their community" runs through all of the subplots and twists of action. *Hunting Badger*, published in 1999, was inspired by an actual manhunt in the Four Corners region in which the search for killers was badly bungled by the FBI. In Hillerman's scenario, there is a robbery at an Ute casino, and the security officer there is killed in the process. Chee is drawn into the case along with Leaphorn. Reviews of this fifteenth book in the series were somewhat mixed. Wilda Williams, writing in *Library Journal*, felt that the novel "offers a paint–by–the–numbers plot with cardboard characters," but that "diehard fans will want this." However a reviewer for *Publishers Weekly* felt that "Hillerman is in top form" with *Hunting Badger*, while *Booklist*'s Bill Ott felt the book was "a return to form for Hillerman." Ott concluded, "Nobody uses the power of myth to enrich crime fiction more effectively than Hillerman."

If you enjoy the works of Tony Hillerman, you might want to check out the following books:

Margaret Coel, *The Ghost Walker*, 1996.
Brian Garfield, *The Threepersons Hunt*, 1974.
Jake Page, *The Stolen Gods*, 1993.
Chelsea Quinn Yarbro, *Ogilvie, Tallant, and Moon*, 1976.

Hillerman has also been commended for his nonfiction works and anthologies that explore the natural beauty and unique history of the Southwest. In *New Mexico, Rio Grande, and Other Essays*, the author discusses a number of topics, including how geographical, political, and historical factors helped the Pueblo Indians thrive when many other tribes fell prey to conquering forces. In *The Mysterious West*, Hillerman as editor pulls together previously unpublished stories from writers such as J. A Jance and Marcia Muller, while in *The Oxford Book of American Detective Stories* and *The Best American Stories of the Century*, he shows his ties to the mystery genre are as strong as those to the Southwest. But in the final analysis, Hillerman is known for his Chee–Leaphorn books and their evocation of Navajo country. In these books, Hillerman explores, as Muhlestein noted in *Dictionary of Literary Biography,* "the themes he cares about most deeply: the question of identity, the tension between the desire to assimilate and the need to retain native traditions, the shortcomings of Anglo justice, and the spiritual illness of white culture." As Fred Erisman commented in *Tony Hillerman,* "Leaphorn and Chee, as Navajos, give readers a sense of the demands of Southwestern life. In a larger sense, though, that they are Navajo is incidental; they are human as well as Navajo, and as they . . . grapple with the realities of their people, their place, and their time, their responsibilities help all readers to decipher the palimpsest of human life in all its complexity and all its majesty."

■ Biographical and Critical Sources

BOOKS

Bulow, Ernie, and Tony Hillerman, *Talking Mysteries: A Conversation with Tony Hillerman,* University of New Mexico Press, 1991.

Contemporary Literary Criticism, Volume 62, Gale, 1990.

Dictionary of Literary Biography, Volume 206: *Twentieth–Century American Western Writers, First Series,* Gale, 1999.

Erisman, Fred, *Tony Hillerman,* Boise State University, 1989.

Fredrikkson, Karl G. and Lilian Fredrikkson, "Tony Hillerman: An Overview," *St. James Guide to Crime and Mystery Writers,* 4th edition, St. James Press, 1996.

Greenberg, Martin, editor, *The Tony Hillerman Companion: A Comprehensive Guide to His Life and Work,* HarperCollins, 1994.

Reilly, John M., *Tony Hillerman: A Critical Companion,* Greenwood Press, 1996.

Sadler, Geoff, "Tony Hillerman: An Overview," *Contemporary Popular Writers,* St. James Press, 1997.

Sobol, John, *Tony Hillerman: A Public Life,* ECW Press, 1994.

PERIODICALS

Armchair Detective, fall, 1990, p. 426.

Atlantic, September, 1990, Phoebe–Lou Adams, review of *Coyote Waits,* p. 121; January, 1992, p. 115.

Booklist, October 1, 1994, p. 243; September 15, 1995, p. 116; March 1, 1996, p. 1125; November 1, 1996, Stephanie Zvirin, review of *The Fallen Man,* p. 459; October 15, 1997, p. 424; November 15, 1998, p. 604; June 1, 1999, p. 1853; July, 1999, Stephanie Zvirin, review of *The First Eagle,* p. 1829; April 1, 2000, p. 1437; May 1, 2000, Bill Ott, review of *Hunting Badger,* p. 1595; September 1, 2000, p. 144.

Cosmopolitan, June, 1989, Louise Bernikow, review of *Talking God,* p. 48.

Economist, August 14, 1993, pp. 83–84.

Entertainment Weekly, April 3, 1992, review of *The Ghostway,* p. 47; January 31, 1992, review of *Coyote Waits,* p. 54; September 17, 1993, Gene Lyons, review of *Sacred Clowns,* p. 82; November 3, 1995, p. 59; November 15, 1996, Sikki Andur, review of *The Fallen Man.*

Kirkus Reviews, February 1, 1996, p. 179.

Library Journal, November 1, 1994, p. 77; March 1, 1996, p. 109; March 15, 1997, p. 102; July, 1998, p. 136; January, 1999, p. 184; November 15, 1999, Wilda Williams, review of *Hunting Badger,* p. 98; April 1, 2000, p. 150.

Los Angeles Times Book Review, January 21, 1990, p. 14; May 27, 1990, p. 10; December 16, 1990; November 17, 1991, p. 12; January 5, 1992, p. 9; October 3, 1993, p. 12.

New Yorker, August 23, 1993, p. 165.

New York Times, June 10, 1989, Herbert Mitgang, "Hillerman Adds Tribal Rites of Washington to the Navajos," p. 15; February 16, 2000, p. B2.

New York Times Book Review, December 23, 1990, p. 20; October 20, 1991, p. 36; February 2, 1992, p. 28; August 30, 1992, p. 14; October 17, 1993, p. 36; October 22, 1995, p. 29; November 21, 1999, p. 80.

People Weekly, February 9, 1987, Campbell Geeslin, review of *Skinwalkers,* p. 16; July 18, 1988, Michael Neill, "A Keen Observer in a World Not His Own," p. 85; August 27, 1990, Michael Neill, review of *Coyote Waits,* p. 22.

Playboy, July, 2000, p. 183.

Publishers Weekly, October 24, 1980; May 11, 1990, review of *Coyote Waits,* p. 250; July 26, 1993, review of *Sacred Clowns,* p. 60; September 12, 1994, p. 85; September 4, 1995, p. 48; February 12, 1996, p. 63; October 21, 1996, review of *The Fallen Man,* p. 73; July 13, 1998, review of *The First Eagle,* p. 65; October 18, 1999, p. 74; November 22, 1999, p. 16; January 3, 2000, review of *Hunting Badger,* p. 40; March 6, 2000, p. 85.

Quadrant, July, 2000, p. 118.

School Library Journal, February, 1994, p. 136; March, 1995, p. 235.

Time, July 4, 1988, review of *A Thief of Time,* p. 71.

Tribune Books (Chicago), September 2, 1990; September 26, 1993, p. 6.

Wall Street Journal, August 13, 1998, p. A12.

Washington Post Book World, May 27, 1990, p. 12; July 26, 1992, p. 1; September 5, 1993, p. 4.

Writer's Digest, January, 2000, pp. 8–9.

—Sketch by J. Sydney Jones

Nalo Hopkinson

■ Personal

Born on December 20, 1960, in Kingston, Jamaica; moved to Toronto, Canada in 1977; daughter of Slade (a poet and actor) and Freda (a library technician) Hopkinson. *Education:* University of York, combined honors graduate, Russian and French; Clarion Science Fiction and Fantasy Writers' Workshop, Michigan State University, 1995.

■ Addresses

Home—Toronto, Canada. *E-mail*—nalo@sff.net.

■ Career

Author, 1997—. Has also worked as a librarian and as a grants officer for a local arts council.

■ Awards, Honors

Short Prose Competition for Developing Writers, Writers' Union of Canada, second place, 1994, for "Midnight Robber" (short story); winner, Warner Aspect First Novel Contest, 1997, for *Brown Girl in the Ring;* Locus Award, First Novel Category and short list selection, James R. Triptree, Jr. Award, both 1998, both for *Brown Girl in the Ring;* finalist, Philip K. Dick Award, for *Brown Girl in the Ring* and *Midnight Robber* (novel); John W. Campbell Award, 1999, for best new writer of 1997–98; Ontario Arts Council Foundation award for emerging writers, 1999; Nebula Award and Philip K. Dick Award finalist, both 2000, both for *Midnight Robber;* short list selections, James R. Triptree, Jr., Award, 2000, for *Midnight Robber* and "The Glass Bottle Trick."

■ Writings

Brown Girl in the Ring, Warner Aspect, 1998.
Midnight Robber, Warner Aspect, 2000.
(Editor) *Whispers from the Cotton Tree Root: Caribbean Fabulist Fiction,* Invisible Cities Press, 2000.
Skin Folk (short story collection), Warner Aspect, 2001.

Short stories by Hopkinson include "Midnight Robber," originally published in *Exile Magazine;* "Ganger: Ball Lightning" and "Greedy Choke Puppy," both published in the anthology, *Dark Matter,* edited by Sheree Thomas and Martin Simmons; "A Habit of Waste," published in 1996 in the feminist journal, *Fireweed,* and anthologized in *Women of Other Worlds,* edited by Helen Merrick and Tess Williams, and *Northern Suns,* edited by David Hartwell and Glenn Grant; "Riding the Red," published in 1997 in the anthology, *Black Swan, White Raven*, edited by Ellen Datlow and Terri Windling; "Precious," published in the anthology, *Silver Birch, Blood Moon*, edited by Datlow and Windling; "Money Tree," published in the 1997 anthology, *Tesseracts 6*, edited by Carolyn Clink and Rob Sawyer; and "Slow Cold Chick," written for Canadian Broadcasting Corporation (CBC) radio in 1997 and included in the anthology, *Northern Frights 5*, edited by Don Hutchinson. *Indicator Species*, a radio play, was produced by CBC radio. Contributor of book reviews to *Science Fiction Weekly*, among other publications.

■ Adaptations

"Greedy Choke Puppy" has been adapted for a play of the same name, produced by Seeing Ear Theatre; "Riding the Red" was adapted for CBC radio as a performance by the author with original music composed and played by William Sperandei.

■ Work in Progress

Griffone, a novel, for Warner Books.

■ Sidelights

Nalo Hopkinson calls her work an attempt at "subverting the [science fiction] genre"; reviewers point to her intriguing blend of African, Caribbean, and Creole folklore with the usual conventions of science fiction and science fantasy; literary analysts put her in the magical realism, post–colonial lit school. Whatever you call Hopkinson's work, speculative fiction, magical realism, or plain old science fiction, the Canadian author has quickly carved out a niche for herself on bookstore shelves with two novels and a handful of short stories. Her 1998 debut novel, *Brown Girl in the Ring*, won the Warner Aspect First Novel contest, and major publication and distribution. This tale of a decaying urban center in the near future, though a well–plowed field, found new life with Hopkinson's spicy mix of Afro–Caribbean folklore and patois. Her protagonist, Ti–Jeanne, is a single mother who is struggling to come to terms with her past and with her heritage. Hopkinson's second novel, *Midnight Robber*, is set on a planet colonized by a Caribbean population and

Winner of a national science–fiction competition, Hopkinson's 1998 fiction–writing debut shows the way of life of primitive peoples resurfacing within abandoned inner cities of a near–future Earth.

employs a hybridized Creole dialect to an even greater extent than her first novel. An allegory of displacement and diaspora, Midnight Robber, "bears evidence that Hopkinson owns one of the more important and original voices in SF," according to a reviewer for *Publishers Weekly*.

Within the space of a few years of writing, Hopkinson has filled enough print–and cyber–space to elevate her science fiction to crossover status, just as another Canadian author, Margaret Atwood, did with a basically science fiction premise in *The Handmaid's Tale*. Hopkinson herself is still reeling from the sudden change in her life and in her career path. "I didn't know it would happen so quickly," she told a group of panelists on a TimeWarnerBookmark chatline, *Talk City.* "I've got a list of things I would like to accomplish, and some of those have happened in wonderful ways and are giving me the impetus to keep me trying to achieve the others." Some of those "others" are a third contracted novel for Warner Books as well as promotional tours for her books and speaking engagements at colleges and conventions around the country.

A Literary Childhood

The hurly–burly of the literary life is nothing new for Hopkinson, daughter of the Guyanese poet, playwright, and actor, Slade Hopkinson. For several

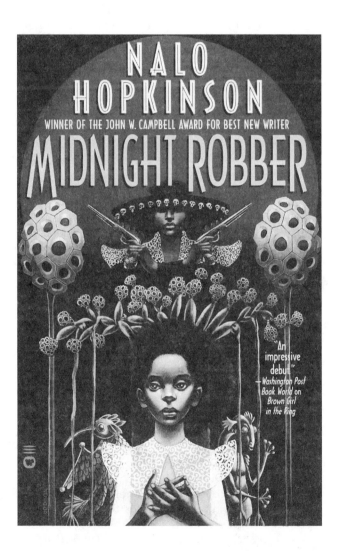

Hopkinson's second SF novel combines Caribbean myth and space–age technology as a young girl living with her father on an planetary outpost is suddenly forced into an alternate universe where she adopts a new identity to free herself from her father's emotional clutches.

years her father was a co–director with the Nobel–winning writer, Derek Walcott, at the Trinidad Theater Workshop which Walcott founded. Even as a child, Hopkinson and her brother experienced a peripatetic life; she was born in Kingston, Jamaica, on December 20, 1960, but at eight months of age her family "started jaunting around from island to island," as she noted in an autobiographical piece for *Locus* magazine. The family traveled from Jamaica to Trinidad to Guyana, her father writing and teaching in high schools and her mother working as a librarian. For a time the family settled in Connecticut while her father was attending Yale Dramatic School, and then it was back to the Caribbean. Hopkinson grew up in a household filled with books and one that had a healthy respect for the arts. "My parents took me to see theater, dance, readings, visual art exhibitions," Hopkinson told Gregory E. Rutledge in *African America Review.*

With one writer in the house already, Hopkinson was loath to come forward with her own dreams of one day becoming a writer. She was a voracious reader as a child, working her way through folk and fairy tales, both Western and African. Some of her particular favorites involved Anansi, the West African trickster. She also devoured *Gulliver's Travels* and *The Iliad* and *The Odyssey.* Living in Kingston again as an adolescent, Hopkinson discovered the world of science fiction, reading Harlan Ellison, Samuel Delany, and Elizabeth Lynn. It was only later she discovered that some of her literary heroes were of her own race. "Some time in my 20s I saw a photograph of Chip Delany," Hopkinson told Rutledge, "and realized he was black. I'd never heard of such a thing before. I wept. It felt as though my universe had just doubled in size. Though my life was surrounded with Caribbean writers of color . . . , none of them wrote sf. I'd only met one other black person who read the literature." As a young child Hopkinson was already experimenting with writing her own tales. At ten she wrote "a vampire murder mystery" as she told the panelists on *Talk City.* "It involved lots of blood and a Catholic priest. I remember my father reading it and saying, 'Nalo, this is very nice. Is there anything bothering you?'" She also played with blank verse when at fifteen she penned a science fiction poem.

Coming of Age in Canada

In her sixteenth year, Hopkinson's family moved to Toronto, Canada, where her father, suffering from kidney failure, found treatment. Hopkinson attended several high schools before graduating, and studied Russian and French at university in Canada, graduating with combined honors. She followed this up with a diploma in recreational management and then went back for more schooling, in the sciences this time as a prelude to a career as a chiropractor. But as she told Rutledge, she was "good at biology but horrible at math, without which I couldn't take physics or chemistry. Whew. I dropped out and abandoned plans to become a chiropractor."

She worked instead for many years as a library clerk and then library supervisor, during which time she discovered other black writers of speculative or science fiction. At her library she discovered the work of Octavia Butler, Samuel Delany, Steve Barnes, Charles Saunders, and Virginia Hamilton; a handful of black writers in a genre in which she believed all the authors to be white. She began to see that much of Western science fiction has been affected by the pulp image of the genre, with as she described it to Rutledge, "a stigma about being adventure stories in which white people use technology to overpower alien cultures." Hopkinson went on to note, "Small wonder that black writers haven't been drawn to [SF] in large numbers." Instead, Hopkinson began to see the appeal of an alternative science fiction: told from a black woman's point of view and dealing the shibboleths of African and Caribbean society rather than the dominant Euro–centered one found in most science fiction books. "I think that a speculative literature from a culture that has been on the receiving end of the colonization glorified in some sf could be a compelling body of writing," she told Rutledge.

So, in 1992, when Hopkinson finally got over her own self–imposed limitations—her doubts that she did not have the talent to write—and started crafting fiction, her stories came out mostly with a science fiction bent to them. Slowly she found her way in short stories and articles, but it was the impetus of a writing group that formed in 1993 that set her on the path to novels. One story refused to stay small and after about 10,000 words, Hopkinson realized she had a novel on her hands. She attended the Clarion Science Fiction and Fantasy Writers' Workshop at Michigan State University in 1995, where one of her early heroes, Delany, was in residence. Returning from that experience she heard about the Warner Aspect First Novel Contest and on a whim, submitted her novel–in–progress. To her surprise, the committee wanted to see the full manuscript. After two solid months of writing and workshopping, she had a draft of the book and sent it off on the day of the deadline. Six months later, she heard she had won.

Brown Girl in the Ring

The result was Hopkinson's first novel, *Brown Girl in the Ring,* with a title from a Caribbean schoolyard game, a dancing variant of "You're It." A dystopian story, the novel is set in inner–city Toronto in the near future. Such cities have all but been abandoned by the government; the rich have fled the urban areas, barricading those inside, and leaving such places to molder away. Inside the city, the folks have rediscovered some old farming and bartering ways. Ti–Jeanne is a recent single mother in the city who is trying to deal with her new baby and her drug–addict boyfriend, Tony. When Tony gets in trouble with the local gang kingpin, Rudy, boss of the Posse, Ti–Jeanne goes to her wise grandmother for help. Gros–Jeanne, or Mami, a healer, herbalist, and a practitioner of Afro–Caribbean spiritual beliefs, helps bring her granddaughter into the spirit world. But soon Ti–Jeanne finds herself battling Rudy and also coming to terms with the mother she lost long ago—the mother that is now Rudy's captive spirit. Thus, Hopkinson sets up a multi–generational novel of people coping against evil in a world that is all too often taken from the evening news. This edgy novel does not shy away from violence when the plot demands it, nor does it over–explain its rich dialogue. Elements of magical realism sit easily alongside fantasy and SF. Additionally, early in the writing, Hopkinson saw the parallels in her story and in the Walcott play, "Ti–Jean and His Brothers," in which three brothers battle the devil. "I wanted to acknowledge that connection to [Walcott's] work," Hopkinson told Rutledge, "so I named the three women Ti–Jeanne, Mi–Jeanne, and Gros–Jeanne," the feminine equivalents of Walcott's characters.

Hopkinson's novel, which involves characters who speak in such a rich blend of Afro–Caribbean patois as, "You just don't let she go, or I go zap the both of allyou one time," received a quick response from reviewers. A critic for *Kirkus Reviews,* for example, called the book a "splendid if gruesome debut, superbly plotted and redolent of the rhythms of Afro–Caribbean speech." *Booklist*'s Bonnie Johnston felt that Hopkinson's "exotically imaginative debut is just realistic enough," while Farren Miller writing in *Locus* noted that "what propels this fast–paced work is the author's gift for passionate, vivid, tale–spinning." Miller concluded, "Hopkinson is a genuine find." Writing in the *New York Times Book Review,* Gerald Jonas commented that Hopkinson "treats spirit–calling the way other science fiction writers treat nanotechnology or virtual reality. . . . I am happy to report that Hopkinson lives up to her advance billing."

Though David Streitfeld, writing in the *Washington Post,* felt that the book "has the usual first novel faults in pacing and plotting," he went on to praise the "richness of language" which "more than compensates" for any such faults. Streitfeld called *Brown Girl in the Ring* "an impressive debut . . . because of Hopkinson's fresh viewpoint." A writer for *Publishers Weekly* focused on Hopkinson's aural/oral heritage: "The musical rhythms of Caribbean voices and the earthy spirit–magic of obeah knit together this unusual fantasy." The same reviewer concluded, "Though the story sometimes turns too easily on coincidence, Hopkinson's writing is smooth and assured, and her characters lively and believable. She has created a vivid world of urban decay and startling, dangerous magic, where the human heart is both a physical and metaphorical key." And Carol DeAngelo, reviewing the novel in *School Library Journal,* called the book an "outstanding science–fiction novel" as well as a "page–turner that builds to an exciting conclusion," and a "quickly read fantasy . . . [with] lots of appeal to young adults."

Midnight Robber

Hopkinson's encore to this critical applause came two years later in a second SF novel about space colonization—with a twist. The planet Toussaint has been colonized by people of the Caribbean, and Antonio Habib is the powerful mayor of Cockpit County; his daughter Tan–Tan is the product of privilege. The planet is the picture of harmony, ministered by "Granny Nanny," an artificial intelligence which monitors everyone through aural implants. Miscreants are exiled to New Half–Way Tree, an alternate universe to Toussaint, so when Habib runs afoul of the law, killing his wife's lover, that is where he and his daughter end up. The father remarries, but his anger gets the better of him. As her father's fortunes dwindle and he spirals into sexual excess and drunkenness, Tan–Tan struggles to find her own way. Suffering his assaults on her, one day she finally kills him, but she is by now pregnant with her father's child. At age sixteen, she goes on the run, hiding from the vengeance of her father's widow. In the bush she learns magical secrets and transforms herself into the Caribbean Carnival figure of the Midnight Robber, a figure who dresses all in black and tells poetic tales to those he waylays; in short, a sort of Caribbean Robin Hood who steals from the rich and gives to the poor. Thus Tan–Tan becomes the Robber Queen, fighting for survival on New Half–Way Tree. Again Hopkinson mixed Caribbean and African myth and folklore with the rich language stew of the region, but this time she went further with a created language, employing it not only in dialogue but also in part of the narration.

In 2000 Hopkinson focused her talents on editing a collection of stories by Caribbean writers that invoke the rich history, lush surroundings, and vivid mythology of the region.

"In the course of only two novels," wrote David Soyka in *SF Site Review,* "Nalo Hopkinson has established herself as a unique voice in the SF and Fantasy genre, largely because that voice is grounded in the rhythms, myths, and vernacular of Caribbean and Creole cultures." Writing in *Library Journal,* Jackie Cassada also noted the exotic mix of cultures in this new novel: "The author of *Brown Girl in the Ring* once again draws from African, Caribbean, and Creole folklore to flavor her tale of a fierce and resourceful young woman determined to make her way in a world she has not chosen." *Booklist*'s Roberta Johnson called special attention to Hopkinson's "exhilarating prose" which "drives an exciting story that continues with Tan–Tan befriending New Half–Way Tree's natives and coming to terms with self–hatred." A *Publishers Weekly* reviewer felt that Hopkinson's "rich and complex Carib English can be hard to follow at times, but is nonetheless quite beautiful." The same reviewer also commented favorably on Tan–Tan; "at once violent and vulnerable," she "is extremely well drawn," and also on Hopkinson's created worlds of Toussaint: "a world awash in nanotechnology," and New Half–Way Tree, both of which are "believable, lushly detailed worlds." *School Library Journal*'s Francisca Goldsmith observed the mythic elements in Hopkinson's second novel, and concluded that the author "provides an engaging nexus of science fiction and folklore."

The Many Worlds of Nalo Hopkinson

Hopkinson is also the author of a handful of short stories which blend genres as much as her longer fiction. "Midnight Robber," a short story published in *Exile Magazine,* was the inspiration for her second novel of the same name. Other ambitious tales include "Ganger: Ball Lightning" and "Greedy Choke Puppy," both anthologized in *Dark Matter.* Hopkinson took for inspiration her father's poem about a Jamaican bag lady and turned it into the short story, "A Habit of Waste." Other short stories include "Riding the Red," "Precious," "Money Tree," and "Slow Cold Chick." Reviewing Hopkinson's additions to *Dark Matter,* Jonas noted in the *New York Times Book Review* that many of her tales "are not only set in black communities, they make use of West African–derived folklore and language patterns to create fresh worlds and emotionally compelling situations." Jonas called Hopkinson a "bold new voice."

If you enjoy the works of Nalo Hopkinson, you might want to check out the following books:

Emma Bull, *War for the Oaks,* 1987.
Terrence M. Green, *Blue Limbo,* 1997.
Ben Okri, *The Famished Road,* 1992.

Hopkinson, for her part, enjoys the sort of voice she is developing, "the way fantastical fiction allows me to use myth, archetype, speculation, and storytell-

ing," as she told Rutledge. "I like the way that it allows me to imagine the impossible." As for theme, Hopkinson insists that she does not have "an agenda" when she writes. "Unless," she explained to Rutledge, "you count it as an agenda that I want the story to be a compelling read. Story themes come to me in later drafts, when I've figured out what the story's about. I start with a word, a phrase, or a snapshot image. I try to marry it with another image and see what comes out of the tension between the two." Hopkinson also has advice for aspiring authors. As she told the panelists of *Talk City,* "I would say develop your inner editor. Learn to look at the work you've written and try to see where it's not working. And to calmly try to address that. A piece of bad writing doesn't make you a bad writer, so you shouldn't be afraid of it."

■ Biographical and Critical Sources

BOOKS

Hopkinson, Nalo, *Brown Girl in the Ring,* Warner Aspect, 1998.

PERIODICALS

African American Review, Winter, 1999, Gregory E. Rutledge, "Speaking in Tongues: An Interview with Science Fiction Writer Nalo Hopkinson," p. 589.
Booklist, May 15, 1998, Bonnie Johnston, review of *Brown Girl in the Ring,* p. 1602; February 15, 2000, Roberta Johnson, review of *Midnight Robber,* p. 1091.
Emerge Magazine, July–August, 1998.
Kirkus Reviews, May 15, 1998, review of *Brown Girl in the Ring.*
Library Journal, February 15, 2000, Jackie Cassada, review of *Midnight Robber,* p. 201.
Locus, May, 1998, Farren Miller, review of *Brown Girl in the Ring;* July, 1998; January, 1999, "Nalo Hopkinson: Many Perspectives."
Magazine of Science Fiction and Fantasy, July, 1998.
New York Times Book Review, July 12, 1998, Gerald Jonas, review of *Brown Girl in the Ring,* p. 26; July 30, 2000, Gerald Jonas, "Science Fiction."
Publishers Weekly, June 8, 1998, review of *Brown Girl in the Ring,* p. 51; January 3, 2000, review of *Midnight Robber,* p. 61.
School Library Journal, November, 1998, Carol DeAngelo, review of *Brown Girl in the Ring,* p. 160; June, 2000, Francisca Goldsmith, review of *Midnight Robber,* p. 173.

Starlog, February, 1999, p. 16.

Washington Post, August 30, 1998, David Streitfeld, "Science Fiction and Fantasy"; July 30, 2000.

ONLINE

Nalo Hopkinson, http://www.sff.net/people/nalo/ (March 11, 2000).

SFF World, http://www.sffworld.com/,(March, 2000), "Interview with Nalo Hopkinson."

SF Site Review, http://www.sfsite.com/ (October 1, 2000), David Soyka, review of *Midnight Robber.*

Talk City, http://www.twbookmark.com/books/ (October 1, 2000), "Interview: Nalo Hopkinson."

—Sketch by J. Sydney Jones

Peg Kehret

Personal

Surname is pronounced "carrot"; born November 11, 1936, in LaCrosse, WI; daughter of Arthur R. (an executive of Geo. A. Hormel Co.) and Elizabeth M. (a homemaker; maiden name, Showers) Schulze; married Carl E. Kehret (a player–piano restorer), July 2, 1955; children: Bob C., Anne M. *Education:* Attended University of Minnesota, 1954–55. *Hobbies and other interests:* Reading, gardening, antiques, watching baseball, animals, cooking.

Addresses

Home—P.O. Box 303, Wilkeson, WA 98396. *Agent*—Emilie Jacobson, Curtis Brown Ltd., 10 Astor Place, New York, NY 10003.

Career

Writer, 1973—.

Member

Authors Guild, Society of Children's Book Writers and Illustrators, Mystery Writers of America.

Awards, Honors

Forest Roberts Playwriting Award, Northern Michigan University, 1978, Best New Play of 1979, Pioneer Drama Service, and Best Plays for Senior Adults, American Theatre Association, 1981, all for *Spirit!*; Children's Choice Award, International Reading Association–Children's Book Council (IRA–CBC), 1988, for *Deadly Stranger*; Recommended Books for Reluctant Young Adult Readers, American Library Association (ALA), 1989, for *The Winner,* and 1992, for *Cages*; Books for the Teen Age, New York Public Library, 1992, for *Cages* and *Winning Monologs for Young Actors: 65 Honest–to–Life Characterizations to Delight Young Actors and Audiences of All Ages*; Maud Hart Lovelace Award, 1995, for *Nightmare Mountain*; Young Adult's Choice Award, IRA, 1992, for *Sisters, Long Ago*; Recommended Books for Reluctant Young Adult Readers, ALA, Books for the Teen Age, New York Public Library, Young Adult's Choice, IRA, Maud Hart Lovelace Award, all 1992, all for *Cages*; Pacific Northwest Writer's Conference Achievement Award, 1992; Young Adult's Choice, IRA, for *Terror at the Zoo*; Quick Picks for Reluctant Young Adult Readers, ALA, and Children's Choices, IRA, both for *Danger at the Fair*; Children's Books of the Year, Child Study Children's Book Committee, 1995, for *The Richest Kids in Town*; Golden Kite Award, Society of Children's Book Writers and Illustrators, 1996, Notable Book, ALA, and PEN Center U.S.A. West Award for children's literature, both 1997, Dorothy Canfield Fisher Award, 1998, and Mark Twain Award, 1999, all for *Small Steps: The Year I Got Polio*; Children's Crown Award, National Christian Schools Association, 1998, and Mark Twain Award list, 1998–99, both for *Earthquake Terror*.

Recipient of numerous state reader awards in the Pacific northwest, and in Alabama, Illinois, Indiana, Iowa, Kansas, Missouri, Nebraska, Nevada, New Hampshire, Oklahoma, Pennsylvania, South Carolina, Tennessee, Texas, Utah, Vermont, Washington, and West Virginia.

■ Writings

FOR CHILDREN AND YOUNG ADULTS

Winning Monologs for Young Actors: 65 Honest–to–Life Characterizations to Delight Young Actors and Audiences of All Ages, Meriwether (Colorado Springs, CO), 1986.

Deadly Stranger, Dodd, Mead, 1987, Troll, 1997.

Encore!: More Winning Monologs for Young Actors: 63 More Honest–to–Life Monologs for Teenage Boys and Girls, Meriwether (Colorado Springs, CO), 1988.

The Winner, Turman (Seattle, WA), 1988.

Nightmare Mountain, Dutton, 1989.

Sisters, Long Ago, Cobblehill, 1990.

Cages, Cobblehill, 1991.

Acting Natural: Monologs, Dialogs, and Playlets for Teens, Meriwether (Colorado Springs, CO), 1991.

Terror at the Zoo, Cobblehill, 1992.

Horror at the Haunted House, Cobblehill, 1992.

Night of Fear, Cobblehill, 1994.

The Richest Kids in Town, Cobblehill, 1994.

Danger at the Fair, Cobblehill, 1995.

Don't Go Near Mrs. Tallie, Pocket Books, 1995.

Desert Danger, Pocket Books, 1995.

Cat Burglar on the Prowl, Pocket Books, 1995.

Bone Breath and the Vandals, Pocket Books, 1995.

Backstage Fright, Pocket Books, 1996.

Earthquake Terror, Cobblehill, 1996.

Screaming Eagles, Pocket Books, 1996.

Race to Disaster, Pocket Books, 1996.

Small Steps: The Year I Got Polio, Albert Whitman, 1996.

The Ghost Followed Us Home, Minstrel, 1996.

Searching for Candlestick Park, Cobblehill, 1997.

The Volcano Disaster, Pocket Books, 1998.

The Blizzard Disaster, Pocket Books, 1998.

I'm Not Who You Think I Am, Dutton, 1999.

Shelter Dogs: Amazing Stories of Adopted Strays, Albert Whitman, 1999.

The Flood Disaster, Pocket Books, 1999.

Don't Tell Anyone, Penguin Putnam Books for Young Readers, 2000.

The Hideout, Pocket Books, 2001.

Saving Lilly, Pocket Books, 2001.

My Brother Made Me Do It, Pocket Books, 2001.

Wally Amos Presents Chip and Cookie: The First Adventure (picture book), illustrated by Leslie Harrington, Addax Publishing Group, 2001.

PLAYS

Cemeteries Are a Grave Matter, Dramatic Publishing, 1975.

Let Him Sleep 'till It's Time for His Funeral, Contemporary Drama Service, 1977.

Spirit!, Pioneer Drama Service, 1979.

Dracula, Darling, Contemporary Drama Service, 1979.

Charming Billy, Contemporary Drama Service, 1983.

Bicycles Built for Two (musical), Contemporary Drama Service, 1985.

FOR ADULTS

Wedding Vows: How to Express Your Love in Your Own Words, Meriwether (Colorado Springs, CO), 1979, second edition, 1989.

Refinishing and Restoring Your Piano, Tab Books (Blue Ridge Summmit, PA), 1985.

Also contributor to periodicals.

■ Work in Progress

The Secret Journey, for Pocket Books.

■ Sidelights

Peg Kehret is the author of over two dozen children's novels; most of them, such as award–winners *Deadly Stranger*, *Nightmare Mountain*, and *Earthquake Terror*, serving up heavy doses of suspense and danger. Kehret has also written nonfiction for adults as well as for children. Her *Winning Monologs for Young Actors* and *Acting Natural* both reflect her own commitment to theater; the multi–talented Kehret has also penned six plays. The winner of the 1998 Dorothy Canfield Fisher Award, Kehret's *Small Steps* documents her own fight with a childhood case of polio that left her temporarily paralyzed. In

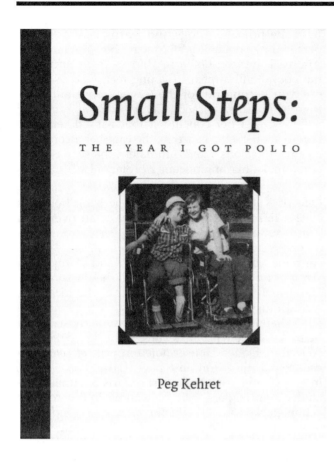

Small Steps:

THE YEAR I GOT POLIO

Peg Kehret

Kehret looks back to 1949, when she was twelve years old, in this sensitive 1996 memoir about coping with her disabling illness and slow recovery.

a *Booklist* review of Kehret's *Earthquake Terror*, Stephanie Zvirin neatly summed up the author's career to date: "Prolific author Kehret has a well–deserved reputation for writing good, solid thrillers for middle–graders."

Born in LaCrosse, Wisconsin in 1936, Kehret formed an early passion for words and writing. Paid three cents a story by her grandfather, she wrote, published, and sold her own newspaper about the dogs in her neighborhood. From this experience she gained valuable knowledge about pleasing an audience: her youthful broadsheet soon went out of business because she continually featured her own dog on the front page.

Kehret's idyllic childhood was shattered when she contracted polio in the seventh grade. As a result, she was paralyzed from the neck down and told that she would never walk again. "Much to everyone's surprise," Kehret once remarked, "I made almost a complete recovery. I vividly remember the

time when I got sick and my months in the hospital and my eventual return to school. Maybe that's why I enjoy writing books for young people; I recall exactly how it felt to be that age. I remember my friends and the books I liked and even what programs I listened to on the radio. When I write, it is easy for me to slip back in my imagination and become twelve years old again."

Beginnings in the Theater

As a teen, Kehret dreamed of being either a veterinarian or writer, finally opting for the wordsmith business. "I'm glad I chose writing," Kehret one stated, "but two of the main characters in my books want to be veterinarians. Dogs, llamas, and elephants have played important parts in my books." With high school came a new direction for Kehret's interest in words: theater. Cast as a hillbilly in a one–act play as a freshman, Kehret was seriously bit by the theater bug, working backstage or in acting roles in every production she could. Kehret briefly attended the University of Minnesota before marrying in 1955. Children soon followed and she lived the busy life of mother and homemaker, also volunteering for the Humane Society.

Kehret began writing in the early 1970s, spurred on by further work in community theater as well as her interest in research of various sorts. She began selling magazine stories, eventually logging over 300 of them before turning her hand to lengthier works. There followed one–act and full–length plays, including the award–winning *Spirit!*, as well as two adult nonfiction titles, before she began writing books for young people. Her initial juvenile title, *Winning Monologs for Young Actors,* appeared in 1986 and was followed by her first novel for young people, *Deadly Stranger.* The story of a kidnaping, this novel was dubbed a "cliffhanger" by a *Kirkus Reviews* contributor. "As soon as I tried writing from a youthful point of view," Kehret once remembered, "I knew I had found my place in the writing world."

Another popular early title from Kehret is *Nightmare Mountain,* a thriller involving young Molly and her visit to her aunt's ranch at the foot of Mt. Baker. The fun visit turns into a nightmare when her Aunt Karen falls into a coma and three valuable llamas are stolen. *Booklist*'s Denise M. Wilms observed that Kehret delivered "a fast–paced mystery–adventure tale with a heroine who, when forced to deal with disaster, shows courage and resourcefulness." Jeanette Larson concluded in *School Library Journal* that the book was a "satisfying novel that will keep readers guessing until the end." Reincarnation in-

THE SECRET JOURNEY

She could never tell anyone what *really* happened....

PEG KEHRET

A work of historical fiction, Kehret's 1999 novel finds spunky Emma Bolton disguising herself as a young boy in order to stow away aboard her parent's ship . . . only to discover that she has boarded a slaver bound for Africa by mistake.

with the homeless dogs and learns lessons about personal responsibility and facing her problems. As Andrea Davidson noted in *Voice of Youth Advocates*, the book "will appeal to young teen readers interested in getting out of the 'cages' represented by their problems." *School Library Journal* reviewer Sylvia V. Meisner concluded that Kit's determination to set herself free from "the cages of alcohol enablement, jealousy, and, ultimately, the secret of her crime make her an appealing protagonist."

One of Kehret's best–selling paperback books is 1992's *Terror at the Zoo*, the story of an overnight camp–out at the zoo which goes very wrong. Another 1992 title is *Horror at the Haunted House*, which continues the adventures of Ellen and Corey from *Terror at the Zoo*. This time around, they help with a Halloween haunted–house project at the local historical museum, only to discover that the house really is haunted. Overcoming her fear of ghosts, Ellen helps find out who is stealing from the museum's collection. Donna Houser noted in *Voice of Youth Advocates* that this "fun, fast–paced novel can be read in an evening," while *Booklist*'s Chris Sherman concluded that readers "will be waiting in line for this action–packed novel, which combines a good mystery with an exciting ghost story, a little danger, and a satisfying ending that ties everything up neatly." Ellen and Corey appear again in *Danger at the Fair*, "this time sharing a thrill–a–minute adventure set at a county fair," according to *Booklist*'s Zvirin. Atop the Ferris wheel, Corey spies a pickpocket at work, but when Corey subsequently trails the thief, he is trapped inside the "River of Fear" ride. Zvirin concluded that the mystery–suspense components of the story, plus "a pair of enthusiastic, heroic, quite likable" protagonists all added up to a book "that won't stay on the shelf for long."

forms Kehret's next book, *Sisters, Long Ago*. When Willow comes close to drowning, she sees herself in another life in ancient Egypt. The girl who saves her seems to be her sister from Egyptian days, while her own sister, Sarah, is fighting a losing battle with leukemia. Bruce Anne Shook, writing in *School Library Journal*, noted that "suspense is maintained up to the very end, making this a page–turner. . . ."

One of Kehret's personal favorites, *Cages,* allowed her to write about a passion of hers, the Humane Society. When young Kit—who has an alcoholic stepfather and a mother in denial—gives in to a momentary urge and shoplifts a bracelet, she sets off a train of events that has lasting repercussions in her life. Caught, she is sentenced to community service at the Humane Society. There she falls in love

Two other personal favorites of Kehret are *The Richest Kids in Town* and *Searching for Candlestick Park*. The former title is a departure for Kehret; a comic novel about Peter's money–making ventures that all go wrong. New in town, Peter desperately wants to save up enough money for a plane ticket to go back and visit his best friend. Peter enlists the help of some other kids, including Wishbone Wyoming, in some of his crazy money–making schemes. Their plans range from an alternative health club to a rubber–duck race, and all fail miserably and rather humorously. Finally Peter comes to see that he no longer needs to make money for a ticket; he has a new best friend in Wishbone. A critic for *Kirkus Reviews* concluded that there were "clever antics in this fun book," while *Horn Book* dubbed it a "read–aloud comedy." In *Searching for Candlestick Park*, 12–year–old Spencer is trying to find the father who left him and his mom three years before. Sure that his dad works for the San Francisco Giants, Spencer sets off on his bicycle from Seattle, accompanied by his cat, Foxey. Lauren Peterson noted in *Booklist* that Spencer's "honesty and integrity are repeatedly tested" in this "fast–paced, exciting adventure." A *Kirkus Reviews* contributor commented that "Spencer's impulsive escapade may give readers infatuated with the notion of running way some second thoughts."

With *Earthquake Terror,* Kehret returned to her more familiar thriller format. When an earthquake destroys the only bridge to the mainland from the tiny island where Jonathan and his disabled sister Abby are staying, the young boy is pitted against nature. With no food or supplies, and unable to contact help, Jonathan must single–handedly save Abby, his dog, and himself. With displaced waters from the quake beginning to flood the island, the clock is ticking on Jonathan's efforts. "It will be a rare thriller fan who won't want to see what happens," Zvirin commented in her *Booklist* review. Roger Sutton, writing in the *Bulletin of the Center for Children's Books,* noted that Kehret's "focus on the action is tight and involving," while Elaine E. Knight concluded in *School Library Journal* that "Jonathan is a sympathetic and realistic character," and that this "exciting tale is a fine choice for most collections."

Kehret has also authored several titles in the "Frightmare" series, a competitor to the popular "Goosebumps" books. Kehret's books feature friends Rosie and Kayo who get involved in all manner of adventures and mysteries, from solving a kidnaping in Arizona in *Desert Danger* to solving a possible poisoning in *Don't Go Near Mrs. Tallie* to discovering vandals in the school with the help of a pet in *Bone Breath and the Vandals.* Using youthful protagonists Warren and Betsy, Kehret has also employed time travel to set up thrilling stories, as in *The Volcano Disaster,* in which Warren must survive the eruption of Mount St. Helens. *Booklist's* Peterson, reviewing *Bone Breath and the Vandals,* noted that "Kehret delivers some likable characters and a thrilling plot that won't disappoint suspense fans."

Nonfiction and a Memoir

Nonfiction for children has also received the Kehret touch. Of her several books of monologues for young actors, one of the most popular is *Acting Natural: Monologs, Dialogs, and Playlets for Teens.* "A wide range of topics is addressed in this sourcebook of 60 original scenes and monologues," noted

MY BROTHER MADE ME DO IT

P E G   K E H R E T

In letters to her elderly pen pal Mrs. Kaplan, preteen Julie reveals how her usually affectionate but sometimes exasperating relationship with her younger brother helps sustain her while she battles juvenile rheumatoid arthritis in Kehret's 2000 novel.

Dianne G. Mahony in *School Library Journal.* Donna Houser commented in *Voice of Youth Advocates* that "all sections have their own merit because they deal with problems that are relevant to today's youth."

Kehret details her own battle with the paralyzing after–effects of polio in her award–winning *Small Steps: The Year I Got Polio.* "This heartfelt memoir takes readers back to 1949 when the author, at age 12, contracted polio," noted Zvirin in *Booklist.* Kehret describes the progress of the illness, the paralysis, and her slow recovery. Christine A. Moesch concluded in *School Library Journal* that Kehret's memoir was an "honest and well–done book." Yet another nonfiction title is Kehret's *Shelter Dogs*, stories of dogs that found a second life after being taken from Humane Society shelters. A *Kirkus Reviews* critic called the book "an amiable collection of short anecdotes," concluding that there was "a ready audience to cry over and gasp at the tale behind every dog."

Kehret returned to children's suspense fiction with the novels *I'm Not Who You Think I Am* and *Don't Tell Anyone*. In the latter title, twelve–year–old Megan cares for a group of feral cats living in a field near her home. When she learns that the land is slated for development, she inadvertently places herself in danger by trying to stop the construction and save the cats. *School Library Journal* critic Julie Ventura praised the book as "a great story with intriguing plot twists and plenty of action." *Booklist* reviewer Debbie Carton noted that Kehret's numerous subplots "all hang together," and that the author delivers a "happy, satisfying ending" to Megan's adventures. Ginger, the young protagonist of *I'm Not Who You Think I Am*, is stalked by psychiatric patient Joyce Enderly, who believes that the girl is her daughter. Ginger's troubles with Joyce are compounded by problems at school—she has information that may help her favorite teacher keep his job, but the evidence could hurt her family's business. Assessing the mystery in *Booklist*, Helen Rosenberg observed that "Kehret skillfully weaves together these two story lines, providing an ending that is both exciting and suspenseful."

If you enjoy the works of Peg Kehret, you might want to check out the following books:

Terence Blacker, *Homebird*, 1993.
Madeleine L'Engle, *Many Waters*, 1986.
Gloria Skurzynski and Alane Ferguson, *Rage of Fire*, 1998.
R. L. Stine, *The First Horror*, 1994.

Kehret has amassed a large body of work and a legion of loyal fans—both girls and boys—for her middle–grade thrillers. Blending exciting action, likable characters, and hi–lo language, Kehret writes books that lead her readers on to more difficult fiction and nonfiction. As she reported in an online source, "I do what I love and get paid for it. It's fun to use my creativity and I like being my own boss. Writing is hard work, but when one of my books wins an award, it's worth it."

■ Biographical and Critical Sources

BOOKS

Science Fiction and Fantasy Literature, 1975–1991, Gale, 1992.

PERIODICALS

Booklist, September 15, 1989, Denise M. Wilms, review of *Nightmare Mountain*, p. 184; February 15, 1990, p. 1166; May 15, 1992, p. 1672; September 1, 1992, Chris Sherman, review of *Horror at the Haunted House*, pp. 56, 60; September 1, 1994, p. 41; December 1, 1994, Stephanie Zvirin, review of *Danger at the Fair*, p. 664; May 1, 1995, Lauren Peterson, review of *Bone Breath and the Vandals*, p. 1573; October 1, 1995, p. 314; January 1, 1996, S. Zvirin, review of *Earthquake Terror*, p. 834; November 1, 1996, S. Zvirin, review of *Small Steps: The Year I Got Polio*, pp. 492–93; August, 1997, L. Peterson, review of *Searching for Candlestick Park*, p. 1901; August, 1998, p. 2005; March 1, 1999, Helen Rosenberg, review of *I'm Not Who You Think I Am*, p. 1202; June 1, 2000, Carolyn Phelan, review of *My Brother Made Me Do It*, p. 1892; August, 2000, Debbie Carton, review of *Don't Tell Anyone*, p. 2140.

Bulletin of the Center for Children's Books, February, 1995, pp. 202–203; March, 1996, Roger Sutton, review of *Earthquake Terror*, p. 231; November, 1996, pp. 100–101; November, 1997, pp. 88–89.

Horn Book, spring, 1995, review of *The Richest Kids in Town*, p. 78.

Kirkus Reviews, March 1, 1987, review of *Deadly Stranger*, p. 373; August 15, 1994, review of *The Richest Kids in Town*, p. 1131; June 1, 1997, review of *Searching for Candlestick Park*, p. 874; April 1, 1999, review of *Shelter Dogs: Amazing Stories of Adopted Strays*, p. 535.

Kliatt, July, 1993, p. 10; March, 1997, p. 40.

Publishers Weekly, March 22, 1999, review of *I'm Not Who You Think I Am*, p. 93.

School Library Journal, October, 1989, Jeanette Larson, review of *Nightmare Mountain*, p. 120; March, 1990, Bruce Anne Shook, review of *Sisters, Long Ago*, pp. 218–19; June, 1991, Sylvia V. Meisner, review of *Cages*, p. 126; August, 1992, Dianne G. Mahony, review of *Acting Natural: Monologs, Dia-*

logs, and Playlets for Teens, p. 182; September, 1994, p. 218; May, 1995, p. 108; December, 1995, p. 104; February, 1996, Elaine E. Knight, review of *Earthquake Terror*, p. 100; November, 1996, Christine A. Moesch, review of *Small Steps: The Year I Got Polio*, p. 114; July, 1998, p. 96; September, 2000, Sharon McNeil, review of *My Brother Made Me Do It*, p. 232; April, 2000, Julie Ventura, review of *Don't Tell Anyone*, p. 138.

Voice of Youth Advocates, June, 1991, Andrea Davidson, review of *Cages*, pp. 97–98; June, 1992, Donna Houser, review of *Acting Natural: Monologs, Dialogs, and Playlets for Teens*, pp. 126–27; October, 1992, D. Houser, review of *Horror at the Haunted House*, p. 224; February, 1996, p. 373

ONLINE

Kids Love Books by Peg Kehret Web site, http://www.pegkehret.com (April 15, 1999).

—*Sketch by J. Sydney Jones*

A. C. LeMieux

▪ Personal

Born Anne Connelly, December 15, 1954 in Bridge-port, CT; daughter of John D., Sr. and Elizabeth (Magee) Connelly; married Charles P. LeMieux III, January 7, 1977 (divorced April, 1996); married Timothy D. Pocock, May, 1997; children: Sarah Elizabeth, Brendan Wolfe. *Education:* Simmons College, B.A., 1976; attended University of Bridgeport School of Music, 1976–78. *Politics:* Democrat. *Religion:* Roman Catholic. *Hobbies and other interests:* Music, acoustic fingerstyle guitar, sailing, golf.

▪ Addresses

Home—490 Pequot Ct., Southport CT 06490. *Agent*—Fran Lebowitz, Writer's House, 21 West 26th St., New York, NY 10010. *E–mail*—Swan522@aol.com.

▪ Career

Freelance journalist, 1982–87; writer, 1987—. Co-founder and co–moderator of the Children's Writer's Chat on America Online.

▪ Member

Authors Guild, Authors League of America, Society of Children's Book Writers and Illustrators, Williams Syndrome Association.

▪ Awards, Honors

Best Book for Young Adults, American Library Association, 1994, and nominated for Garden State Teen Book Award, 1996, both for *The TV Guidance Counselor;* Children's choice, International Reading Association, 1994, for *Super Snoop Sam Snout: The Case of the Missing Marble;* Notable Book, Society of School Librarians International, and Silver Honors Award, Parents' Choice, both 1995, both for *Do Angels Sing the Blues?; Fruit Flies, Fish and Fortune Cookies* was named to the Sequoya Young Adult Master List by the Oklahoma Library Association, 1996–97.

▪ Writings

The TV Guidance Counselor, Tambourine, 1993.
Super Snoop Sam Snout: The Case of the Yogurt Poker, Avon, 1994.
Super Snoop Sam Snout: The Case of the Stolen Snowman, Avon, 1994.
Super Snoop Sam Snout: The Case of the Missing Marble, Avon, 1994.

Fruit Flies, Fish and Fortune Cookies, illustrated by Diane de Groat, Tambourine, 1994.

Do Angels Sing the Blues?, Tambourine, 1995.

Dare to Be, M.E.!, Avon, 1997.

Fairy Lair: A Special Place, Aladdin, 1997.

Fairy Lair: A Hidden Place, Aladdin, 1998.

Fairy Lair: A Magic Place, Aladdin, 1998.

All the Answers, Avon, 2000.

Contributor to anthologies, including a poem to *Food Fight,* Harcourt, 1996, a short story, "Just Say . . .," to *New Year, New Love,* Avon, 1996, *My America: A Poetry Atlas of the United States,* Simon & Schuster, 2000. Contributor to *Family Issues* volume of the "Using Literature to Help Troubled Teens" series, edited by Joan Katwell, Greenwood Press, 1999. Author of unpublished screenplays, including *Music of the Sphere, The TV Guidance Counselor,* and *Mulligans.*

■ Work in Progress

Jester's Quest, Lovespeed, and *Brewtopia,* young adult novels, *Sea–Sar Salad,* a poetry collection, and *Being and Becoming: Journeying Though Life with a Special Child,* adult nonfiction.

■ Sidelights

"For me, writing is a process of finding connections," A. C. LeMieux once commented. "It's not only connecting words, but connecting ideas, symbols, events—and connecting them all to people." LeMieux further elaborated on the act of writing in *ALAN Review:* "If I had to characterize the core of my writing process, I'd describe it as making connections. Connecting small graphic symbols into groupings which carry meaning. Connecting words into ordered strings which hopefully compound the meaning. Connecting sentences until the constructs of language are as laden with meaning as I can make them—ideas, events, symbols, all connected to character—the whole hopefully forming a conduit for human meaning, leading to a reader, the final connection." In this "final connection," LeMieux has been eminently successful, attracting loyal teenage and preteen readers for problem novels like *The TV Guidance Counselor,* which deals with teen depression and suicide, and *Do Angels Sing the Blues?,* which looks at the impact of the death of a friend. LeMieux also employs humor to connect her readers to lighter novels such as *Fruit Flies, Fish and Fortune Cookies* and its sequel, *Dare to Be, M.E.!,* and to

the comedy–laden *All the Answers.* Or perhaps LeMieux connects with a younger audience with her trio of easy to read mysteries featuring "Super Snoop Sam Snout," or with early middle grade readers into fantasy with her "Fairy Lair" trilogy. With all of her books, LeMieux follows the edict of the British writer, E. M. Forster: "only connect." "I interpret this," LeMieux wrote in *ALAN Review,* "as a call to unite our ideals with our daily efforts and second, as a call to reach out and cultivate relationship."

Born in Fairfield, Connecticut, in 1954, LeMieux was the second oldest of seven children—six boys and one girl. Growing up with so many boys around inevitably led to a deeper understanding of the young male psyche and may, as LeMieux once commented, "have contributed to the fact that I often write from a boy's point of view." An avid reader as a child, she would often run out of her own titles and have to borrow one of her brothers' more guy–oriented tales. Something of a tomboy, she and the rest of the neighborhood congregated at the local golf course, sledding on the fairways in the winter and dodging golf balls in the summer, and generally using the space like a giant backyard.

As a seventh grader, LeMieux first ventured into novel writing, "a neighborhood saga called *From My Porch,*" as she once stated. "It was one of those tell–all exposes, written from the point of view of a crow who spied on all the neighborhood kids, and it got more than a few people mad at me when Sister Robert Ann read it out loud to the English class at school." In high school LeMieux read Harper Lee's *To Kill a Mockingbird,* and studying it with her freshman English teacher is what LeMieux credits as being most influential in making her a writer herself. "Immersed in the story, I first encountered a living concept of justice in the unshakable ethics of the gentle Atticus Finch," LeMieux noted in the *ALAN Review.* "I first realized the complexity of morality, and the decisions we face, and the choices we must make, witnessing, through Scout's perception, the renegade against–the–rules heroism of Boo Radley." Already a patient observer as a teenager, LeMieux filed away one character she encountered for future use. While working after school as a cashier in a supermarket, she observed one young man who came into the store continually, went to the magazine rack, and then skimmed through the pages of *TV Guide* with a worried look on his face. For two years the young man did this, without ever buying the magazine. Much later LeMieux would use this character in her first young adult novel, *The TV Guidance Counselor.*

Attending Simmons College in Boston, LeMieux majored in writing and minored in illustration. Intimidated by the idea of writing fiction, she stuck with nonfiction and journalism, publishing an article on Arthurian legends while still in college. Graduating from Simmons in 1976, she went on to study music for two years at the Bridgeport School of Music. Married in 1977, she soon had a daughter. In the 1980s, LeMieux worked part time as a freelancer, writing about sailing and music. "Doing freelance journalism, I also learned another important writing rule: writing is rewriting," LeMieux once commented. With the birth of a son in 1987, LeMieux finally felt she had lived enough and experienced enough to actually have something to say in fiction. To that end, she signed up for a children's book writing course at Fairfield University; after a dozen manuscripts and five years of slogging away at the writing process, LeMieux finally published her first work, *The TV Guidance Counselor.*

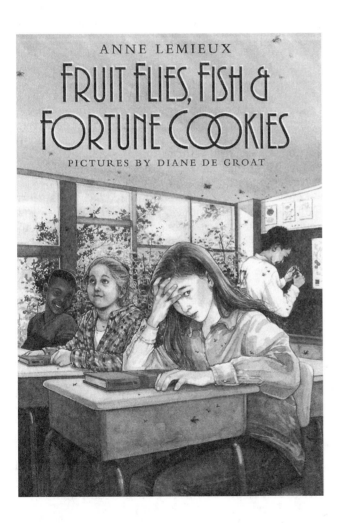

Mary Ellen is convinced that her spurt of bad luck—not only is she sprayed by a skunk, but her best friend in the whole world is moving to France—is caused by a fortune cookie in this 1994 novel.

A Published Writer

The narrator of LeMieux's first novel, seventeen–year–old Michael Madden, relates the events that led to his suicide attempt and hospitalization. Employing both flashbacks and conversations with his psychiatrist, Michael tells the reader about his parent's divorce which turned his life upside down, and his ultimate withdrawal from society. Michael and his mother live much less affluently than they had when his photographer father was part of the family. Michael takes a job at a supermarket to help out, and here he comes across the "guidance counselor" of the title, dubbed so by his best friend, Ricky. LeMieux made this character a central metaphor of her first novel. Soon Michael is taking more and more photos with a camera his father once gave him and discovers he has a real talent for photography. Despite his new hobby, encouraged by the photography teacher, Mr. Dorio, and the attentions of a girlfriend, Melissa, Michael becomes increasingly withdrawn and is finally a victim to sadness and despair which, in the end, brings him to a near–fatal jump off a bridge.

"That such an ordinary young man can find himself plunging off a bridge will shock readers," observed a contributor for *Kirkus Reviews.* However, this same writer felt that the first–person narration "offers enough insights into Michael's world, and into the depth of his feelings, to make his actions comprehensible," and concluded that this was a "well–wrought first novel." A writer for *Publishers Weekly* applauded LeMieux for her excellent handling of "adolescent anguish," saying "this first novel admirably explores a young man's injured soul." While criticizing LeMieux for having Michael recite "adult pop psychology," Kathy Piehl, in *School Library Journal,* nevertheless commended the author for creating a character with "an authentic teen voice" and "masterfully depict[ing] various aspects of depression." Reviewing this debut novel in *Booklist,* Karen Hutt wrote that readers would "appreciate Michael's vulnerability and understand his despondency," while the first–person narration "will sweep them into the goings–on."

LeMieux's next novel, the 1994 *Fruit Flies, Fish and Fortune Cookies,* deals with teen and preteen issues of a less serious nature. One evening, Mary Ellen Bobowick has the misfortune of eating a fortune cookie which warns, "Reflect carefully, or your deeds will bring bad luck." Shrugging off the ominous prediction, Mary Ellen notices that suddenly nothing seems to go her way: she shatters her mother's antique mirror, gets sprayed by a skunk, and learns that her best friend is moving to France for a year. After she drops a jar of fruit flies at school on

Career Day, Mary Ellen becomes convinced that the cookie was telling the truth. However, Mary Ellen's luck eventually improves, and she even finds a new boyfriend. Leslie Barban, in *School Library Journal,* called *Fruit Flies, Fish and Fortune Cookies* a "light-hearted, funny novel" and enjoyed LeMieux's "believable, likable . . . characters." Carolyn Phelan, writing in *Booklist,* maintained that some of the minor characters in the story "are not well developed," but added that Mary Ellen is an "easily identifiable" heroine for middle–grade readers.

"For me, writing is a process of finding connections. It's not only connecting words, but connecting ideas, symbols, events—and connecting them all to people."

—A. C. LeMieux

LeMieux has also written a trio of easy to read mysteries featuring "Super Snoop Sam Snout" which earned a place on the International Reading Association Children's Book Choice List. However, in 1995, she returned to a world where teenagers must overcome more serious problems in their lives with *Do Angels Sing the Blues?* "I knew I wanted the book to be about the death of a best friend," LeMieux once stated. "My own best friend, who grew up across the street from me in my neighborhood, died when I was twenty–six. And I knew I wanted the book to be about music. I was listening to Stevie Ray Vaughan one day, singing 'Life Without You,' and that's when the connection clicked: I knew that the music in the book had to be the blues." The result is a book about friendship, a story of love and loss, and also a musical tale all told from the point of view of a sixteen–year–old narrator, James "Boog" Buglioni.

Boog recounts the events of one year in high school and his friendship with Theodore Haley Stone, his buddy since grade school. Together Boog and Theo formed a band called "Blues Thing," and the two are basically inseparable until the advent of Carey Harrigan. Seeing her one day in Mrs. Brockmeyer's class, Theo falls instantly in love with her, and then everything changes between Boog and Theo. A depressive girl from a troubled family, Carey forms an unlikely triangle with Theo and Boog at first. She begins writing lyrics for the band, and for a time

Boog and Carey try to get along well together. Pressure plays on the triangle when Theo gets into trouble in a bid to protect Carey, caught drinking at school. Grounded, Theo cannot play in the local "Battle of the Bands." Carey subsequently runs away when she learns that old family friends have died in a fire. Boog and Theo go looking for her and find her alongside the road. Crossing the misty road to get Carey a hot chocolate at a shop, Theo is hit by a passing car and killed. Boog cannot forgive Carey for what he sees as her responsibility for his buddy's death; he confronts her at the funeral, where she is drunk. Thereafter, he leaves his music behind and spends the summer tucked away in his room. Finally, letters from Theo's mother and from Carey give him some perspective on the incidents and allow him to put the death of Theo behind him and forgive Carey.

Again, critics generally responded favorably to LeMieux's problem novel. Although criticizing the slightly heavy–handed foreshadowing of Theo's death, Renee Steinberg in *School Library Journal* believed that LeMieux created teenagers who "can deal with unexpected tragedy" in a way that is neither condescending or unbelievable. Maeve Visser Knoth in *Horn Book Magazine* complimented LeMieux for the emotional depth of her characters, describing Boog and Theo as "sympathetic, richly drawn characters with human complexities," and concluding that LeMieux presented "an emotional but never maudlin story of tragedy and growth." "LeMieux writes well," commented *Booklist*'s Merri Monks, "evoking some favorite teen fantasies in a believable first–person male voice." A reviewer for *Publishers Weekly* felt that *Do Angels Sing the Blues?* surpassed LeMieux's first novel "in its power and sensitivity," and was an "absorbing exploration of adolescent hopes, dreams and vulnerability" which "contains undertones as resonant and melancholy as a blues melody."

Such resonance is not a matter of chance in LeMieux's books. "Especially in the early stages of a book," LeMieux once commented, "I often feel my way into a story with a pen—I see what it's about as it emerges on the page. I write all my drafts longhand, then edit them into the word processor. Using the computer actually seems to activate a different part of my 'writing brain'—a part that's as tuned into the sounds of language as the sense itself, and that thinks hypertextually, associatively. In fact, I write all my poetry directly on the computer.

"I find the act of writing to be a process of exploration and discovery. Much of the 'think–work' I do as a writer involves asking questions and postulating answers. When I sit down to write the first draft of the story, I consider two things: what is going to happen, a general plot, but even more important, to whom it is going to happen. I spend a lot of time getting to know my characters, who they are, what they're like, how they think, so that they really do take on a life of their own inside my head. Parts of me wind up in all my characters, both male and female, adult and young people."

Laughter is the Best Medicine

LeMieux lets laughter do the work in her sequel to *Fruit Flies, Fish and Fortune Cookies,* the 1997 *Dare to Be, M.E.!.* Reprising the gang from *Fruit Flies,* LeMieux brings Mary Ellen to stage center, initially saddened by the departure of friend Ben just before the start of the seventh grade. However, Mary Ellen soon has something to be happy about when she learns that another friend is coming back into her life. Recently returned from Paris where her parents split up, Justine is having difficulty re–adjusting to her old life. She insists on dieting, even though she does not need to lose weight, and obsesses about her looks. Only slowly does Mary Ellen come to understand that her friend's obsession with dieting is really a sickness—bulimia. Touching on issues from nose rings to peer pressure and body image, the book follows Mary Ellen and Justine through a difficult readjustment until Justine is finally willing to admit her problem and see a therapist.

"In a story filled with subplots and modeled behavior, LeMieux offers a primer for students entering junior high," wrote a contributor for *Kirkus Reviews,* who also felt that "the lessons slide down easily." *Booklist*'s Ilene Cooper thought that even though some of the writing in *Dare to Be, M.E.!* was "cliched," and despite an over–easy resolution, "the story does bring the issue of eating disorders to the forefront . . . ." A *Publishers Weekly* reviewer also commented on the "issues–oriented" nature of the story, touching on eating disorders, body image and other "sources and symptoms of preteen angst."

With *All the Answers,* LeMieux once again let laughter do the work for her in a preteen novel. Witty, eighth–grade Jason at first appears to have all the answers, except for those that he desperately needs to pass algebra class. His stressed–out dad is becoming alienated from wise–cracking Jason, and at school things are not going so rosy outside of algebra class, either. The arrival of twins, Philip and Phelicia, is putting another strain on Jason's life: Philip is something of a bully to Jason, both on the basketball court and off, and the beautiful though shallow Phelicia becomes the object of Jason's flirt-

Inspired by a song by blues performer Stevie Ray Vaughan, LeMieux's 1995 novel finds high school buddies Theo and Boog at odds when a troubled young woman threatens both their garage band and their friendship.

ing attentions. Things come to a head when Jason pays a friend to copy her math homework and then must face the wrath of his teacher when she finds out about the cheating.

Reviewing the novel in *Publishers Weekly,* a contributor noted that male and female readers alike would find Jason "both likable and authentic; his incessant string of wisecracks would make any standup comic envious." A writer for *Kirkus Reviews* found the novel "[b]riskly engaging though strictly skin deep," with LeMieux's narrative "consistently amusing and peppered with witty dialogue." *Booklist*'s Shelle Rosenfeld also noted LeMieux's "snappy dialogue," but felt in addition that Jason's troubles "are insightfully portrayed," and that the "well–written novel champions the value of honesty and integrity."

The versatile LeMieux has also penned a trilogy of fantasy novels aimed at early middle grade readers. Her "Fairy Lair" novels take readers on a magical trip to a fairy glade, featuring Sylvia and Dana who learn with bitter results that man can upset the fragile balance of the fairy realm. Additionally, LeMieux has written poetry and short stories that have been anthologized in young adult story collections.

If you enjoy the works of A. C. LeMieux, you might want to check out the following books:

Hadley Irwin, *Can't Hear you Listening,* 1990.
Eloise McGraw, *The Moorchild,* 1996.
Leslea Newman, *Fat Chance,* 1994.
Lee Robinson, *Gateway,* 1996.

"As a writer, I think of myself as a miner of life," LeMieux once observed, "digging for meaning, for raw ore to refine into characters of genuine mettle, and forge into building blocks to create a world. My aim is to produce work that will be so genuinely evocative of and so true to life, that a reader will experience it as real." In *ALAN Review* she expounded on her use of humor in her books. "How to connect with today's adolescent readers by means of laughter and literature?" she wrote. "As a writer, my foremost aim is to write with honesty, and without condescension, with humor which encompasses the paradoxes, incongruities, and even absurdities of life. My hope is that my characters' voices will catch kids' attention, and connect with their hearts, and that my stories might help expand their emotional vocabularies. I believe a writer can be an agent of connection. . . ."

■ Biographical and Critical Sources

PERIODICALS

ALAN Review, spring, 1998, A. C. LeMieux, "The Problem Novel in a Conservative Age"; winter, 2000, Anne C. LeMieux, "Only Connect," pp. 11–16.

Booklist, December 15, 1993, Karen Hutt, review of *The TV Guidance Counselor,* p. 746; March 15, 1994, p. 1358; November 1, 1994, Carolyn Phelan, review of *Fruit Flies, Fish and Fortune Cookies,* p. 497; September 1, 1995, Merri Monks, review of *Do Angels Sing the Blues?,* p. 66; June 1 & 15, 1997, Ilene Cooper, review of *Dare to Be, M.E.!,* p. 1703; January 1 & 15, 2000, Shelle Rosenfeld, review of *All the Answers,* p. 906.

Bulletin of the Center for Children's Books, October, 1993, p. 50; February, 2000, p. 213.

Horn Book, November–December, 1995, Maeve Visser Knoth, review of *Do Angels Sing the Blues?,* p. 746.

Horn Book Guide, fall, 1997, p. 304.

Kirkus Reviews, August 15, 1993, review of *The TV Guidance Counselor,* p. 1075; November 15, 1994, p. 1534; July 1, 1995, p. 949; May 15, 1997, review of *Dare to Be, M.E.!,* p. 802; December 1, 1999, review of *All the Answers,* p. 1887.

Kliatt, January, 1995, p. 9; November, 1996, p. 9.

Publishers Weekly, July 12, 1993, review of *The TV Guidance Counselor,* p. 81; July 10, 1995, review of *Do Angels Sing the Blues?,* p. 58; June 2, 1997, review of *Dare to Be, M.E.!,* p. 73; January 17, 2000, review of *All the Answers,* p. 57.

School Library Journal, October, 1993, Kathy Piehl, review of *The TV Guidance Counselor,* p. 151; October, 1994, Leslie Barban, review of *Fruit Flies, Fish and Fortune Cookies,* p. 124; September, 1995, Renee Steinberg, review of *Do Angels Sing the Blues?,* p. 219; June, 1997, p. 94; July, 1997, p. 94; February, 2000, p. 122.

Voice of Youth Advocates, February, 1994, p. 370; August, 1995, p. 160.

—Sketch by J. Sydney Jones

Leonardo da Vinci

■ Personal

Born Leonardo di Ser Piero da Vinci, in Vinci, Italy, April 15, 1452; died in Amboise, France, May 2, 1519.

■ Career

Probably studied with Verrocchio in Florence, Italy, c. 1470–77; member of the Florence guild, 1472; lived in Verrocchio's house, 1476; set up studio, late 1470s; worked for Ludovico Sforza in Milan, c. 1482–99 on both artistic and scientific projects (including a bronze horseman, not completed); worked in Florence, 1500–06; worked for Louis XII of France, 1507–19, as painter and engineer. *Exhibitions:* A major collection of da Vinci's work is located in Paris, France. Other collections are located in Cracow, Poland; Florence, Italy; Leningrad, Russia; London, England; Milan, Italy; Münich, Germany; the Vatican; and Washington, DC.

■ Writings

I manoscritti e i disegni di Leonardo, seven volumes, edited by Adolfo Venturi, [Italy], 1928–52.

Literary Works, two volumes, edited by J. P. Richter, commentary by Carlo Pedretti, University of California Press (Berkeley, CA), 1977.

Notebooks, two volumes, edited by J. P. Richter, Peter Smith Publisher, Inc. (Magnolia, MA), 1970.

Paragone: A Comparison of the Arts, edited by Irma A. Richter, Oxford University Press (New York), 1949.

Scritti scelti, edited by Anna Maria Brizio, [Italy], 1952, 1966.

Treatise on Painting, two volumes, edited by L. H. Heydenreich and A. Philip McMahon, Princeton University Press, 1956.

Fragments at Windsor Castle from the Codex Atlanticus, edited by Carlo Pedretti, Phaidon Press (London), 1957.

The Madrid Codices of Leonardo da Vinci, translated by Ladislao Reti, McGraw–Hill, 1974.

Il Codice Atlantico della Biblioteca Ambrosiana di Milan, twelve volumes, edited by Augusto Marinoni, [Italy], 1975–80.

I pensieri, edited by Bruno Mardini, [Italy], 1977.

■ Sidelights

Often hailed as the archetypal Renaissance Man, a creative genius equally adept at art, engineering, architecture, and invention, Leonardo da Vinci is still perhaps best known for paintings such as the *Mona Lisa* and *The Last Supper.* Though his artistic output was not great, his influence was, and his artistic breakthroughs in perspective and in shading quite literally changed the vision of future painters. Leonardo also wrote a treatise on art and left thousands of pages of drawings on architecture, the human face, botany, physics, engineering, cartography, and anatomy—a rich treasure trove which modern-day researchers still consult. The numerous notebooks Leonardo produced in his lifetime contain not only this wealth of drawing, but also an accompanying spider–like, mirror text that is still being translated five centuries after his death.

"Jack of all trades, master of none," is a criticism often leveled at Leonardo. So talented was the man, that many say he squandered his talents in a relentless search for new forms of self–expression. Indeed, his earliest biographer, the painter–turned–chronicler Giorgio Vasari, had this to say about Leonardo's talents: "He was a man of regal spirit and tremendous breadth of mind" but "he was always setting himself to learn many things only to abandon them almost immediately. . . . He would have made great advances in knowledge and in the foundations of learning had he not been of such a various and changeable nature." It was this mercurial nature that kept Leonardo, for many years after his death, from achieving the same degree of fame as other High Renaissance artists slightly younger than he, such as Michelangelo, Titian, and Raphael. Leonardo had a mind so open to inquiry that it cost him even his greatest artistic creation, *The Last Supper.* In order to work in more detail in this fresco, he invented a new technique, the downside of which is that the fresco began disintegrating not long after it was painted. What is left today in Milan is the cumulative work of generations of restorers.

Only at the turn of the nineteenth century with the re–discovery of his notebooks and their subsequent translation and publication did Leonardo join the ranks of Michelangelo. With a scant twenty–five known paintings to his credit, less than a dozen of which remain today, Leonardo's fame relies upon his drawings and the ten thousand pages of manuscript that are quite literally scattered around the world. If early critics accused him of squandering his artistic talents by his many projects, Leonardo himself, it seemed, could not do otherwise. For Leonardo there could be no art without science; he insisted that the artist should possess knowledge of nature or else he would be a mere draughtsman. His endeavor to create a codified body of scientific knowledge was Herculean, his accomplishments astounding.

Florentine Upbringing

Born on April 15, 1452, just west of Florence in the village of Vinci, Leonardo was the illegitimate son of Ser Piero da Vinci, a well–known notary in Florence. He was brought up in the home of his father, otherwise childless until Leonardo was well into his twenties. Many writers have made much of Leonardo's illegitimacy, but the fact is that Renaissance Italy was surprisingly open about such matters. "Leonardo had all the advantages and disadvantages of an only child in a well–to–do family," wrote R. Langton Douglas in *Leonardo da Vinci: His Life and Pictures.* "He was good looking, and had unusual physical strength and a quick intelligence. It cannot be doubted that he was a spoiled child, the idol of his grandmother, and perhaps even of his childless stepmother." Douglas went on to postulate that this only child upbringing could have been responsible for Leonardo's later nature, growing bored with one toy or project before it was brought to a conclusion and forever moving on to the next. "Leonardo was the victim of a fickle sincerity," wrote Douglas. "And this failing grew with the years."

A talent in drawing resulted in an apprenticeship to Andrea del Verrocchio, a personal friend of Leonardo's father and one of the bright lights of Florentine art at the time, a sculptor, painter, and goldsmith. Leonardo was a teenager when his family moved from Vinci to Florence and he entered Verrocchio's workshop. He studied with Verrocchio for several years, learning the fundamentals of painting and sculpting. In 1472, Leonardo was entered in the painter's guild in Florence and four years later was still mentioned as Verrocchio's assistant. One of his earliest known public works was the painting of the kneeling angel in Verrocchio's *Baptism of Christ,* now at the Uffizi Museum in Florence. Already as a young man, Leonardo was known for his talent in illustrating skin, draperies, animal fur, and plant foliage. His first complete painting, the Uffizi *Annunciation,* done while still an apprentice for Verrocchio, shows Leonardo's characteristic soft focus background accomplished with a bluish misty light on the horizon. His skill with drapery, foliage and with metaphor are also fully developed in this early painting. "In spite of certain faults," wrote the art critic Kenneth Clark in his *Leonardo da Vinci,* "the 'Annunciation' remains a lovely and original picture, in which shortcomings of composition are outweighed by beauties of detail and of mood." Clark further commented, "No other work of Leonardo does so much to support Vasari's account of his early sympathy with nature. . . . Leonardo has given to his flowers and grasses something of the turbulence he felt to be the essence of nature."

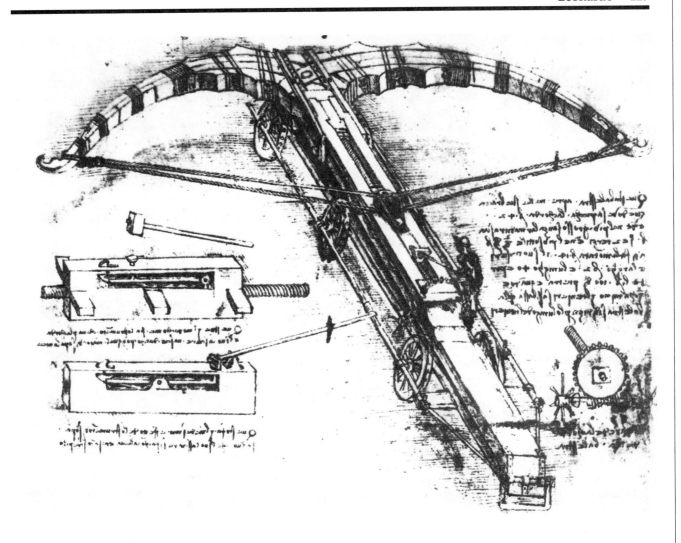

This rendering of a giant mechanical crossbow, developed in the 1490s while the artist lived in Milan, was published in da Vinci's *Codex Atlanicus,* c. 1500.

Shortly after this time, Leonardo completed his first portrait, that of a young Florentine woman, Ginevra de'Benci. The portrait of the same name now hangs in the National Gallery in Washington, D.C., "the best preserved of all Leonardo's early pictures," according to Clark, who went on to observe that "this pale young woman has become one of the memorable personalities of the Renaissance," and was something of a foreshadowing—especially in the mysterious dark trees in the background—of his much more famous portrait of a woman, the *Mona Lisa.*

In 1478 Leonardo set up his own studio and his first major commission was for an altar–piece for the Chapel of Saint Bernard in Florence, but it was—as became characteristic of Leonardo—never completed. The *Benois Madonna,* a painting of the Virgin and baby Jesus, comes from this same period. In 1481, Leonardo received a second altarpiece commission, likewise never finished. The unfinished painting, however, *Adoration of the Magi,* is among his most famous works. In this painting he joins mere linear perspective with the perspective of clarity—in which more distant objects have a less distinct outline—and of color—in which distant objects appear more uniformly gray in tone. Clark noted that the *Adoration* "is an overture to all Leonardo's work, full of themes that will recur." Though left unfinished, the *Adoration of the Magi* with its ambitious sixty–seven characters and complex structure, influenced many contemporary painters, including the German, Albrecht Dürer, whose later *Adoration* owed much in content to Leonardo's.

That the *Adoration* was left unfinished by Leonardo is due not totally to his impatient nature, for he was hired away to Milan in 1482. By this time his reputation had been growing in Florence, not only as a painter, but also as a musician, as he was an accomplished composer and lute player. Also, increasingly, scientific, mathematical, and architectural matters were beginning to concern this young man, and it was not only as court artist but also as a skilled military engineer and court architect that Leonardo presented himself to Ludovico Sforza, Duke of Milan.

Milan, 1482–1499

Leonardo's first stay in Milan is perhaps the most creative period of his life. It was during these years that his name became known all over Italy and during which he undertook the greatest number of important works, many of them admittedly left uncompleted. During this period he ceased to be a Florentine painter, but developed his own unique style that later had both its champions and imitators. His first Milanese painting is the altarpiece *Virgin of the Rocks*, in two separate versions, one now found in Paris, and the other in London. Commissioned in 1483, the painting portrays the holy family in a cave or grotto–like setting which in turn serves as a vehicle for Leonardo's use of dimmed light to blur object differentiation. Many art historians and critics have pointed out that this is one of the earliest examples of his use of *sfumato*, or blue and misty shadows along with blurred outlines in the background which serve to bring subjects in the foreground more to prominence and give a slightly mysterious feel to the entire work.

Other important works from this time include the unfinished *St. Jerome*, and *Lady with an Ermine*, which depicted the mistress of the Duke of Milan. There are also *Portrait of a Musician*, and *La belle Ferroniere*, perhaps the portrait of another of Ludovico's mistresses. In all of these Leonardo displays amazingly intricate detail in hair, knots ('vinci' is Italian for 'knot' and the artist loved to play puns on his own name), lace, fur, skin, and garments. He was also one of the first painters to strive, in his portraits, to bring out the personality of his subjects, emphasizing unique physical qualities in each. But by far the most important work of these Milanese years was *The Last Supper,* a fresco for the refectory of a convent in Milan.

Begun in about 1493, *The Last Supper* has been called by some the high point of Renaissance art. The art historian and Leonardo expert, Martin Kemp, writing in the *Grove* art encyclopedia on–line, noted that it was "[h]ailed originally as a triumph of illusionistic naturalism," but that "it may now be described as the most famous wreck in the history of art." Leonardo demanded a wider range of artistic effects than could be achieved with normal fresco technique in which the artist painted onto fresh plaster. Using a method similar to tempera painting on panel and employing a layering effect, Leonardo all but insured the temporality of his masterwork: it started crumbling, chipping, and fading within his own lifetime. Continually renovated by an assortment of artists over the years, a restoration campaign was begun in 1980 to get back to the original of Leonardo. However, by the end of the restoration in 1999, it was found that in some large areas only scattered bits of the original paint was left. Yet, according to Kemp, "Even in its unhappy state, the grandeur and ingenuity of the conception of *The Last Supper* remain discernible."

Entire books have been written on this one painting, notable among which is that by Ludwig H. Heydenreich, *Leonardo: The Last Supper.* Heydenreich observed that *The Last Supper* "stands supreme among" artworks which have "entered into the general consciousness and become, in a certain sense, the spiritual possession of the whole world." Heydenreich further commented, "The perfection of the work lies not only in the formal or purely artistic merits of the composition, but also in Leonardo's expressive mastery, in his deeply human and profoundly felt exposition of the subject." The subject, in this case, is the final supper with Jesus and the apostles. In contrast to traditional depictions of the subject in earlier paintings, Leonardo's *Supper* is full of movement and action. The twelve apostles are reacting to the prophetic words of Jesus: "One of you will betray me." The apostles are broken into four groups of three with Jesus in the middle of them. In Leonardo's painting, the apostles are individual personalities, displaying anger, despair, and horror at Christ's prediction of betrayal. Jesus is set off serenely from these men, and Judas, who would betray him, sits to his immediate right, isolated from the other two apostles in his group. In addition to this novel patterning of subjects, Leonardo's own sense of atmosphere, color, and surroundings served to make the fresco famous even during the years he was working on it. In terms of composition, Leonardo worked and reworked the trinity metaphor, in his groups of apostles in threes, in the three windows in back of Jesus, in the triangle Christ himself forms with his arms outstretched in front of him. The arch over the window in back forms a symbolic halo over Christ's head; the viewers eyes are drawn into the painting, beyond the turbulence of emotions displayed by the apostles, to Christ at the center, calm and in control. "Unity and drama," ex-

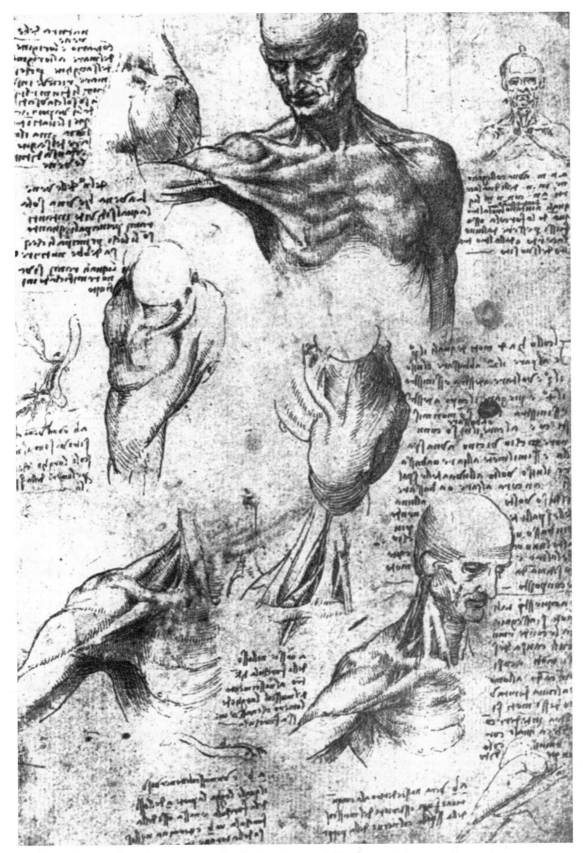

Based on dissections he witnessed, da Vinci's anatomical studies were included in his notebooks which, after resurfacing in the early nineteenth century, have served as valuable resources to generations of art students.

plained Clark, "these are the essential qualities by which Leonardo's 'Last Supper' is distinguished from earlier representations of the subject." Assessing its important not only to art history but to world history as well, Heydenreich wrote: "Thus Leonardo's *Last Supper* is one of the very few pictures of a Christian subject—perhaps the only one—that has become identified with its theme throughout the world. No other version . . . has been able to affect the absolute preeminence of Leonardo's achievement. His work has remained untouched by interdenominational strife and has maintained its effect unimpaired right down to the present."

During this same period, Leonardo also left many drawings for a bronze equestrian statue of the previous Duke of Milan. Though the sculpture was never completed, the huge clay model was said to have been finished. Leonardo did not, however, confine himself solely to artistic concerns alone while in Milan. He also built machinery for pageants and artillery, and was an active architect. His studies included in the notebooks range from anatomy to optics to hydraulics. These notebooks also suggest that Leonardo worked on various architectural and engineering schemes near the birthplace of Ludovico, including the canalization of the region. Assisting the mathematician Luca Pacioli, he helped produce a classic work on geometry, *Divina Proportione*. During these Milan years he also wrote, for the many pupils which he had, large sections of what would later become his *Treatise on Painting*. When the Sforza family was driven from Milan by rival French forces, Leonardo too left this city which had been his home for almost two decades, returning to Florence. His clay model for an equestrian statue was left behind, providing target practice for French archers who ultimately destroyed it.

The Second Florentine and Milanese Periods

Leonardo stayed in Florence from roughly 1500 to 1508 and then went back to Milan again from 1508 to 1513. In Florence he soon entered the service of Cesare Borgia, Duke of Romagna and the son and chief general of Pope Alexander VI. Leonardo was taken on not for his artistic abilities, but as chief architect and engineer to supervise the fortification of central Italy's papal territories, and his work often took Leonardo away from Florence, to Urbino and other cities in central Italy. It appears that, in 1503, he was one of the engineers to take part in the unsuccessful rerouting of the Arno around Pisa, while Florence was at war with that city.

That same year he won a commission for a wall painting of the *Battle of Anghiari*, for the Council Hall in Florence's Palazzo della Signoria, commemo-

rating a Florentine victory over Milan. Though executed and partially finished, it was later painted over and only drawings remain to tease future generations. From copies and sketches, it can be seen that Leonardo was working on the grand scale, in which a group of cavalry skirmish with one another, and horses and men become a swirl of activity. Studied by Raphael, the painting in its day proved very influential with a new generation of artists, setting as Kemp explained, "new standards of figural complexity."

Other works of art from this period include the unfinished *St. John the Baptist* and *Leda and the Swan*, the latter which is lost and known only through copies. But by far the most important work to grow out of this period was the *Mona Lisa*, perhaps "the most famous, most visited, and most studied portrait ever painted," according to G. Aimee Ergas in *Artists: From Michelangelo to Maya Lin*. Millions of words have been written on it; it has inspired lovers and novellas alike and is surely the single most famous painting in the history of art. As well known as the painting is, its origins on the other hand are as mysterious as the background in one of Leonardo's paintings. Some claim that the painting was done as early as 1498, others, including Clark, place it in 1503, while still others say it is a later production. And the subject of the portrait is as shrouded in mystery and controversy as its age. The painting is also known as *La Gioconda*, after the presumed name of the wealthy Florentine who commissioned this painting of his young wife. Others claim it is of Isabelle of Aragon, who might also have been the subject for Leonardo's earlier *La Belle Ferroniere*. Still others suggest it might be of Isabelle d'Este, Duchess of Mantua, one of the great art patrons of the age and a woman who had hounded Leonardo for years to do a portrait of her. Some say a Neapolitan lady; some the Duchess of Francavilla. Some call the painting *Mona Lisa*, after the woman's name, Madonna, or Mona, Lisa del Giocondo; the art historian Kemp calls it *Portrait of a Lady on a Balcony*.

Whatever the year of provenance or the true identity of the subject, the result is a painting that is at once recognizable to a viewer who would not otherwise know an oil painting from a watercolor. The female subject is seen in half–length, seated, turned slightly to her left and gazing outward at the spectator. Two features of her face in particular have been noted over the centuries: her smile, which is either just beginning or just fading, and her eyes, which seem to follow the viewer around the room. Her delicate, finely wrought hands are held in her lap, which may or may not be bulged in early pregnancy. In the background is a dreamlike, misty landscape with a river or body of water situated

This drawing by da Vinci depicts a bust of a Renaissance warrior, his helmet and breastplate decorated with embellishments typical of the period.

among jagged peaks. Writing in *Leonardo: A Portrait of the Renaissance Man*, Roger Whiting noted of this landscape that is "is a masterpiece of the sfumato style, the blending of vague colors and shades to produce a misty appearance." Commenting also on the "delicate streaks of paint in the drapery and landscape" which "underline the sense of identity between the background and the foreground," Whiting further claimed that this reveals the true meaning of the painting: "nothing less than the genesis of the macrocosm and the microcosm, the birth of the world and mankind in the womb of time." This theory is reinforced by several other referents: at the time of painting, Leonardo was busy with anatomical studies which included dissections of a pregnant uterus and drawings of babies in the womb. Additionally, Leonardo believed that the earth came out of the sea, and some historians would argue it is the sea we observe in the background; and finally there is the lady herself in the foreground who is, many agree, pregnant. Leonardo worked on this painting for many years, carrying it with him and adding to it bit by bit. In the end, it, like so many other works of his, was left unfinished.

From 1508 to 1513 Leonardo once again took up residence in Milan, working initially for the French ruler of the city, Charles d'Amboise, under much the same terms as he had for the Sforzas earlier. He provided architectural plans and designs for court entertainments and also worked on a second bronze equestrian statue, this one life–sized, a plan which came far short of completion. During this period in Milan his interests turned solidly to scientific matters, and his anatomical drawings of the human skeletal and musculature systems are some of the most outstanding of his complete oeuvre of drawings. He also continued his studies on water in motion and extended this to the flow of blood in the human body. His fascination with flight led to the design of numerous flying machines, including a prototype of the helicopter; military designs included an early tank, a submarine, and a weapon that resembled what would later be the machine gun. These were all accompanied by meticulous notes in mirror writing, perhaps more a result of Leonardo's left–handedness than of any purely secretive nature.

During his second Milan period, Leonardo also produced a piece of art that is considered among his masterworks, *Virgin and Child and St. Anne* from 1510. Here again is the prototypical Leonardesque style: the beatific women in foreground, one behind the other with Anne bending to her right to hold the infant Jesus who in turn holds onto the sacrificial lamb. There is also the delicate working of fabric and intricate details in nature so typical of the mature Leonardo style, and in the background are the mysterious depths of perspective achieved by line and color. Clark in his study of Leonardo contended that only the background coloring was actually from the hand of Leonardo; again the painting is left unfinished with the drapery covering the Virgin's leg little more than an outline. Clark also commented on the final design and composition, the genesis of which is possible to develop through the examination of many studies Leonardo did for the painting. Clark wrote: "By considerable distortion he has achieved a perfect balance throughout. The design has the exhilarating quality of an elaborate fugue: like a masterpiece of Bach it is inexhaustible. We are always discovering new felicities of movement and harmony, growing more and more intricate, yet subordinate to the whole; and, as with Bach, this is not only an intellectual performance; it is charged with human feeling." The father of psychoanalysis, Sigmund Freud, also had something to say about this painting. In his study of Leonardo, he commented upon the closeness in age which mother and daughter seemed to have in the painting, something many others have observed, as well. For Freud, this was an unconscious memory of the two mothers Leonardo had as a young boy: both his biological mother with whom he spent time as a youth, and his childless stepmother who raised him.

With the fall of the French and the return of the Sforza family to Milan in 1511, Leonardo's livelihood and very life were in danger, for he was considered a collaborator, having worked for the French. Another move was in order. Happily the new pope in Rome, Leo X, was one of the three sons of Leonardo's old Florentine patron, Lorenzo de' Medici. The pope's brother, Giuliano de' Medici, a lover of both art and science, was also in Rome gathering men ingenious men around him, and by 1513 Leonardo was off to that city to begin another phase of his life.

Rome and France: The Final Years

Giuliano was called, like his father, the Magnificent, and he installed Leonardo in rooms in the Belvedere Palace on top of Vatican hill. Here Leonardo established a workshop where he could continue his vast array of studies into the physical world—from aviation and properties of flight, to optics and the work of lenses to a camera obscura which acted as projector of images utilizing a candle as light source. Work in his voluminous notebooks also went apace, but there was scant artistic work produced in his three years in Rome. Leonardo reportedly kept to himself during these years; uninterested in the great building project of the Basilica of St. Peter, such work went instead to a younger generation, including Michelangelo and Raphael, the latter who was widely known to borrow from Leonardo's ideas. Leonardo's health began to fail and he also ran afoul of the pope when that man learned of his many dissections and ordered them stopped. Finally, with the death of Giuliano de' Medici in 1516, Leonardo's hopes for advancement in Rome also died.

Fortunately for Leonardo at this same time, a new king of France, Francis I, took the throne. Francis was not only a vigorous political man, he was also a patron of the arts and Leonardo came into his service in 1516, taking up residence at a small manor house, Cloux, near the king's own favorite chateau in the Loire valley. Here Leonardo was left to his own devices; the king only demanded of him occasional conversation. In his last years at Cloux, Leonardo lived relatively simply, following his own rules of living moderately: eat lightly and only when hungry, chew your food well, avoid medicine and anger, be temperate with wine. During these years he worked on his scientific schemes mostly: developing a plan for a canal that would connect the Loire River and the Cher; designing a village of prefabricated houses; sketching plans for a hunting lodge and palace for the king; and one design—carried out—for a gala pageant at court. But there was no further production of great paintings or wonderful drawings in these final years. Leonardo died on May 2, 1519, only days after he had made out his will and made arrangements for his own funeral even down to the weight of candles to be burned.

Upon his death, the king of France is reputed to have said that no man knew so much as Leonardo. Over the centuries the rightness of that judgment has been happily vindicated. First and foremost, Leonardo was a painter of major talents who brought the static line of quattrocento or early Renaissance painting into a new world with his work on perspective and sfumato and with his ability to allow personality to come through in his portraits. The founding father of what is known as the High Renaissance style, Leonardo left behind a handful of paintings cherished by the world: *Portrait of Ginevra de' Benci, Annunciation, Lady with an Ermine, La Bell Ferroniere, The Last Supper, Mona Lisa, Madonna of the Rocks,* and *Virgin and Child and St. Anne* among them. His writings on art helped, according to Kemp, "to establish the ideals of representation and expression that were to dominate European academies for the next 400 years." And then there are the drawings, over a thousand of them from studies of nature. "The standards he set," Kemp further wrote, "in figure draughtsmanship, handling of space, depiction of light and shade, representation of landscape, evocation of character and techniques

The bemused gaze of da Vinci's *La Giaconda*—more well known as the *Mona Lisa*—was likely painted between 1498 and 1503, while its creator lived and worked in Florence.

of narrative radically transformed the range of art." So many projects, so many left uncompleted.

With his scientific work, as well, there was this same incredible energy of creation. Like his paintings, these were based on careful observation and precise documentation. And like his artwork, most of these scientific and engineering projects were left incomplete. Indecipherable in his lifetime, Leonardo's notebooks demonstrate exactly what a genius he was. The notebooks contain work on architecture, botany, physics, engineering, cartography, a catalogue of facial expressions, and incredibly accurate anatomical drawings. Leonardo was by turns painter, writer, inventor, architect, botanist, engineer, mathematician, musician, city planner, philosopher, and costume and set designer. Many of his scientific discoveries anticipated much later discoveries, as in meteorology, geology, the circulation of the blood and the workings of the eye. Additionally he studied the effect of the moon on the tides, understood what has become the modern theory of plate tectonics and continent building, and was one of the first to surmise the importance of fossil shells in the geological record. His studies in hydraulics were truly groundbreaking; he was one of the founders of that science and is most likely the inventor of the hydrometer. His many projects for canalization of rivers influenced future generations of engineers and his manifold mechanical devices—including flying machines embodying sound principles of aviation and an underwater diving suit—had applications for the future, as well.

Leonardo well earned the appellation of Renaissance Man or Universal Man. Though some quibble at his small output of paintings and his many unfinished projects, there is no denying the range of his achievement. The American art critic Bernard Berenson wrote perhaps one of the soundest tributes to Leonardo in *The Italian Painters of the Renaissance*: "We forget that genius means mental energy, and that Leonardo, for the self–same reason that prevents his being merely a painter—the fact that it does not exhaust a hundredth part of energy—will, when he does turn to painting, bring to bear a power of seeing, feeling and rendering . . . utterly above that of the ordinary painter. . . . No, let us not join the reproaches made to Leonardo for having painted so little; because he had much more to do than paint, he has left all of us heirs to one or two of the supremest works of art ever created."

If you enjoy the works of Leonardo da Vinci, you might want to check out the following:

The architecture of Donato Bramante, whose work may have been inspired in part by Leonardo's drawings.
The works of architect and artist Filippo Brunelleschi, whose interests included mechanics and hydraulics as well as art.
The sculpture and painting of Michelangelo, another renowned master of the Italian Renaissance period.
The Renaissance paintings of Andrea del Sarto, who was influenced by Leonardo's work.

The biographer Robert Payne, writing in his *Leonardo*, felt that Leonardo "gave dignity to mankind" in his art. "To see a painting or drawing by Leonardo is to see through the veils, to be aware of a perfection beyond the reach of our ordinary senses." But Payne also paid tribute to the universal man in Leonardo: "Above all, he was the father of the modern age: the visionary inventor of machines, the student of flowing water, of the power that comes from water and winds and burning glasses and the sun. He saw man as the master of nature, the superb conqueror of the earth's resources. In the silence of the night, writing in his endless notebooks, he conjured up the future, and sometimes it seems that we are only the dreams of his teeming brain." Payne concluded, "The great bird spread his wings and flew farther and higher than any man had flown before, and even today we live in his shadow."

■ Biographical and Critical Sources

BOOKS

Beck, James, *Leonardo's Rules of Painting,* Viking (New York City), 1979.

Brown, David Alan, *Leonardo's Last Supper: The Restoration,* National Gallery of Art (Washington, DC), 1983.

Berenson, Bernard, *The Italian Painters of the Renaissance,* Phaidon (London), 1957.

Calder, Ritchie, *Leonardo and the Age of the Eye,* Simon & Schuster (New York City), 1970.

Chastel, Andre, *Leonardo par lui–même,* Paris, 1952, published as *The Genius of Leonardo,* Orion Press, 1961.

Clark, Kenneth, *A Catalogue of the Drawings of Leonardo . . . at Windsor Castle,* two volumes, Cambridge, 1935, revised three–volume edition with Carlo Pedretti, Phaidon (London), 1968.

Clark, Kenneth, *Leonardo da Vinci,* Cambridge, 1939, 5th edition, revised with introduction by Martin Kemp, Viking (New York City and London).

Cooper, Margaret, *The Inventions of Leonardo,* Macmillan, 1965.

Douglas, Robert Langton, *Leonardo: His Life and His Pictures,* University of Chicago Press, 1944.

Ergas, G. Aimee, "Leonardo da Vinci," *Artists: From Michelangelo to Maya Lin,* Gale, 1995, pp. 250–256.

Goldscheider, Ludwig, *Leonardo: Paintings and Drawings,* Phaidon (London), 1944.

Gould, Cecil, *Leonardo: The Artist and the Non–Artist,* New York Graphic Society, 1975.

Hart, Ivor B., *The World of Leonardo, Man of Science, Engineer, and Dreamer of Flight,* University of California Press, 1963.

Heydenreich, Ludwig H., *Leonardo: The Last Supper,* Viking, 1974.

Heydenreich, Ludwig H., *Leonardo Studies,* Münich, 1987.

Keele, Kenneth, *Leonardo's Elements of the Science of Man,* Academic Press (New York City), 1983.

Kemp, Martin, *Leonardo: The Marvelous Works of Nature and Man,* Harvard University Press (Cambridge, MA), 1981.

MacCurdy, Edward, *The Mind of Leonardo,* [London], 1928, Dodd, Mead, 1940.

McLanathan, Richard B. K., *Images of the Universe: Leonardo: The Artist as Scientist,* Doubleday, 1966.

O'Malley, Charles D., and J. B. de C. M. Saunders, *Leonardo on the Human Body,* Henry Schuman, 1952.

O'Malley, Charles D., editor, *Leonardo's Legacy,* University of California Press, 1969.

Panofsky, Erwin, *The Codex Huygens and Leonardo's Art Theory,* Warburg Institute (London), 1940.

Payne, Robert, *Leonardo,* Doubleday, 1978.

Pedretti, Carlo, *Leonardo: A Study in Chronology and Style,* University of California Press, 1973.

Pedretti, Carlo, *Leonardo architetto,* Milan, 1978, published as *Leonardo, Architect,* translated by Sue Brill, Rizzoli (New York City), 1985.

Pedretti, Carlo, and Kenneth Keele, *Leonardo: Corpus of Anatomical Drawings in the Collection of Her Majesty the Queen,* three volumes, Harcourt, Brace, (New York City), 1979–80.

Popham, Arthur E., *The Drawings of Leonardo,* Reynal Hitchcock, 1945, London, 1946, 1964.

Vasari, Giorgio, *Lives of the Artists,* Modern Library, 1959.

Wallace, Robert, *The World of Leonardo,* Time Inc., 1966.

Wasserman, Jack, *Leonardo,* Abrams, 1975.

Whiting, Roger, *Leonardo: A Portrait of the Renaissance Man,* Knickerbocker Press, 1998.

ONLINE

Grove On–Line, http://www.groveart.com/ (March 15, 2001), Martin Kemp, "Leonardo da Vinci."*

—*Sketch by J. Sydney Jones*

Peter Matthiessen

■ Personal

Surname is pronounced "*Math*–e–son"; born May 22, 1927, in New York, NY; son of Erard A. (an architect) and Elizabeth (Carey) Matthiessen; married Patricia Southgate, February 8, 1951 (divorced, 1958); married Deborah Love, May 16, 1963 (deceased, 1972); married Maria Eckhart, November 28, 1980; children: (first marriage) Lucas, Sara C.; (second marriage) Rue, Alexander. *Education:* Attended Sorbonne, University of Paris, 1948–49; Yale University, B.A., 1950.

■ Addresses

Home—527 Bridge Lane, P.O. Box 392, Sagaponack, NY 11962. *Agent*—Donadio Olsen Associates, Inc., 231 West 22nd St., New York, NY 10011.

■ Career

Writer, 1950 ; *Paris Review,* New York City (originally Paris, France), cofounder, 1951, editor, 1951—. Former commercial fisherman; captain of deep–sea charter fishing boat, Montauk, Long Island, NY, 1954–56; member of expeditions to Alaska, Canadian Northwest Territories, Peru, Nepal, East Africa, Congo Basin, Siberia, India, Bhutan, China, Japan, Namibia, Botswana, and Outer Mongolia and of Harvard–Peabody Expedition to New Guinea, 1961; National Book Awards judge, 1970. *Military service:* U.S. Navy, 1945–47.

■ Member

American Academy and Institute of Arts and Letters, New York Zoological Society (trustee, 1965–78), American Academy of Arts and Sciences.

■ Awards, Honors

Atlantic Prize, 1951, for best first story; permanent installation in White House library, for *Wildlife in America*; National Institute/American Academy of Arts and Letters grant, 1963, for *The Cloud Forest: A Chronicle of the South American Wilderness* and *Under the Mountain Wall: A Chronicle of Two Seasons in the Stone Age*; National Book Award nomination, 1966, for *At Play in the Fields of the Lord*; Christopher Book Award, 1971, for *Sal si Puedes: Cesar Chavez and the New American Revolution*; National Book Award nomination, 1972, for *The Tree Where Man Was Born/ The African Experience*; elected to National Institute of Arts and Letters, 1974; "Editor's Choice" citation, *New York Times Book Review*, 1975, for *Far Tortuga*; Brandeis Award and National Book Award for contemporary thought for *The Snow Leopard*, both 1979; American Book Award, 1980, for paperback edition of *The Snow Leopard*; John Burroughs Medal and African Wildlife Leadership Foundation Award, both 1982, both for *Sand Rivers*; gold medal for distinction in natural history, Academy of Natural Sciences, Philadelphia, 1985; Ambassador Award, English–speaking Union, 1990, for *Killing Mister Watson*; John Steinbeck Award, Long Island University, Southampton, elected to Global 500 Honour Roll, United Nations Environment Programme, and designated fellow, Academy of Arts and Science, all 1991.

■ Writings

FICTION

Race Rock, Harper (New York City), 1954.

Partisans, Viking (New York City), 1955.

Raditzer, Viking (New York City), 1961.

At Play in the Fields of the Lord, Random House (New York City), 1965.

Seal Pool (juvenile), illustrated by William Pene Du Bois, Doubleday (Garden City, NY), 1972, published as *The Great Auk Escape*, Angus & Robertson (London), 1974.

Far Tortuga, Random House (New York City), 1975.

Midnight Turning Gray, Ampersand, 1984.

On the River Styx, and Other Stories, Random House (New York City), 1989.

Killing Mister Watson, Random House (New York City), 1990.

Lost Man's River, Random House (New York City), 1997.

Bone by Bone, Random House (New York City), 1999.

NONFICTION

Wildlife in America, Viking, 1959, Penguin (London), 1977, revised edition, Viking (New York City), 1987.

The Cloud Forest: A Chronicle of the South American Wilderness, Viking (New York City), 1961.

Under the Mountain Wall: A Chronicle of Two Seasons in the Stone Age, Viking (New York City), 1962.

Oomingmak: The Expedition to the Musk Ox Island in the Bering Sea, Hastings House (New York City), 1967.

(With Ralph S. Palmer and Robert Verity Clem) *The Shorebirds of North America*, edited by Gardner D. Stout, Viking (New York City), 1967, published as *The Wind Birds*, illustrated by Robert Gillmor, 1973, reprinted as *The Wind Birds: Shorebirds of North America*, Houghton Mifflin, 1999.

Sal si Puedes: Cesar Chavez and the New American Revolution, Random House (New York City), 1970.

Blue Meridian: The Search for the Great White Shark, Random House (New York City), 1971.

Everglades: With Selections from the Writings of Peter Matthiessen, edited by Paul Brooks, Sierra Club–Ballantine (New York City), 1971.

The Tree Where Man Was Born/The African Experience, photographs by Eliot Porter, Dutton (New York City), 1972, revised edition, Penguin, 1995.

The Snow Leopard, Viking (New York City), 1978.

Sand Rivers, photographs by Hugo van Lawick, Viking (New York City), 1981.

In the Spirit of Crazy Horse, Viking (New York City), 1983.

Indian Country, Viking (New York City), 1984.

Men's Lives: The Surfmen and Baymen of the South Fork, Random House (New York City), 1986.

Nine–Headed Dragon River: Zen Journals 1969–1982, Shambhala (Boulder, CO), 1986.

African Silences, Random House (New York City), 1991.

Shadows of Africa, illustrated by Mary Frank, Abrams (New York City), 1992.

Baikal, Sacred Sea of Siberia, photographs by Boyd Norton, Sierra Club Books (San Francisco), 1992.

East of Lo Monthang: In the Land of Mustang, Shambhala (Boulder, CO), 1995.

The Peter Matthiessen Reader: Nonfiction 1959–1991, edited by McKay Jenkins, Vintage Books, 2000.

Tigers in the Snow, photographs by Maurice Hornocker, North Point Press, 2000.

Contributor to books, including *The American Heritage Book of Natural Wonders*, edited by Alvin M. Josephy, American Heritage Press, 1972 and *Crackers in the Glade: Life and Times in the Old Everglades*, by Rob Storter, edited by Betty S. Briggs, University of Georgia Press, 2000. Contributor of numerous short stories, articles, and essays to popular periodicals, including *Atlantic, Audubon, Conde Nast Traveler, Esquire, Geo, Harper's, Nation, Newsweek, New Yorker, New York Review of Books*, and the *Saturday Evening Post*.

■ Adaptations

Adventure: Lost Man's River—An Everglades Journey with Peter Matthiessen was produced by the Public Broadcasting System (PBS) in 1991; *At Play in the*

Fields of the Lord was produced as a motion picture by Saul Zaentz, directed by Hector Babenco, starring Aidan Quinn, Tom Berenger, Tom Waits, Kathy Bates, Darryl Hannah, and John Lithgow, and released by Metro–Goldwyn–Mayer, 1992; *Men's Lives* was adapted by Joe Pintauro and was performed on Long Island at the Bay Street Theater Festival on July 28, 1992.

■ Sidelights

Peter Matthiessen is widely considered one of the most important wilderness writers of the twentieth century. In fiction and nonfiction alike, he explores endangered natural environments and human cultures threatened by encroaching technology. As Conrad Silvert notes in *Literary Quarterly*, Matthiessen "is a naturalist, an anthropologist and an explorer of geographies and the human condition. He is also a rhapsodist who writes with wisdom and warmth as he applies scientific knowledge to the peoples and places he investigates. Works of lasting literary value and moral import have resulted." Matthiessen also writes of the inner explorations he has undertaken as a practitioner of Zen Buddhism. His National Book Award–winning memoir *The Snow Leopard* combines the account of a difficult Himalayan trek with spiritual autobiography and contemplations of mortality and transcendence. According to Terrance Des Pres in the *Washington Post Book World*, Matthiessen is "a visionary, but he is very hardminded as well, and his attention is wholly with abrupt detail. This allows him to render strangeness familiar, and much that is menial becomes strange, lustrous, otherworldly." *Dictionary of Literary Biography* contributor John L. Cobbs concludes: "In fiction and in nonfiction, Peter Matthiessen is one of the shamans of literature. He puts his audience in touch with worlds and forces which transcend common experience."

Critics contend that despite his pessimistic forecasts for the future of natural areas and their inhabitants, Matthiessen imbues his work with descriptive writing of high quality. According to Vernon Young in the *Hudson Review*, Matthiessen "combines the exhaustive knowledge of the naturalist . . . with a poet's response to far–out landscapes. . . . When he pauses to relate one marvel to another and senses the particular merging into the general, his command of color, sound and substance conjures the resonance of the vast continental space." *New York Times Book Review* contributor Jim Harrison feels that Matthiessen's prose has "a glistening, sculpted

Considered a modern classic, Matthiessen's haunting 1965 novel juxtaposes the native South American Niarunu people with the white Europeans who have been sent to alternately kill or convert them.

character to it. . . . The sense of beauty and mystery is indelible; not that you retain the specific information on natural history, but that you have had your brain, and perhaps the soul, prodded, urged, moved into a new dimension." Robert M. Adams offers a concurrent assessment in the *New York Review of Books*. Matthiessen, Adams writes, "has dealt frequently and knowingly with natural scenery and wild life; he can sketch a landscape in a few vivid, unsentimental words, capture the sensations of entering a wild, windy Nepalese mountain village, and convey richly the strange, whinnying behavior of a herd of wild sheep. His prose is crisp, yet strongly appealing to the senses; it combines instinct with the feeling of adventure."

Kathy Bates portrays troubled missionary Hazel Quarrier in the 1991 adaptation of *At Play in the Fields of the Lord*, filmed on location in the rainforests of Brazil.

Early Writings and Wild Places

Although Matthiessen was born in New York City, he spent most of his youth in rural New York state and in Connecticut, where he attended the Hotchkiss School. His father, an architect, was a trustee of the National Audubon Society, and Matthiessen took an early interest in the fascinations of the natural world. "I had always been interested in nature," he remembered in *Publishers Weekly*. "My brother and I started with a passion for snakes, and he went into marine biology, while I took courses in [zoology and ornithology] right up through college." After service in the U.S. Navy, Matthiessen attended Yale University, spending his junior year at the Sorbonne in Paris. Having realized that a writing vocation drew him strongly, he began writing short stories, one of which won the prestigious *Atlantic* Prize

in 1951—several of his works of short fiction would be collected in *On the River Styx, and Other Stories*, published in 1989. Matthiessen also received his degree in 1950, and after teaching creative writing for a year at Yale, he returned to Paris.

When *Race Rock* was published in 1954, Matthiessen returned to the United States, where he continued to write while eking out a livelihood as a commercial fisherman on Long Island. Reflecting on the early stages of his writing career in the *Washington Post*, Matthiessen said: "I don't think I could have done my writing without the fishing. I needed something physical, something non–intellectual." The friendships Matthiessen formed with Long Island's fishermen enabled him to chronicle their vanishing lifestyle in his book *Men's Lives: The Surfmen and Baymen of the South Fork*. Although tourism threatens the solitude of the far reaches of Long Island, Matthiessen still makes his home there when he is not traveling.

Matthiessen embarked on his first lengthy journey in 1956. Loading his Ford convertible with textbooks, a shotgun, and a sleeping bag, he set off to visit every wildlife refuge in the United States. He admitted in *Publishers Weekly* that he brought more curiosity than expertise to his quest. "I'm what the 19th century would call a generalist," he said. "I have a lot of slack information, and for my work it's been extremely helpful. I've always been interested in wildlife and wild places and wild people. I wanted to see the places that are disappearing." Nearly three years of work went into Matthiessen's encyclopedic *Wildlife in America*, published in 1959 to high critical acclaim. A commercial success as well, *Wildlife in America* initiated the second phase of Matthiessen's career, a period of two decades during which he undertook numerous expeditions to the wild places that captured his curiosity. Since 1959, he has supported himself solely by writing.

The popularity of Matthiessen's nonfiction somewhat overshadows his equally well–received fiction. Three of his first four books are novels, and critics have found them commendable and promising works. In a *New York Herald Tribune Book Review* piece about *Race Rock*, Gene Baro comments: "Mr. Matthiessen's absorbing first novel, apart from being a good, well–paced story, offers the reader some depth and breadth of insight. For one thing, *Race Rock* is a vivid but complex study of evolving character; for another, it is a narrative of character set against a variously changed and changing social background. Mr. Matthiessen has succeeded in making from many strands of reality a close–textured book." *New York Times* contributor Sylvia Berkman contends that with *Race Rock*, Matthiessen "assumes immediate place as a writer of disciplined craft, perception, imaginative vigor and serious temperament. . . . He commands also a gift of flexible taut expression which takes wings at times into a lyricism beautifully modulated and controlled." Cobbs feels that although *Race Rock* "does not anticipate the experimental techniques or exotic subject matter of Matthiessen's later fiction, the novel shows the author's early concern with fundamental emotions and with the tension between primitive vitality and the veneer of civilization."

Partisans and *Raditzer,* Matthiessen's second and third novels, have garnered mixed reviews. According to M. L. Barrett in the *Library Journal,* the action in *Partisans,* "notable for its integrity and dramatic quality, is realized in real flesh–and–blood characters." *New York Times* contributor William Goyen conversely states: "The characters [in *Partisans*] seem only mouthpieces. They are not empowered by depth of dramatic conviction—or confusion. They do, however, impress one with this young author's thoughtful attempt to find answers to ancient and serious questions." Critics have been more impressed with the title character in *Raditzer,* a man Cobbs finds "both loathsome and believable." In the *Nation,* Terry Southern describes *Raditzer*'s anti–hero as "a character distinct from those in literature, yet one who has somehow figured, if but hauntingly, in the lives of us all. It is, in certain ways, as though a whole novel had been devoted to one of [Nelson] Algren's sideline freaks, a grotesque and loathsome creature—yet seen ultimately, as sometimes happens in life, as but another human being." Cobbs concludes: "A skillful ear for dialect and an immediacy in sketching scenes of violence and depravity saved *Raditzer*'s moral weightiness from being wearisome, and the novel proved Matthiessen's ability to project his imagination into worlds far removed from that of the intellectual upper–middle class."

Based on two decades of observations of the world's remaining wild spaces, Matthiessen's 1991 work of nonfiction describes the slow destruction of the African wilderness, a result of unstable political regimes and the rapaciousness of the industrialized world.

More Novels and a Film

At Play in the Fields of the Lord enhanced Matthiessen's reputation as a fiction writer when it was issued in 1965; the novel would increase his renown still further after it was filmed as a motion picture directed by Hector Babenco in 1992. Set in a remote jungle village in the Amazon region, the work is, in the words of *New York Times Book Review* contributor Anatole Broyard, "one of those rare novels that satisfy all sorts of literary and intellectual hungers while telling a story that pulls you along out of sheer human kinship." The story recounts the misguided efforts of four American missionaries and an American Indian mercenary to "save" the isolated

Niaruna tribe. Cobbs suggests that the book shows "a virtuosity and richness that few traditional novels exhibit. There is immense stylistic facility in shifting from surreal dream and drug sequences to scrupulous realistic descriptions of tropical nature." *Nation* contributor J. Mitchell Morse voices some dissatisfaction with *At Play in the Fields of the Lord,* claiming that Matthiessen "obviously intended to write a serious novel, but . . . he has unconsciously condescended to cheapness." Conversely, Granville Hicks praises the work in the *Saturday Review:* "[Matthiessen's] evocation of the jungle is powerful, but no more remarkable than his insight into the people he portrays. He tells a fascinating story, and tells it well. . . . It is this firm but subtle evocation of strong feeling that gives Matthiessen's book its power over the imagination. Here, in an appallingly strange setting, he sets his drama of familiar aspirations and disappointments."

Matthiessen's 1975 novel, *Far Tortuga,* presents a stylistic departure from his previous fictional works. As Cobbs describes it, "the deep penetration of character and psychology that characterized *At Play in the Fields of the Lord* yields to an almost disturbing objectivity in *Far Tortuga,* an absolute, realistic reproduction of surface phenomena–dialogue, noises, colors, shapes." In *Far Tortuga* Matthiessen creates a fictitious voyage of a Caribbean turtling schooner, using characters' conversations and spare descriptions of time, weather and place. "The radical format of *Far Tortuga* makes the novel a structural tour de force and assured a range of critical reaction," Cobbs notes. Indeed, the novel's use of intermittent blank spaces, wavy lines, ink blots, and unattributed dialogue has elicited extreme critical response. *Saturday Review* contributor Bruce Allen calls the work an "adventurous failure. . . . It exudes a magnificent and paradoxical radiance; but beneath the beautiful surface [it lacks] anything that even remotely resembles a harmonious whole." Most reviewers express a far different opinion, however. *Newsweek*'s Peter S. Prescott praises the book as "a beautiful and original piece of work, a resonant, symbolical story of nine doomed men who dream of an earthly paradise as the world winds down around them. . . . This is a moving, impressive book, a difficult yet successful undertaking." And *New York Review of Books* contributor Thomas R. Edwards feels that the novel "turns out to be enthralling. Matthiessen uses his method not for self–display but for identifying and locating his characters. . . . What, despite appearances, does *not* happen in *Far Tortuga* is a straining by literary means to make more of an acutely observed life than it would make of itself."

Killing Mister Watson, published in 1990, details, through the linked recollections of ten individuals, life in the Florida Everglades a century ago. Basing his story on actual events, Matthiessen novelizes the life of Edgar J. (Jack) Watson, who settled in the area in 1892 and became a successful sugar–cane farmer. Tales of a dark past begin to circulate among his neighbors: stories of murder, of past wives, of illegitimate children. People are mysteriously murdered, and Watson's volatile temper and mean streak are common knowledge. Despite, or perhaps because of, his wealth, strong physical charisma, and the golden tongue of a born politician, Watson eventually becomes the object of resentment and even fear in his community—a man approached with submission. Eventually, Watson is killed by a

group of his neighbors—shot with thirty–one bullets—upon returning to town after the hurricane of 1910. "Aggressive and gregarious, without ethics or introspection, both hugely talented and dangerously addicted to untamed power, Edgar Watson finally seems to represent great potential gone awry, or America at its worst," notes Ron Hansen in the *New York Times Book Review.* But the act of his murder remains incomprehensible: "since accounts of the man differ so radically, we are left, like the detective–historian, with more questions than answers, and with a sense of frustration," remarks Joyce Carol Oates in the *Washington Post Book World.* "The more we learn about Watson, this 'accursed' figure, the less we seem to know."

Lost Man's River, published in 1997, picks up on the story of Edgar Watson and forms the second installment in the trilogy. While *Killing Mr. Watson* approached the tale of the central figure through patching together many documentary sources, *Lost Man's River* retraces this forceful man's life and his death through the single perspective of his son Lucius. Lucius, an academic and self–proclaimed failure, is haunted by his father's legacy, and fifty years later he begins to research the circumstances surrounding his death and comes across a new piece of evidence. The quest leads him into a dark and complicated family past and a tragic history, which is tied, as always, to the exploitation of the wilderness. The *New York Times Book Review*'s Janet Burroway, while praising Matthiessen for his "perfect ear for the cadences of Southern speech," suggested that the complex maze of familial connections and impostures was "hard on the reader. . . . Our involvement depends very much on our sharing Lucius's determination to thread this maze, and *Lost Man's River* does not entirely persuade us to do so." However, Kit Miniclier, a critic for the *Denver Post,* asserted that Matthiessen "pulls his readers through the darkness of those human souls occupying the morose, flickering light of the deep Florida Everglades." And a *Kirkus Reviews* writer described Matthiessen's accomplishment in these glowing terms: "Interweaving a lament for the lost wilderness, a shrewd, persuasive study of character, and a powerful meditation on the sources of American violence, Matthiessen has produced one of the best novels of recent years."

Matthiessen concluded the Watson trilogy in 1999, with the publication of the final volume, *Bone by Bone.* Unlike the previous novels in the series, which told Watson's story through the voices of different characters, this book is Watson's own account of his troubled upbringing in Civil War–era South Carolina. Matthiessen depicts the childhood of his protagonist as one shaped by poverty, physical abuse, and the innate violence and degradation of institutionalized slavery. Watson endures his father's beatings and his mother's indifference, and goes on to make his fortune as a sugar cane grower in the Florida Everglades. Watson's success, Matthiessen's narrative suggests, is forever marked by the dysfunction of his boyhood, which manifests itself in his adult life in his drunken rages and occasional violence. Moreover, Matthiessen reveals the environmental price paid for such pioneering land development: the destruction of the pristine beauty of the Florida wilderness; and the spirit–crushing labor required of slaves and prison chain–gangs in order to make the plantations prosper. A *Publishers Weekly* critic called the novel "a triumph of characterization and historical recreation," while a *Booklist* contributor noted that *Bone by Bone* is a satisfying

A sequel to the quasi–fictional *Killing Mister Watson*, Matthiessen returns readers to the Florida Everglades of the early 1900s as a young man attempts to learn the truth of his father's violent life—and death—in this 1997 novel.

conclusion to a "magnificent epic." While *Library Journal*'s Barbara Hoffert acknowledged that the book is "sometimes overwritten," another *Publishers Weekly* reviewer found Watson to be "a monumental creation, and in bringing him and his amazing period to life with such vigor Matthiessen has created an unforgettable slice of deeply true and resonant American history."

Human victims form the core of much of Matthiessen's writings about the United States. In his 1970 title, *Sal si Puedes: Cesar Chavez and the New American Revolution*, Matthiessen chronicles the efforts of migrant worker Cesar Chavez to organize farm laborers in California. In a review for the *Nation*, Roy Borngartz expresses the opinion that in *Sal si Puedes* Matthiessen "brings a great deal of personal attachment to his account of Chavez and his fellow organizers. . . . He makes no pretense of taking any objective stand between the farm workers and the growers. . . . But he is a good and honest reporter, and as far as he was able to get the growers to talk to him, he gives them their say. . . . Matthiessen is most skillful at bringing his people to life." A similar sympathy for oppressed cultures provides the focus for *Indian Country* and *In the Spirit of Crazy Horse*.

New Republic contributor Paul Zweig notes that the author "has two subjects in *Indian Country*: the destruction of America's last open land by the grinding pressure of big industry, in particular the energy industry; and the tragic struggle of the last people on the land to preserve their shrinking territories, and even more, to preserve the holy balance of their traditions, linked to the complex, fragile ecology of the land." According to David Wagoner in the *New York Times Book Review*, what makes *Indian Country* "most unusual and most valuable is its effort to infuse the inevitable anger and sorrow with a sense of immediate urgency, with prophetic warnings. . . . Few people could have been better equipped than Mr. Matthiessen to face this formidable task. He has earned the right to be listened to seriously on the ways in which tribal cultures can teach us to know ourselves and the earth."

The focus of *In the Spirit of Crazy Horse*, while still directed toward the historic treatment of Native Americans, was much more journalistic in nature than *Indian Country*. In fact, the book itself was the subject of much press when it became the subject of a lawsuit the year after its publication. Claiming that they were libeled in the book, both an FBI agent and then–governor of South Dakota, William Janklow, sued Matthiessen and Viking, the book's pub-

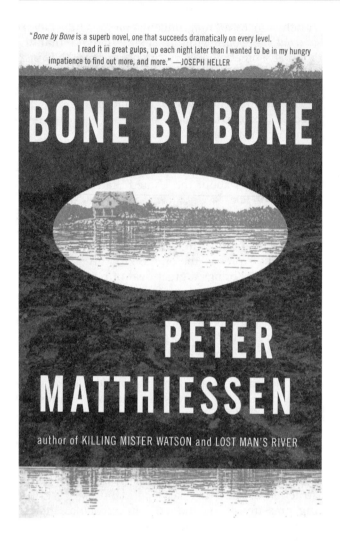

"*Bone by Bone* is a superb novel, one that succeeds dramatically on every level. I read it in great gulps, up each night later than I wanted to be in my hungry impatience to find out more, and more." —JOSEPH HELLER

BONE BY BONE

PETER MATTHIESSEN

author of KILLING MISTER WATSON and LOST MAN'S RIVER

The concluding volume in a trilogy about Floridian Edgar Watson, Matthiessen's 1999 novel reveals the cause of the murdered man's violent temperament, his inner demons rooted in a life shattered by Civil War and fed on a desire to regain his Southern family's wealth and social standing.

lisher, for a combined $49 million. While the two lawsuits were eventually thrown out by a federal appeals court, the actions of the two men effectively kept the book out of circulation for several years. A reading of the work makes their efforts understandable: *In the Spirit of Crazy Horse* presents an effective indictment of the FBI and other government offices in crushing the efforts of the American Indian Movement (AIM) to recover sacred Sioux lands illegally confiscated by the U.S. government. The discovery of uranium and other mineral deposits on the land prompted federal officials to go to desperate lengths including, Matthiessen claims, framing AIM activist

Leonard Peltier for murder. *In the Spirit of Crazy Horse* was reissued by Matthiessen in 1991, after new evidence came to light further reinforcing the author's contentions.

Physical and Spiritual Journeys

The Snow Leopard integrates many of Matthiessen's themes—the abundance and splendor of nature, the fragility of the environment, the fascinations of a foreign culture—with contemplations of a more spiritual sort. The book is an autobiographical account of a journey Matthiessen took, in the company of wildlife biologist George Schaller, to a remote part of Nepal. *New York Times* columnist Anatole Broyard writes of Matthiessen: "On this voyage he travels to the outer limits of the world and the inner limits of the self. . . . When he looks in as well as outward, the two landscapes complement one another." Harrison likewise notes in a review in the *Nation*: "Running concurrent to the outward journey in *The Snow Leopard* is an equally torturous inward journey, and the two are balanced to the extent that neither overwhelms the other." As part of that "inward journey," Matthiessen remembers his second wife's death from cancer and opens himself to the spiritual nourishment of Zen. Des Pres suggests that as a result of these meditations, Matthiessen "has expressed, with uncommon candor and no prospect of relief, a longing which keeps the soul striving and alert in us all."

The Snow Leopard elicited wide critical respect and received both a National Book Award and an American Book Award. In the *Saturday Review,* Zweig comments that the book "contains many . . . passages, in which the naturalist, the spiritual apprentice, and the writer converge simply and dramatically." *Atlantic Monthly* contributor Phoebe–Lou Adams concludes of the work: "It is as though [Matthiessen] looked simultaneously through a telescope and a microscope, and his great skill as a writer enables the reader to share this double vision of a strange and beautiful country." Harrison contends that the author "has written a magnificent book: a kind of lunar paradigm and map of the sacred for any man's journey." As a conclusion to his review, Des Pres calls *The Snow Leopard* "a book fiercely felt and magnificently written, in which timelessness and 'modern time' are made to touch and join."

Though Matthiessen writes about Zen in *The Snow Leopard* and in *Nine–Headed Dragon River: Zen Journals 1969–1982,* he still expresses reservations about offering his personal philosophies for public perusal. "One is always appalled by the idea of wearing your so–called religion on your sleeve," he told *Publishers Weekly*. "I never talked about Zen much. . . . If people come along and want to talk about Zen, that's wonderful, but I don't want to brandish it. It's just a quiet little practice, not a religion . . . just a way of seeing the world. . . . And I find myself very comfortable with it." He elaborated briefly: "Zen is a synonym for life, that's all. Zen practice is life practice. If you can wake up and look around you, if you can knock yourself out of your customary way of thinking and simply see how really miraculous and extraordinary everything around you is, that's Zen."

If you enjoy the works of Peter Matthiessen, you might want to check out the following books:

Philip Caputo, *The Voyage,* 1999.
Barry Lopez, *Arctic Dreams,* 1986.
Paul Theroux, *The Mosquito Coast,* 1982.

Matthiessen's 2000 offering, *Tigers in the Snow,* showcased his interest in the fate of Amur (or Siberian) tigers in Siberia, Indonesia, India, Thailand, and China. The book, which includes more than sixty photographs by renowned biologist and tiger expert Maurice Hornocker, documents many attempts by governments and conservationists to save shrinking tiger populations. Matthiessen's text combines eyewitness reports, tiger facts, and thoughtful meditations on the power and beauty of the big cats. His focus is on the labors of the Siberian Tiger Project, a collaborative effort between American and Russian researchers to maintain tiger habitats and stop illegal hunting. In a review of the book in *The Amicus Journal,* Andrew Wingfield commends the author for his "holistic approach" in telling the story of the Amur tigers. Rather than simply considering the problem of the cats' survival from a scientific perspective, Matthiessen also accounts for the local Siberian population's fear of the tigers in his narrative. Wingfield notes that "this method helps point up how deeply interwoven are the lives of people and tigers," concluding that "the only real chance for wild tigers' survival is quick, decisive, and intelligent human action." Calling *Tigers in the Snow* "a marvelously effective brief in favor" of the big cats, a *Publishers Weekly* critic praised Matthiessen for his "graceful prose and attentive descriptions." *New Statesman* reviewer Martyn Bedford summed up

Matthiessen's chronicle of the tiger's struggle for survival as "a beautiful book [that] is at once a celebration of the tiger, a lament for its decline, and a warning that, without action, all tigers—not just the Siberian—face extinction."

■ Biographical and Critical Sources

BOOKS

Contemporary Literary Criticism, Gale, Volume 7, 1977, Volume 11, 1979, Volume 32, 1985, Volume 64, 1991.

Dictionary of Literary Biography, Volume 6: *American Novelists since World War II, Second Series,* Gale, 1980.

Dowie, William, *Peter Matthiessen,* Twayne (Boston), 1991.

Nicholas, D., *Peter Matthiessen: A Bibliography,* Orirana (Canoga Park, CA), 1980.

Parker, William, editor, *Men of Courage: Stories of Present–Day Adventures in Danger and Death,* Playboy Press, 1972.

Styron, William, *This Quiet Dust and Other Writings,* Random House, 1982.

PERIODICALS

Amicus Journal, fall, 2000, Andrew Wingfield, review of *Tigers in the Snow,* p. 35.

Atlantic Monthly, June, 1954; March, 1971; November, 1972; June, 1975; September, 1978; March, 1983, Robert Scherrill, review of *In the Spirit of Crazy Horse,* p. 112; June, 1984, Phoebe–Lou Adams, review of *Indian Country,* p. 124.

Bloomsbury Review, September–October, 1990, pp. 22, 24.

Booklist, January 1, 1996, Raul Nino, review of *East of Lo Monthang,* p. 779; September 15, 1997, Benjamin Segedin, review of *Lost Man's River,* p. 180; February 15, 1999, B. Segedin, review of *Bone by Bone,* p. 1004; December 1, 1999, Nancy Bent, review of *Tigers in the Snow,* p. 660; January 1, 2000, review of *Bone by Bone,* p. 817.

Buzzworm, March–April, 1993, Deborah Houy, "A Moment with Peter Matthiessen," p. 28.

Chicago Tribune Book World, April 5, 1981; March 13, 1983; June 24, 1990, pp. 1, 5; July 28, 1991, pp. 6–7.

Christian Science Monitor, March 11, 1983.

Denver Post, December 7, 1998, Kit Miniclier, review of *Lost Man's River.*

Hudson Review, winter, 1975–76; winter, 1981–82.

Guardian, October 26, 1999, Andrew Clements, "Wild at Heart," p. T14.

Kirkus Reviews, September 15, 1997.

Library Journal, August, 1955; August, 1997, Michael Rogers, review of *Blue Meridian,* p. 142; October 15, 1997, Marc A. Kloszewski, review of *Lost Man's River,* p. 93; March 15, 1999, Barbara Hoffert, review of *Bone by Bone,* p. 110; January, 2000, Edell Marie Schaefer, review of *Tigers in the Snow,* p. 152.

Literary Quarterly, May 15, 1975.

Los Angeles Times, March 22, 1979; November 16, 1990, p. E4; May 30, 1991, p. E1; November 8, 1992, p. L9.

Los Angeles Times Book Review, May 10, 1981; March 6, 1983; May 18, 1986; August 24, 1986; May 14, 1989, pp. 2, 11; July 8, 1990, pp. 1, 5; July 28, 1991, p. 4; December 6, 1992, p. 36.

Maclean's, August 13, 1990, John Bemrose, review of *Killing Mr. Watson,* p. 59; July 22, 1991, Victor Dwyer, review of *In the Spirit of Crazy Horse,* p. 41.

Nation, February 25, 1961; December 13, 1965; June 1, 1970; May 31, 1975; September 16, 1978.

New Republic, June 7, 1975; September 23, 1978; March 7, 1983; June 4, 1984, Paul Zweig, review of *Indian Country,* p. 36; November 5, 1990, Verlyn Klinkenborg, review of *Killing Mr. Watson,* pp. 43–45.

New Statesman, April 10, 2000, Martyn Bedford, "The Hunted," p. 59.

Newsweek, April 26, 1971; May 19, 1975; September 11, 1978; December 17, 1979; April 27, 1981; March 28, 1983; August 11, 1986; June 11, 1990, p. 63.

New Yorker, May 19, 1975; April 11, 1983; June 4, 1984.

New York Herald Tribune Book Review, April 4, 1954.

New York Review of Books, December 23, 1965; January 4, 1968; August 31, 1972; January 25, 1973; August 7, 1975; September 28, 1978; April 14, 1983; September 27, 1984; January 31, 1991, p. 18.

New York Times, April 4, 1954; October 2, 1955; November 8, 1965; April 23, 1971; August 24, 1978; March 19, 1979; May 2, 1981; March 5, 1983; June 19, 1986; October 11, 1986; July 7, 1990, p. A16; August 22, 1991; July 26, 1992.

New York Times Book Review, April 4, 1954; October 2, 1955; November 22, 1959; October 15, 1961; November 18, 1962; November 7, 1965; December 3, 1967; February 1, 1970; November 26, 1972; May 25, 1975; May 29, 1977; August 13, 1978; November 26, 1978; May 17, 1981; March 6, 1983; July 29, 1984; June 22, 1986; May 14, 1989, p. 11; June 24, 1990, p. 7; August 18, 1991, p. 3; December 6, 1992, p. 52; December 3, 1995, p. 49; November 23, 1997, p. 16.

New York Times Magazine, June 10, 1990, pp. 30, 42, 94–96.

People Weekly, August 11, 1986, Campbell Geeslin, review of *Men's Lives,* p. 14.

Progressive, April, 1990, pp. 28–29.

Publishers Weekly, May 9, 1986; September 1, 1989, p. 8; April 27, 1990, review of *Killing Mr. Watson,* p. 52; November 9, 1990, p. 12; May 17, 1991, review of *African Silences,* p. 49; September 7, 1992, review of *Shadows of Africa,* p. 87; September 14, 1992, review of *Baikal,* p. 92; October 13, 1997, review of *Lost Man's River,* p. 56; March 15, 1999, review of *Bone by Bone,* p. 47; November 1, 1999, review of *Bone by Bone,* p. 46; January 10, 2000, review of *Tigers in the Snow,* p. 57.

Saturday Review, April 10, 1954; November 6, 1965; November 25, 1967; March 14, 1970; October 28, 1972; June 28, 1975; August, 1978; April, 1981.

Sciences, January–February, 1993, Laurence A. Marschall, review of *Shadows of Africa,* p. 43.

Sierra, May–June, 1994, Jonathan White, "Talking on the Water," p. 72.

Spectator, June 13, 1981; May 23, 1992, p. 34.

Sports Illustrated, December 3, 1990, Nicholas Dawidoff, "Earthbound in the Space Age," p. 119.

Time, May 26, 1975; August 7, 1978; March 28, 1983, J. D. Reed, review of *In the Spirit of Crazy Horse,* p. 70; July 7, 1986, review of *Men's Lives,* p. 63; July 16, 1990, Martha Duffy, review of *Killing Mr. Watson,* p. 82; January 11, 1993, Pico Iyer, "Laureate of the Wild," pp. 42–43; November 24, 1997, John Skow, review of *Lost Man's River,* p. 106; May 17, 1999, J. Skow, "Lost Man's Tale," p. 89.

Times Literary Supplement, October 23, 1981; March 21, 1986, p. 299; September 22, 1989, p. 1023; August 31, 1990; July 17, 1992, p. 6.

Vanity Fair, December, 1991, p. 114.

Washington Post, December 13, 1978.

Washington Post Book World, August 20, 1978; April 19, 1981; March 27, 1983; May 20, 1984; June 29, 1986; June 24, 1990, p. 5; July 14, 1991, p. 1.

Whole Earth Review, fall, 1987, Sallie Tisdael, review of *Men's Lives,* p. 99.

Wilson Library Bulletin, March, 1964.

World and I, October, 1999, Peter Filkins, review of *The Dark Side of Paradise,* p. 276.

Sharan Newman

Personal

Born April 15, 1949, in Ann Arbor, MI; daughter of Charles William (a U.S. Air Force captain) and Betty (a psychologist; maiden name, Martin) Hill; married Paul Richard Newman (a physicist), June 12, 1971; children: Allison. *Education:* Antioch College, B.A., 1971; Michigan State University, M.A., 1973, in Medieval Literature; additional study, 1973–75.

Addresses

Home—Portland, OR.

Career

Writer and freelance lecturer. Temple University, Philadelphia, PA, instructor in English as a second language and director of evening program, 1976; Oxford College, Oxnard, CA, instructor in English as a second language, 1977–79; Asian Refugee Committee, Thousand Oaks, CA, director of and teacher in English school; University of California, Santa Barbara, instructor.

Member

Authors Guild, Leo Baeck Institute, Medieval Academy of the Pacific, Medieval Academy of America, Science Fiction Writers of America, PEN.

Awards, Honors

Philadelphia Children's Reading Round Table Award, for *The Dagda's Harp.*

Writings

The Dagda's Harp, St. Martin's, 1977.
Guinevere, St. Martin's, 1981, Tor, 1996.
The Chessboard Queen, St. Martin's, 1983, Tor, 1996.
Guinevere Evermore, St. Martin's, 1985, Tor, 1998.

"CATHERINE LEVENDEUR" SERIES

Death Comes as Epiphany, Tor, 1993.
The Devil's Door, Forge, 1994.
The Wandering Arm, Forge, 1995.
Strong as Death, Forge, 1996.
Cursed in the Blood, Forge, 1998.
The Difficult Saint, Forge, 1999.
To Wear the White Cloak, Forge, 2000.

"Spectacular...exotic...rich historical setting."
— Faye Kellerman, author of *The Quality of Mercy*

"Newman has delivered Ellis Peters some fierce competition for her Brother Cadfael novels."
— *Booklist*

Newman's 1993 mystery weaves a tale of murder into the legendary story of Heloise and Abelard, as Catherine LeVendeur, a young novice at a French convent, is tempted by the outside world as she investigates a charge of heresy.

OTHER

(Editor and contributor) *Crime through Time*, Berkeley, 1997.

(Editor) *Crime through Time II*, Berkeley, 1998.

(Editor) *Crime through Time III*, Berkeley, 1999.

■ Sidelights

Sharan Newman has plumbed medieval history—that enormous and dimly known region of time from the fall of Rome to the Renaissance—to serve up two series of novels that deal with the Middle Ages, warts and all. Her "Guinevere" trilogy takes a novel look at the Arthurian legend, from the point of view of Guinevere, his bride, while her "Catherine LeVendeur" mystery series takes a scalpel to the twelfth century through the adventures and investigations of a French woman. "I believe that human beings have changed little emotionally in recorded history," Newman wrote in the *Ricardian Register*. "Greed, fear, love, hate and revenge are all understandable today. So the reader has something familiar to hold on to while I take them into the medieval permutations of these traits." For Newman, writing historical mysteries "is another way of teaching about a time I love and intend to continue studying for the rest of my life."

Newman was born in Ann Arbor, Michigan, and did her masters work at Michigan State University in medieval literature. While working on a scholarly paper for graduate school, she came across some intriguing details about fourth–century Ireland that would not neatly fit into such an academic paper. Deciding to turn the material into a novel, Newman came up with her first published work, the young adult tale, *The Dagda's Harp*, winner of a Philadelphia Children's Round Table Award. The same approach led to her "Guinevere" trilogy. As she noted in an interview with Raymond H. Thompson for *Authors of Modern Arthurian Literature*, "About 1973, I was doing research on Guinevere for a scholarly paper. I went through the academic libraries and the MLA lists, but I found nothing on her to speak of: she was a very neglected part of the legend at that time." Out in the hurly–burly of the real world after graduate studies, Newman saw that what she had to say about Guinevere could best be done in a novel rather than in a scholarly paper. "I thought, alright, given that this is a woman who behaves like this, what would make her do it? I started from there, working out how she could have grown up, what kind of life she might have had."

The result was Newman's second novel, *Guinevere*, in which the author traces the childhood of this golden child whose closest friend was a saint who heard spirits singing. Soon she meets the proud King Arthur, whose wife she will become. Newman continues the story in *The Chessboard Queen*. Now married to King Arthur, Guinevere soon discovers that she is passionately attracted to her husband's most trusted knight and the most beloved of all at the Round Table, Lancelot. Judith Szarka, writing in the *Los Angeles Times*, noted that "in the story of Lancelot and Guinevere, the ideal love is stronger than marriage, but marriage is sacred and indissoluble; herein lies the inevitable, tragic dilemma." Szarka further observed that Newman's major contribution to the legend "is to humanize Lancelot

In her 1994 novel Newman returns readers to twelfth–century France as novice–scholar Catharine LeVendeur is forced to decide between abandoning her vocation for the man she loves and staying at her convent to solve a murder.

and Guinevere; they are not wicked or haughty, but good, kind people powerless to withstand their great love." A *Publishers Weekly* reviewer remarked that in *The Chessboard Queen*, Newman "shows Lancelot and Guinevere [as they] struggle painfully with honor and commitment." The same reviewer felt that Newman "evokes an intriguing ambiance, blending the magical and the historical in this fresh perspective on the Arthurian romance." And a critic writing in *Library Journal* thought that Newman gave this ageless story "a fresh viewpoint, excellent writing, and delightful humor." Newman completed her trilogy with *Guinevere Forever,* in which Guinev-

ere and Lancelot's affair eventually leads to tragedy at Camelot. It not only chronicles the failure of a romance, but also the end of an era.

"I was twenty–five or twenty–six when I started the first book [of the trilogy]," Newman told Thompson in her interview. "By the time I wrote the third, I was in my thirties, had a child, was out of school, and was in the suburbs where I was living an entirely different kind of life and looking at people in a very different way . . . . As a result I viewed the Arthurian story with more acceptance. I recognized that you can't accomplish everything you want to, but that if you can sweep up your own little corner, that may be enough."

"Catherine LeVendeur" Series

Newman resisted all temptations to continue writing on the Arthurian theme, despite encouragement to do so by fans and her editor. Instead, she turned her interests to another subject: twelfth–century France and the exploits of one Catherine LeVendeur. In the LeVendeur series, as Margaret Flanagan wrote in *Booklist*, "Newman expertly vivifies twelfth–century Europe" in "extremely intelligent, highly suspenseful, and richly textured historical fiction."

In the series' first novel, *Death Comes as Epiphany*, LeVendeur, a novice and scholar at the Convent of the Paraclete, is sent by the (real–life) Abbess Heloise to discover who is trying to discredit her convent with slanderous stories of heresy. These stories also touch on the reputation of Heloise's former lover, the theologian Peter Abelard. Catherine must leave the convent and re–enter everyday life in order to pursue her investigation and also solve the murder of a local stonemason. Catherine, daughter of a wealthy merchant, has taken up service at the convent in order to conquer the sin of pride. Now, in the course of her investigations, Catherine rediscovers the outside, material world and all its temptations, some of which are found in the person of a young apprentice sculptor, Edgar, son of a Scots family, with whom she eventually joins forces to uncover the evil doings. A critic for *Publishers Weekly*, reviewing this first novel in the series, commented that "Newman skillfully depicts historical figures and issues in a very different age, one in which piety and great beauty co–exist with cruelty." The same reviewer further noted that Newman "breathes life and vigor into the scholastic debates and religious controversies of 12th–century France," and called Newman's mystery debut "entrancing." A writer for *Kirkus Reviews* described Catherine as a "spunky, sensible, determined novice nun," and also noted the "[g]entle humor and a popping plot" which keep things going in the book. "Like the author's Guinevere trilogy," the same reviewer concluded, "this offers a most likable heroine who wears well in the stretch."

The second LeVendeur adventure, *The Devil's Door*, finds Catherine on the trail of the person who brutally beat a wealthy countess. The countess lies at death's door at the Convent of the Paraclete, yet refuses to name her assailant. Into this brew comes another conflicting need: Edgar has come to fetch the woman he loves from her chaste life and soon Catherine must choose between her love for the young man and the sanctity of the convent she has come to love. Together Catherine and Edgar "will take on the dangers with derring–do," according to a contributor for *Kirkus Reviews*. The same writer concluded, "With richly satisfying settings, this smooth mystery is tight as a tambour. Top–notch sleuthing, classy with Latin saws and observations."

The Wandering Arm finds LeVendeur leaving the convent to marry. But her wedded bliss is short–lived as she discovers herself called upon to find a missing church relic. Her investigation exposes her to "the manifold perils of the Paris nether world," according to Flanagan in *Booklist*. Flanagan concluded that *The Wandering Arm* is "an extremely intelligent narrative that expertly captures and conveys the authentic flavor of medieval life and thought."

This unique sleuth's adventures continue in *Strong as Death*, the fourth book in the series. Edgar and Catherine, desperate to have a healthy baby after a stillbirth and two miscarriages, travel to Santiago de Compostela, to pray for a child at this shrine. Among their traveling party are Catherine's father, Hubert, who converted from Judaism to Christianity, more of the family, some knights, and even a one–time prostitute. When two of the knights are murdered, Catherine is led to investigate; more deaths ensue until finally Catherine traces them all back to a crime in the past. A reviewer for *Publishers Weekly* called the climax in a cave near Compostela a "hair–raising finale," and further commented on Newman's "vivid depiction of medieval life." *Booklist*'s Flanagan dubbed this "another masterful medieval mystery featuring the indefatigable Catherine LeVendeur." However, not all critics were so generous with this title. A writer for *Kirkus Reviews* noted the "clutter of subplots," "the coyly repetitive chronicles of hardships . . . the coyly described sex life of Edgar and Catherine," as well as the "frequently leaden dialogue" which make for what that critic found to be a "long, wearying journey—for the reader as well as the pilgrim."

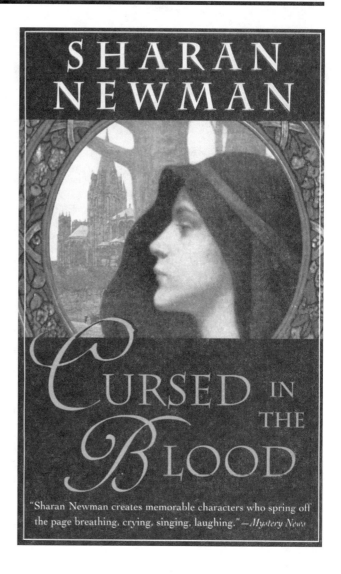

Although a new baby and a murder with few clues keeps her mind off her discomfort, Catherine regrets her decision to leave her native France and accompany her husband to far more primitive Scotland in Newman's 1998 novel.

In *Cursed in the Blood*, LeVendeur has had a child, and the young family journey to her husband's homeland of Scotland where there is religious strife between his noble family and their serfs. LeVendeur soon discovers a prisoner in the family castle, survives a fire, and works out just who is trying to destroy her husband's family. "If the pace is slow and the language sometimes anachronistically modern," wrote a *Publishers Weekly* reviewer, "Newman nevertheless manages to render the complicated matters of state and church interesting and comprehensible."

With her sixth entry, *The Difficult Saint*, Newman sets her heroine investigating matters close to home. When her sister's marriage to a German noble ends with her being accused of the man's murder, Catherine does everything she can to clear her sibling, despite the fact that they have long been estranged from one another. Such estrangement came as the result of her sister, Agnes, rejecting her Jewish past and renouncing ties to her family. Traveling to Germany, Catherine discovers dangerous undercurrents of anti–Semitism and a mixture of conflicting demands and personalities that all confuse the issue of who killed Agnes's husband. "The mystery develops slowly," observed a critic for *Publishers Weekly*, "which allows the reader to savor the customs, practices and beliefs that inform the lives of the French, German, and English." The same writer concluded that Newman translates her wide knowledge "into an absorbing and entertaining narrative." Pam Johnson, reviewing the title in *School Library Journal*, felt that "With several plots intermingling and a constant flow of major crises, the interest stays at a consistently high level." "Teens," Johnson concluded, "will find much to appreciate here."

A Knight Templar is discovered brutally murdered after Catherine and her family return to France after long absence in *To Wear the White Cloak*. Worse yet, the knight in question is in her father's home, and suspicion quickly falls on Catherine's family and the secret of their Jewish roots. Edgar and Catherine, now married for a decade, are approaching midlife in this seventh tale in the series, dealing with parental and financial responsibilities. However, they must now, with the help of Catherine's cousin, Solomon, focus on solving the mystery of the dead knight in order to save their family. "Besides providing an intriguing mystery," a reviewer for *Publishers Weekly* wrote, "the author touches on such issues of life in 12th–century France as Jewish–Christian relations . . . [and] child rearing and birth control." The same writer concluded, "Seasoned with wit and humor, this is a recommended read for mystery lovers and historical devotees alike."

1999 saw publication of the sixth volume in the "Catherine LeVendeur" series, as Newman's popular heroine travels to Germany in the face of rising anti–Semitism to support her sister Agnes against accusations that she caused her husband's death.

If you enjoy the works of Sharan Newman, you might want to check out the following books:

Marion Zimmer Bradley, *The Mists of Avalon*, 1983.
Veronica Black, *A Vow of Poverty*, 1996.
Candace Robb, *The Apothecary Rose*, 1993.
Persia Woolley, *Guinevere: The Legend in Autumn*, 1991.

Such reviews are music to Newman's ears, for one of her aims in the series is to reach people who might not otherwise be exposed to much history. "My goal is to interest people in my field enough so that they will hunt out the primary material," she wrote in *Ricardian Register*, "and perhaps even return to the university to learn more about the reality of the Middle Ages. There are plenty of fine professors there who would love to fill them in."

■ Biographical and Critical Sources

PERIODICALS

Booklist, October 15, 1995, Margaret Flanagan, review of *The Wandering Arm,* p. 388; September 1, 1996, Margaret Flanagan, review of *Strong as Death,* p. 68.

Kirkus Reviews, May 1, 1993, review of *Death Comes as Epiphany;* March 15, 1994, review of *The Devil's Door;* July 1, 1996, review of *Strong as Death.*

Library Journal, April 1, 1981, p. 815; February 15, 1983, review of *The Chessboard Queen;* April 15, 1985, p. 87; May 15, 1994, p. 128; August, 1996, p. 117.

Los Angeles Times, May 29, 1983, Judith Szarka, review of *The Chessboard Queen.*

Publishers Weekly, December 19, 1980, p. 38; January 14, 1983, review of *The Chessboard Queen;* June 7, 1993, review of *Death Comes as Epiphany,* p. 54; June 10, 1996, review of *Strong as Death,* p. 88; June 29, 1998, review of *Cursed in the Blood,* p. 39; October 4, 1999, review of *The Difficult Saint,* p. 67; September 18, 2000, review of *To Wear the White Cloak,* p. 90.

School Library Journal, February, 1994, p. 136; May, 2000, Pam Johnson, review of *The Difficult Saint,* p. 192.

ONLINE

Authors of Modern Arthurian Literature, http://www.ub.rug.nl (November 19, 2000), Raymond H. Thompson, "Interview with Sharan Newman."

Ricardian Register, http://www.r3.org/fiction/rpses/newman.html (November 19, 2000), Sharan Newman, "Why Write History?"

Sharan Newman Web site, http://www.hevanet.com/sharan/Levendeur1.htm (March 26, 2001).

—Sketch by J. Sydney Jones

Francine Pascal

■ Personal

Born May 13, 1938, in New York, NY; daughter of William and Kate (Dunitz) Rubin; married John Robert Pascal (a journalist and author), August 18, 1965 (died, 1981); children: Laurie, Susan, Jamie (daughter). *Education:* New York University, B.A., 1958. *Hobbies and other interests:* Travel, reading.

■ Addresses

Home—New York, NY, and France. *Agent*—Amy Berkower, Writers House, 21 West 26th St., New York, NY 10010.

■ Career

Writer and lecturer.

■ Member

International Creative Writers League, PEN, Dramatists Guild, Authors League of America, National Organization for Women, Writers Guild of America.

■ Awards, Honors

New York Public Library Books for the Teen Age citation, 1978–85, for *Hangin' out with Cici;* American Library Association (ALA) Best Books for Young Adults citation, 1979, for *My First Love and Other Disasters;* Dorothy Canfield Fisher Children's Book Award, Vermont Congress of Parents and Teachers, *Publishers Weekly* Literary Prize list, both 1982, and Bernard Versele Award, Brussels, 1988, all for *The Hand–Me–Down Kid;* Milner Award, Atlanta Public Library, 1988; ALA Quick Picks for Reluctant Readers citation, 2001, for *Fearless.*

■ Writings

(With husband, John Pascal) *The Strange Case of Patty Hearst,* New American Library, 1974.

Hangin' out with Cici, Viking, 1977, paperback edition published as *Hangin' out with Cici; or, My Mother Was Never a Kid,* Dell, 1985.

My First Love and Other Disasters, Viking, 1979.

The Hand–Me–Down Kid, Viking, 1980.

Save Johanna! (adult novel), Morrow, 1981.

Love and Betrayal and Hold the Mayo! (sequel to *My First Love and Other Disasters*), Viking, 1985.

If Wishes Were Horses, Crown, 1994.

"SWEET VALLEY HIGH" SERIES

Double Love, Bantam, 1984.
Secrets, Bantam, 1984.

Playing with Fire, Bantam, 1984.
Power Play, Bantam, 1984.
All Night Long, Bantam, 1984.
Dangerous Love, Bantam, 1984.
Dear Sister, Bantam, 1984.
Heartbreaker, Bantam, 1984.
Racing Hearts, Bantam, 1984.
Wrong Kind of Girl, Bantam, 1984.
Too Good to Be True, Bantam, 1984.
When Love Dies, Bantam, 1984.
Kidnapped!, Bantam, 1984.
Deceptions, Bantam, 1984.
Promises, Bantam, 1985.
Rags to Riches, Bantam, 1985.
Love Letters, Bantam, 1985.
Head over Heels, Bantam, 1985.
Showdown, Bantam, 1985.
Crash Landing!, Bantam, 1985.
Runaway, Bantam, 1985.
Too Much in Love, Bantam, 1986.
Say Goodbye, Bantam, 1986.
Memories, Bantam, 1986.
Nowhere to Run, Bantam, 1986.
Hostage!, Bantam, 1986.
Lovestruck, Bantam, 1986.
Alone in the Crowd, Bantam, 1986.
Bitter Rivals, Bantam, 1986.
Jealous Lies, Bantam, 1986.
Taking Sides, Bantam, 1986.
The New Jessica, Bantam, 1986.
Starting Over, Bantam, 1987.
Forbidden Love, Bantam, 1987.
Out of Control, Bantam, 1987.
Last Chance, Bantam, 1987.
Rumors, Bantam, 1987.
Leaving Home, Bantam, 1987.
Secret Admirer, Bantam, 1987.
On the Edge, Bantam, 1987.
Outcast, Bantam, 1987.
Caught in the Middle, Bantam, 1988.
Pretenses, Bantam, 1988.
Hard Choices, Bantam, 1988.
Family Secrets, Bantam, 1988.
Decisions, Bantam, 1988.
Slam Book Fever, Bantam, 1988.
Playing for Keeps, Bantam, 1988.
Troublemaker, Bantam, 1988.
Out of Reach, Bantam, 1988.
In Love Again, Bantam, 1989.
Against the Odds, Bantam, 1989.
Brokenhearted, Bantam, 1989.
Teacher Crush, Bantam, 1989.
Perfect Shot, Bantam, 1989.
White Lies, Bantam, 1989.

Two–Boy Weekend, Bantam, 1989.
That Fatal Night, Bantam, 1989.
Lost at Sea, Bantam, 1989.
Second Chance, Bantam, 1989.
Ms. Quarterback, Bantam, 1990.
The New Elizabeth, Bantam, 1990.
The Ghost of Tricia Martin, Bantam, 1990.
Friend against Friend, Bantam, 1990.
Trouble at Home, Bantam, 1990.
Who's to Blame, Bantam, 1990.
The Parent Plot, Bantam, 1990.
Boy Trouble, Bantam, 1990.
Who's Who?, Bantam, 1990.
The Love Bet, Bantam, 1990.
Amy's True Love, Bantam, 1991.
Miss Teen Sweet Valley, Bantam, 1991.
The Perfect Girl, Bantam, 1991.
Regina's Legacy, Bantam, 1991.
Rock Star's Girl, Bantam, 1991.
Starring Jessica!, Bantam, 1991.
Cheating to Win, Bantam, 1991.
The Dating Game, Bantam, 1991.
The Long–Lost Brother, Bantam, 1991.
The Girl They Both Loved, Bantam, 1991.
Rosa's Lie, Bantam, 1992.
Kidnapped by the Cult, Bantam, 1992.
Steven's Bride, Bantam, 1992.
The Stolen Diary, Bantam, 1992.
Soap Star, Bantam, 1992.
Jessica against Bruce, Bantam, 1992.
My Best Friend's Boyfriend, Bantam, 1992.
Love Letters for Sale, Bantam, 1992.
Elizabeth Betrayed, Bantam, 1992.
Don't Go Home with John, Bantam, 1993.
In Love with a Prince, Bantam, 1993.
She's Not What She Seems, Bantam, 1993.
Stepsisters, Bantam, 1993.
Are We in Love, Bantam, 1993.
The Morning After, Bantam, 1993.
The Arrest, Bantam, 1993.
The Verdict, Bantam, 1993.
The Wedding, Bantam, 1993.
Beware the Babysitter, Bantam, 1993.
The Evil Twin, Bantam, 1993.
The Boyfriend War, Bantam, 1994.
Almost Married, Bantam, 1994.
Operation Love Match, Bantam, 1994.
A Date with a Werewolf, Bantam, 1994.
Beware the Wolfman, Bantam, 1994.
Jessica's Secret Love, Bantam, 1994.
Death Threat, Bantam, 1994.
Left at the Altar, Bantam, 1994.
Elizabeth's Secret Diary, Bantam, 1994.
Double–Crossed, Bantam, 1994.

Love and Death in London, Bantam, 1994.
College Weekend, Bantam, 1995.
The Cousin War, Bantam, 1995.
Jessica's Older Guy, Bantam, 1995.
Jessica Quits the Squad, Bantam, 1995.
Jessica the Genius, Bantam, 1995.
Meet the Stars of Sweet Valley High, Bantam, 1995.
The Morning After, Bantam, 1995.
Nightmare in Death Valley, Bantam, 1995.
The Pom–Pom Wars, Bantam, 1995.
She's Not What She Seems, Bantam, 1995.
"V" for Victory, Bantam, 1995.
The Treasure of Death Valley, Bantam, 1995.
When Love Dies, Bantam, 1995.
The Arrest, Bantam, 1996.
Beware of the Babysitter, Bantam, 1996.
Camp Killer, Bantam, 1996.
Dance of Death, Bantam, 1996.
Elizabeth's Rival, Bantam, 1996.
Elizabeth's Secret Diary, No. 2, Bantam, 1996.
The High School War, Bantam, 1996.
In Love with the Enemy, Bantam, 1996.
Jessica's Secret Diary, Vol. 1, Bantam, 1996.
Jessica's Secret Diary, Vol. 2, Bantam, 1996.
A Kiss Before Dying, Bantam, 1996.
Kiss of a Killer, Bantam, 1996.
Meet Me at Midnight, Bantam, 1996.
Out of Control, Bantam, 1996.
Tall, Dark, and Deadly, Bantam, 1996.
Cover Girls, Bantam, 1997.
Elizabeth's Secret Diary, No. 3, Bantam, 1997.
Fashion Victim, Bantam, 1997.
Happily Ever After, Bantam, 1997.
Jessica's Secret Diary, Vol. 3, Bantam, 1997.
Lila's New Flame, Bantam, 1997.
Model Flirt, Bantam, 1997.
Once Upon a Time, Bantam, 1997.
To Catch a Thief, Bantam, 1997.
Too Hot to Handle, Bantam, 1997.
The Big Night, Bantam, 1998.
Elizabeth Is Mine, Bantam, 1998.
Fight Fire with Fire, Bantam, 1998.
Picture Perfect Prom, Bantam, 1998.
Please Forgive Me, Bantam, 1998.
What Jessica Wants, Bantam, 1998.
Party Weekend, Bantam, 1998.

"SWEET VALLEY HIGH" SUPER EDITIONS

Perfect Summer, Bantam, 1985.
Malibu Summer, Bantam, 1986.
Special Christmas, Bantam, 1986.
Spring Break, Bantam, 1986.

Spring Fever, Bantam, 1987.
Winter Carnival, Bantam, 1987.
Falling for Lucas, Bantam, 1996.
Jessica Takes Manhattan, Bantam, 1997.
Mystery Date, Bantam, 1997.
Last Wish, Bantam, 1998.
Earthquake, Bantam, 1998.

"SWEET VALLEY HIGH" SUPER THRILLER SERIES

Double Jeopardy, Bantam, 1987.
On the Run, Bantam, 1988.
No Place to Hide, Bantam, 1988.
Deadly Summer, Bantam, 1989.
Murder on the Line, Bantam, 1992.
Beware the Wolfman, Bantam, 1993.
A Deadly Christmas, Bantam, 1994.
A Killer on Board, Bantam, 1995.
Murder in Paradise, Bantam, 1995.
A Stranger in the House, Bantam, 1995.
"R" Is for Revenge, Bantam, 1997.

"SWEET VALLEY HIGH" SUPER STAR SERIES

Lila's Story, Bantam, 1989.
Bruce's Story, Bantam, 1990.
Enid's Story, Bantam, 1990.
Olivia's Story, Bantam, 1991.
Todd's Story, Bantam, 1992.

"SWEET VALLEY" MAGNA EDITIONS

A Night to Remember, Bantam, 1993.
The Evil Twin, Bantam, 1993.
Elizabeth's Secret Diary, Bantam, 1994.
Jessica's Secret Diary, Bantam, 1994.
Return of the Evil Twin, Bantam, 1995.
Elizabeth's Secret Diary Volume II, Bantam, 1996.
Jessica's Secret Diary Volume II, Bantam, 1996.
The Fowlers of Sweet Valley, Bantam, 1996.
The Patmans of Sweet Valley, Bantam, 1997.
Elizabeth's Secret Diary Volume III, Bantam, 1997.
Jessica's Secret Diary Volume III, Bantam, 1997.

"SWEET VALLEY UNIVERSITY" SERIES

College Girls, Bantam, 1993.
Love, Lies, and Jessica Wakefield, Bantam, 1993.
What Your Parents Don't Know, Bantam, 1994.
Anything for Love, Bantam, 1994.
A Married Woman, Bantam, 1994.
The Love of Her Life, Bantam, 1994.

Home for Christmas, Bantam, 1994.
Good–Bye to Love, Bantam, 1994.
Behind Closed Doors, Bantam, 1994.
College Cruise, Bantam, 1995.
Deadly Attraction, Bantam, 1995.
No Means No, Bantam, 1995.
The Other Woman, Bantam, 1995.
Shipboard Wedding, Bantam, 1995.
Sorority Scandal, Bantam, 1995.
S.S. Heartbreak, Bantam, 1995.
Take Back the Night, Bantam, 1995.
Billie's Secret, Bantam, 1996.
Broken Promises, Shattered Dreams, Bantam, 1996.
Busted, Bantam, 1996.
Elizabeth's Summer Love, Bantam, 1996.
For the Love of Ryan, Bantam, 1996.
Here Comes the Bride, Bantam, 1996.
His Secret Past, Bantam, 1996.
Sweet Kiss of Summer, Bantam, 1996.
The Trial of Jessica Wakefield, Bantam, 1996.
Beauty and the Beach, Bantam, 1997.
The Boys of Summer, Bantam, 1997.
Elizabeth and Todd Forever, Bantam, 1997.
Elizabeth's Heartbreak, Bantam, 1997.
One Last Kiss, Bantam, 1997.
Out of the Picture, Bantam, 1997.
Spy Girl, Bantam, 1997.
The Truth about Ryan, Bantam, 1997.
Undercover Angels, Bantam, 1997.
Breaking Away, Bantam, 1997.
Elizabeth Loves New York, Bantam, 1998.
Escape to New York, Bantam, 1998.
Good–Bye Elizabeth, Bantam, 1998.
Have You Heard about Elizabeth?, Bantam, 1998.
Private Jessica, Bantam, 1998.
Sneaking In, Bantam, 1998.
The Price of Love, Bantam, 1998.
Love Me Always, Bantam, 1998.
Dropping Out, Bantam, 1999.
Don't Let Go, Bantam, 1999.
I'll Never Love Again, Bantam, 1999.
Fooling Around, Bantam, 1999.
Rush Week, Bantam, 1999.
Truth or Dare, Bantam, 1999.
You're Not My Sister, Bantam, 1999.
The First Time, Bantam, 1999.
Stranded, Bantam, 1999.
Summer of Love, Bantam, 1999.
Living Together, Bantam, 1999.
No Rules, Bantam, 1999.
Who Knew?, Bantam, 1999.
The Dreaded Ex, Bantam, 2000.
Elizabeth in Love, Bantam, 2000.
Secret Love Diaries: Jessica, Bantam, 2000.

Secret Love Diaries: Sam, Bantam, 2000.
Secret Love Diaries: Chloe, Bantam, 2000.

"SWEET VALLEY UNIVERSITY" THRILLER EDITIONS

Kiss of the Vampire, Bantam, 1995.
Wanted for Murder, Bantam, 1995.
He's Watching You, Vol. 2, Bantam, 1995.
The House of Death, Bantam, 1996.
The Roommate, Bantam, 1996.
Running for Her Life, Bantam, 1996.
Dead Before Dawn, Bantam, 1996.
Killer at Sea, Bantam, 1997.
What Winston Saw, Bantam, 1997.
Don't Answer the Phone, Bantam, 1998.
Channel X, Bantam, 1998.
Love and Murder, Bantam, 1998.
Cyberstalker: The Return of William White, Part I, Bantam, Bantam, 1999.
Cyberstalker: The Return of William White, Part II, Bantam, Bantam, 1999.
Loving the Enemy, Bantam, 1999.
Killer Party, Bantam, 2000.
Very Bad Things, Bantam, 2000.
Face It, Bantam, 2000.

"SWEET VALLEY TWINS" SERIES

Best Friends, Bantam, 1986.
Teacher's Pet, Bantam, 1986.
The Haunted House, Bantam, 1986.
Choosing Sides, Bantam, 1986.
Sneaking Out, Bantam, 1987.
The New Girl, Bantam, 1987.
Three's a Crowd, Bantam, 1987.
First Place, Bantam, 1987.
Against the Rules, Bantam, 1987.
One of the Gang, Bantam, 1987.
Buried Treasure, Bantam, 1987.
Keeping Secrets, Bantam, 1987.
Stretching the Truth, Bantam, 1987.
Tug of War, Bantam, 1987.
The Bully, Bantam, 1988.
Playing Hooky, Bantam, 1988.
Left Behind, Bantam, 1988.
Claim to Fame, Bantam, 1988.
Center of Attention, Bantam, 1988.
Jumping to Conclusions, Bantam, 1988.
Second Best, Bantam, 1988.
Boys against Girls, Bantam, 1988.
The Older Boy, Bantam, 1988.
Out of Place, Bantam, 1988.
Elizabeth's New Hero, Bantam, 1989.

Standing Out, Bantam, 1989.
Jessica Onstage, Bantam, 1989.
Jessica, the Rock Star, Bantam, 1989.
Jessica's Bad Idea, Bantam, 1989.
Taking Charge, Bantam, 1989.
Teamwork, Bantam, 1989.
Jessica and the Brat Attack, Bantam, 1989.
April Fool!, Bantam, 1989.
Princess Elizabeth, Bantam, 1989.
Elizabeth's First Kiss, Bantam, 1990.
The War between the Twins, Bantam, 1990.
Summer Fun Book, Bantam, 1990.
The Twins Get Caught, Bantam, 1990.
Lois Strikes Back, Bantam, 1990.
Mary Is Missing, Bantam, 1990.
Jessica's Secret, Bantam, 1990.
Jessica and the Money Mix–Up, Bantam, 1990.
Danny Means Trouble, Bantam, 1990.
Amy's Pen Pal, Bantam, 1990.
Amy Moves In, Bantam, 1991.
Jessica's New Look, Bantam, 1991.
Lucy Takes the Reins, Bantam, 1991.
Mademoiselle Jessica, Bantam, 1991.
Mandy Miller Fights Back, Bantam, 1991.
The Twins' Little Sister, Bantam, 1991.
Booster Boycott, Bantam, 1991.
Elizabeth the Impossible, Bantam, 1991.
Jessica and the Secret Star, Bantam, 1991.
The Slime That Ate Sweet Valley, Bantam, 1991.
The Big Party Weekend, Bantam, 1991.
Brooke and Her Rock–Star Mom, Bantam, 1992.
The Wakefields Strike It Rich, Bantam, 1992.
Big Brother's in Love, Bantam, 1992.
Elizabeth and the Orphans, Bantam, 1992.
Barnyard Battle, Bantam, 1992.
Ciao, Sweet Valley!, Bantam, 1992.
Jessica the Nerd, Bantam, 1992.
Sarah's Dad and Sophia's Mom, Bantam, 1992.
Poor Lila!, Bantam, 1992.
The Charm School Mystery, Bantam, 1992.
Patty's Last Dance, Bantam, 1993.
The Great Boyfriend Switch, Bantam, 1993.
Jessica the Thief, Bantam, 1993.
The Middle School Gets Married, Bantam, 1993.
Won't Someone Help Anna?, Bantam, 1993.
Psychic Sisters, Bantam, 1993.
Jessica Saves the Trees, Bantam, 1993.
The Love Potion, Bantam, 1993.
Lila's Music Video, Bantam, 1993.
Elizabeth the Hero, Bantam, 1993.
Jessica and the Earthquake, Bantam, 1994.
Yours for a Day, Bantam, 1994.
Todd Runs Away, Bantam, 1994.
Steven and the Zombie, Bantam, 1994.

Jessica's Blind Date, Bantam, 1994.
The Gossip War, Bantam, 1994.
Robbery at the Mall, Bantam, 1994.
Steven's Enemy, Bantam, 1994.
Amy's Secret Letter, Bantam, 1994.
The Cousin War, Bantam, 1995.
Deadly Voyage, Bantam, 1995.
Don't Go in the Basement, Bantam, 1995.
Elizabeth the Seventh–Grader, Bantam, 1995.
Escape from Terror Island, Bantam, 1995.
It Can't Happen Here, Bantam, 1995.
Jessica's Cookie Disaster, Bantam, 1995.
The Mother–Daughter Switch, Bantam, 1995.
Romeo and Two Juliets, Bantam, 1995.
Steven Gets Even, Bantam, 1995.
The Battle of the Cheerleaders, Bantam, 1996.
The Beast Is Watching You, Bantam, 1996.
The Beast Must Die, Bantam, 1996.
Don't Talk to Brian, Bantam, 1996.
Elizabeth the Spy, Bantam, 1996.
The Incredible Madame Jessica, Bantam, 1996.
The Mysterious Dr. Q, Bantam, 1996.
Too Scared to Sleep, Bantam, 1996.
Twins in Love, Bantam, 1996.
Big Brother's in Love Again, Bantam, 1997.
Breakfast of Enemies, Bantam, 1997.
Cammi's Crush, Bantam, 1997.
Elizabeth Solves It All, Bantam, 1997.
Jessica's Lucky Millions, Bantam, 1997.
Pumpkin Fever, Bantam, 1997.
Sisters at War, Bantam, 1997.
The Twins Hit Hollywood, Bantam, 1997.
The Boyfriend Game, Bantam, 1998.
The Boyfriend Mess, Bantam, 1998.
Down with Queen Janet, Bantam, 1998.
Happy Mother's Day, Lila, Bantam, 1998.
If Looks Could Kill, Bantam, 1998.
Jessica Takes Charge, Bantam, 1998.
No Escape!, Bantam, 1998.

"SWEET VALLEY TWINS" SUPER SERIES

The Class Trip, Bantam, 1988.
Holiday Mischief, Bantam, 1988.
The Big Camp Secret, Bantam, 1989.
The Unicorns Go Hawaiian, Bantam, 1991.
Lila's Secret Valentine, Bantam, 1994.
The Twins Take Paris, Bantam, 1996.
Jessica's Animal Instincts, Bantam, 1996.
Jessica's First Kiss, Bantam, 1997.
The Twins Go to College, Bantam, 1997.
The Year without Christmas, Bantam, 1997.

Good–Bye Middle School, Countdown to Junior High,
   Bantam, 1997.
Jessica's No Angel, Bantam, 1998.

"SWEET VALLEY TWINS" MAGNA SERIES

The Magic Christmas, Bantam, 1992.
A Christmas without Elizabeth, Bantam, 1993.
BIG for Christmas, Bantam, 1994.
If I Die before I Wake, Bantam, 1996.

"SWEET VALLEY TWINS" SUPER CHILLER SERIES

The Carnival Ghost, Bantam, 1990.
The Christmas Ghost, Bantam, 1990.
The Ghost in the Graveyard, Bantam, 1990.
The Ghost in the Bell Tower, Bantam, 1992.
The Curse of the Ruby Necklace, Bantam, 1993.
The Curse of the Golden Heart, Bantam, 1994.
The Haunted Burial Ground, Bantam, 1994.
The Secret of the Magic Pen, Bantam, 1995.
Evil Elizabeth, Bantam, 1995.

"SWEET VALLEY KIDS" SERIES

Surprise! Surprise!, Bantam, 1989.
Runaway Hamster, Bantam, 1989.
The Twins' Mystery Teacher, Bantam, 1989.
Lila's Secret, Bantam, 1990.
Elizabeth's Valentine, Bantam, 1990.
Elizabeth's Super–Selling Lemonade, Bantam, 1990.
Jessica's Big Mistake, Bantam, 1990.
Jessica's Cat Trick, Bantam, 1990.
Jessica's Zoo Adventure, Bantam, 1990.
The Twins and the Wild West, Bantam, 1990.
Starring Winston Egbert, Bantam, 1990.
Sweet Valley Trick or Treat, Bantam, 1990.
Crybaby Lois, Bantam, 1990.
Bossy Steven, Bantam, 1991.
Jessica the TV Star, Bantam, 1991.
Carolyn's Mystery Dolls, Bantam, 1991.
Fearless Elizabeth, Bantam, 1991.
Jessica and the Jumbo Fish, Bantam, 1991.
The Twins Go to the Hospital, Bantam, 1991.
Jessica the Babysitter, Bantam, 1991.
Jessica and the Spelling Bee Surprise, Bantam, 1991.
Lila's Haunted House Party, Bantam, 1991.
Sweet Valley Slumber Party, Bantam, 1991.
Cousin Kelly's Family Secret, Bantam, 1991.
Left–Out Elizabeth, Bantam, 1991.
Jessica's Snobby Club, Bantam, 1991.
The Sweet Valley Clean–Up, Bantam, 1992.

Elizabeth Meets Her Hero, Bantam, 1992.
Andy and the Alien, Bantam, 1992.
Jessica's Unburied Treasure, Bantam, 1992.
Elizabeth and Jessica Run Away, Bantam, 1992.
Left Back, Bantam, 1992.
Caroline's Halloween Spell, Bantam, 1992.
The Best Thanksgiving Ever, Bantam, 1992.
Elizabeth's Broken Arm, Bantam, 1993.
Elizabeth's Video Fever, Bantam, 1993.
The Big Race, Bantam, 1993.
Good–bye, Eva?, Bantam, 1993.
Ellen Is Home Alone, Bantam, 1993.
Robin in the Middle, Bantam, 1993.
The Missing Tea Set, Bantam, 1993.
Jessica's Monster Nightmare, Bantam, 1993.
Jessica Gets Spooked, Bantam, 1993.
The Twins' Big Pow–Wow, Bantam, 1993.
Elizabeth's Piano Lessons, Bantam, 1994.
Get the Teacher!, Bantam, 1994.
Elizabeth, the Tattletale, Bantam, 1994.
Lila's April Fool, Bantam, 1994.
Jessica's Mermaid, Bantam, 1994.
Steven's Twin, Bantam, 1994.
Lois and the Sleepover, Bantam, 1994.
Julie and the Karate Kid, Bantam, 1994.
The Magic Puppets, Bantam, 1994.
Star of the Parade, Bantam, 1994.
The Halloween War, Bantam, 1995.
The Jessica and Elizabeth Show, Bantam, 1995.
Jessica + Jessica = Trouble, Bantam, 1995.
Jessica Plays Cupid, Bantam, 1995.
Lila's Birthday Bash, Bantam, 1995.
Lila's Christmas Angel, Bantam, 1995.
No Girls Allowed, Bantam, 1995.
Scaredy–Cat Elizabeth, Bantam, 1995.
The Amazing Jessica, Bantam, 1996.
And the Winner IS . . . Jessica Wakefield, Bantam, 1996.
Elizabeth's Horseback Adventure, Bantam, 1996.
A Roller Coaster for the Twins!, Bantam, 1996.
The Secret of Fantasy Forest, Bantam, 1996.
Steven's Big Crush, Bantam, 1996.
Class Picture Day!, Bantam, 1997.
Good–Bye, Mrs. Otis, Bantam, 1997.
Jessica's Secret Friend, Bantam, 1997.
The Macaroni Mess, Bantam, 1997.
The Witch in the Pumpkin Patch, Bantam, 1997.
Danger: Twins at Work!, Bantam, 1998.
Little Drummer Girls, Bantam, 1998.
Sweet Valley Blizzard!, Bantam, 1998.

"SWEET VALLEY KIDS" SUPER SNOOPER SERIES

The Case of the Secret Santa, Bantam, 1990.
The Case of the Magic Christmas Bell, Bantam, 1991.
The Case of the Haunted Camp, Bantam, 1992.
The Case of the Christmas Thief, Bantam, 1992.
The Case of the Hidden Treasure, Bantam, 1993.
The Case of the Million–Dollar Diamonds, Bantam, 1993.
The Case of the Alien Princess, Bantam, 1994.

"SWEET VALLEY KIDS" SUPER SPECIAL SERIES

Trapped in Toyland, Bantam, 1994.
Save the Turkey, Bantam, 1995.
A Curse on Elizabeth, Bantam, 1995.
The Easter Bunny Battle, Bantam, 1996.
Elizabeth Hatches an Egg, Bantam, 1996.

"CAITLIN" SERIES

The Love Trilogy, Volume 1: *Loving,* Volume 2: *Love Lost,* Volume 3: *True Love,* Bantam, 1986.
The Promise Trilogy, Bantam, Volume 1: *Tender Promises,* 1986, Volume 2: *Promises Broken,* 1986, Volume 3: *A New Promise,* 1987.
The Forever Trilogy, Volume 1: *Dreams of Forever,* Volume 2: *Forever and Always,* Volume 3: *Together Forever,* Bantam, 1987.

"UNICORN CLUB" SERIES

Save the Unicorns, Bantam, 1994.
Maria's Movie Comeback, Bantam, 1994.
The Best Friend Game, Bantam, 1994.
Lila's Little Sister, Bantam, 1994.
Unicorns in Love, Bantam, 1994.
Unicorns at War, Bantam, 1995.
Too Close for Comfort, Bantam, 1995.
Kimberly Rides Again, Bantam, 1995.
Ellen's Family Secret, Bantam, 1996.
Lila on the Loose, Bantam, 1996.
Mandy in the Middle, Bantam, 1996.
Who Will Be Miss Unicorn?, Bantam, 1996.
Angels Keep Out, Bantam, 1996.
Five Girls and a Baby, Bantam, 1996.
Too Cool for the Unicorns, Bantam, 1997.
Bon Voyage, Unicorns!, Bantam, 1997.
Boyfriends for Everyone, Bantam, 1997.
The Most Beautiful Girl in the World, Bantam, 1997.
Rachel's In, Lila's Out, Bantam, 1997.
Snow Bunnies, Bantam, 1997.
In Love with Mandy, Bantam, 1997.

Jessica's Dream Date, Bantam, 1998.
Trapped in the Mall, Bantam, 1998.

"SWEET VALLEY SENIOR YEAR" SERIES

Boy Meets Girl, Bantam, 1999.
Broken Angel, Bantam, 1999.
Can't Stay Away, Bantam, 1999.
I've Got a Secret, Bantam, 1999.
If You Only Knew, Bantam, 1999.
Maria Who?, Bantam, 1999.
Say It to My Face, Bantam, 1999.
So Cool, Bantam, 1999.
Take Me On, Bantam, 1999.
The One That Got Away, Bantam, 1999.
Your Basic Nightmare, Bantam, 1999.
Bad Girl, Bantam, 2000.
Three Girls and a Guy, Bantam, 2000.
The It Guy, Bantam, 2000.
Split Decision, Bantam, 2000.
So Not Me, Bantam, 2000.
On My Own, Bantam, 2000.
All about Love, Bantam, 2000.
As If I Care, Bantam, 2000.
Backstabber, Bantam, 2000.
Falling Apart, Bantam, 2000.
Nothing is Forever, Bantam, 2000.
It's My Life, Bantam, 2000.
Never Let Go, Bantam, 2000.
Straight Up, Bantam, 2001.
Too Late, Bantam, 2001.
Playing Dirty, Bantam, 2001.
Meant To Be, Bantam, 2001.

"SWEET VALLEY JUNIOR HIGH" SERIES

Boy. Friend., Bantam, 1999.
Cheating on Anna, Bantam, 1999.
Get Real, Bantam, 1999.
Got a Problem?, Bantam, 1999.
How to Ruin a Friendship, Bantam, 1999.
Lacey's Crush, Bantam, 1999.
One 2 Many, Bantam, 1999.
Soulmates, Bantam, 1999.
The Cool Crowd, Bantam, 1999.
Too Popular, Bantam, 1999.
Twin Switch, Bantam, 1999.
Third Wheel, Bantam, 1999.
What You Don't Know, Bantam, 2000.
Wild Child, Bantam, 2000.
Whatever, Bantam, 2000.
True Blue, Bantam, 2000.
Three Days, Two Nights, Bantam, 2000.

She Loves Me . . . Not, Bantam, 2000.
Hands Off!, Bantam, 2000.
My Perfect Guy, Bantam, 2000.
Keepin' It Real, Bantam, 2000.
Invisible Me, Bantam, 2000.
I'm So Outta Here, Bantam, 2000.
Clueless, Bantam, 2000.
Drama Queen, Bantam, 2001.
No More Mr. Nice Guy, Bantam, 2001.
She's Back . . ., Bantam, 2001.
Dance Fever, Bantam, 2001.

"ELIZABETH" SERIES

University, Interrupted, Bantam, 2001.
London Calling, Bantam, 2001.
Royal Pain, Bantam, 2001.
Downstairs, Upstairs, Bantam, 2001.

"FEARLESS" SERIES

Fearless, Pocket Books, 1999.
Sam, Pocket Books, 1999.
Run, Pocket Books, 2000.
Twisted, Pocket Books, 2000.
Kiss, Pocket Books, 2000.
Payback, Pocket Books, 2000.
Rebel, Pocket Books, 2000.
Heat, Pocket Books, 2000.
Blood, Pocket Books, 2000.
Liar, Pocket Books, 2000.
Trust, Pocket Books, 2000.
Killer, Pocket Books, 2000.
Bad, Pocket Books, 2001.
Missing, Pocket Books, 2001.
Tears, Pocket Books, 2001.
Naked, Pocket Books, 2001.

OTHER

(With husband, John Pascal, and brother, Michael Stewart) *George M!* (musical), produced on Broadway, 1968.

(With J. Pascal) *George M!* (television special based on musical of same title), American Broadcasting Companies, Inc. (ABC–TV), 1970.

Creator for television of *The See–through–Kids*, a live-action family series; adapter of television scripts; co-writer with J. Pascal of television scripts for soap–opera serial *The Young Marrieds*, ABC–TV. Has contributed humor, nonfiction, and travel articles to *True Confessions, Modern Screen, Ladies' Home Journal,* and *Cosmopolitan.*

■ Adaptations

Hangin' out with Cici was filmed by ABC–TV and broadcast as "My Mother Was Never a Kid," an *ABC Afterschool Special,* 1981; *The Hand–Me–Down Kid* was filmed by ABC–TV and broadcast as an *ABC Afterschool Special,* 1983; the "Sweet Valley High" series began syndication as a television series in 1994. Books that have been recorded onto audio-cassette and released by Warner Audio include: *Double Love, Secrets,* and *Playing with Fire,* all 1986, *All Night Long, Dangerous Love,* and *Power Play.*

■ Sidelights

With over six hundred titles to her credit in a half–dozen different series, Francine Pascal is one of the most successful publishing phenomena ever in juvenile and young adult literature. She made publishing history in 1985 when *Perfect Summer,* the first "Sweet Valley High" super edition, became the first young adult novel to make the *New York Times* bestseller list. Since that time the "Harry Potter" books have eclipsed such a feat, yet with over one hundred twenty million books in print in over twenty languages, Pascal and the mythical middle-class suburb of Sweet Valley, California, are still something to make a publishers mouth water, for her books draw a huge and loyal readership from middle grade readers on through high school.

Although many critics maintain that the various "Sweet Valley" series are simplistic, unbelievable, and sexist, their popularity with young adults is undeniable. The various series revolve around Elizabeth and Jessica Wakefield, beautiful and popular identical twins with completely opposite personalities—while Elizabeth is sweet, sincere, and studious, Jessica is arrogant, superficial, and devious. The events in each story usually focus on relationships with boys or other personal issues, and adults are nearly nonexistent. "Sweet Valley is the essence of high school," asserted Pascal in a *People* interview with Steve Dougherty. "The world outside is just an adult shadow going by. The parents barely exist. Action takes place in bedrooms, cars and school. It's that moment before reality hits, when you really do believe in the romantic values—sacrifice, love, loyalty, friendship—before you get jaded and slip off into adulthood."

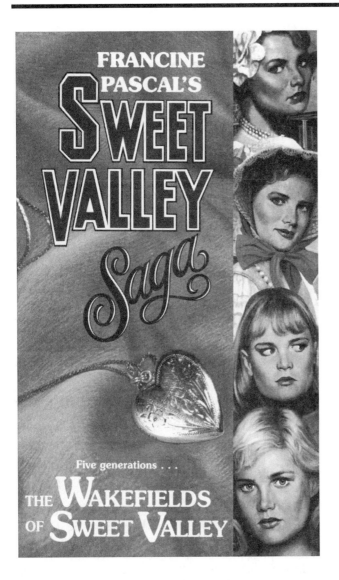

Pascal's 1991 epic traces the bloodline of nineteenth–century Swedish immigrant Alice Larsen and her beau Theodore Wakefield through five generations of hard–working American families to its culmination in late–twentieth–century teen twins Jessica and Elizabeth Wakefield.

A Writer in the Making

Born in New York City, Pascal moved from Manhattan to Jamaica, Queens, when she was five. Movies, adventure comics, and fairy tales were among Pascal's many passions, and because there was no young adult literature at the time, she read the classics. "I have always had a very active imagination—my retreat when things don't go right," Pascal once told *Authors and Artists for Young Adults* (*AAYA*). "I realized early that this set me apart from

most people. For example, it wasn't my habit to confide in others very much, particularly my parents. As far back as I can recall, I kept a diary. Important thoughts, imaginings, and events were recounted in my diaries, not to people."

Other forms of writing that Pascal attempted at an early age included poetry and plays. Her brother was a writer, so Pascal wanted to write too, but her parents did not take her writing as seriously as they did his. Her teachers and classmates encouraged her, though, and she even performed her plays, casting and directing her friends for neighborhood audiences. Moving from childhood into adolescence, Pascal, unlike her "Sweet Valley" characters, had a less than ideal high school experience. "Going to high school in the fifties, as I did, was not appreciably different from going to high school in the eighties," pointed out Pascal to *AAYA*. "Both decades are conservative and full of nostalgia. Adolescence is pretty awful no matter when you go through it. And all of us think high school is wonderful for everyone else. The 'Sweet Valley' series came out of what I fantasized high school was like for everyone but me."

College, on the other hand, was something Pascal looked forward to and thoroughly enjoyed. It was a couple of days after her last class that she met her future husband, John Pascal, who was then a journalist working for a number of papers. "He was an excellent writer," Pascal recalled, "and in many ways my mentor. He loved everything I wrote and encouraged me unceasingly." In their early years together, Pascal's husband free–lanced while she began her own writing career with articles for such magazines as *True Confessions* and *Modern Screen,* eventually moving up to *Ladies' Home Journal* and *Cosmopolitan.* They began working together as second writers for the soap opera *The Young Marrieds* in 1965, staying with the show until it moved to California. The musical *George M!* and the nonfiction work *The Strange Case of Patty Hearst* were among the other writings they collaborated on before Pascal turned her attention to the young adult audience.

Focuses on Young Adult Books

The idea for Pascal's first young adult novel, *Hangin' out with Cici,* came to her early one morning while she was lying in bed. She had never written a novel before, and at the time had no idea what young adult novels were. Upon hearing her idea, Pascal's husband encouraged her to sit down and begin writing immediately, so she did. When the manuscript was finished she mailed it off to three agents, and the book sold within two weeks. *Hangin' out with Cici* introduces Victoria, a spoiled and selfish young girl who has just been caught smoking a joint during a weekend visit to her aunt. On the train ride home, Victoria somehow wishes herself back in time to 1944, where she makes friends with a girl named Cici. Even wilder than Victoria, Cici shoplifts and sneaks cigarettes before being caught trying to buy a science test with stolen money. Over time, Victoria realizes that Cici is really her mother as a young girl and urges her to confess to her crime. She then wakes up to find herself on the train, where she had been all along—everything was just a dream. From that point on, however, Victoria and her mother have a stronger relationship. "The story contains some funny episodes," commented Ann A. Flowers in *Horn Book*, adding that *Hangin' out with Cici* is "an amusing fantasy with realistic adolescent characters."

Adolescence is pretty awful no matter when you go through it. And all of us think high school is wonderful for everyone else. The 'Sweet Valley' series came out of what I fantasized high school was like for everyone but me."

—Francine Pascal

A few other novels followed before Pascal came up with the idea for the "Sweet Valley High" series. *My First Love and Other Disasters*, published in 1979, is the story of Victoria as she takes a summer job as a mother's helper on Fire Island to be close to her first love. Barbara Elleman, writing in *Booklist*, maintained that the novel is "wittily told in the first person vernacular of a 15–year–old" and "captures the kaleidoscopic complexities of living through a first love." *The Hand–Me–Down Kid* offers a younger protagonist. Eleven–year–old Ari Jacobs is the youngest child in her family, and has a distinctly negative view of life until she meets Jane, who is in the same position as herself, yet exudes positiveness. "Narrated in the slightly skewed grammatical style typical of today's adolescent, the story is an amusing contemporary novel with an urban setting, which maintains a perspective on everything from training bras to older brothers and sisters and offers hand–me–down kids a believable example of assertiveness training," remarked Mary M. Burns in *Horn Book*.

Pascal's husband died in 1981, shortly after the 1980 publication of *The Hand–Me–Down Kid*. "It seems unfair that he isn't alive to enjoy the success of my 'Sweet Valley' series," Pascal told *AAYA*. "He would have gotten a real kick out of it, and could have retired on the money I've made. The house is too quiet now." The idea for this incredibly successful series was not a completely new one. In the late 1970s, Pascal wanted to do something similar, but in the form of a television soap opera for teenagers. No one was interested, but a few years later one of Pascal's editors suggested she try a teenage book series instead, maybe something similar to the television show *Dallas*.

When this first attempt failed, Pascal examined the reasons why, coming up with the elements she thought must be present to make a teenage series work. "Each book, I concluded," Pascal explained to *AAYA*, "would have to be a complete story in itself, but with a hook ending to lead you to the sequel. The series would have to have vivid continuing characters. When I came up with the idea for Elizabeth and Jessica, the Jekyll and Hyde twins, I was off and running. I did a proposal over the course of several days, wrote about six pages and that was that."

A Place Called Sweet Valley

Bantam immediately bought the project and, with successful marketing and packaging, made it a publishing sensation. At the beginning of the series, Pascal presented Sweet Valley as a completely idealized fantasy world. But when she started getting letters from readers telling her how "real" the books were to them, Pascal decided to include some aspects of reality, such as minority characters. "I didn't intend Sweet Valley to be realistic," Pascal commented to *AAYA*, "so I'm a little puzzled. It is a soap opera in book form, after all. I guess what these readers mean is that there is emotional reality in the relationship between the characters."

Despite the success of the various "Sweet Valley" series, Pascal has received a great deal of criticism. She argues, however, that her "books encourage young people to read. 'Sweet Valley High' opened a market that simply didn't exist before," points out Pascal. "It is not that those millions of girls were not reading my books, they weren't reading any books. I have gotten many, many letters from kids saying that they never read before 'Sweet Valley High.' If nine out of ten of those girls go on to read Judith Krantz and Danielle Steel, so be it, they are still reading. . . . The reality is that not everyone is able, or wishes to read great literature. There should be books for all types of readers. Reading time is precious; it's a time for privacy, fantasy, learning, a time to live in our imaginations. No one should be denied that."

The popularity of the "Sweet Valley High" series prompted a number of spin–off series, including "Sweet Valley Twins," which aims at younger readers by placing Elizabeth and Jessica in sixth grade, "Sweet Valley Kids," which presents the twins as six–year–olds, and "Sweet Valley High" super thriller series, which attempts to compete with other young adult mystery and horror writers. In 1991, Pascal brought a new twist to the series with the publication of *The Wakefields of Sweet Valley*. This full–length novel covers one hundred years as it traces five generations of the Wakefield family. It begins in 1860 with the sea voyage of sixteen–year–old Alice Larson of Sweden and eighteen–year–old Theodore Wakefield from England, following the family through wagon trains, earthquakes, the Roaring Twenties, love, courage, and heartbreak. In addition to this new saga, a television series based on the Sweet Valley books began airing in 1994, and a musical about the series is in the works.

Other new additions to the Sweet Valley stable include "Sweet Valley University," "Sweet Valley Junior High," Sweet Valley Senior Year," and the edgier non–Sweet Valley series, "Fearless." Inaugurated in 1993, "Sweet Valley University" follows the twins to college. "It had to happen," announced a reviewer for *Publishers Weekly*. "Jessica and Elizabeth Wakefield, the darlings of Sweet Valley High, have graduated to swinging college life. The two experience the gambit of emotions and adventures of college–age girls in this series, while in "Sweet Valley Junior High" more adolescent scenarios come into play. Reviewing *Get Real*, an early title in the "Sweet Valley Junior High" series, Lisa Denton noted in *School Library Journal* that Pascal capitalizes on the "popular teen–soap genre," producing a book with "humorous moments, fast switches in narrative voices, and fun characters." All in all, Denton concluded, the book "has that quick–read quality sought after by many busy preteens."

More mature matters are dealt with in the "Sweet Valley Senior Year," such as the death of a classmate during an earthquake in *Can't Stay Away*. Karen Hoth of *School Library Journal* noted an "interesting break from standard [Sweet Valley High] style here in that there are 'diary' entries from the key players, in an attempt to create three–dimensional characters." With her "Fearless" series, Pascal attempts to capture a more daring reader, using a New York city teenager, seventeen–year–old Gaia, who appears to have been born "without the gene for fear," according to *Booklist*'s Frances Bradburn. A black belt in kung fu, Gaia is also trained in a welter of other martial arts, and continually puts herself in harm's way to test herself. Bradburn felt "Pascal has created a fascinating, complex character," and that the lead book, *Fearless*, "is a winning set piece for this new series." Reviewing *Twisted*, the fourth book in the series, Bradburn noted in *Booklist* that readers "hooked on Gaia and her mixture of teen angst and the darkness that surrounds her" would keep "clamoring for the next book."

If you enjoy the works of Francine Pascal, you might want to check out the following books:

Katherine A. Applegate, *Sand, Surf, and Secrets*, 1996.
Elizabeth Cage, *License to Thrill*, 1998.
Elizabeth Chandler, *I Do*, 1999.
Sheri Cooper Sinykin, *A Matter of Time*, 1998.

With so many series in progress, Pascal is unable to write the books herself. "It would be impossible to do them without a stable of writers," Pascal told *AAYA*. "They come out at the rate of one a month plus periodic super editions. I do all the plot outlines, descriptions of characters, time setting, and so forth. I love plot twists and the conflicts between the good and bad twin. Creating Sweet Valley was a real 'high.' I loved making up the history of the place, visualizing it in great detail. We have a stable of authors each of whom generally does one title every three months. I maintain artistic control over every aspect of these novels. I may not write every word, but they are very much mine."

■ Biographical and Critical Sources

BOOKS

Children's Literature Review, Volume 25, Gale, 1991, pp. 175–82.
St. James Guide to Young Adult Fiction, edited by Tom Pendergast and Sara Pendergast, St. James Press, 1999.

PERIODICALS

Booklist, February 15, 1979, Barbara Elleman, review of *My First Love and Other Disasters,* p. 936; January 15, 1994, p. 901; February 1, 2000, Frances Bradburn, review of *Fearless,* p. 1016; April 1, 2000, Frances Bradburn, review of *Twisted,* p. 1451.

Chicago Tribune, June 1, 1987.

Growing Point, September, 1984, pp. 4311–4312.

Horn Book, September–October, 1977, Ann A. Flowers, review of *Hangin' out with Cici,* p. 541; May–June, Mary M. Burns, review of *The Hand–Me–Down Kid,* pp. 302–303.

Library Journal, June 15, 1981, pp. 1323–1324; January, 1994, p. 163.

Los Angeles Times, April 20, 1986, section 6, pp. 1, 10–11.

New York Times Book Review, April 29, 1979, p. 38.

People, March 30, 1981; July 11, 1988, Steve Dougherty, "Heroines of 40 Million Books, Francine Pascal's 'Sweet Valley' Twins Are Perfection in Duplicate," pp. 66–68.

Publishers Weekly, January 8, 1979, p. 74; July 26, 1985; May 29, 1987, p. 30; September 27, 1993, review of *College Girls,* p. 64; November 29, 1993, p. 55.

School Library Journal, September, 1977, p. 134; March, 1979, pp. 149–150; September, 1980, p. 76; September, 1984, p. 136; September, 1985, p. 148; March, 1990, pp. 137–140; February, 1999, Karen Hoth, review of *Can't Stay Away,* p. 111; February, 1999, Lisa Denton, review of *Get Real,* p. 111.

Variety, August 7, 2000, p. 23.

Voice of Youth Advocates, October, 1980, p. 27; August, 1984, p. 146; October, 1985, p. 264; December, 1986, pp. 231–232; June, 1987, p. 87.

Rick Reilly

Personal

Born Richard Paul Reilly, February 3, 1958, in Denver, CO; son of Jack and Betty (Guiry) Reilly; married Linda Campbell, December 30, 1983; children: Kellen, Jake (sons), Rae (daughter). *Education:* University of Colorado, B.A., 1981. *Politics:* Democrat. *Hobbies and other interests:* Snowboarding, skiing, scuba diving, basketball, mountain biking, piano, magic.

Addresses

Home—Denver, CO. *Office*—*Sports Illustrated,* Time & Life Building, Rockefeller Center, New York, NY 10020–1393. *Agent*—The Marquee Group, New York, NY. *E-mail*—milesofriles@earthlink.net.

Career

Sports writer, columnist, and novelist. *Daily Camera,* Boulder, CO, writer, 1979–81; *Denver Post,* Denver, CO, writer, 1981–83; *Los Angeles Times,* Los Angeles, CA, writer, 1983–85; *Sports Illustrated,* New York City, senior writer, 1985—, author of the weekly column "Life of Reilly."

Awards, Honors

Page One Award, New York Newspaper Guild, for best magazine story; named National Sportswriter of the Year six times; First–Place Award, Golf Writ-er's Association of America, received six times; *The Boz: Confessions of a Modern Anti–Hero* was number two among the top–ten books in the nonfiction category of the *New York Times* Best–Seller List, 1988.

Writings

(With Brian Bosworth) *The Boz: Confessions of a Modern Anti–Hero,* Doubleday, 1988.

(With Wayne Gretzky) *Gretzky: An Autobiography,* HarperCollins, 1990.

(With Marv Albert) *I'd Love to but I Have a Game: Twenty–Seven Years without a Life,* Doubleday, 1993.

(With Charles Barkley) *Sir Charles: The Wit and Wisdom of Charles Barkley,* Warner Books, 1994.

Missing Links (novel), Doubleday, 1996.

Slo–Mo! My Untrue Story (novel), Doubleday, 1999.

Life of Reilly, Total/Sports Illustrated, 2000.

Also author, with Richard Brenne, of episode "The Changing of the Guard" for the program *Arli$$.* Co–author of *Leatherheads,* a screenplay.

Adaptations

Sir Charles: The Wit and Wisdom of Charles Barkley was adapted for audio cassette.

■ **Work in Progress**

Three screenplays for Warner Bros.

■ **Sidelights**

Rick Reilly has been described as a combination of sports analyst, stand–up comic, and satirist whose journalism and book–length works have led a writer for *Publishers Weekly* to declare that Reilly "may well be the funniest sportswriter in America." A senior writer and columnist for the magazine *Sports Illustrated,* Reilly has received six National Sportswriter of the Year designations during his career as sports writer and author. He has co–written autobiographies and compilations with the famous sports figures Brian Bosworth, Wayne Gretzky, Charles Barkley, and Marv Albert. In addition to his nonfiction sports writing, Reilly is also the author of two novels, *Missing Links* and *Slo–Mo! My Untrue Story,* and a collection of his weekly columns for *Sports Illustrated* has also been published in book form as *Life of Reilly.*

Reilly was born in 1958 in Denver, Colorado, and at a young age he demonstrated the eager go–getter aptitude of a journalist in search of a story. At age twelve, he sneaked into a football game at the University of Colorado and managed to get a field pass to help out a photographer for *Sports Illustrated* mule around his heavy equipment. This led to a cover shot for the October 5, 1970 edition of the magazine and a $9 payment to the young Reilly. There was no stopping him after that. While a sophomore at the University of Colorado, he took phoned–in volleyball scores from local high schools for the *Boulder Daily Camera.* After graduation in 1981, he spent two years at the *Denver Post* and then two years at the *Los Angeles Times* before he moved on to the prestigious desk of *Sports Illustrated* in 1985. In 1983, Reilly married his high school sweetheart and the couple ultimately had three children.

Early on in his career with *Sports Illustrated,* Reilly demonstrated his ability for humor that has become a trademark of his work. As publisher Donald J. Barr wrote in an issue of *Sports Illustrated* in 1986, "In just nine months as a staff writer, Rick Reilly has become one of this magazine's most distinctive voices. Fresh insights and deft turns of phrase have enlivened his profiles . . . ." It was his ability to inject fun into the pithiest of stories that began to earn Reilly a loyal readership. One of his early breakthrough stories at *Sports Illustrated* was a profile of the East German ice skater Katarina Witt, but

he also profiled such figures as Pete Rose and Michael Jordan. Over the years, Reilly has written columns on topics as diverse as the wrestling priests in Mexico City, women caddies in Japan, and playing golf with President Clinton. His range stretches from a profile of a high school athlete battling Obsessive–Compulsive Disorder, to the presidential election of 2000 competing with the annual Florida–Florida State football game. "God, it was electric in Tallahassee, Fla., last weekend," Reilly wrote in the November 21, 2000 issue of *Sports Illustrated.* "The anticipation. The tension. The fate of the free world on a simple tally. Plus, there was that little vote thingy." Such contretemps are a favored technique of the irreverent Reilly. "Everything stopped come game time," Reilly noted of the post–election proceedings, "including the hand count in Palm Beach County. Two Florida Supreme Court justices arrived at Doak Campbell Stadium, neither looking as if he gave a pitcher of possum spit about picking the leader of the free world."

Forays into the World of Books

Reilly's first venture into the authorship of books involved the 1988 autobiography *The Boz: Confessions of a Modern Anti–Hero,* which was included among the top–ten books in the nonfiction category of the *New York Times* Best-Seller List that year. Reilly co–wrote the book with its subject of focus, Brian Bosworth, a former football player at the University of Oklahoma who signed with the National Football League (NFL) on an eleven–million dollar contract and stirred public interest for always speaking his opinion. In the book, Bosworth relates his views concerning such matters as the National Collegiate Athletic Association (NCAA), the NFL, and his time in Oklahoma. A *Publishers Weekly* reviewer asserted that Bosworth displays his "public persona" throughout the autobiography, but the reviewer also mentioned that the athlete at times "offers insights into what we are to accept as the *real* Boz." Charles Salzberg in the *New York Times Book Review* said that the athlete "has reaped the scorn of 'adults,' the adulation of 'kids.'" Salzberg added that Bosworth's autobiography "takes the form of a long, sometimes rambling monologue," though he credited the book for its "occasional insight into college and pro sports."

In 1990, *Gretzky: An Autobiography* was published, the second work focusing on a well–known sports figure to be co–written by Reilly. The book details the life and career of the famous National Hockey League (NHL) legend, including Gretzky's childhood days playing hockey, his early career as a professional athlete, the influences and motivations that

Reilly's 1996 saga concerns four disgruntled golfers who plan the clandestine infiltration of an exclusive country club near their run–down municipal putting green.

for *Sporting News*, Steve Gietschier called *Gretzky: An Autobiography* a "self–effacing book by hockey's humblest star," though adding that despite the "bitterness, Gretzky looks lightheartedly to the future."

Reilly's next effort, *I'd Love to but I Have a Game: Twenty–Seven Years without a Life*, was co–written with sports broadcaster Marv Albert. The book details the thirty–year career of Albert, who has worked as an announcer covering basketball, football, and boxing matches for the National Broadcasting Company (NBC), as well as announcing the games of the New York Knicks and the New York Rangers. Albert provides depictions of various events and encounters he has experienced during his career, involving such famous figures in the sports world as Kareem Abdul–Jabbar, Howard Cosell, and William Perry. Reviewers reacted favorably to the work, often noting its humor. Michael Lichtenstein, in a review for the *New York Times Book Review*, deemed the book an "anecdote–filled memoir" that "tells many a good story." A reviewer for *Publishers Weekly* maintained that *I'd Love to but I Have a Game* "contains a humorous and perceptive look at the life of a professional sports broadcaster." *Library Journal* reviewer Albert Spencer advised, "This book of light reading is recommended for libraries serving sports fans (and comedians)."

In his *Sir Charles: The Wit and Wisdom of Charles Barkley*, Reilly once again teams up with a sports personality to co–write an introduction to that person's life and attitudes. The audiotape version of the book, simultaneously published, was "markedly different in format and content from the book," observed a writer for *Publishers Weekly*. On tape, Reilly "asks openly confrontational questions," according to the same reviewer, and Barkley speaks out candidly on "racial identity, the stupidity of drug use and the importance of family."

Reilly As Novelist

Besides his efforts at nonfiction sports writing, Reilly has authored two novels that incorporate the subject of sports: *Missing Links* and *Slo–Mo! My Untrue Story*. The first of these novels was developed from an article Reilly, a golf nut, wrote for *Sports Illustrated* about a blue collar golf course in Massachusetts, the Ponkapoag Gold Club, also known as the Ponky to its habitues. Reilly sets the 1996 *Missing Links* in a working class suburb of Boston and renames the course the Ponkaquogue Municipal Course and Deli, portraying a group of working–class individuals who, in the process of golfing at the run–down public course, discover a nearby golf

made him a talented athlete, and the trade that took him away from his longtime affiliation with the Edmonton Oilers. Gretzky criticizes his former coach on the Oilers, Glen Sather, and the team's owner, Peter Pocklington, for various reasons, and this criticism partly led to some reviewers reacting negatively to the book. Tom Fennell, reviewing the book for *Maclean's*, commented that in the autobiography "Gretzky grumbles—and hides behind cliches," adding that "Gretzky's account of his controversial blockbuster trade to the [Los Angeles] Kings is largely a rehash of previously published information. And in describing the deal, he contradicts himself." Fennell further maintained that the book "reads like a dizzying blur of between–period interviews," and said that "Gretzky fails to reveal anything new about his personal life." In a review

course located at a nice country club, the Mayflower Club. The friends, envious of the Mayflower's golf course, begin a bet to see who can be the first to tee off for a round at the club. "The day The Bet began to assume its hideous form," wrote Reilly in his novel, "was the day Hoover lost $208 to his shadow, which is a lot of cash to drop for a man who takes the bus to the golf course. Hoover wasn't much to look at. Dannie said his mother must've had to borrow a baby to take to church. He sort of looked like that skinny guy in Westerns, the one that's always first out of the saloon whenever it looks there's gonna be gunplay . . . . Hoover apparently had all his luck surgically removed as a small boy . . . .

Still, Hoover had a will. You could beat him like egg whites and the next day he'd be back, convinced his breakthrough was just around the corner." A subplot develops for one of the group's members, narrator Raymond Lee Hart, as he must deal with the problems in his life, including a rocky relationship with his father—a member of the Mayflower Club.

Rick Reilly "may well be the funniest sportswriter in America."

—Publishers Weekly

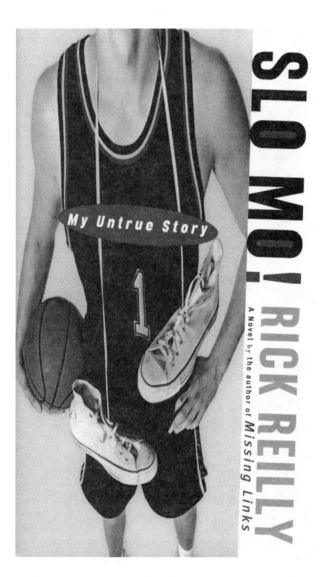

When Reilly's spoof about seventeen–year–old basketball ace Maurice Finsternick reached the public in 1999, it was cited by several critics as a transparent but effective satire of professional sports.

Booklist contributor Bill Ott commented of Missing Links: "For at least 16 of its 18 holes, this is the funniest, most unpretentious golf novel since Dan Jenkins' Dead Solid Perfect (1974)." A reviewer for Publishers Weekly called the novel "a rollicking tale," but mentioned "[t]he humor occasionally flags," adding that "a working knowledge of golf is required to appreciate much of the funny stuff." However, the same reviewer lauded the work as a "wry tribute to the game." Bill Kent of the New York Times Book Review, though saying that Reilly's novel "becomes annoyingly solemn when family values come into play," maintained that the book is an "enjoyable spoof of country–club class warfare." Kent also commented that in the novel one can "find at least three laughs per page." Los Angeles Times Book Review critic Michael Harris assured, "Reilly knows enough not to belabor the moralizing; it's the social satire and pure irreverence that keep this story in the groove." A contributor for Kirkus Reviews called Missing Links "easily the wittiest golf novel yet," with a "gaggle of loopy characters plucked off the country's municipal courses." The same reviewer concluded, "A loving, knowledgeable, laugh–out loud portrait of the Hardest Sport There Is, as practiced by the blue–collar rakes who compose golf's most devoted fans."

Reilly's second novel, Slo–Mo! My Untrue Story, is a fictitious autobiography (as told to Reilly) of basketball star Maurice Finsternick, nicknamed "Slo Mo." Slo Mo, a 7'8" seventeen–year–old who is unaware of the ways of the world, was raised by a Colorado cult living in a cave. The biographical novel follows the young man's life and career, including the discovery of Slo Mo by a man who would become his agent, Slo Mo's duped entry into the National Basketball Association (NBA), and the young talented player's distinct personality from his teammates. "Dear Kind Reader," Reilly/Finsternick introduce their story. "Well, I can't believe I'm writing a book and this is because I've hardly ever even read a book much less wrote one before, on account of evil surface trappings like books, TVs, and automobiles weren't allowed in the Spelunkarium where I grew up." Dubbed Slo Mo because he has "the same speed and agility of the Istanbul Hilton," the lovable large one bares all in this faux biography, and lovers of his reputed thirty–foot hook shot should eat it up.

Wes Lukowsky of *Booklist,* though commenting that *Slo–Mo! My Untrue Story* "was probably more fun to write than it is to read," added that the novel "attempts to poke fun at everything NBA." Reilly's targets of ridicule include various types of fans, coaches, agents, sports writers, shoe companies, athletes, and recruiters involved with the NBA. A *Publishers Weekly* reviewer noted that the novel is "a dead–on parody of the inner workings of big–time basketball," and added that the book "will bring tears of laughter once readers make the leap of faith and adjust to Slo Mo's tenacious, angelic personality." Not all critics agreed on the merits of the book, however. Writing in *Sport,* Scott Burton called *Slo–Mo!* "an obvious, sophomoric and cynical satire of the NBA," but Charles Hirshberg noted in *Sports Illustrated* that Reilly's "heavy–handed moral—that mutual respect and decency ought to rule pro sports as much as any other sphere of life—doesn't make the book any less funny." Hirshberg also felt "this could be a wonderful book for teenagers, especially those who idolize pro athletes to excess." *Library Journal*'s Marylaine Block called *Slo–Mo!* "a funny tale of a likable, amazingly naive 17–year–old . . . who is plucked out of a high school to play for the NBA." Block concluded, "Even your nonsports fans will enjoy this one."

If you enjoy the works of Rick Reilly, you might want to check out the following books:

Alden R. Carter, *Bull Catcher,* 1997.
Susan E. Cayleff, *Babe Didrikson: The Greatest All–Sport Athlete of All Time,* 2000.
Troon McAllister, *The Foursome,* 2000.
John Tessitore, *Muhammed Ali: The World's Champion,* 1998.

Reilly's sport columns, collected over a number of years, were also published in 2000 as *Life of Reilly.* The only opinion columnist in the history of *Sports Illustrated,* Reilly sounds off in this book on topics from Jack Nicholson and his obsession with the Los Angeles Lakers, to the arduous task of accompanying models for the annual swimsuit issue. Reilly has his hands full with a multitude of projects from his sports columns and books, to screenplays. Making his home in downtown Denver, Colorado, with his wife and three children, Reilly has noted that his eight handicap in golf keeps him from concentrating on anything very important.

■ Biographical and Critical Sources

BOOKS

Reilly, Rick, *Missing Links,* Doubleday, 1996.
Reilly, Rick, *Slo–Mo! My Untrue Story,* Doubleday, 1999.

PERIODICALS

Booklist, November 1, 1993, Wes Lukowsky, review of *I'd Love to but I Have a Game: Twenty–Seven Years without a Life,* p. 498; June 1, 1996, Bill Ott, review of *Missing Links,* p. 1677; September 1, 1998, review of *Missing Links,* p. 168; October 1, 1999, Wes Lukowsky, review of *Slo–Mo! My Untrue Story,* p. 344.
Entertainment Weekly, July 26, 1996, review of *Missing Links,* p. 50.
Kirkus Reviews, May 1, 1996, review of *Missing Links,* p. 630.
Library Journal, November 15, 1993, Albert Spencer, review of *I'd Love to but I Have a Game: Twenty–Seven Years without a Life,* p. 83; June 15, 1994, Cliff Glaviano, review of cassette recording of *Sir Charles: The Wit and Wisdom of Charles Barkley,* p. 111; November 15, 1999, Marylaine Block, review of *Slo–Mo!,* p. 100.
Los Angeles Times Book Review, May 26, 1996, Michael Harris, review of *Missing Links,* p. 11.
Maclean's, October 1, 1990, Tom Fennell, review of *Gretzky: An Autobiography,* p. 58.
New York Times Book Review, October 2, 1988, Charles Salzberg, review of *The Boz: Confessions of a Modern Anti–Hero,* p. 27; December 26, 1993, Michael Lichtenstein, review of *I'd Love to but I Have a Game: Twenty–Seven Years without a Life,* p. 15; August 4, 1996, Bill Kent, review of *Missing Links,* p. 18; June 15, 1997, review of *Missing Links,* p. 36; November 7, 1999, p. 26.

Publishers Weekly, July 15, 1988, review of *The Boz: Confessions of a Modern Anti–Hero,* p. 50; November 22, 1993, review of *I'd Love to but I Have a Game: Twenty–Seven Years without a Life,* p. 57; April 4, 1994, review of cassette recording of *Sir Charles: The Wit and Wisdom of Charles Barkley,* p. 33; May 13, 1996, review of *Missing Links,* p. 57; September 13, 1999, review of *Slo–Mo! My Untrue Story,* p. 63.

Sport, September, 1988, James Cholakis, "Fall Line: Gossip and Good Old Days," p. 74; January, 2000, Scott Burton, review of *Slo–Mo!,* p. 84.

Sporting News, October 22, 1990, Steve Gietschier, review of *Gretzky: An Autobiography,* p. 53.

Sports Illustrated, June 3, 1985, p. 4; January 20, 1986, Donald J. Barr, "Staff Writer Rick Reilly, author of Katarina Witt Story," p. 4; April 27, 1992, p. 1; May 12, 1997, p. 4; November 15, 1999, Charles Hirshberg, review of *Slo–Mo!,* p. R12.

ONLINE

Sports Illustrated, http://sportsillustated.cnn.com/ (November 21, 2000) "Hangin' with the Chads in Tallahassee."

—*Sketch by J. Sydney Jones*

Luis J. Rodriguez

■ Personal

Born July 9, 1954, in El Paso, TX; son of Alfonso (a laboratory technician) and Maria Estela (a seamstress and homemaker; maiden name, Jimenez) Rodriguez; married Camila Martinez, August, 1974 (divorced November, 1979); married Paulette Theresa Donalson, November, 1982 (divorced February, 1984); married Maria Trinidad Cardenas (an editor and interpreter), March 28, 1988; children: (first marriage) Ramiro Daniel, Andrea Victoria; (third marriage) Ruben Joaquin, Luis Jacinto. *Education:* Attended California State University, 1972–73, Rio Hondo Community College, California Trade–Technical Institute, Watts Skills Center, Mexican–American Skills Center, East Los Angeles College, 1978–79, University of California at Berkeley, 1980, and University of California at Los Angeles. *Politics:* "Revolutionary." *Religion:* "Catholic/Indigenous Spirituality."

■ Addresses

Home and Office—716 Orange Grove Ave., San Fernando, CA 91340.

■ Career

Worked variously as a school bus driver, lamp factory worker, truck driver, paper mill utility worker, millwright apprentice, steel mill worker, foundry worker, carpenter, and chemical refinery worker, 1972–79; Eastern Group Publications, Los Angeles, CA, photographer and reporter for seven East Los Angeles weekly newspapers, 1980; reporter in San Bernadino, CA, 1980–82; *People's Tribune,* Chicago, IL, editor, 1985–88; computer typesetter for various firms in the Chicago area, including the Archdiocese of Chicago, 1987–89; writer, lecturer, and critic, 1988—; part–time news writer for WMAQ–AM in Chicago, 1989–92.

Director of the mural project for the Bienvenidos Community Center, 1972; public affairs associate for the American Federation of State, County, and Municipal Employees, AFL–CIO, 1982–85; publisher and editor of *Chismearte,* 1982–85; facilitator of the Barrio Writers Workshops, Los Angeles, 1982–85; board member of KPFK–FM, Pacifica Station in Los Angeles, 1983–85; founder and director of Tia Chucha Press, 1989—; writer in residency, Shakespeare and Company, Paris, France, 1991; writer in residence, North Carolina's "Word Wide," 2000; founder of the following organizations: Rock a Mole (rhymes with guacamole) Productions, League of Revolutionaries for a New America, the Guild Complex, Youth Struggling for Survival, and Tia Chucha's Café Cultural. Conductor of talks, readings, and workshops in prisons, juvenile facilities, public and private schools, migrant camps, churches, universities, community centers, and homeless shelters throughout the United States, Canada, Mexico, Puerto Rico, Central America, and Europe, 1980—.

■ Member

PEN USA West, Poets and Writers, American Poetry Society, National Writers Union, Los Angeles Latino Writers Association (director/publisher, 1982–85).

■ Awards, Honors

Honorable mention for the Quinto Sol Chicano Literary Award, 1973; second place for the best freelance story, from the Twin Counties Press Club, 1982; honorable mention for the Chicano Literary Award, from the University of California at Irvine, Department of Portuguese and Spanish; second place for the Corazon de Aztlan Literary Award, 1984; best of the *Los Angeles Weekly*, 1985; honorable mention for the Patterson Poetry Prize and PEN West/Josephine Miles Award for Literary Excellence, both for *The Concrete River*; Poetry Center Book Award from San Francisco State University, for *Poems Across the Pavement*, 1989; Illinois Arts Council Poetry Fellowship, 1992, 2000; Lannan Fellowship in Poetry, 1992; Dorothea Lange/Paul Taylor Prize, from the Center for Documentary Studies, Duke University, 1993; Carl Sandburg Literary Award for nonfiction, *New York Times Book Review* Notable Book, both 1993, and *Chicago–Sun Times* Book Award for nonfiction, 1994, all for *Always Running: La Vida Loca, Gang Days in L.A.*; Hispanic Heritage Award for literature, 1998; Lila Wallace–*Reader's Digest* Writers' Award, 1996; National Association for Poetry Therapy Public Service Award, 1997; Paterson Prize for Books for Young Adults, 1999; "Skipping Stones" Magazine Honor Award, 1999 and 2000; *Foreword Magazine*'s Silver Book Award, 1999; Parent's Choice Books for Children Award, 1999; Illinois Author of the Year Award, 2000; Americas Award for Children's and Young Adult Literature Commended Title, 2000; Premio Fronterizo of the Border Book Festival, Las Cruces, New Mexico, 2001; "Unsung Heroes of Compassion" Award, 2001.

■ Writings

Poems Across the Pavement, Tia Chucha Press, 1989.
The Concrete River (poems), Curbstone Press, 1991.

Always Running: La Vida Loca—Gang Days in L.A. (memoir), Curbstone Press, 1993, Touchstone Books, 1994.
America Is Her Name, illustrated by Carlos Vazquez, Curbstone Press, 1998.
Trochemoche: Poems, Curbstone Press, 1998.
It Doesn't Have to Be This Way: A Barrio Story, illustrated by Daniel Galvez, Children's Book Press, 1999.

Contributor of articles, reviews, and poems to periodicals, including *Los Angeles Times, Nation, U.S. News and World Report, Utne Reader, Philadelphia Inquirer Magazine, Chicago Reporter, Poets and Writers, Chicago Tribune, American Poetry Review, TriQuarterly, Bloomsbury Review, Rattle Magazine*, and *Latina Magazine*. Also contributor to anthologies, including *The Outlaw Bible of American Poetry, Letters of a Nation: A Collection of Extraordinary American Letters, Las Christmas: Favorite Latino Authors Share Their Holiday Memories, Inside the L.A. Riots: What Happened and Why It Will Happen Again, Mirrors Beneath the Earth: Short Fiction by Chicano Writers, After Aztlan: Latino Writers in the '90s, Fifty Ways to Fight Censorship, With the Wind at My Back and Ink in My Blood: A Collection of Poems by Chicago's Homeless, Unsettling America: An Anthology of Contemporary Multicultural Poetry, Power Lines: A Decade of Poetry at Chicago's Guild Complex*, and *Voices: Readings from El Grito*. Rodriquez's work has been translated into German, French, Arabic, and Spanish.

■ Work in Progress

Hearts and Hands: Imagining Peace and Community in a Time of Violence and Chaos, a nonfiction book to be published by Seven Stories/Ciete Cuentos Press; *Sometimes You Dance with a Watermelon and Other Stories*, a short story collection to be published by HarperCollins/Rayo Books in early 2002; *My Nature is Hunger: New & Selected Poems*, to be published by Curbstone Press; "Nations," an original treatment for a possible TV pilot and series for Shore Media Productions, registered with the Writers Guild.

■ Sidelights

In his 1993 memoir, poet–author–journalist Luis J. Rodriguez encapsulates the trapped feeling of the Latino in East Los Angeles: "It never stopped this running. We were constant prey, and the hunters soon became big blurs: The police, the gangs, the junkies, the dudes on Garvey Boulevard who took our money, all smudge into one." But the enemy was not always on the street for young Mexican Americans like Rodriguez: "Sometimes they were teachers who jumped on us Mexicans as if we were born with a hideous stain. We were always afraid, always running." It was this feeling of persecution, of being the target of others, that led young men like Rodriguez into gang membership.

Always Running: La Vida Loca, Gang Days in L.A. was Rodriguez's personal statement, his mea culpa, both a cautionary tale and gut–wrenching personal document. Written two decades after his own gang activity, the book was partly inspired by his own son, Ramiro, who was himself becoming involved in gangs at the time Rodriguez was writing his book. In the event, the memoir was not enough of a palliative to keep Ramiro out of trouble: Rodriguez's son was sent to prison in 1998 for attempted murder. However, despite school bans on the book and a mini–controversy over its content, Rodriguez still believes his book is essential reading for many. "I actually hope my book will lose its validity some day," he told Patrick Sullivan in an interview for the *Sonoma County Independent*, "that there isn't a need for a book like *Always Running*. . . . . But right now that's not the case. The book is very relevant, and as long as that's the case, then we should make sure that people can get access to it."

Rodriguez has written three books of poetry and two children's books in addition to this partly fictionalized memoir, and has also contributed journalistic articles to national publications such as the *Los Angeles Times*, *Nation*, and *U.S. News and World Reports*, chronicling the Mexican–American experience and speaking out articulately for social justice and equity in the country. But he continues to view himself primarily as a poet. As he told Aaron Cohen in an interview for *Poets and Writers*, "Poetry is the foundation of everything I do. It's poetry with a sense of social engagement. The written, powerful expressive language of poetry is the springboard for everything I want to write."

Growing Up on Mean Streets

Rodriguez is no stranger to the mean streets he depicts in all his work. Born in El Paso, Texas, on July 9, 1954, he spent two years in Ciudad Juarez, Mexico, before his family immigrated to the United States in 1956. His father, Alfonso Rodriguez, a school principal in Mexico, brought his family north because the pay was so poor in his native country that he could not support his children. But once

settled in the Watts community of south central Los Angeles, Alfonso and his family were presented with the cruel reality of low–status work and constant racism. The father held a number of jobs, ultimately working as a laboratory custodian, while Rodriguez's mother, Maria Estela Jimenez, worked as a seamstress. Rodriguez grew up with three siblings and three nieces, the daughters of his half–sister, and in 1962 the family moved to the East Los Angeles community of South San Gabriel. Rodriguez's teenage years were spent in the barrio there.

These were turbulent years for the young Rodriguez, who felt always on the outside, harassed by both Anglo children and the police. To find a sense

"An absolutely unique work: richly literary and poetic, yet urgent and politically explosive at the same time.... A permanent testament to human courage and transcendence."
— Jonathan Kozol, author of *Savage Inequalities*

ALWAYS RUNNING

LA VIDA LOCA: GANG DAYS IN L.A.

LUIS J. RODRIGUEZ

An award–winning memoir of his teen years as part of a Chicano gang cruising East Los Angeles streets, Rodriguez's 1993 book was part of the author's effort to keep his own young son from a life of violence on the streets.

of solidarity and belonging, Rodriguez joined the gangs of East Los Angeles. Dropping out of school at fifteen, he led a life during the 1960s and 1970s characterized by ever–escalating violence and mayhem. Jailed for attempted murder, he was released only to take part in a fire bombing of a home and in store robberies. Sex and drugs formed a continual base line to his life. "Everything lost its value for me," Rodriguez wrote in *Always Running*, describing the nihilism of those days. "Death seemed the only door worth opening, the only road toward a future."

But Rodriguez was one of the fortunate ones. From his early youth he had tried to find a safe haven in books, in an interior life. Even as a very young child, as he told Cohen, "I found refuge in books because I was a shy, broken–down little kid. They were fairytale books, Walt Disney books, whatever. I would go inside and hide myself in books and not have to worry about the yelling and screaming and bullets flying." Even as a gang member, he was composing verses based on his experiences on the streets. This propensity for self–reflection came in handy when, at the height of the Chicano Movement, Rodriguez was pulled from the gangs by the lure of education and political activism. A recreational leader at a local youth center introduced Rodriguez to Mexican history and a new way of looking at himself, while a counselor at school, when he returned to graduate in 1970, also helped to make the young man into a student leader instead of a gang dupe, taking pride in his culture, in his race, in his heritage. Slowly Rodriguez turned away from violence to the world of words.

Graduating from high school in 1970, Rodriguez won his first literary award two years later, the Quinto Sol Literary Award, which earned him $250 and a trip to Berkeley. Throughout the 1970s Rodriguez continued writing while holding down blue collar jobs. He also married for the first time and became the father of two children. Then in 1980 he became a full time writer, working as a journalist and photographer for several Los Angeles newspapers.

Budding Poet and Journalist

Rodriguez became heavily involved in the east Los Angeles political and literary scene, serving as director of the Los Angeles Latino Writers Association and publishing the literary magazine, *Chismearte*, in whose pages some of the bright and rising stars of Latino literature were first introduced to a wider public. By the mid 1980s, divorced, remarried, and

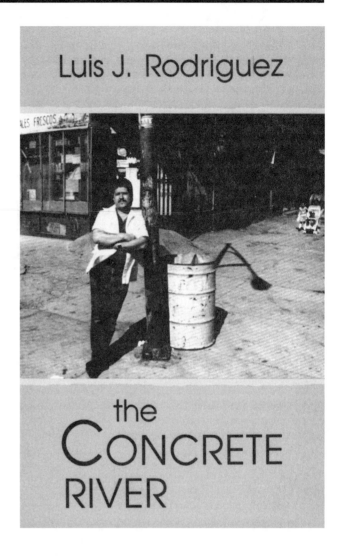

Rodriguez's 1991 poetry collection, his second to be published, contains what its author describes as "poetry with a sense of social engagement."

divorced again, Rodriguez had resettled in Chicago, where he worked as an editor on the *People's Tribune*, a weekly leftist journal. He also became deeply involved in not only literary matters, giving poetry workshops and crafting his journalism, but also in social issues, working with gang members, the homeless, convicts, and migrants. During this time he also established Tia Chucha Press, the publishing house of the Guild Complex, an arts center in Chicago focusing on Multicultural issues. In 1988, he married for a third time and has two children by this marriage in addition to two from his first.

In 1989, his Tia Chucha Press published his first collection of poetry, *Poems Across the Pavement*, verses that focus on "life in America," according to Dina G. Castillo, writing in *Dictionary of Literary Biography*, "but his America is one that relatively few people want to acknowledge." Castillo described the America Rodriguez portrays as "an environment fraught with economic oppression, racism, cultural alienation, class battles, industrial displacement, strained human relations, and street turmoil in Los Angeles and Chicago." Rodriguez depicts this situation in poems in the collection such as "'Race' Politics," "No Work Today," "Tombstone Poets," and "Alabama," which take the reader on "an emotional roller coaster," according to Castillo. Some of the poems were written when Rodriguez was still a teenager, and all display the influence of his own favorite writers, poets from Walt Whitman to Pablo Neruda, and Latino and African American authors such as Claude Brown and Piri Thomas, whose work portrayed the hard lives of society's outcasts and downtrodden.

A second collection, *The Concrete River*, appeared in 1991, confirming Rodriguez's early promise and delving more deeply into the themes of urban violence, race relations, gender conflicts, and drug addiction which he explored in his first volume of poetry. An interesting development in *The Concrete River* was the use of both poetry and prose in longer pieces, ones that tie together to provide a witnessing of his own past, from Mexico to Watts to East Los Angeles to Chicago. In the first of five sections, with the poem "Prelude to a Heartbeat," Rodriguez talks of his youth in Watts "Where fear is a deep river. / Where hate is an overgrown weed." His dangerous gang years are dealt with in the second section while his failed first marriage comes to center stage in the third, "Always Running": "When all was gone, / the concrete river / was always there / and me, always running." Other sections deal with his life as a blue–collar worker and with his new life in Chicago, away from the city that spawned him and nearly destroyed him.

Castillo noted that Rodriguez uses the "motifs of concrete and pavement to represent all that has limited him in the past but that nevertheless became the source of his literary creativity." For Rodriguez there is some value, some resiliency to be gained from such a hard life. "He views poetry as the water that runs through the concrete river," Castillo observed, "cleansing and restoring life." A reviewer for *Publishers Weekly* felt that Rodriguez "writes eloquently of . . . a populace locked out of privilege and prosperity." The same writer concluded, "This poetry is of the barrio yet stubbornly refuses to be confined in it—Rodriguez's perceptive gaze and sto-

ryteller's gift transport his world across neighborhood boundaries." Audrey Rodriguez, writing in *Bilingual Review*, noted that *The Concrete River* "involves a return to and recovery of the past . . . and a recognition of chaos, death, and the reality of a place that locks in or jeopardizes the thinking–feeling self." Rodriguez, the critic, concluded that Luis J. Rodriguez "is one of Chicano literature's most gifted and committed artists today . . . . His is a refreshing voice—of rebellion and beauty—in an increasingly narrow age of literature's disengagement from the ground of great art and true history." *The Concrete River* won an honorable mention for the Patterson Poetry Prize and the PEN West/Josephine Miles Award for Literary Excellence. In 1992, Rodriguez received both an Illinois Arts Council Poetry Fellowship and a Lannan Fellowship in Poetry.

Always Running

For his next work, Rodriguez moved away from poetry, but not from the lyrical inspiration, to tell in prose form the story of his own years in the Los Angeles gangs. He dedicated his book to twenty–five childhood friends of his who died victims of gang violence before the author reached the age of eighteen. In *Always Running: La Vida Loca—Gang Days in L.A.*, Rodriguez also explains the needs out of which the Hispanic gang culture springs. As Dale Eastman reported of the book in *New City* magazine: "Socially ostracized and economically segregated from their white counterparts, the young children of mostly migrant workers who had come north to earn a living, first formed clicas, or clubs, to create some sense of belonging." These Mexican youths were denied, for the most part, membership in other organizations, be it the Boy Scouts or even athletic teams. These alternate, ad hoc youth clubs slowly evolved into the gangs of today, many of them simply another way to hang out with friends. Eastman further noted: "As increasing numbers of Mexicans moved into the barrio areas, the clubs adopted a more dangerous profile, offering much–needed protection from rival groups and a sense of power in an increasingly powerless world."

As Rodriguez grew older, he became increasingly involved in drugs and gang violence. Gary Soto, critiquing *Always Running* in the *New York Times Book Review*, noted that "the body count rises page by page. The incidents become increasingly bizarre and perversely engaging. Mr. Rodriguez is jailed for attempted murder, then let go. He participates in the firebombing of a home. He robs stores. He experiments with heroin. He wounds a biker with a shotgun blast, is arrested, then let go. When police officers beat him to the ground, his 'foot inadvertently came up and brushed one of them in the chest,' and he is booked for assault and eventually tried and jailed." But Rodriguez also tells how he escaped the gang life, and he brings *Always Running* up to date by discussing the role of gangs in the 1992 riots in Los Angeles, and his own son's gang involvement in Chicago. Soto concluded that *Always Running* "is a chilling portrait of gang life during the 1960s, a gang life that haunts us even now. . . . The book is fierce and fearless."

Castillo noted that while some critics call the book "a memoir, others have qualified it as a novel of redemption because of its fictional/poetic qualities." As Rodriguez noted to Cohen, the book is a little of both, for he "synthesized events and reorganized the material so that it would work as literature [fiction] but still maintain the truth and reality of the situation." Castillo further observed: "Often poetic, the narration is nevertheless a straight presentation of life as it was for Rodriguez. Readers witness a childhood and adult behavior that is surprising for its violence." Ultimately, Rodriguez was saved from the violence by two mentors who showed him a different path; such a path was not open to Chava, a former gang leader whom Rodriguez meets at the end of the book, outside a party. Battered and wounded—Chava carries a colostomy bag as a result of a stabbing—this once feared enemy is "a fragment of the race, drunk, agonized, crushed, and I can't hate him anymore; I can't see him as the manifestation of craziness and power he once possessed; he's a caricature, an apparition, but also more like me, capable of so much ache beneath the exterior of so much strength . . . ."

Other reviewers lauded Rodriguez's gritty tale, while a storm of controversy began to brew over its use in the schools. Suzanne Ruta called the book "beautifully written and politically astute" in an *Entertainment Weekly* review, while Floyd Salas, writing in the *Los Angeles Times,* felt it was "a pilgrim's progress, a classic tale of the new immigrant in the land of the melting pot." Salas went on to describe *Always Running* as "a tome of the torturous, faltering, sometimes progressing, sometimes repressing journey of a gifted migrant. With this memorable, often tragic story, Rodriguez has fulfilled that journey by achieving the American dream of success in art and life." Fred Whitehead, reviewing the book in *National Catholic Reporter,* concluded, "By expressing the pain of those most destroyed, Rodriguez never lets us forget where we need to go together. He thinks it is possible for us all to deal with these problems, not by way of patching here and there,

but through fundamental change." Echoing these sentiments, a reviewer for *The Progressive* wrote that this "beautifully written insider's account of what it's like to live in the desolation of America's urban ghettoes" tells "how our society leaves minorities and the poor no viable alternatives. . . . The problem, Rodriguez makes clear, is not with the gangs but with the society that creates gangs."

In artistic content, Rodriguez was perhaps too successful in his reproduction of the climate of violence in which he grew up. Several school boards around the country banned the book from its library shelves, criticizing it for promoting violence. But Rodriguez is steadfast. The book neither glorifies nor demonizes gang involvement, for as Rodriguez told Sullivan, "[b]oth views distort reality." The book contains, according to its many supporters, a message that will reach kids in gangs, that touches their lives directly and that may lead them—as a similar approach did for Rodriguez himself—out of the violence and into the light. Ilan Stavans, reviewing the book in *The Nation,* posed this very desire: "Although gang life may be impossible to eradicate fully, one hopes that *Always Running* (a fortunate title) will be read where it most counts, and widely, and have an impact."

Man of Letters and Social Activist

Rodriguez has maintained a busy schedule of writing and speaking in schools since the publication of *Always Running,* becoming a spokesman for Latino causes, as well as for youth and the dispossessed. Deeply involved in social causes, Rodriguez has also continued to publish distinguished and innovative verse and prose. In 1998, he added to his poetry publications with *Trochemoche,* or "helter–skelter" in Spanish. These verses are once again highly autobiographical in nature and explore the phases of Rodriguez's life from gang member to "his more sedate role as a Chicago publisher," as Lawrence Olszewski noted in a *Library Journal* review of the collection. In the poem "Notes of a Bad Cricket," Rodriguez assays his inner worlds: "There is a mixology of brews within me; I've tasted them all, still fermenting / as grass–high anxieties. I am rebel's pen, rebel's son, father of revolution in verse." Olszewski went on to observe the "head–on, no-holds barred style" which "smacks more of newspaper accounts than lyricism without succumbing to sensationalism." Susan Smith Nash described the collection as "raw, honest, hard–hitting" in *World Literature Today,* with voices that "are dissident, angry, raised in protest." Nash further commented that these voices "are truly unforgettable."

Additionally, Rodriguez has branched out into new territory with his children's books, *America Is Her*

Name and *It Doesn't Have to Be This Way*. Castillo called the former book "a sensitive story for young children" in *Dictionary of Literary Biography*. The story of nine–year–old America Soliz, an illegal Mexican immigrant living in a Chicago barrio, the book takes young readers inside the head and heart of this young girl whose greatest wish is simply to

return to her native Oaxaca. But when a Puerto Rican poet visits her ESL class one day, she is inspired to become a citizen of the world through poetry.

Writing in *School Library Journal*, Denise E. Agosto felt that the "story is generally well told, and its

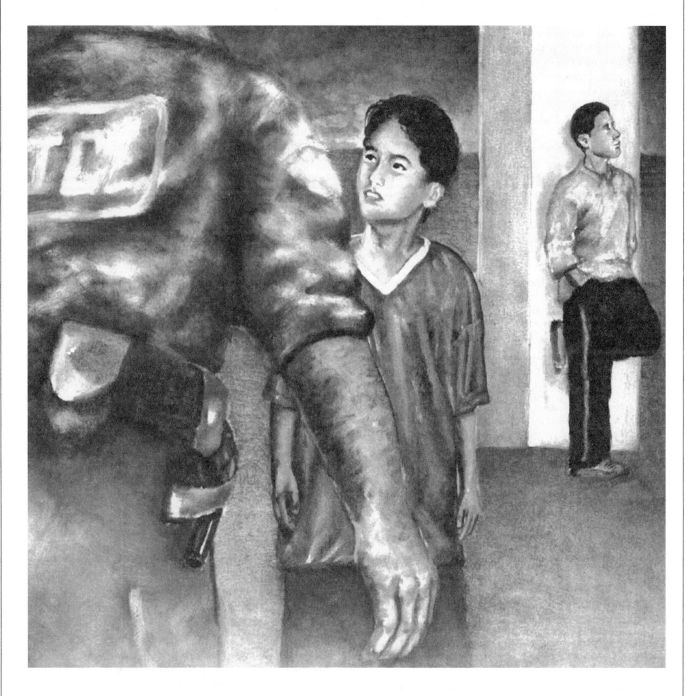

A collaboration with award–winning muralist Daniel Galvez, Rodriguez's 1999 bilingual children's book, *It Doesn't Have to Be This Way*, depicts a young, impressionable boy's initiation into gang life.

message is an important one." Agosto concluded that *America Is Her Name* is a "solid choice for bilingual and ESL collections." Though a reviewer for *Publishers Weekly* thought the book "ponderous" and "wordy," *Skipping Stones'* Beth Erfurth called the book a "story about hopes, memories, and dreams amid a reality of discrimination and despair," and found it to be an "inspiration to readers of all ages."

In a second picture book, *It Doesn't Have to Be This Way*, Rodriguez tells another cautionary tale about gangs. Ten–year–old Monchi relates his own near miss with joining a gang—saved by the shooting of his older girl cousin who has advised him to avoid the gangs. Dreamer, the older cousin, is left in a wheelchair as a result of the shooting, but Monchi refuses to be drawn into the cycle of retribution that others demand. "The message is spelled out," wrote Hazel Rochman in a *Booklist* review, "but Rodriguez's personal experience, as a teenage gang member and now as an adult counselor, gives the story immediacy." *School Library Journal's* Reina Huerta felt the book could be "a springboard for discussion."

Rodriguez once commented: "Despite great odds, today I'm a poet and writer of note, driven by the great social upheavals of our day. I say to any young person—especially one linked to a great cause such as the fundamental progress of humanity—never give up. We all have the capabilities of great art and poetry. It's a matter of tapping into that creative reservoir we contain as human beings. Once tapped, this reservoir is inexhaustible. Skills and technique can always be learned. Opening up to our innate powers as communicators and artists is a strong foundation for obtaining such skills."

If you enjoy the works of Luis J. Rodriguez, you might want to check out the following books:

S. Beth Atkin, *Voices from the Streets: Young Former Gang Members Tell Their Stories,* 1996.
Yxta Maya Murray, *Locas,* 1999.
Gary Soto, *Petty Crimes,* 1998.

And the poet also once noted in an autobiographical essay that after a life lived through cultural and economic hardships, his "resolve has only strength-

ened" and his "vision has only sharpened." Sober, reconciled with family members and the world at large, Rodriguez faces the future with optimism. He concluded his essay: "There are difficult roads ahead; if anything, I'm more prepared for them than I have ever been. According to the ancient Mexican people, we are living under the Fifth Sun. Nahui Ollin. A time of change. Of movement, From the heart of a person to the heart of the universe."

■ Biographical and Critical Sources

BOOKS

Castillo, Dina G., "Luis J. Rodriguez," *Dictionary of Literary Biography,* Volume 209: *Chicano Writers, Third Series,* Gale, 1999, pp. 243–250.
Contemporary Authors Autobiography Series, Volume 29, Gale, 1998.
Rodriguez, Joseph, "La Vida Loca: Joseph Rodriguez and Luis J. Rodriguez on 'The Crazy Life,'" *East Side Stories: Gang Life in East LA,* Powerhouse Books, 1998, pp. 175–185.
Schwartz, Michael, *Luis J. Rodriguez,* Raintree/Steck–Vaughn, 1997.

PERIODICALS

Bilingual Review, September–December, 1996, Audrey Rodriguez, "Contemporary Chicano Poetry," pp. 203–207.
Booklist, August, 1999, Hazel Rochman, review of *It Doesn't Have to Be This Way,* p. 2059.
Chicago Tribune, February 25, 1993.
Entertainment Weekly, February 12, 1993, Suzanne Ruta, review of *Always Running,* p. 51.
Hartford Courant, March 5, 1993, pp. C1, C8.
Hispanic, June, 1993, p. 72.
Hungry Mind Review, summer, 1993.
Library Journal, June 15, 1998, Lawrence Olszewski, review of *Trochemoche,* p. 82.
Los Angeles Times, March 7, 1993, Floyd Salas, "Leaving the Gang Behind," p. 2; March 31, 1993; June 18, 1998.
Los Angeles Weekly, March 7, 1993, Floyd Salas, "Leaving the Gang Behind," p. 2.
Nation, April 12, 1993, Ilan Stavans, review of *Always Running,* pp. 494–498.
National Catholic Reporter, January 8, 1993, Fred Whitehead, review of *Always Running,* p. 61.
New City, February 8, 1993, Dale Eastman, review of *Always Running,* pp. 10, 12.

New York Times Book Review, February 14, 1993, Gary Soto, "The Body Count in the Barrio," p. 26.

Poets and Writers, January–February, 1995, Aaron Cohen, "An Interview with Luis J. Rodriguez," pp. 50–55.

Progressive, September, 1993, review of *Always Running,* p. 43.

Publishers Weekly, May 17, 1991, review of *The Concrete River,* p. 58; February 1, 1993, p. 86; September 23, 1996, p. 12; April 13, 1998, review of *American Is Her Name,* p. 75; August 16, 1999; p. 85.

Rattle Magazine, winter, 1999, interview with Luis Rodriguez.

School Library Journal, September, 1998, Denise E. Agosto, review of *America Is Her Name,* p. 180; October, 1999, Reina Huerta, review of *It Doesn't Have to Be This Way,* p. 124.

Skipping Stones, May–August, 1999, Beth Erfurth, review of *America Is Her Name,* p. 6.

Sojourners, March, 1999, p. 57.

Sonoma County Independent, February 4–10, 1999, Patrick Sullivan, "Class War: Luis J. Rodriguez Casts a Skeptical Eye on Attempts to Ban His Autobiography," pp. 21–22.

Sun Magazine, April, 2000, Derrick Jensen, interview with Luis Rodriguez.

World Literature Today, winter, 1999, Susan Smith Nash, review of *Trochemoche,* p. 156.

OTHER

The Choice of a Lifetime: Returning from the Brink of Suicide (video), New Day Films, 1996.

In Their Own Voices: A Century of Recorded Poetry (audio cassette), Ehino/Word Beat Records, 1996.

Luis Rodriguez (video), Lannan Foundation, 1992.

Making Peace: Youth Struggling for Survival (video), Moira Productions, 1997.

A Snake in the Heart: Poems and Music by Chicago's Spoken Word Performers (audio cassette), Tia Chucha Press, 1994.

La Vida Loca: El Testimonio de un Pandillero en Los Angeles (audio cassette), AudioLibros del Mundo, 1998.

—*Sketch by J. Sydney Jones*

Shel Silverstein

Best Books, *School Library Journal*, 1981, Buckeye awards, 1983 and 1985, George G. Stone award, 1984, and William Allen White award, 1984, all for *A Light in the Attic;* International Reading Association's Children's Choice award, 1982, for *The Missing Piece Meets the Big O.*

■ Personal

Born Sheldon Allan Silverstein, September 25, 1930, in Chicago, IL; died on May 10, 1999, in Key West, FL; son of Nathan and Helen Silverstein; divorced; children: Matthew.

■ Career

Cartoonist, songwriter, recording artist, and writer. *Playboy* magazine, Chicago, IL, writer and cartoonist, 1956–96. Appeared in film *Who Is Harry Kellerman and Why Is He Saying Those Terrible Things about Me?*, 1971; composer of soundtracks for motion pictures. *Military service:* Served in the U.S. Army in the Korean War; cartoonist for *Pacific Stars and Stripes.*

■ Awards, Honors

New York Times Notable Book designation, 1974, Michigan Young Readers award, 1981, and George G. Stone award, 1984, all for *Where the Sidewalk Ends;*

■ Writings

FICTION; SELF–ILLUSTRATED

Uncle Shelby's Story of Lafcadio, the Lion Who Shot Back, Harper (New York City), 1963.

The Giving Tree, Harper, 1964.

Uncle Shelby's Giraffe and a Half, Harper, 1964, published as *A Giraffe and a Half*, J. Cape (London), 1988.

Uncle Shelby's Zoo: Don't Bump the Glump!, Simon & Schuster (New York City), 1964.

(Under pseudonym Uncle Shelby) *Who Wants a Cheap Rhinoceros?*, Macmillan (New York City), 1964, revised edition, 1983.

Where the Sidewalk Ends: Poems and Drawings, Harper, 1974.

The Missing Piece, Harper, 1976.

The Missing Piece Meets the Big O, Harper, 1981.

A Light in the Attic (poems), Harper, 1981.

Falling Up: Poems and Drawings, HarperCollins (New York City), 1996.

The Giving Tree, Where the Sidewalk Ends, A Light in the Attic, and *Falling Up* have been translated into twenty languages.

FOR ADULTS; SELF-ILLUSTRATED

Now Here's My Plan: A Book of Futilities, foreword by Jean Shepherd, Simon & Schuster, 1960.
Uncle Shelby's ABZ Book: A Primer for Tender Minds (humor), Simon & Schuster, 1961.
A Playboy's Teevee Jeebies (cartoons), Playboy Press (Chicago), 1963.
More Playboy's Teevee Jeebies: Do-It-Yourself Dialogue for the Late Late Show, Playboy Press, 1965.

PLAYS

The Lady or the Tiger Show (one-act; based on the short story by Frank Stockwell), produced in New York City, 1981.
(And director) *Gorilla,* produced in Chicago, 1981.
Wild Life (includes one-acts *I'm Good to My Doggies, Nonstop, Chicken Suit Optional,* and *The Lady or the Tiger Show*), produced in New York City, 1983.
Remember Crazy Zelda?, produced in New York City, 1984.
The Crate, produced in New York City, 1985.
The Happy Hour, produced in New York City, 1985.
One Tennis Shoe, produced in New York City, 1985.
Little Feet, produced in New York City, 1986.
Wash and Dry, produced in New York City, 1986.
(With David Mamet) *Things Change: A Screenplay,* Grove Press (New York City), 1988.
The Devil and Billy Markham (produced with David Mamet's *Bobby Gould in Hell* under collective title *Oh, Hell,* at Lincoln Center, New York City, 1989), published in *Oh, Hell: Two One-Act Plays,* S. French (New York City), 1991.

Contributor to *The Best American Short Plays, 1992–1993: The Theatre Annual since 1937,* edited by Billy Aronson, Applause (Diamond Bar, CA), 1993.

RECORDINGS

Dirty Feet, Hollis Music, 1968.
Shel Silverstein: Songs and Stories, Casablanca, 1978.
Where the Sidewalk Ends, Columbia, 1984.

Also recorded *Drain My Brain* and *The Great Conch Train Robbery.*

OTHER

Different Dances (drawings), Harper, 1979.
(With David Mamet) *Things Change* (screenplay), Grove Press, 1988.

Contributor to *I Like You, If You Like Me: Poems of Friendship,* edited by Myra Cohn Livingston, McElderry Books, 1987, and *Spooky Poems,* collected by Jill Bennett, illustrated by Mary Rees, Little, Brown, 1989. Also writer of lyrics for popular songs, including "A Boy Named Sue," "Sylvia's Mother," "Hey Loretta," "Boa Constrictor, "The Unicorn," and "I'm My Own Grandpa." Albums of Silverstein's songs recorded by other artists include *Freakin' at the Freakers Ball,* Columbia, 1972; *Sloppy Seconds,* Columbia, 1972; *Dr. Hook,* Columbia, 1972; and *Bobby Bare Sings Lullabies, Legends, and Lies: The Songs of Shel Silverstein,* RCA Victor, 1973.

■ Adaptations

Several of Silverstein's books have been recorded on audio cassette.

■ Sidelights

Upon Shel Silverstein's death from a heart attack in 1999, his long-time editor at HarperCollins, Robert Warren, noted in a *Publishers Weekly* obituary that the poet, illustrator, playwright, songwriter, and humorist "had a genius that transcended age and gender, and his work probably touched the lives of more people than any writer in the second half of the 20th century." Blending the zaniness of Dr. Seuss with the cheek of Edward Lear, and wrapping it all up with a darker edged ribbon than either possessed, Silverstein transformed the genre of nonsense verse and absurdist drawing with his four best-selling books, *The Giving Tree, Where the Sidewalk Ends, A Light in the Attic,* and *Falling Up.* Together these books have sold, according to *Publishers Weekly,* over eighteen million copies in twenty languages around the world. His many creative outlets—as writer, illustrator, playwright, actor, performer, composer of country, pop, and children's songs, and author of movie soundtracks—have earned Shel Silverstein the title of "Renaissance Man": a man of many talents. While his self-illustrated volumes of prose and poetry are frequently relegated to children's literature collections, many critics have embraced his work as speaking to readers of all ages. In music, he penned and recorded such country classics as "A Boy Named Sue," made popular by the singer Johnny Cash. As a cartoonist for *Playboy*, Silverstein amused an entire post–war generation, and as a playwright he produced such popular works as *The Lady or the Tiger Show*. Collaborating with the playwright and director, David Mamet, Silverstein produced, among others, the screenplay for Mamet's 1988 movie, *Times Change*.

Born in Chicago, Illinois, in 1930, the young Silverstein grew up in the Logan Square neighborhood, a somewhat low–class area at the time. Silverstein once noted that he fell sideways into art. "When I was a kid—12, 14, around there—I would much rather have been a good baseball player or a hit with the girls," he once told *Publishers Weekly*'s Jean F. Mercier in a rare interview. "But I couldn't play ball, I couldn't dance. Luckily, the girls didn't want me; not much I could do about that. So, I started to draw and to write. . . . By the time I got to where I was attracting girls, I was already into work, and it was more important to me." One of two siblings, Silverstein graduated from Roosevelt High School and then went on to the University of Illinois as an art student, where he lasted only one year before withdrawing, and then attended the Chicago Academy of Fine arts. Drafted into the Army in September, 1953, he served in both Japan and Korea, working during that period as a cartoonist for *Stars and Stripes,* a Pacific–based U.S. military publication. By this time, his cartoons already contained a heavy dose of satire, lampooning various features of military life. Not known as a model soldier, Silverstein had the stubborn habit of getting into trouble with superior officers.

Returning to civilian life in 1956, he took a job with *Playboy* as a cartoonist, his first cartoon appearing in the August, 1956 edition of the magazine. The following December, he published his first article for *Playboy*, "Confessions of a Button Down Man." Eventually Silverstein's work for the magazine was anthologized in the collections *Playboy's Teevee Jeebies* and *More Playboy's Teevee Jeebies; Do–It–Yourself Dialog for the Late Late Show*. Along with his drawing, Silverstein began writing songs, which made him well known in country music circles. Singer Johnny Cash made a number–one hit out of the Silverstein–penned "A Boy Named Sue" in 1969, and Silverstein himself recorded a country music album, *The Great Conch Train Robbery*, in 1980. He also wrote lyrics for Loretta Lynn, Kris Kristofferson, and the Serendipity Singers, among many others, and his folk and country music is still available on CD.

Retooling for a Juvenile Audience

Meanwhile, in 1963, at the suggestion of fellow illustrator Tomi Ungerer, Silverstein wrote and illustrated his first book for young readers: *Uncle Shelby's Story of Lafcadio, the Lion Who Shot Back*. The story of a lion who gets hold of a hunter's gun, practices until he becomes a crack shot, and then joins a circus where he can exhibit his talent, *Lafcadio* was praised by a *Publishers Weekly* reviewer as "a wild, free–wheeling, slangy tale that most children and many parents will enjoy immensely."

Although *Lafcadio, the Lion Who Shot Back* was a successful debut for the newly minted children's writer, it was 1964's *The Giving Tree* that made the name Shel Silverstein well known to children and adults across the country. A simple story that has since attained the status of a childhood classic, *The Giving Tree* follows a young boy as he grows up. The stages of maturation into adulthood are marked by the boy's relationship with a tree, which gives the boy shade and a branch to swing from when he is young, apples to sell when he is a teenager in need of money, wood for a house when he becomes the head of a family, and a log from which to carve a boat when he wants to escape from the rat race. Finally, with its fruit, branches, and trunk now gone, the tree continues to serve the boy; now grown to a bent old man, he uses the tree's stump as a place to rest.

The deceptive simplicity of Silverstein's poignant parable has left it open to varied interpretations. While, as Richard R. Lingeman noted in the *New York Times Book Review*, "many readers saw a religious symbolism in the altruistic tree; ministers preached sermons on *The Giving Tree*; it was discussed in Sunday School." Other critics have maintained that the allegorical tale conceals a more sinister message. "By choosing the female pronoun for the all–giving tree and the male pronoun for the all–taking boy, it is clear that the author did have a prototypical master/slave relationship in mind," critic Barbara A. Schram argued in *Interracial Books for Children*. "How frightening," she later added, "that little boys and girls who read *The Giving Tree* will encounter this glorification of female selflessness and male selfishness." For his part, Silverstein told Lingeman that the parable–like tale was "just a relationship between two people: one gives and the other takes." Critics have remained divided on the true message behind the story, some reading depths into it, others taking it as a bit of whimsy from Silverstein. Eric A. Kimmel, writing in *Twentieth–Century Children's Writers*, called *The Giving Tree* "a deceptively simple parable about a tree that gives all it has to the little boy who loves it." Noting that the book had been alternately praised by ministers and denounced by feminists, Kimmel imagined that Silverstein for his part was "laughing in his beard." And writing about *The Giving Tree* in a humorous vein ten years on in the *New York Times Book Review*, William Cole observed, "My interpretation is that that was one dum–dum of a tree, giving everything and getting nothing in return. Once beyond boyhood, the boy is unpleasant and ungrateful, and I wouldn't give him the time of day, much less my bole."

Silverstein's "poems read like those a fourth grader would write in the back of his notebook when the teacher's eye was turned. That may be precisely their appeal."

—Eric A. Kimmel

Equally controversial was *The Missing Piece*, which Silverstein published in 1976. Together with its sequel, 1981's *The Missing Piece Meets the Big O*, Silverstein relates the efforts of a partial circle, missing a pie–shaped piece, to search for that part that will make it complete. After the circle finds its missing wedge, it realizes that the process of the search was more enjoyable than reaching its goal; that the missing piece wasn't really necessary after all. In contrast, the wedge's point of view serves as the basis for *The Missing Piece Meets the Big O*. One reading of these books reveals a moral along the lines of "too much togetherness turns people into bores—that creativity is preserved by freedom to explore from one relationship to another," according to critic Anne Roiphe in her *New York Times Book Review* commentary. Roiphe also added, however, that another interpretation could be made: "no one should try to find all the answers, no one should hope to fill all the holes in themselves . . . because a person without a search, loose ends, internal conflicts and external goals becomes too smooth to enjoy or know what's going on." Lingeman paired *The Missing Piece* together with its predecessor, *The Giving Tree,* as "almost parables, with a kind of wise–fool simplicity." Silverstein expounded to Lingeman on the interpretation of the ending of *The Missing Piece*. Deciding not to stop the book where the whole seemed to have found its missing mate and as a result could no longer sing its happy–go–lucky song, Silverstein

continued the parable. "Instead it goes off singing," Silverstein told Lingeman. "It's still looking for the missing piece. That's the madness of the book, the disturbing part of it." Something of a foe to the traditional happy endings in children's books, Silverstein felt that such endings "create an alienation " in children, as he put it to Lingeman, for most children do not have that same level of happiness and joy in their own lives. Reviewing *The Missing Piece Meets the Big O* in the *New York Times Book Review*, Joyce Milton felt that "the title of Shel Silverstein's new cartoon fable is definitely the best part." Milton called Silverstein a "witty man" and "not so much an author of children's books as a publishing phenomenon."

Blockbuster Light Verse

Where The Sidewalk Ends: Poems and Drawings, published in 1974, marked a new direction for Silverstein. Following in the footsteps of such popular writers as Dr. Seuss, Roald Dahl, and limerick–writer Edward Lear, Silverstein infused a generous dose of nonsense into his rhymes, many of which were based on song lyrics. With such gloriously titled verses as "Sarah Cynthia Sylvia Stout" (who "would not take the garbage out"), "With His Mouth Full of Food," and "Band–Aids," *Where the Sidewalk Ends* was instantly popular with the younger set. "With creatures from the never–heard, Ickle Me Pickle Me, Tickle Me Too, the Mustn'ts, Hector the Collector, and Sarah Cynthia Sylvia Stout . . . Silverstein's funny bone seems to function wherever he goes," exclaimed reviewer Kay Winters in *Reading Teacher*.

Reviewing the title in *New York Times Book Review*, Sherwin D. Smith commented, "Here's a volume of verse for children labeled 'all ages.' It's either the ultimate in silliness or the ultimate in good sense, quite possibly the latter." Smith ticked off a number of "rollicking patter songs," including 'Sarah Cynthia Sylvia Stout,'" but went on to debunk what he saw as a myth about Silverstein being a "Renaissance Man." For Smith, Silverstein was "a very facile 20th–century man with a sense of where the market is. The result is a sense of derivativeness." Smith pointed out the obvious parallels between "Sarah Cynthia Sylvia Stout" and A. A. Milne's "Disobedience," as well as between Silverstein's "Dreadful" and Harry Graham's "Ruthless Rhymes for Heartless Children." In spite of all of this, however, Smith concluded, "there's some nice, lively stuff in here, good for reading aloud on a sleety weekend afternoon. Just don't make it the only book of verse on the children's shelves."

A follow–up collection of poetry, *A Light in the Attic*, was published in 1981, to the joy of growing numbers of Silverstein devotees. With one hundred thirty–six poems, *Light* is even more substantial than *Sidewalk.* "Both cartoons and verses in this new bunch seem just about as lively as those in *Sidewalk,*" noted X. J. Kennedy in the *New York Times Book Review.* "In his verse for children . . . , Shel Silverstein displays a certain startling quirkiness," Kennedy further commented. Kennedy pointed to "a streak of the weird" in poems such as "Who Ordered the Broiled Face" and "Quick Trip," among others. "In some of his most memorable nonsense," according to Kennedy, "Mr. Silverstein is playfully disruptive of parental authority." Further poems include a fresh take on fairy tales with "In Search of Cinderella." Here the prince searches from "dusk to dawn" to find the "slender foot" that fits the crystal shoe: "From dusk to dawn, / I try it on / Each damsel that I meet / And I still love her so, but oh, / I've started hating feet." Kennedy concluded his review of *A Light in the Attic* by writing, "Mr. Silverstein's work remains a must for lovers of good verse for children. Quite like nobody else, he is still a master of delectable outrage and the proprietor of a surprisingly finely tuned sensibility." Kimmel wrote, "It is easy to dismiss Shel Silverstein as a facile versifier with the knack of combining just the right amount of sentiment and impudence to assure mass appeal, but that would not be doing him justice." Noting the immense popularity of both *Where the Sidewalk Ends* and *A Light in the Attic,* Kimmel declared, "For better or worse, the monumental success of these two books has transformed the way poetry is taught in American schools. . . . His poems read like those a fourth grader would write in the back of his notebook when the teacher's eye was turned. That may be precisely their appeal."

Versifying Hiatus

It was another fifteen years before devoted fans could relish new Silverstein verse nonsense. In addition to writing several plays, which included the 1981 stage hit *The Lady or the Tiger Show,* 1984's *Remember Crazy Zelda?,* and the 1986 stage debut of *Wash and Dry,* Silverstein collaborated with film director David Mamet on the upbeat play *Oh, Hell!* and a screenplay for the Mamet–directed film *Things Change,* released in 1988. Reviewing *The Lady or the Tiger Show* in the *New York Times,* Mel Gussow called the play "a cynical satire of our acquisitive, amoral society," and the "highlight" of an annual festival of one–act plays at the Ensemble Studio Theater for 1981. A game show contestant is faced with choosing between two doors: behind one is a vicious tiger, and behind the other is the girl of the contestant's dreams. A reviewer for *Variety* called the one–act play "a hilarious harpooning of media hype and

show biz amorality." Gussow, reviewing Silverstein's 1985 one–act, *One Tennis Shoe,* called it "a wild card of a comedy," and his 1986 one–act, "Little Feet," "smart, mischievous and very quick." Reviewing a performance of four of his one–act plays, Frank Rich commented in the *New York Times,* "Whoever the ubiquitous Shel Silverstein is, he's certainly unpredictable . . . . Now we have Shel Silverstein the playwright, and this may eventually prove his most fruitful career to date." Writing of his 1985 play, *The Crate,* Rich noted, "Whatever else is to be said about Mr. Silverstein, he's a man who marches to his own unpredictable beat . . . . [H]e has been testing the theatrical waters for a few years now. The result has been a steady flow of antic one–act plays—some wonderful . . . some less so."

Finally, in 1996, a new work of nonsense verse by Silverstein arrived in bookstores. *Falling Up: Poems and Drawings,* a collection of verses with line drawings, was met by mostly positive reviews and eager readers. Calling the one–hundred–fifty poems included in *Falling Up* an "inspired assemblage of cautionary tales, verbal hijinks, and thoughtful observations, deftly inserted," a *Kirkus Reviews* critic dubbed Silverstein's latest an irresistible read. Other reviewers have agreed; commenting on the author's interjection of social commentary, Susan Dove Lempke noted in *Booklist* that "It's been a long wait for fans of *A Light in the Attic* . . . but it was worth it. . . . As always, Silverstein has a direct line to what kids like, and he gives them poems celebrating the gross, the scary, the absurd, and the comical." A mouse in the hair is conjured up in "Imagining," and wordplay takes over in "The Gnome, the Gnat, and the Gnu," with it's silly line, "That Gnat ain't done gnothing to you." Other verses range the gamut from an ode to Pinocchio to a lament over a "Stone Airplane": "I made an airplane out of stone . . . / I always did like staying home."

A reviewer for *Publishers Weekly* observed, "All the things that children loved about *A Light in the Attic* and *Where the Sidewalk Ends* can be found in abundance in this eclectic volume." The same reviewer further commented, "By turns cheeky and clever and often darkly subversive, the poems are vintage Silverstein." The humorously seditious poems of this volume, like his earlier ones, give voice to a child's desperate need for empowerment, as in "Remote–a–Dad," with which a child can instantly control his parent. Reviewing *Falling Up* in *Horn Book,* Nancy Vasilakis noted that while the book "is patterned . . . after Silverstein's two phenomenally successful earlier volumes," it was not up to the standard of those. "An occasional touch of the old spark appears here and there, but these are less frequent than the cheap bathroom humor which will make adults, at least, wince." Yet as with all of Silverstein's work, such critical judgment varied. Lempke concluded her *Booklist* review, "[I]n addition to all the laughs, [Silverstein] slips in some thought–provoking verses about animal rights, morality, and the strange ways humans behave."

If you enjoy the works of Shel Silverstein, you might want to check out the following books:

Jack Prelutsky, *It's Raining Pigs and Noodles*, 2000.
Maurice Sendak, *In the Night Kitchen*, 1970.
Dr. Suess, *Green Eggs and Ham*, 1960.

Silverstein died three years after publication of this last book of verse, leaving a legacy of silliness and fun for generations of children of all ages. On a more material level, his legacy to his son was an estate worth $20 million. Despite varying critical opinions of his work, the fact remains that Silverstein helped introduce painless poetry to kids. As Kimmel summed up, "Whatever his literary shortcomings, by convincing millions of children that poetry is neither difficult nor threatening, Silverstein has earned himself an honorable place among the great names in writing for children."

■ Biographical and Critical Sources

BOOKS

Children's Literature Review, Volume 5, Gale (Detroit), 1983.

Kimmel, Eric A., "Shel Silverstein: Overview," *Twentieth–Century Children's Writers*, 4th edition, St. James Press (Detroit), 1995.

Legends in Their Own Time, Prentice–Hall (Upper Saddle River, NJ), 1994.

PERIODICALS

Booklist, July, 1996, Susan Dove Lempke, review of *Falling Up*, p. 1824.

Horn Book, September–October, 1996, Nancy Vasilakis, review of *Falling Up*, p. 606.
Interracial Books for Children, Volume 5, number 5, 1974, Barbara A. Schram, "Misgivings about *The Giving Tree*," pp. 1, 8.
Kirkus Reviews, May 1, 1996, review of *Falling Up: Poems and Drawings*.
Language Arts, January, 1982, p. 53.
New Republic, January 29, 1990, p. 28.
New York Times, May 29, 1981, Mel Gussow, review of *The Lady and the Tiger Show*; May 4, 1983, Frank Rich, "Choosing a Door"; February 15, 1985, Frank Rich, "Flights of Crate–ivity"; June 10, 1985, Mel Gussow, review of *One Tennis Shoe*; June 3, 1986, Mel Gussow, review of *Little Feet*.
New York Times Book Review, September 9, 1973, William Cole, "About Alice, a Rabbit, a Tree," p. 8; November 3, 1974, Sherwin D. Smith, review of *Where the Sidewalk Ends*, pp. 24 25; May 2, 1976, Anne Roiphe, review of *The Missing Piece*, p. 28; April 30, 1978, Richard R. Lingeman, "The Third Mr. Silverstein," p. 57; October 11, 1981, Joyce Milton, review of *The Missing Piece Meets the Big O*, p. 39; November 15, 1981, X. J. Kennedy, "A Rhyme Is a Chime," pp. 51, 60; March 9, 1986, pp. 36–37; May 19, 1996, p. 29.
People, August 18, 1980.
Publishers Weekly, October 28, 1963, review of *Uncle Shelby's Story of Lafcadio, the Lion Who Shot Back*, p. 52; December 9, 1974, p. 68; January 24, 1975, Jean F. Mercier, "Shel Silverstein," pp. 50, 52; September 18, 1981, p. 155; November 16, 1992, p. 25; April 29, 1996, review of *Falling Up*, p. 73.
Reading Teacher, February, 1976, Kay Winters, review of *Where the Sidewalk Ends: Poems and Drawings*, p. 515.
School Library Journal, September, 1976, p. 125; April, 1981, p. 143; July, 1996.
Time, December 18, 1989, p. 78.
Time for Kids, May 17, 1996, p. 8.
Times Educational Supplement, November 23, 1984, p. 37.
Variety, May 11, 1983, review of *The Lady and the Tiger Show*.
Voice of Youth Advocates, February, 1982, p. 45.
Wilson Library Bulletin, November, 1987, p. 65.

ONLINE

Shel Silverstein, http://www.banned–width.com/ (December 13, 2000).

■ Obituaries

PERIODICALS

Chicago Tribune, May 11, 1999, Section 1, p. 16.
Horn Book, July–August, 1999, p. 494.

London Times, May 12, 1999.

New York Times, May 11, 1999, p. B10.

Publishers Weekly, May 17, 1999, p. 32.

Washington Post, May 11, 1999, p. B5.*

—Sketch by J. Sydney Jones

Orson Welles

■ Personal

Born May 6, 1915, in Kenosha, WI; died October 10, 1985, in Los Angeles, CA; son of Richard Head (an inventor and manufacturer) and Beatrice (a pianist; maiden name, Ives) Welles; married Virginia Nicholson (an actress), December 20, 1934 (divorced, 1940); married Rita Hayworth (an actress), September 7, 1942 (divorced, 1948); married Paolo Mori (an actress), May 8, 1955; children: Christopher, Rebecca, Beatrice. *Education:* Graduated from Todd High School in Woodstock, IL, 1930. *Hobbies and other interests:* Gourmet food, magic.

■ Career

Actor, director, producer, and writer of productions for radio, stage, television, and motion pictures. Actor in stage productions, including *The Jew Suss,* 1931, *Romeo and Juliet,* 1933, *Macbeth,* 1936, *Doctor Faustus,* 1937, *Julius Caesar,* 1937, *Five Kings,* 1939, *The Unthinking Lobster,* 1950, *King Lear,* 1956, and *Chimes at Midnight,* 1960; actor in radio productions, including *The Shadow,* 1935, and in motion pictures, including *Citizen Kane,* 1941, *Jane Eyre,* 1944, *The Third Man,* 1949, *Othello,* 1952, and *Falstaff,* 1966; actor in television productions, including *King Lear,* 1953, and *The Immortal Story,* 1968. Director of stage productions, including *Horse Eats Hat,* 1936, *The Cradle Will Rock,* 1937, *Moby Dick,* 1955, and *Rhinoceros,* 1960, radio productions, including *Dracula,*

1938, and *Invasion From Mars,* 1938, and motion pictures, including *Citizen Kane,* 1941, *The Magnificent Ambersons,* 1942, *Othello,* 1952, *The Trial,* 1962, and *Falstaff,* 1966. Narrator of numerous productions for radio, stage, television, and motion pictures. Co-director with John Houseman of Federal Theatre Project's Negro People's Theatre, 1936–37; co-founder with Houseman of Mercury Productions, 1937. Announcer for radio program *Hello, Americans,* 1942; toured in *The Mercury Wonder Show,* 1943.

■ Awards, Honors

Claire M. Senie Plaque from Drama Study Club, 1938; co-winner with Herman Mankiewicz of Academy Award for best screenplay from Academy of Motion Picture Arts and Sciences and nominations for best actor and best director, all 1941, all for *Citizen Kane;* Golden Palm award for best film from Cannes Film Festival, 1956, for *Othello;* Grand Prize from Brussels Film Festival, 1958, for *Touch of Evil;* co-winner of best actor award from Cannes Film Festival, 1959, for *Compulsion; Citizen Kane* was selected as "best film in motion picture history" by international film critics in polls taken in 1962 and 1972; Twentieth Anniversary Special Prize from Cannes Film Festival, 1966, for *Chimes at Midnight;* Special Academy Award from Academy of Motion Picture Arts and Sciences, 1971; Life Achievement Award from American Film Institute, 1974; and numerous other film awards.

■ Writings

The Free Company Presents . . . His Honor, the Mayor (radio play; first broadcast by Columbia Broadcasting System, April 6, 1941), [New York], 1941.

(Compiler) *Invasion From Mars, Interplanetary Stories: Thrilling Adventures in Space*, Dell, 1949.

(With others) *The Lives of Harry Lime*, News of the World, 1952.

Mr. Arkadin (novel), Crowell, 1956.

(And director) *Moby Dick—Rehearsed* (two-act play; produced in London at Duke of York's Theatre, June 16, 1955; adapted from the novel by Herman Melville), Samuel French, 1965.

(And director) *The Trial* (screenplay; produced by Paris Europa Productions/FI–C–IT/Hisa–Films, 1962; adapted from the novel by Franz Kafka), translated by Nicholas Fry, Simon & Schuster, 1970.

(With Herman Mankiewicz) *The Citizen Kane Book* (contains shooting script and screenplay by Welles and Mankiewicz for *Citizen Kane*, Mercury, 1941), introduction by Pauline Kael, Little, Brown, 1971.

Also co–editor with R. Hill of *Everybody's Shakespeare*, 1934, and *The Mercury Shakespeare*, 1939. Other screenplays; all as director, except as noted: *The Magnificent Ambersons* (adapted from the novel by Booth Tarkington), Mercury, 1942; (screen story only) Charles Chaplin, *Monsieur Verdoux*, United Artists, 1947; *The Lady From Shanghai* (adapted from the novel by Sherwood King, *If I Die Before I Wake*), Mercury, 1946; *Macbeth* (adapted from the play by William Shakespeare), Mercury, 1948; *Othello* (adapted from the play by Shakespeare), Mercury, 1952; *Mr. Arkadin* (released in England as *Confidential Report*; adapted from own novel), Cervantes Film Organization/Sevilla Studios, 1955; *Touch of Evil* (adapted from the novel *Badge of Evil* by Whit Masterson), Universal, 1958; *Falstaff* (released in England as *Chimes at Midnight*; adapted from various plays by Shakespeare), International Films Espanola/Alpine, 1966; *The Immortal Story* (adapted for French television from the novel by Isak Dinesen), ORTF/Albina Films, 1968; *F for Fake* (documentary), Specialty Films, 1975; *Filming Othello* (documentary), 1979. Also author and director of unreleased motion picture *Too Much Johnson*, Mercury, 1938, and unfinished films including *It's All True*, with Norman Foster and John Fante, Mercury, 1942, and *The Deep*, adapted from the novel *Dead Calm* by Charles Williams, 1967–69. Author of numerous unproduced screenplays, including *Operation Cinderella*.

OTHER

Author of libretto for ballet *The Lady in Ice*, 1953. Co–author and narrator of adaptations of novels for radio and for recordings. Author of column, *Orson Welles' Almanac*, for New York Post, 1945.

■ Sidelights

Considered an artistic genius, Orson Welles was involved in productions for radio, theatre, film, and television in a career spanning more than forty years. He was found to be exceptional as a child—reading at age two, playing Igor Stravinsky's music on the violin at seven, performing William Shakespeare's plays at ten—and by the time he reached his mid–twenties he had acted on Dublin and New York stages and had created a sensation with his radio adaptation of H.G. Well's *War of the Worlds.* Broadcast on Halloween, 1938, by the Mercury Theatre of the Air—which Welles and actor John Houseman had founded the previous year. The drama unintentionally convinced many Americans that Martians were invading the earth, causing widespread panic.

Also the onetime voice of the popular radio character *The Shadow*, Wells was dubbed the "boy wonder" of radio, and his success attracted the attention of the motion picture industry. In 1940 RKO studios brought Welles to Hollywood, and that year he began work on his film *Citizen Kane*, based on the life of publishing magnate William Randolph Hearst. Believed by many to be the greatest film ever made, *Citizen Kane* earned Welles a 1941 Academy Award for best screenplay as well as nominations for best actor and best director. The film is credited with technical innovations that set new creative standards for cinematic arts. Welles proceeded to write and direct a number of other films, including *The Magnificent Ambersons, The Lady From Shanghai,* in which he starred with his second wife, actress Rita Hayworth, *A Touch of Evil,* and *Chimes at Midnight/ Falstaff.*

But in later years Welles's filmmaking career languished, due at least in part to his inability to raise sufficient financial backing for his projects. He left many projects unfinished, acted in the films of others, rendered some unremarkable television appearances, and endorsed products in commercial advertising. Most notable among the latter was his pitch for Paul Masson vineyards, in which Welles proclaimed the vineyard would "sell no wine before its time."

Beginnings in the Theater

Although Welles is probably best known for his film *Citizen Kane* and his 1938 radio broadcast of the Martian "invasion," he first received recognition for

Welles in the title role of his best–known film, *Citizen Kane* (1941), a fictionalization of the life of newspaper tycoon William Randolph Hearst.

his work in the theatre. As a youth Welles exhibited precocity as an actor, artist, and magician (he studied under Houdini); at ten he had already read Nietzsche and all of Shakespeare. Upon graduation from high school at fifteen he decided to tour Ireland and sketch his impressions. There he attended a performance by the Gate Players, after which he convinced the troupe's director to cast him in *The Jew Suss.* Welles toured briefly with the players before arriving in London, where his roles were assumed by British actors.

He returned to America and then abruptly departed for Morocco, where he lived in a tent writing plays and stories. After returning to the United States, he submitted his writings to publishers and magazines but with little success. Then he attended a party and met Thornton Wilder, who had heard of Welles's accomplishments as an actor in Ireland. With Wilder's assistance, Welles managed to land the roles of Tybalt and Mercutio in *Romeo and Juliet.*

After *Romeo and Juliet,* Welles distinguished himself in productions of *Candida* and *Panic,* the latter produced by John Houseman. Welles then directed and acted at the Woodstock Dramatic Festival, and afterwards teamed with Houseman to establish an independent theatre. Welles's parents were both wealthy but his father, alarmed by his son's financial nonchalance, had stipulated that young Orson turn twenty–five before collecting his inheritance. Undaunted, Welles, who possessed an impressive voice, began working for radio programs to obtain funds for the theatre. Among his best–known roles for the radio shows was that of The Shadow in the program of the same title.

In 1935, Welles and Houseman accepted a position with the Federal Theatre Project as co–directors of the Negro People's Theatre. Some of Welles's most impressive innovations derived from this association. *Macbeth,* his initial production as director with the company, was marked by daring use of an all black cast in Haitian setting. Welles also replaced the witches with voodoo doctors. The play was an enormous critical success, and Welles followed it with an even greater one, *Doctor Faustus.* Directing himself in the title role, Welles astonished audiences by replacing conventional props and backgrounds with huge, wandering columns of light and exaggerated shadows. Critics began hailing Welles as the theatre's "boy genius."

But critical success was not enough to perpetuate the project. Welles had to fund much of *Doctor Faustus* himself, and his association with the project closed in grandiose fashion when the company was left without a theatre for the first performance of *The Cradle Will Rock.* Since the audience had already arrived, Welles led them through New York City with cast in tow and eventually performed the play in another theatre.

With the Negro People's Theatre defunct, Welles and Houseman created their own company, Mercury Theatre. They chose *Julius Caesar* as their first effort, in which Welles played Brutus and directed. By now the public was expecting radical interpretations from Welles and Houseman, and *Julius Caesar* was no disappointment. Caesar appeared in Fascist uniform while other characters wore modern dress (Welles wore "intellectual's" garb). The background was the brick wall surrounding the stage.

Julius Caesar was produced in 1938 when Welles was twenty–six. The same year Mercury Theatre began presenting a radio program, *Mercury Theatre of the Air,* which Welles edited, directed, broadcast, and co–wrote. The show is remembered for its adaptation of the H. G. Wells novel, *The War of the Worlds.* By presenting the program as a series of newscasts covering an invasion of Earth by Martians, the Mercury Theatre unintentionally created a minor panic: listeners actually believed that Martians were attacking! People fled their homes and caused traffic jams while armed citizens patrolled the streets for signs of alien life. The public swamped Welles with complaints and threats. The Mercury Theatre survived the incident, though, only to fold the following year.

The telling blow for the Mercury Theatre was the play *Five Kings,* an amalgam of five historical plays by Shakespeare. Welles had worked intermittently on it since childhood but was overwhelmed by its demands. The production proved disastrous and in 1940 he left New York City for Hollywood and movies, taking the Mercury Theatre ensemble with him.

Hollywood Success with *Citizen Kane*

Welles was greeted less than enthusiastically upon arrival in the film capital. Members of the movie industry, infuriated by Welles's arrogance, hoped he would fail in his filmmaking debut; some columnists suggested in print that film moguls were overestimating his talents, and they lambasted RKO Pictures for signing Welles to a contract that granted him total control of his films.

At first it seemed as if Welles's critics were correct. His first two proposals, including an adaptation of Joseph Conrad's *Heart of Darkness* in which Welles planned to substitute the narrator with subjective

Captured by a row of mirrors in true Hollywood style, Welles and then wife Rita Hayworth cautiously embrace in the 1946 release *The Lady from Shanghai*.

camera, were both rejected by RKO. The studio finally agreed on the third offer, *Citizen Kane,* for which Welles would write, produce, direct, and act.

Welles began writing a version of the screenplay in Hollywood while his collaborator, Herman Mankiewicz, was miles away doing the same under Houseman's guidance. Explaining why the two writers worked separately, Welles told Peter Bogdanovich: "I left him on his own finally, because we'd started to waste too much time haggling. So, after mutual agreements on storyline and character, Mank went off with Houseman and did his version, while I stayed in Hollywood and wrote mine." Years later, Pauline Kael accused Welles of underplaying Mankiewicz's contribution to the script. But Welles informed Bogdanovich, "At the end, naturally, I was

the one making the picture, after all—who had to make the decisions. I used what I wanted of Mank's and, rightly or wrongly, kept what I liked of my own."

Filming *Citizen Kane* took ten weeks. The pace was a hectic one for Welles who, aside from his acting and directing duties, was constantly revising the script. "Orson was always writing and rewriting," recalled his secretary, Katherine Trosper. "I saw scenes written during production. Even while he was being made up, he'd be dictating dialogue."

Welles received assistance throughout the filming from his cinematographer, Gregg Toland, whom Welles later called "the fastest cameraman who ever lived." He revealed that Toland had volunteered to film *Citizen Kane.* "He asked me who did the lighting," Welles said. "I told him in the theater most directors have a lot to do with it . . . and he said, 'Well, fine. I want to work with somebody who never made a movie.' Now partly because of that, I somehow assumed that movie lighting was supervised by movie directors. And, like a damned fool, for the first few days of *Kane* I 'supervised' like crazy. Behind me . . . Gregg was balancing lights and telling everybody to shut their faces . . . He was quietly fixing it so as many of my notions as possible would work. Later he told me, 'That's the only way to learn anything—from somebody who doesn't know anything.'" Although Kael also accused Welles of taking credit from Toland, Welles acknowledged, "It's impossible to say how much I owe to Gregg. He was superb."

Citizen Kane was hailed as a masterpiece when first shown in 1941. It concerns newspaper tycoon Charles Foster Kane who, as a child, is sent to live with a banker. Upon reaching adulthood, Kane inherits a newspaper business and enormous wealth. For all his wealth, though, Kane never really finds what he wants most: "Love on my own terms." The story unfolds in flashback fashion, with a dying Kane speaking the word "rosebud." Then the film cuts sharply to "News on the March," a parody of the popular "March of Time" newsreels, which delivers a capsule biography of the millionaire. The

Welles portrayed bootlegger Harry Lime in the 1949 thriller *The Third Man,* a classic film noir based on a novel by Graham Greene.

story centers around a reporter's efforts to discover why Kane said "rosebud" as his dying words by discover why Kane's friends and associates. The interviews present a composite portrait of the tycoon. In the final scene, "rosebud" is revealed to be the name of Kane's childhood sled.

Although it was virtually ignored at the Academy Awards, *Citizen Kane* is now hailed as one of the greatest films ever made. Andrew Sarris called it "the work that influenced the cinema more profoundly than any American film since *Birth of a Nation*."

Welles's good fortune began to turn after his highly regarded first film. *The Magnificent Ambersons,* adapted from the novel by Booth Tarkington, traces the lives of two prestigious families at the turn of the century. The changing values of the time are reflected in George Minaver, a brash young man who scorns the coming of the automobile and plans to devote his life to yachting. Eventually, his family's fortunes depleted, George must work on a dangerous job. After his injury in an explosives accident, George realizes that times have changed and surrenders his affections to the daughter of Eugene Morgan. George has despised Mr. Morgan through most of the film because Morgan signifies the changing times (he favors use of the automobile) and because he was once romantically involved with George's mother. Welles's misfortune regarding *The Magnificent Ambersons* occurred while he was filming a documentary in Latin America. When he returned to the United States he discovered that RKO had ended his contract and had confiscated the film. Dissatisfied with its tone (Welles had intended a less "all's well" ending than George falling in love), and displeased with its length, the studio made its own ending and inserted it into the film after cutting out more than forty minutes.

The revised version of *The Magnificent Ambersons* altered Welles's intentions with the film. However, he bore little grudge against the studio and, except for the ending, he believed *The Magnificent Ambersons* to be superior to *Citizen Kane.* In the early 1960s, Welles entertained the notion of gathering the film's cast and remaking the end. Unfortunately, while he was occupied with other business, one of the film's actors died.

During World War II, Welles involved himself in a number of projects. He was the announcer for the radio program *Hello, Americans,* and an entertainer in *The Mercury Wonder Show.* He also distinguished himself as an actor in such films as *Journey Into Fear* and *Jane Eyre.* His next directing effort, *The Stranger,* was released in 1946. It details the uncovering of a fugitive Nazi posing as a professor in a New England town. After the professor, played by Welles, resorts to murder to preserve his identity, he is discovered by an FBI agent. In an exciting climax, the Nazi is spotted atop the town clock, whereupon he tries to escape only to become impaled on a rotating statue.

Because *The Stranger* was more to the audience's liking than *Citizen Kane* and *The Magnificent Ambersons,* Welles found himself in good standing with the Hollywood moguls. He was hired by Columbia as writer, producer, director, and star of *The Lady From Shanghai.* The release of that film signified Welles's final days in "movieland." When the Columbia upper–echelon viewed Welles's concoction of double–crosses and deceptions, they confessed that they couldn't follow the story. Upon seeing it, even Welles admitted having the same problem. The studio added footage, but it didn't matter: nothing, it seemed, could reduce its incoherence. Defined by James Naremore in *The Magic World of Orson Welles* as "essentially a dark, grotesquely stylized comedy, a film that takes us beyond expressionism toward absurdity," *The Lady from Shanghai* contains at least one memorable scene: a bizarre shoot–out in an abandoned funhouse involving Welles (who plays an Irish sailor duped into a fake–murder, fraud, and blackmail scheme), the woman who involved him in the scheme, and her crippled husband, a famous criminal lawyer. "For all its imperfections," noted Naremore, "it manages to retain many of the qualities of Welles's best work."

Abandons Movieland for Work in Europe

But Welles was now financially strapped. In 1946 he had sunk much of his own money into an elaborate staging of *Around the World in Eighty Days* that managed to last only seventy–five performances. Welles lost $350,000. And the poorly received *The Lady From Shanghai* had left him persona non grata in Hollywood. Welles decided to work in Europe, where he could seek independent financing and thus control his own films.

Before Welles left America he made a low–budget film of *Macbeth* for Republic Pictures. Welles made the whole film in three weeks using sets from westerns. In order to save time and money, he performed the play from beginning to end and recorded the dialogue. Then, during filming, he played the recording over the loudspeakers and had the actors mouth the dialogue they were hearing. As a result, some of the dialogue seems to come from characters who aren't moving their mouths.

Adapted by Welles from the play by William Shakespeare, 1952's *Othello* **stars director Welles as the Moor of Venice, playing opposite Suzanne Cloutier as his ill–fated wife.**

Also, Welles omitted more than one–third of the play and introduced an entirely new character, the "Holy Father." Some critics suggested that the film be called *Welles's Macbeth*, claiming that Shakespeare would scarcely have recognized his play. But Welles defended his actions by contending, "I use Shakespeare's words and characters to make motion pictures." Welles called these motion pictures "variations on [Shakespeare's] themes."

The critical standing of *Macbeth* has improved through recognition of its virtues as a character study. "It is not surprising that Welles' experiment did not wholly succeed," wrote Michael Mullin. "Nonetheless, his treatment of the play is true to the major concerns of his art, in both style and substance: his simplifications—or clarifications—of moral complexities, his obsession with a single, superhuman character . . . ., and, ultimately, his need to break with the conventional in everything he did. In his *Macbeth* Welles suggests an expressionistic alternative to the realism that makes many Shakespeare films . . . seem bad mixtures of intense poetry and prosaic filming. At its best moments, Welles' *Macbeth* leads us deep into the nightmare realms where Macbeth lives, where nothing is but what is not, where fair is foul and foul is fair."

After arriving in Europe, Welles appeared in a number of British films, including *Prince of Foxes* and *Trouble in the Glen*. At the same time, he was directing and starring in his own production of Shakespeare's *Othello*. This film proved extremely troublesome in production. Welles began making *Othello* in 1949 but quickly ran into funding difficulties. When financial stipulations forced a change in locations, Welles then had to recast certain roles. Throughout the next three years he traveled from locations in Morocco and Rome and back to Britain to fulfill acting obligations.

Welles's most noteworthy achievement as an actor during this turbulent time was as Harry Lime in Carol Reed's film, *The Third Man*. Lime lives in the sewers of Vienna while bootlegging watered–down penicillin. Believed to be dead, Lime is eventually discovered by a friend who is then faced with a moral dilemma: should he protect Lime or turn him over to the police? After visiting a hospital ward full of children crippled by Lime's diluted penicillin, the friend cooperates with the police. Lime is finally shot by him after a furious chase through the sewers. Although Welles only had one scene with dialogue, he carried it off with such aplomb that many critics consider *The Third Man* one of his most memorable film appearances.

In 1954, Welles finished *Othello* and rushed it to the Cannes Film Festival, where it won the Grand Prize. As with *Macbeth*, Welles took many liberties with

Controversial because of its interpretation of the novel by Franz Kafka, *The Trial*, starring Anthony Perkins (left), was released in 1963.

the text of *Othello*. He eliminated some scenes, condensed others, and placed most of the action outdoors. Because he was forced to substitute so many actors, Welles shot much of the film from a distance to make the replacements less noticeable. The dialogue is once again a source of irritation, however, since much of it was postsynchronized. Welles used his own voice for many of the characters.

The film is now considered to be one of the finest Shakespearean adaptations. "Full of flamboyant cinematography, composed and edited in what has been called the 'bravura style,' *Othello* transcends categories," wrote Jack J. Jorgens, "blending the deep focus 'realistic' photography hailed by Bazin with the expressionist montage of Eisenstein. What the film lacks in acting—subtle characterization and emotional range—it makes up in rich, thematically significant compositions."

Upon completion of *Othello*, Welles turned to British television to produce a pair of shows and star in a special performance of *King Lear*. He also presented his adaptation of Moby Dick at this time. All three projects were enormously successful, but Welles's good fortune did not last long. In 1956, while starring in another production of *King Lear,* Welles injured his leg and was forced to deliver the first several performances from a wheelchair. The critics denounced the show vehemently.

Shortly after *Othello,* Welles made *Mr. Arkadin,* a film about a wealthy European, Gregory Arkadin, who hires another man, Van Stratten, to investigate his past. Whenever Van Stratten discovers anyone who has knowledge about how Arkadin acquired his wealth, Arkadin has them killed. Eventually Van Stratten falls in love with Arkadin's daughter. Arkadin, thinking Van Stratten has told his daughter about his unscrupulous actions, jumps from an airplane. The film has enjoyed cult status in Europe for many years, especially among the French critics. Français Truffaut observed in *Les Films de Ma Vie:* "In this gorgeous film, once again we find Welles's inspiration behind every image, that touch of madness and of genius, his power, his brilliant heartiness, his gnarled poetry. There isn't a single scene which isn't based on a new or unusual idea."

In 1957 Welles agreed to direct *Touch of Evil* for Universal, provided he be allowed to write the screenplay. The film details a confrontation between a corrupt American cop named Quinlan, played by Welles, and a Mexican officer, Vargas. Thinking that Quinlan has planted evidence on a bombing suspect, Vargas sets a trap for him using bugging devices. Quinlan discovers the device taped to an associate whom he then kills. Before dying though, the associate also kills Quinlan. Ironically, Vargas learns at films's end that Quinlan's suspect has confessed.

Following the release of *Touch of Evil,* a film virtually ignored by American distributors and critics, Welles was unable to find financiers for his own film projects. But he was approached by foreign producers anxious to have him direct one of their projects. As Welles related: "A man came to see me and told me he believed he could find money so that I could make a film in France. He gave me a list of films and asked that I choose. And from that list of fifteen films I chose the one that, I believe, was the best: *The Trial.* Since I couldn't do a film written by myself, I chose Kafka."

The Trial proved to be another of Welles's controversial films. He altered the mood from the novel so that the film resembled a dream and he exaggerated the death–by–stabbing climax of the novel by having his protagonist destroyed by dynamite. Critics were sharply divided on the possible merits of the film. Andrew Sarris called it "the most hateful, the most repellent, and the most perverted film Welles ever made." Writing in *A Ribbon of Dreams,* Peter Cowie, however, called it "Welles' finest film since *Kane* and, far from being a travesty of Kafka's work, achieves an effect through cinematic means that conveys perfectly the terrifying vision of the modern world that marks every page of the original book." Welles justified the changes by stating: "When I make a film . . ., the critics habitually say, 'This work is not as good as the one of three years ago.' And if I look for a criticism of that one, three years back, I find an unfavourable review that says that that isn't as good as what I did three years earlier. And so it goes. I admit that experiences can be false but I believe that it is also false to want to be fashionable. If one is fashionable for the greatest part of one's career, one will produce second class work. Perhaps by chance one will arrive at being a success but this means that one is a follower and not an innovator. An artist should lead, blaze trails."

Mixed Reviews

Welles returned to Shakespeare for his next film, *Falstaff* (released in England as *Chimes at Midnight*), an adaptation of his play *Chimes at Midnight* which was, in turn, culled from various plays by Shakespeare that featured the portly character. The filming circumstances were similar to *Othello:* with Welles shooting scenes from afar to mask stand–in actors, substituting his own voice for several characters, and enduring countless delays due to sporadic funding and short–term contracts for some of the actors.

When the film was finally released in 1966, it received the most praise of any Welles film since *Citizen Kane* and *The Magnificent Ambersons.* Joseph McBride hailed it as "Welles' masterpiece, the fullest, most completely realized expression of everything he had been working toward since *Citizen Kane.*" In her *Kiss Kiss Bang Bang,* Kael referred to it as "Welles's finest Shakespearean production to date—another near masterpiece." Welles himself deemed it one of his most successful film ventures. "*The Ambersons* and *Chimes at Midnight* [*Falstaff*] represent more than anything else what I would like to do in films," he said.

Falstaff also marked a high point for Welles as an actor. In earlier films, critics often accused him of being "wooden" and "unemotional." He especially failed to impress critics with his characterizations in *Macbeth* and *Othello.* In a review of Welles's acting in the latter, Jorgens cited Eric Bentley's observation that Welles "never acts, he is photographed." And his *King Lear* performed from a wheelchair drew

In 1966's *Falstaff* (released in England as *Chimes at Midnight*) Welles starred as the title character opposite popular French actress Jeanne Moreau, scripting the film from a collection of scenes involving the portly Shakespearean creation.

jeers from many New York City critics. Other performances, however, drew raves. His portrayal in *Doctor Faustus* during the mid–1930s was considered a classic, as was his *King Lear* done in England prior to the wheelchair fiasco. He was nominated for an Academy Award for his performance in *Citizen Kane*. Perhaps his most noteworthy role, though, aside from Harry Lime in *The Third Man*, is that of Falstaff. As Kael noted, "Welles as an actor has always been betrayed by his voice. It was too much and it was inexpressive; there was no warmth in it, no sense of a life lived. It was just an instrument that he played, and it seemed to be the key to something shallow and unfelt even in his best performances, and most fraudulent when he tried to make it tender." She added, "In *Falstaff*, Welles seems to have grown into his voice; he's not too young for it anymore, and he's certainly big enough. And his emotions don't seem fake anymore; he's grown into them, too."

Welles's themes are closely related to the roles he chooses. His characters are almost always victims—men doomed by their own actions and those of others—and their actions usually lead to death. Kane, Macbeth, Othello, Arkadin, Quinlan, and Falstaff all die in their films' ends and, except for Falstaff, they are all great men who have brought about their own undoing. Even in *The Magnificent Ambersons*, in which Welles does not appear, there is a concern for the once–great. Stephen Farber, in an article on that film, inquired, "But how does one explain this obsession with rot and decay in a man of 26, who seemed to the world to be the most youthful and vigorous of artists, the 'boy genius?' The scenes of death in *The Magnificent Ambersons* seem to transfix the young Welles. Is this the famous 'self–destructiveness' of the Welles legend evidence of a morbid, irresistible attraction to decadence?" And in a review of *Falstaff*, a film made more than twenty years after *The Magnificent Ambersons*, McBride noted, "Death hangs over the entire film, and the gaity seems forced." After *Falstaff*, Welles expressed his fear of decadence. He told McBride that he was becoming more interested in forms: "That's what I'm reaching for, what I hope is true. If it is, then I'm reaching maturity as an artist. If it isn't true, then I'm in decadence, you know?"

In 1968 Welles made *The Immortal Story*, a film for French television. This story of an aging man who "directs" a film in which his wife and a young sailor make love was dismissed by most critics as a disappointment. The lighting, sound, and sets were all inferior, even when compared to those of Welles's previous low–budget films. But Charles Silver felt that the film was important as "one of the most poignantly personal works in all cinema." He explained that "most of what is important about

Welles, in the role of English Cardinal Wolsey, shares the window with Paul Scofield as Sir Thomas More in the 1966 film *A Man for All Seasons*.

The Immortal Story . . . is the extent to which the director makes the film an expression of self. . . . In no previous film . . . has Welles' conception of himself been so crucial to the essence of the work."

Welles's later films included *F for Fake* and *Filming Othello*, both documentaries. The former deals with forgeries in the art world and includes an interview with expert Clifford Irving, ironic since Irving was later revealed as a forger himself in a fraudulent "collaboration" with Howard Hughes. Another irony of *F for Fake* is that Welles actually directed little of the film—most of it was culled from a documentary by François Reichenbach. *Filming Othello* is much less complex, dealing instead with the chaotic period in which Welles made his second Shakespearean film.

Throughout the 1970s, Welles managed to sustain interest in his incomplete films, *Don Quixote* and *The Other Side of the Wind*, by screening clips from each at retrospectives honoring his accomplishments. According to Todd McCarthy, *Don Quixote* can be edited into "an allegorical tale about fascism in Spain" or a "moon trip." In fact, Welles's original ending to his adaptation of Cervantes's classic featured Quixote and Sancho Panza on the moon. Welles insisted that he scrapped that ending, though, after moon landings became reality. He also publicized his intentions to make the film into an "essay about the pollution of the old Spain." But when queried about the film's eventual shape, Welles responded: "That's really my business. . . . I am making it for myself, with my own money. I keep changing my approach, the subject takes hold of me and I grow dissatisfied with the old footage."

The Other Side of the Wind, Welles's study of decadence in the filmmaking industry, was plagued by financial difficulties. Prevented by the Internal Revenue Service from funding the film himself, Welles accepted payments from Iranian investors. However, that country became embroiled in a revolution towards the end of the decade, leaving knowledge concerning the lone print of the film (which Welles contended was 96 percent finished) considerably vague.

If you enjoy the works of Orson Welles, you might want to check out the following films:

The Big Sleep, a film noir classic starring Humphrey Bogart and Lauren Bacall, 1946.
Cradle Will Rock, directed by Tim Robbins, 1999.
Richard III, an innovative adaptation of the Shakespeare play starring Ian McKellen, 1995.
RKO 281, a docudrama about the making of *Citizen Kane,* 1999.

Welles was most visible in the 1970s as an actor in other filmmakers' works, including *It Happened One Christmas* and *The Muppet Movie.* In addition, he appeared on numerous talk shows, where he entertained with humorous anecdotes and magic tricks. He also became well-known to Americans as the celebrity spokesperson for the Paul Masson winery. While few filmmakers have suffered the same hardships as Welles, including the confiscation and remaking of *The Magnificent Ambersons* and *The Lady*

From Shanghai and financial difficulties with numerous others, he remained reluctant to complain. Referring to his first years as a filmmaker, he once commented, "I had luck as no one had; afterwards I had the worst bad luck in the history of the cinema, but that is the order of things: I had to pay for having had the best luck in the history of the cinema." He also told McBride, "I'd like to think I wouldn't have made all bad films if I could have stayed in Hollywood. But of course you don't know." Perhaps Kael put Welles's career in proper perspective when she wrote that he "might have done for American talkies what D. W. Griffith did for the silent film. But when he lost his sound and his original, verbal wit, he seemed to lose his brashness, his youth, and some of his vitality. . . . An *enfant terrible* defeated ages very fast."

Welles died from complications of cardiovascular disease, October 10, 1985, in Los Angeles. Despite its decline, Welles's career was a distinguished one, and he was honored in 1970 with a special Academy Award for "superlative artistry and versatility in the creation of motion pictures," in 1975 with the Lifetime Achievement Award of the American Film Institute, and in 1984 with the D. W. Griffith Award, the highest honor of the Directors Guild.

■ Biographical and Critical Sources

BOOKS

Bazin, Andre, *Orson Welles,* Editions Chavane, 1950, translation by Jonathan Rosenbaum published as *Orson Welles: A Critical View,* Harper, 1978.
Cowie, Peter, *A Ribbon of Dreams: The Cinema of Orson Welles,* A. S. Barnes, 1973.
France, Richard, *The Theatre of Orson Welles,* Bucknell University Press, 1977.
Gottesman, Ronald, editor, *Focus on Citizen Kane,* Prentice–Hall, 1971.
Gottesman, Ronald, editor, *Focus on Orson Welles,* Prentice–Hall, 1976.
Kael, Pauline, *Kiss Kiss Bang Bang,* Little, Brown, 1976.
Higham, Charles, *The Films of Orson Welles,* University of California Press, 1970.
Higham, Charles, *Orson Welles: The Rise and Fall of An American Genius,* St. Martin's, 1985.
Houseman, John, *Run–Through: A Memoir,* Simon & Schuster, 1972.
Leaming, Barbara, *Orson Welles: A Biography,* Viking, 1985.

MacLiammoir, Michael, *Put Money in Thy Purse,* preface by Orson Welles, Methuen, 1952.

McBride, Joseph, *Orson Welles,* Viking, 1972.

McBride, Joseph, *Orson Welles: Actor and Director,* Harcourt, 1978.

Naremore, James, *The Magic World of Orson Welles,* Oxford University Press, 1978.

Noble, Peter, *The Fabulous Orson Welles,* Hutchinson, 1956.

Sarris, Andrew, editor, *Hollywood Voices: Interviews With Film Directors,* Bobbs–Merrill, 1967.

Sarris, Andrew, *The American Cinema: Directors and Direction: 1929–1968,* Dutton, 1968.

Truffaut, François, *Les Films de Ma Vie,* Flammarion, 1975, translation by Leonard Mayhew published as *The Films of My Life,* Simon & Schuster, 1978.

Welles, Orson, and Herman Mankiewicz, *The Citizen Kane Book,* introduction by Pauline Kael, Little, Brown, 1971.

PERIODICALS

Collier's, January 29, 1938.

Film Comment, summer, 1971, November, December, 1978, March–April, 1979.

Film Quarterly, spring, 1970.

Newsweek, January 20, 1941.

New Yorker, October 8, 1938.

New York Times, September 13, 1969, August 30, 1970.

Show, October–November, 1961.

Sight and Sound, autumn, 1961.

■ **Obituaries**

PERIODICALS

Chicago Tribune, October 11, 1985, October 12, 1985.

Los Angeles Times, October 11, 1985.

New York Times, October 11, 1985, October 20, 1985.

New York Times Magazine, July 14, 1985.

Time, October 21, 1985.

Times (London), October 12, 1985.

Washington Post, October 11, 1985.*

Lois–Ann Yamanaka

■ Personal

Born September 7, 1961, in Ho'olchua, Molokai, HI; daughter of Harry (a taxidermist) and Jean (a primary school teacher); married John (a teacher); children: John. *Education:* University of Hawaii at Manoa, B.Ed., 1983, M.Ed., 1987.

■ Addresses

Home—Honolulu, HI.

■ Career

Writer. Hawaii Department of Education, language arts resource teacher and English teacher.

■ Awards, Honors

National Endowment for the Humanities grant, 1990; Pushcart Prize XVIII, 1993, for "Saturday Night at the Pahala Theatre"; Elliot Cades Award for Literature, 1993; Carnegie Foundation grant, 1994; Asian American Studies National Book Award, 1994, for *Saturday Night at the Pahala Theatre*; National Endowment for the Arts creative writing fellowship, 1994; Pushcart Prize XIX, 1994, for "Yarn Wig"; Rona Jaffe Award for Women Writers, 1996; Lannan Literary Award, 1998.

■ Writings

Saturday Night at the Pahala Theatre (verse novellas), Bamboo Ridge Press (Honolulu, HI), 1993.
Wild Meat and the Bully Burgers, Farrar, Straus (New York City), 1996.
Blu's Hanging, Farrar, Straus, 1997.
Heads by Harry, Farrar, Straus, 1999.
Name Me Nobody, Hyperion (New York City), 1999.
Father of the Four Passages, Farrar, Straus, 2000.

Author of the short works "Saturday Night at the Pahala Theatre" and "Yarn Wig."

■ Sidelights

Dubbed "one of the most original voices on the American literary scene" by Jamie James in the *Atlantic Monthly*, Lois–Ann Yamanaka explores what it means to grow up Asian American in Hawaii, looking behind the usual tourist–brochure image of those islands. She is the author of such hard–hitting, humorous, insightful, and probing fictional works as the trilogy including *Wild Meat and the Bully Burgers, Blu's Hanging,* and *Harry's Head,* as well as stand–alone novels such as the young adult title, *Name Me Nobody,* and *Father of the Four Passages.* "Yamanaka's novels possess a unique and riotous energy as they conjure Hawaii's spiky cultural brew that roils within the green embrace of a gorgeous and vulnerable land," wrote *Booklist's* Donna Seaman. Focusing on young, working–class Japanese Americans from Hawaii who struggle with such typical issues of adolescence as sexual development and peer acceptance while coming to terms with their cultural identity as the descendants of Japanese immigrant laborers, Yamanaka has validated the use of pidgin English in her stories and novels, giving voice to an entire segment of the Hawaiian population and that of the U.S. who previously had been outside the bounds of literature. "Linguistic and cultural identity are skin and flesh," Yamanaka told Valerie Takahama of the *Orange County Register.* "When you sever one from the other, you make it not OK to be who you are. You cannot discuss your grandmother, people who suck fish eye, the customs in your family. . . . That stuff is all severed once they say 'Don't speak the language.'" The language in question is known as Hawaii Creole English, otherwise called pidgin, a dialect developed by immigrants to Hawaii from China, the Philippines, Japan and other countries. And it is a language Yamanaka uses to fine effect in most of her novels and prose works.

Yamanaka grew up in Pahala, a sugar–plantation town on Hawaii's big island, one of four daughters. The use of pidgin was discouraged at her school. "My youngest sister and I were very much like our mother," Yamanaka told Takahama, describing her childhood. "Talk too much, wore strange clothes, did strange things. We always thought things that we shouldn't have been thinking or said things that we shouldn't have been saying. Little weirdos. . . . It was very painful not being able to fit in with what was middle class–class Japanese." Attending the University of Hawaii at Manoa, Yamanaka earned a master's degree in education and later enrolled in a writing class where she read African–American women writers who were writing in their dialect. "That's when I came to terms that pidgin was not an ignorant language, that I was speaking a dialect and that my feelings and thoughts were so connected to the language that in order of me to write truthfully, I needed to write in that voice," Yamanaka further commented to Takahama.

Yamanaka's debut work, *Saturday Night at the Pahala Theatre,* which Kiana Davenport described as "witty" and "street–smart" in the *Women's Review of*

In Yamanaka's debut novel, published in 1996, Japanese American Lovey Nariyoshi grows up in Hawaii knowing she could be the perfect All–American teen ... if only she could change her looks, her pidgin dialect, and her working–class family.

Books, was published in 1993. Composed of four verse novellas focusing on and narrated by working–class Hawaiian teenagers, *Saturday Night* explores such subjects as ethnic identity, sexual awakening, drug use, and abusive relationships. Marilyn Kallet, writing in the *American Book Review,* enthusiastically praised the work, commenting that Yamanaka's "characters speak in dramatic monologues as tight and fierce as anything Browning might have dreamed of, but their voices hold true to the idiomatic language of tough, vulnerable preteen girls holding private talks." Mallet further observed, "Self–hatred that can torture adolescents attacks here with even more fury as questions about cultural identity are stirred into the conflicts about personal identity." According to Lawrence Chua in the *Voice Literary Supplement,* "Saturday Night emerges from the abandoned debris of paradise, a Hawaii of carjackings and cruel girlhoods in small plantation towns. But Yamanaka is not content to merely transcribe the sexy argot of equatorial poverty. Her poetry is enabled by its elegant structure as much as its indolent diction. *Saturday Night* is not a lonely specimen of street life but a bold push at the borders of meaning and memory."

While *Saturday Night* earned Yamanaka critical praise and awards, it also brought objections from educators in Hawaii who criticized both her use of pidgin English as well as the inclusion of doses of profanity. Suddenly Yamanaka, who had been a regular speaker in schools, was "uninvited," as she put it to Takahama, and teachers were urged not to use her work in classes. This was not the last time her works would cause such a debate.

A Trio of Novels

Wild Meat and the Bully Burgers, published in 1996, is a series of connected vignettes narrated in the pidgin dialect of Lovey Nariyoshi, a Japanese–American teenager in Hilo, Hawaii, during the 1970s. A coming–of–age story that illustrates Lovey's adolescent self–consciousness and her desire for a better life while examining larger issues of class and ethnicity, *Wild Meat and the Bully Burgers* was judged "funny, poignant, scathingly authentic and often stabbingly beautiful" by Davenport in the *Women's Review of Books.* While Lauren Belfer in the *New York Times Book Review* found the colloquial text to be somewhat impenetrable, she concluded that "Yamanaka delivers moments of stinging clarity, creating haunting images as she sketches Lovey's search for a spiritual home." Calling Yamanaka's "a fresh, distinctive and authentic voice," a *Publishers Weekly* reviewer noted that although the author presents a harshly realistic view of life among her characters, she also balances her novel with images of "the bonds of love and understanding that can create poignant, epiphanic moments of reconciliation." Alice Joyce, writing in *Booklist,* dubbed this first novel "vibrant," and one that "resoundingly affirms the dialect spoken within her own family and around Hawaii." "Yamanaka's voice demands to be heard," concluded Joyce.

Yamanaka's follow–up novel, *Blu's Hanging,* was published in 1997. Focusing on the lives of the thirteen–year–old narrator, Ivah Ogata, her brother, Blu, and her younger sister, Maisie, the novel depicts their attempts to cope with the death of their mother and the physically impoverished and morally bankrupt conditions of their daily life. Narrated in pidgin, the novel won praise from a reviewer in *Publishers Weekly.* According to the critic, "In presenting issues of race, violence and neglect through the filtered lenses of these children, Yamanaka gives us a textured picture of their society and of the tensions that exist beyond the borders of a troubled family." Calling *Blu's Hanging* a "well–wrought but painful work," Anna Quan Leon in *Library Journal* noted that Ivah's decision to leave her siblings in order to attend college sends the story "deeper into a cycle of despair from which there is no escape." Lan N. Nguyen, writing in *People Weekly,* felt that *Blu's Hanging* was "a touching tale of an impoverished family's disintegration in spite of their love for each other," while Jessica Hagedorn called it a "poignant novel" in a *Harper's Bazaar* review. Hagedorn further commented, "Yamanaka's scrappy characters endure poverty, racism, and sexual and emotional abuse, but never lose their capacity for humor." This second novel also launched a storm of controversy when the Association for Asian American Studies (AAAS) first awarded it a fiction prize and then rescinded the award because of alleged racism in the book involving the use of a Filipino sexual predator whom some critics found to be insulting to that ethnic group. Yamanaka's defenders, including novelists Amy Tan and Maxine Hong Kingston, however, have found the AAAS decision to smack of censorship and to deny the writer her freedom of expression.

Critical firestorm or no, Yamanaka continued her coming–of–age trilogy with the 1999 *Heads by Harry,* set in a taxidermist shop in Hilo as the three children of Harry O. and Mary Alice find their precarious road to adulthood. The heroine is the older daughter, Toni, who often accompanies her father on his hunting expeditions. Then there is younger sister Bunny, "beautiful and manipulative," according to *Booklist's* Seaman, and their gay brother, Sheldon, a constant irritation to his macho dad. "This frank and tragicomic novel completes Yamanaka's trilogy about growing up in Hawaii," noted a reviewer for *Publishers Weekly.* Again employing pidgin to tell her tale, Yamanaka creates a "stirring novel," according to the same reviewer, who also noted that "the potency and honesty of Yamanaka's view of Hawaiian life achieves the haunting force of myth." *Library Journal's* Shirley N. Quan felt that Yamanaka's writing "is emotionally gripping and filled with harsh realism but at the same time liberally sprinkled with sensitivity and humor." Quan concluded, "Fans of her work will not be disappointed." Some critics, however, found that Yamanaka had run her course with her series of Hawaiian Bildungsroman. Writing in *Nation,* Mindy Pennybacker noted that "the last installment in Yamanaka's trilogy about coming of age in Hawaii replays many characters (with names changed) and themes from the earlier books," but also noted that *Heads by Harry* "is a lot funnier than *Blu's Hanging,*" with its rape and leprosy. Pennybacker went on to wonder, "When does a souvenir become literature

H Y P E R I O N

Name Me Nobody

"...absolutely essential reading for Yamanaka fans."
—Multicultural Review

LOIS-ANN YAMANAKA

In this 1999 novel, overweight teen Emi–Lou Kaya's whole world seems on the verge of collapse after her best friend announces she is moving.

and not a sitcom?" In partial answer to her own question, Pennybacker concluded, "Without turning the deep scrutiny on racism that it does on the taxidermist's art, this author's facile, glib prose could lose its edge to farce. Now that her trilogy is over, these are questions Yamanaka ought to ask herself for her next book."

Explores Other Fiction

As if anticipating Pennybacker's criticism, Yamanaka changed course with her next novel, presenting a young adult tale, *Name Me Nobody*. Emi–Lou Kaya feels out of it in her middle school in Hawaii, like an overweight "dorky Jap nobody," as Yamanaka writes. Since her mother deserted her,

she is being raised by her grandmother. Emi–Lou's one contact to the mainstream world of school is her best friend, Yvonne, who tries to get her into softball and cheerleading. This friend also tries to get Emi–Lou to lose weight, even going to the extreme of shoplifting diet pills in this endeavor. But when Yvonne suddenly abandons her—not for a cute guy, but for Babes, an even cuter girl—things get decidedly strange in this coming of age novel. Babes is the catcher on the Hilo Astros, a woman's softball team that Yvonne, or Von, belongs to. Emi–Lou, shedding pounds now, is desperate to get her best friend back, to make her be 'normal' again. Interesting plot twists also ensue when Emi–Lou suddenly attracts the attention of two boys on the volleyball team, one of whom has genuine feelings for Emi–Lou but caves to peer pressure, and another who only wants to use her. Finally, with a little help from her no–nonsense grandmother, Emi–Lou sees that she cannot control other people, cannot force people to become things which they are not. This includes not only Emi–Lou's neglectful mother, but also Yvonne.

Reviewing the novel in *Booklist*, Hazel Rochman commented that Yamanaka "draws a diverse community with rich vitality and no false reverence." Rochman further noted that teens "will recognize the outsider story, the vicious name–calling . . . as well as the elemental drama of friendship, betrayal, and love." A contributor to *Horn Book* observed that in "subject, structure, and style, the novel resembles the writer's notable works for adults—vignettes of young girlhood, praised for their vivid images and expert distillation of language." The same reviewer noted the "respectful homage" Yamanaka pays to Hawaii Creole English and concluded, "[Yamanaka] is a welcome new YA voice noteworthy for its complexity and richness."

With *Father of the Four Passages*, Yamanaka returned to adult fiction, this time set both in Hawaii and on the mainland, in Las Vegas. Sonia Kurisu is a streetwise young mother who struggles to raise her child, Sonny Boy, and also to come to terms with the three abortions she has had. Employing a dual timeline, both present and past, Yamanaka tells the story of Sonia's early life—the abandonment by both her parents and warring relationship with her sister, Celeste. The reader also learns of failed loves and substance abuse and Sonia's desire to make a truce with her father. She seeks a sort of absolution from all this in her role of parent, and is doubly challenged when Sony Boy shows developmental problems. "Readers devoted to Yamanaka's Hawaiian trilogy . . . will be pleased with her fourth novel, an uncompromising story of the tenaciousness of motherly love amid the chaos of drugs and dysfunction," wrote a critic for *Publishers Weekly*. Thus,

Yamanaka continued her investigations into the troubled lives of Asian Americans and into the world of dysfunctional families in Hawaii. The writer for *Publishers Weekly* further noted, "Harsher than ever in its unflinching depiction of stifled rage and twisted love, and charged with a fervid yet earthy mysticism, this is Yamanaka's most challenging work to date."

If you enjoy works by Lois–Ann Yamanaka, you might want to check out the following books:

Sherman Alexie, *The Lone Ranger and Tonto Fistfight in Heaven,* 1993.
Christina Chui, *Troublemaker and Other Saints,* 2001.
Milton Murayama, *All I Asking for Is My Body,* 1988.

Yamanaka has created controversy, drawn high praise, and built a loyal readership with her uncompromising tales—written in the language of the people—of growing up in Hawaii. She is confident that her reading of life in the islands provides a more accurate semblance than any conjured up by the media. As she concluded to Takahama, "It's a big industry, the exotification of Hawaii and its people. 'Hawaii 5-0,' 'The Hawaiians,' James Michener's *Hawaii,* making Hawaii into every white man's dream, 'Magnum PI,' 'Byrds of Paradise.' It goes on and on. It's nice now that we have ownership of our own stories."

■ Biographical and Critical Sources

PERIODICALS

American Book Review, September 11, 1995, Marilyn Kallet, review of *Saturday Night at the Pahala Theatre,* p. 11.

Atlantic Monthly, February, 1999, Jamie James, "This Hawaii Is Not for Tourists," pp. 90–92.
Booklist, December 1, 1995, Alice Joyce, review of *Wild Meat and the Bully Burgers,* p. 611; January 1, 1999, Donna Seaman, review of *Heads by Harry,* p. 835; August, 1999, Hazel Rochman, review of *Name Me Nobody,* p. 2045.
Christian Science Monitor, January 19, 1996, p. 14.
Current Biography, June, 1999, pp. 57–60.
Harper's Bazaar, April, 1997, Jessica Hagedorn, review of *Blu's Hanging,* p. 164.
Horn Book, July–August, 1999, review of *Name Me Nobody,* p. 476.
Library Journal, November 15, 1995, p. 101; March 1, 1997, Anna Quan Leon, review of *Blu's Hanging,* p. 105; February 1, 1999, Shirley N. Quan, review of *Heads by Harry,* p. 124.
Los Angeles Times, July 23, 1998, p. E1.
Ms. Magazine, July–August, 1996, p. 85.
Nation, March 1, 1999, Mindy Pennybacker, review of *Heads by Harry,* pp. 28–29.
Newsweek, August 17, 1998, p. 63.
New York Times, February 8, 1999, p. E1.
New York Times Book Review, December 31, 1995, Lauren Belfer, review of *Wild Meat and the Bully Burgers,* p. 11; May 4, 1997, p. 21; March 14, 1999, p. 23.
Orange County Register, February 28, 1996, Valerie Takahama, "Hawaiian Writer Lois–Ann Yamanaka Draws Praise, Criticism for Her Novel Using Pidgin English."
People Weekly, May 26, 1997, Lan N. Nguyen, "Hawaiian Eye–Opener: Talking with Lois–Ann Yamanaka," p. 42.
Publishers Weekly, August 21, 1995, p. 35; October 2, 1995, review of *Wild Meat and the Bully Burgers,* p. 51; February 24, 1997, review of *Blu's Hanging,* p. 62; December 21, 1998, review of *Heads by Harry,* p. 54; October 30, 2000, review of *Father of the Four Passages,* p. 45.
Review of Contemporary Fiction, Fall, 1999, p. 160.
Voice Literary Supplement, December, 1993, Lawrence Chua, review of *Saturday Night at the Pahala Theatre,* pp. 7–8.
Women's Review of Books, July, 1996, Kiana Davenport, review of *Saturday Night at the Pahala Theatre,* p. 37.*

—Sketch by J. Sydney Jones

Chelsea Quinn Yarbro

cartographer, 1963–70; program director for Sampo Productions, 1970–71, 1973; Magic Cellar, San Francisco, CA, tarot reader, 1974–79. Voice teacher and composer.

■ Personal

Born September 15, 1942, in Berkeley, CA; daughter of Clarence Elmer (a cartographer) and Lillian (an artist; maiden name, Chatfield) Erickson; married Donald Paul Simpson (an artist and inventor), November 3, 1969 (divorced, January, 1982). *Education:* Attended San Francisco State College (now University), 1960–63. *Politics:* Democrat. *Religion:* Atheist. *Hobbies and other interests:* Music, horseback riding.

■ Member

Science Fiction Writers of America (secretary, 1970–72), Mystery Writers of America, Horror Writers of America (president, 1988–89).

■ Awards, Honors

Mystery Writers of America scroll, 1973, for novelette *The Ghosts at Iron River,* and 1986, for novel *Floating Illusions;* World Fantasy Award nomination, 1979, for novel *The Palace,* 1980, for novel *Ariosto* and story "Cabin 33," and 1987, for story "Do I Dare to Eat a Peach?"

■ Addresses

Agent—Ellen Levine Literary Agency, Inc., 432 Park Ave. S., New York, NY 10016.

■ Writings

NOVELS

Time of the Fourth Horseman, Doubleday (Garden City, NY), 1976.

■ Career

Writer. Mirthmakers Children's Theatre, San Francisco, CA, theatre manager and playwright, 1961–64; counselor of mentally disturbed children, 1963–64; C. E. Erickson and Associates, Oakland, CA,

False Dawn, Doubleday (Garden City, NY), 1978.

Sins of Omission, New American Library (New York City), 1980.

Ariosto, Pocket Books (New York City), 1980.

Dead and Buried (novelization of screenplay by Ronald Shusett and Dan O'Bannon; Doubleday Book Club, Mystery Guild, and Science Fiction Book Club selection), Warner Books (New York City), 1980.

The Godforsaken, Warner Books (New York City), 1983.

Hyacinths, Doubleday (Garden City, NY), 1983.

Nomads (novelization of screenplay by John McTiernan), Bantam (New York City), 1984.

A Mortal Glamour, Bantam (New York City), 1985.

To the High Redoubt, Warner Books (New York City), 1985.

A Baroque Fable, Berkley Publishing (New York City), 1986.

Firecode, Warner Books (New York City), 1987.

Taji's Syndrome, Popular Library (New York City), 1988.

The Law in Charity, Doubleday (Garden City, NY), 1989.

Charity, Colorado, M. Evans (New York City), 1993.

Crown of Empire, Baen (New York City), 1994.

Sisters of the Night: The Angry Angel, Avon (New York City), 1998.

Magnificat, Hidden Knowledge, 2000.

"SAINT—GERMAIN" SERIES

Hotel Transylvania: A Novel of Forbidden Love (Literary Guild, Doubleday Book Club, Mystery Guild, and Science Fiction Book Club selection), St. Martin's, 1978.

The Palace: A Historical Horror Novel (Literary Guild, Doubleday Book Club, Mystery Guild, and Science Fiction Book Club selection), St. Martin's, 1979.

Blood Games: A Novel of Historical Horror (Literary Guild, Doubleday Book Club, Mystery Guild, and Science Fiction Book Club selection), St. Martin's, 1980.

Path of the Eclipse: A Historical Horror Novel (Literary Guild, Doubleday Book Club, Mystery Guild, and Science Fiction Book Club selection), St. Martin's, 1981.

Tempting Fate (Literary Guild, Doubleday Book Club, Mystery Guild, and Science Fiction Book Club selection), St. Martin's, 1982.

The Saint—Germain Chronicles (story collection; Literary Guild, Doubleday Book Club, Mystery Guild, and Science Fiction Book Club selection), Pocket Books (New York City), 1983.

Signs and Portents (story collection), Dream Press (Santa Cruz, CA), 1984.

Out of the House of Life, Tor Books (New York City), 1990.

The Spider Glass (story collection), Pulphouse (Eugene, OR), 1991.

Better in the Dark, Tor Books (New York City), 1993.

Darker Jewels, Tor Books (New York City), 1993.

Mansions of Darkness, Tor Books (New York City), 1996.

Writ in Blood, Tor Books (New York City), 1997.

Blood Roses, Tor Books (New York City), 1998.

Communion Blood, Tor Books (New York City), 1999.

Come Twilight, Tor Books (New York City), 2000.

A Feast in Exile, Tor Books (New York City), 2001.

"MYCROFT HOLMES" SERIES; WITH BILL FAWCETT, UNDER JOINT PSEUDONYM QUINN FAWCETT

The Adventures of Mycroft Holmes: Against the Brotherhood, Tor Books (New York City), 1997.

The Further Adventures of Mycroft Holmes: Embassy Row, Tor Books (New York City), 1998.

The Further Adventures of Mycroft Holmes: The Flying Scotsman, Tor Books (New York City), 1999.

The Further Adventures of Mycroft Holmes: The Scottish Ploy, Forge, 2000.

The Further Adventures of Mycroft Holmes: Glastonbury Haunts, Tor Books (New York City), 2001.

"MME. VICTOIRE VERNET" SERIES; WITH BILL FAWCETT, UNDER JOINT PSEUDONYM QUINN FAWCETT

Napoleon Must Die, Avon, 1993.

Death Wears a Crown, Avon, 1993.

"BRIDES OF DRACULA" TRILOGY

Kelene: The Angry Angels, Avon, 1998.

Fenice: Soul of an Angel, Avon, 1999.

Zhameni: The Angel of Death, Avon, 2000.

"OLIVIA" SERIES

A Flame in Byzantium, Tor Books (New York City), 1987.

Crusader's Torch, Tor Books (New York City), 1988.

A Candle for D'Artagnan, Tor Books (New York City), 1989.

"CHARLIE MOON" SERIES; UNDER NAME C. Q. YARBRO

Ogilvie, Tallant & Moon, Putnam (New York City), 1976.
Music When Sweet Voices Die, Putnam (New York City), 1979.
Poison Fruit, Jove (New York City), 1991.
Cat's Claw, Jove (New York City), 1992.

YOUNG ADULT NOVELS

Locadio's Apprentice, Harper (New York City), 1984.
Four Horses for Tishtry, Harper (New York City), 1985.
Floating Illusions, Harper (New York City), 1986.
Monet's Ghost, Atheneum, 1997.

SHORT STORY COLLECTIONS

Cautionary Tales, Doubleday, 1978, expanded edition, Warner Books (New York City), 1980.
On Saint Hubert's Thing, Cheap Street (Newcastle, VA), 1982.

NONFICTION

Messages from Michael on the Nature of the Evolution of the Human Soul, Playboy Paperbacks (Chicago, IL), 1979.
More Messages from Michael, Berkley Publishing (New York City), 1986.
Michael's People: Continuing the Michael Studies, Berkley Publishing (New York City), 1988.
Michael for the Millennium, Berkley Publishing (New York City), 1995.

OTHER

(Editor with Thomas N. Scortia, and contributor) *Two Views of Wonder,* Ballantine (New York City), 1973.
The Little Girl Dragon of Alabaster–on–Fenwick (play), first produced in San Francisco at the St. Francis Hotel, July, 1973.
CQY, Cheap Street, 1982.
(Under Pseudonym Vanessa Pryor) *A Taste of Wine,* Pocket Books, 1982.
(Under Pseudonym Terry Nelsen Bonner) *The Making of Australia #5: The Outback,* Dell (New York City), 1983.
Dark Light (second volume in "Shattered Light" series), Pocket Books, 1999.

Also author of musical works, including *Stabat Mater, Sayre Cycle, Alpha and Omega, Cinque Ritratti, Nightpiece for Chamber Orchestra, Mythologies,* and *If Wishes Were Horses.* Contributor to numerous anthologies, including *Generation,* Dell, 1972; *Infinity 3,* Lancer, 1972; *Strange Bedfellows,* Random House (New York City), 1972; *Men and Malice,* Doubleday, 1973; *The Best Detective Fiction of the Year 1974,* Dutton (New York City), 1974; *Anthropology through Science Fiction,* St. Martin's (New York City), 1974; *Vampires, Werewolves, and Other Monsters,* Curtis Publishing (Indianapolis, IN), 1974; *Women of Wonder,* Vintage (New York City), 1975; *Tomorrow Today,* Unity Press, 1975; *Beyond Time,* Pocket Books, 1976; *Faster Than Light,* Harper, 1976; *You and Science Fiction,* National Textbook Co. (Lincolnwood, IL), 1976; *Chrysalis,* Zebra Books (New York City), 1977; *Sleight of Crime,* Regnery (New York City), 1977; *Dark Sins, Dark Dreams,* Doubleday, 1978; *Cassandra Rising,* Doubleday, 1978; *Nightmares,* Playboy Paperbacks, 1979; *Chrysalis 3,* Zebra Books, 1979; *Against Tomorrow,* Fawcett (New York City), 1979; *Horrors,* Playboy Paperbacks, 1979; *Shadows 3,* Doubleday, 1980; *Shadows 4,* Doubleday, 1981; *Seventh World Fantasy Convention Program Book,* Seventh World Fantasy Convention, 1981; *Ghouls!,* Arbor House (New York City), 1982; *Shadows 5,* Doubleday, 1982; *Terrors,* Playboy Paperbacks, 1982; *Fears,* Berkley Publishing, 1983; *The Dodd, Mead Gallery of Horror,* Dodd (New York City), 1983; *Shadows 7,* Doubleday, 1984; *Shadows 8,* Doubleday, 1985; *Young Monsters,* Harper, 1985; *The World Fantasy Program Book,* World Fantasy Convention, 1985; *Masters of Darkness,* Tor Books, 1986; *The Cutting Edge,* Doubleday, 1986; *Greystone Bay,* Tor Books, 1986; *Invitation to Camelot,* Berkley Publishing, 1987; *Terrorists from Tomorrow,* Tor Books, 1988; *The Fleet II,* Berkley Publishing, 1988; *The Best of Shadows,* Doubleday, 1989; *A Whisper of Blood,* 1991. Contributor to magazines, including *If, Galaxy, Writer,* and *Washington Post Book World. Yclept Yarbro,* a fanzine, comes out in May and December of each year.

Also author of numerous novellas. The manuscripts of Yarbro are archived as the Popular Culture Library of the University of Bowling Green, Bowling Green, OH. Yarbro's works have been translated into French, Dutch, German, Italian, Spanish, and Portuguese.

■ Work in Progress

In the Face of Death, an e–book featuring Madelaine de Montalia, for Hidden Knowledge; fifteenth "Saint–Germain" novel, dealing with Charlemagne, for Tor Books.

■ Adaptations

The "Saint–Germain" series has been optioned for film adaptation.

■ Sidelights

From Paris in the eighteenth century to Saxony in the tenth, and from ancient Rome to even more ancient Greece, spanning centuries and continents, Chelsea Quinn Yarbro's character, the Comte de Saint–Germain follows a sanguine trail of vampire adventures. But Saint–Germain is not just any toothsome bloodsucker; he stands apart from the vampire genre in his desire to do good. Saint–Germain believes in justice, honor, and human dignity; he is the opposite of the usual Draculan dark force. The count is a tragic figure who, because he is immortal, suffers the agony of watching those he loves age and die. Each title in the series focuses on a particular historical period and tells of the count's romantic adventures during that time. Roland Green of *Booklist* noted that Yarbro's books are "delectable to the history buffs among fantasy readers."

In over a dozen adventures from the 1978 debut *Hotel Transylvania*, Yarbro has shuttled her unlikely and undying hero through the corridors of time, much to the delight of a legion of readers. But the series featuring Comte de Saint–Germain, or Count Saint–Germain, is only a small part of the production of this prolific writer who deals in genres including horror, romance, fantasy, gothic, science fiction, suspense, historical mysteries, and even westerns. Writing under a variety of pen names, Yarbro has crafted over sixty tales for both adults and young adults.

Yarbro's 1996 novel, from her "Saint–Germain" series, finds the vampire Count in South America where he travels under the name San Germanno while searching for refuge from those who would do him harm.

From Maps to Novels

Born in Berkeley, California in 1942, Yarbro wanted to be a writer from an early age. Attending San Francisco State College, she took a playwriting course that taught her an elemental fact about heroes: they are only as good as the villain is bad. This advice she tucked away; meanwhile she worked in children's theater in the San Francisco Bay area and then for her parent's cartography firm until that business failed in 1970. In 1969 she married and also began writing and composing music.

Yarbro was soon selling her stories to science fiction magazines and anthologies. Her first novel, *Time of the Fourth Horseman,* a suspense story, was published in 1976. Also that same year she published the first of four books in her "Charlie Moon" series, about the adventures of a Native American detective who uses shaman–like powers to aid in his investigations. Yarbro's own interest in the occult began to inform her fiction, and nonfiction alike, as in the "Michael" books she penned, which relate the wisdom of a spirit she channels through a Ouija board. She also branched out into science fiction, historical fantasy, westerns, and mysteries.

By 1972 she had hit on an idea that, little suspected by Yarbro herself, would continue to form the core of her writing endeavors for decades. In her wide reading, she came across a historical character that began to fascinate her, an eighteenth century self–

styled count who claimed descent from Francis Racoczi II, prince of Transylvania, and the widow of Charles II of Spain. A suave cosmopolitan, Count Saint–Germain dressed all in black and white, spoke thirty languages, and was rumored to have married for money in Mexico and then absconded to Constantinople with his bride's wealth. Writers of the era hypothesized that the man was a priest, a fiddler, a nobleman; some called him a Spaniard, others a Pole or Italian. The Count himself claimed occult powers and extreme longevity. It seems he may have been one of the great charlatans of his age, but Yarbro changed this charming huckster into her own creation, the Comte de Saint–Germain, with a lifetime four thousand years long. In Yarbro's version, he is now a vampire, which explains his undying nature. And Yarbro's vampire is unique: one possessed and motivated by altruism. Writing her first novel about Saint–Germain in 1972, it took Yarbro six years to find a publisher.

The "Saint–Germain" Novels

The Saint–Germain novels are undoubtedly Yarbro's best known works. Because each book is set in a different historical period, the series is as much historical fiction as horror. "Yarbro's Count Saint–Germain made his debut in *Hotel Transylvania,* a suave aristocratic figure in mid–18th–century France, actually a vampire who has forsworn the taking of human life for the sake of blood, and who has succeeded in blending into the world of the living," wrote Don D'Ammassa in the *St. James Guide to Horror, Ghost and Gothic Writers.* "Yarbro was one of the first to exploit the inherent sexuality of the vampire and anticipated Anne Rice by using historical settings and a strong romantic element."

In her first Saint–Germain novel, set in Paris in 1743, the Count is pitted against Satanists to save one Madelaine de Montalia from imminent ruin. This book sets the tone for much of the series to follow: a subtle blending of history, fiction, and a touch of horror. Subsequent novels in the series have dealt with other historical periods. *The Palace* uses Renaissance Florence and the rise of the fanatical Savonarola as a backdrop; *Blood Games* is set in the Rome of Nero, and introduces the vampire Atta Olivia Clemens, who later featured in her own series of books; *Path of the Eclipse* finds Saint–Germain in the China and Tibet of Genghis Khan, while the Russian Revolution and the end of World War I sends Saint–Germain into a Germany just witnessing the rise of the Nazis.

Madelaine de Montalia makes a reprise in *Out of the House of Life,* when she joins a French expedition to Egypt to excavate ruins at Thebes. The Count, from

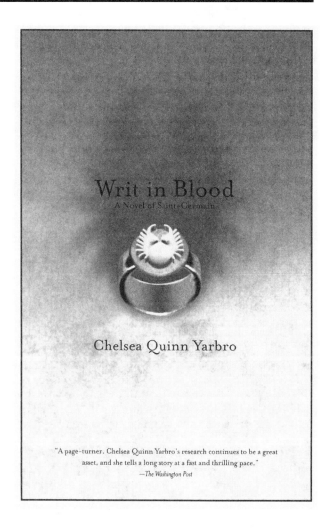

This 1997 installment in the continuing saga of Count Saint–Germain finds Yarbro's nocturnal hero balancing the demands of a new love interest with efforts at international diplomacy in an attempt to prevent World War I.

offstage, sends Madelaine letters describing his millennium spent in Egypt as slave, servant, physician, and finally high priest of Imhotep. Meanwhile, Madelaine is having her own adventures, both in dreams and real life, "besieged by lecherous misogynists and by the bribery of local officials," as Sybil Steinberg explained in a *Publishers Weekly* review. Steinberg felt, however, that Yarbro's "promising story materials flounder in a plotless narrative."

Darkness is the theme of a trio of Saint–Germain novels: *Darker Jewels,* set at the Russian court of Ivan the Terrible, *Better in the Dark,* in tenth–century Lubeck, and *Mansions of Darkness,* in which San Germanno (as he is now called) becomes the lover of the last of the Inca nobility. A reviewer for *Publishers Weekly* assessing *Darker Jewels* felt that Yarbro "brings to vivid life the dark and bloody 16th–century court of Ivan IV or, more commonly, Ivan the Terrible." Attempting to win Russian aid in its war against the Turks, the Polish king sends Saint–Germain as emissary to Ivan, hoping that the Count's alchemical skill will win over the Russian. Saint–Germain, true to form, gets entangled in the human element at the Czar's court. "Underlying this absorbing and historically accurate work is a deep melancholy," observed the reviewer for *Publishers Weekly*, "reflecting both the immortal vampire's lost past and the tortured workings of the Russian soul." *Better in the Dark* is an "entertaining but uninvolving addition to the Count Saint–Germain series," according to a contributor for *Publishers Weekly*. Shipwrecked on the coast of Saxony, the Count is found by the princess of a local castle and then held at the castle until a ransom can be paid. While there, the Count falls in love with the young princess and joins her in battle against the hordes that threaten her. The same reviewer also felt that the book was "[s]mooth and well–crafted," and "showcases Yarbro's eye for historical detail." Traveling to seventeenth–century Spanish America in *Mansions of Darkness*, the Count is, as usual, in search of a refuge from those who pursue vampires. Roland Green observed in a *Booklist* review that Yarbro's "genuine historical gifts make this one livelier reading," while a writer for *Publishers Weekly* noted that Saint–Germain's vampirism "is low key; his presence acts mainly as a catalyst for the treacheries around him," and concluded that those who enjoy "well–researched historical fiction will relish the detailed setting and the tangled plottings."

Blood forms a thematic line in three further novels in the series, *Writ in Blood, Blood Roses,* and *Communion Blood*. With the first of these, Saint–Germain shuttles back and forth between Imperial Russia, London, and Berlin in a desperate effort to save Europe from World War I. The Count's love interest in this book is the English painter, Rowena, and his enemy is the German arms dealer, Baron von Wolgast. Russian Czar Nicholas II asks Saint–Germain to visit his British uncle, Edward VII, and his cousin, Kaiser Wilhelm of Germany, to propose an arms reduction treaty. But such a mission inflames the arms dealer, von Wolgast, who is not above any dastardly ploy to keep such a treaty from happening. One such ploy includes the kidnapping of the young painter for whom Saint–Germain has formed an attachment. Assassination attempts on Saint–Germain are another; these reveal his undead nature and threaten his relationship with Rowena. A reviewer for *Publishers Weekly* felt that Yarbro's "fluent style carries this story to its satisfying con-

clusion," while Patricia Altner, in *Library Journal*, commented, "Much is happening on the European stage at this time, and Yarbro does a credible job of making sense of the often Byzantine intrigues." *Booklist*'s Green observed that Count Saint–Germain "undoubtedly founded his creator's fortunes, and Yarbro is now an expert at giving the count's fans what they expect." Green further noted, "By no means, however, is she writing the same book again and again. . . . There is enough intrigue to fill a book half again as long."

Blood Roses finds the Count living in fourteenth–century Provence, in relative peace and harmony for once. Then the Plague or Black Death reaches Europe and anybody just the tiniest bit odd comes under suspicion as a possible perpetrator of the deadly calamity. The Count is forced to flee and his lands are confiscated. Disguised as a roving jongleur, the Count soon is attached to a noble house and becomes the secret lover of its lady. "Yarbro moves her story along swiftly," observed a reviewer for *Publishers Weekly*, filling each page with the period detail for which her work has become known." The reviewer concluded that as with most of her books, Yarbro's "well–told tale is less about vampirism than about the texture of life during a pivotal moment in time long ago." Writing in *Booklist*, Green called *Blood Roses* "a briskly paced, highly readable historical fantasy," while *Library Journal*'s Jackie Cassada described the same book as a "well–researched, sumptuously written tale of honor and compassion in the midst of death and suspicion."

The Inquisition in seventeenth–century Rome forms the backdrop for *Communion Blood*, in which the Count is trying to settle the affairs of his true love, Olivia Clemens, dead thirty years before. An impostor who says he is the long–lost son of Olivia's husband claims the land that Olivia has willed to her faithful servant, Niklos. One problem: Olivia had no such husband. However, to divulge that fact would also open up all of Olivia's life to more scrutiny than either the Count or Niklos feel advisable. Saint–Germain thus has to tread his way lightly through legal, court, and papal intrigue to ensure that justice is done. "As usual," commented a contributor to *Publishers Weekly*, "Saint–Germain's vampirism forms only a minor footnote to the story." The same reviewer went on to describe the book as "a finely wrought tapestry of lives in grim historical context," and a "richly textured tale of political intrigue spiced with hot blood."

With *Come Twilight*, the thirteenth in the series, Yarbro chose a different format. Instead of focusing on one historical period, she "presents a plot that sprawls across 500 years," according to a *Publishers*

Weekly reviewer. And instead of human villains, Yarbro uses as a counterpoint to the Count's goodness, another vampire as bad as the Count is good. Traveling in seventh–century Spain, Saint–Germain saves the life of a mortally wounded woman, young Csimenae, by mingling his blood with hers. Despite the Count's instructions on living a good life, Csimenae relishes power and frightens the populace into worshipping her. Over the next five hundred years, Saint–Germain and Csimenae butt heads many times; her rise to power roughly parallels that of the Muslim conquest of Spain. The reviewer for *Publishers Weekly*, while noting that the series was thirteen books long, felt that "the unexpectedly original angle of this novel offers an infusion of fresh blood that could make it one of the series' most popular entries."

Yarbro does extensive research before writing her Saint–Germain novels, and she keeps her research materials near at hand while working. The result is fiction that vividly re–creates bygone places and events. Roger C. Schlobin, writing in *Fantasy Newsletter*, maintained that "all the [Saint–Germain] novels are thoroughly researched, and further pointed out that each of her Saint–Germain titles is "really more of a historical novel with a vampire in it than it is a pure work of fantasy or horror." The Count is, Susan M. Shwartz observed in the *Washington Post Book World*, "immensely appealing," while Schlobin commented that Saint–Germain possesses "deep love, enlightenment, physical and artistic skills, sensuality, charm, intellectuality, insight, and much more. Even his blood consumption is gracefully handled . . . and we see none of the traditional, erotic bestiality of fanged feedings." The stories focus on the count's vain efforts to assist the suffering mortals he befriends. He is, Schlobin stated, "a good person trying to make the best of awkward and frequently insoluble problems and incurable agonies."

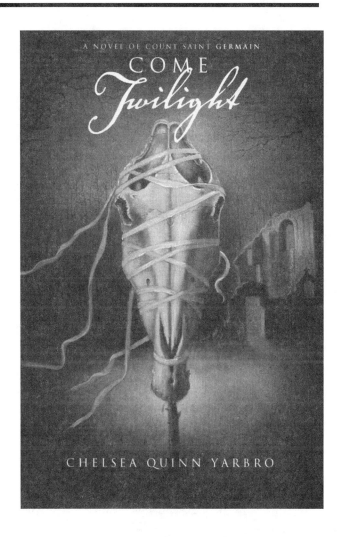

An act of kindness performed in fifteenth–century Spain results in centuries of regret in this 2000 novel, as Yarbro's immortal Count Saint–Germain is plagued by a female vampire as ruthless as he is compassionate.

Of History and Mystery

Among Yarbro's most successful non–series novels is *A Mortal Glamour*, set in a fourteenth–century French convent. The nuns of the convent are being visited at night by a sensuous and evil demon. When word of the visits reaches the church authorities, an inquisitor is sent out to investigate. His brutal interrogations transform the convent into a place of horror. "This is a grim, unsettling novel," wrote Parke Godwin in the *Washington Post*, "that mirrors the fear–filled adolescence of the western mind and the suppressed place of women within it." Paul McGuire of the *Science Fiction Review* called *A Mortal Glamour* "a well–researched novel of manners with powerful characterizations of men and women

sinking through hopeless depression into madness. . . . This is a fascinating and realistic work [by] a superb author of mature horror fiction."

Writing specifically for young adults, Yarbro has created several intriguing tales, including *Monet's Ghost*, which explores a unique talent which young Geena Howe has: she is able to think herself into a painting. This happens at first by accident with a Mondrian canvas, then two weeks later she wills it to happen when viewing a Vermeer painting. Geena's real adventures begin, however, when she enters a Monet painting of water lilies floating on a castle moat. At the castle she encounters a boy named Crispin, his aunt, a cook, and a ghost. Things get sticky, however, when suddenly the moat vanishes and Geena can no longer find her exit from the picture. "Readers with an interest in painters and paintings will especially enjoy the story," wrote Sally Estes in a *Booklist* review.

Another stand–alone title is *Magnificat,* which Yarbro published as an e–book to be downloaded from the Internet. Here Yarbro presents alternate history: in 1997, a new pope needs to be elected and the cardinals who cast their votes are affected as they decide by a mysterious power. They subsequently elect a non–Catholic, the widow of a Chinese communist who reluctantly agrees to take on the job. Pope An, as she is called, takes Jesus's teachings literally and rids the Church of any rulings that, in her opinion, Jesus never directly specified. These include, among others, the ban on divorce and women in the priesthood. Some of the cardinals love her, others hate her, and public unrest breaks out each time she speaks. "The novel," noted a reviewer for *Publishers Weekly,* "features a compelling cast of characters and a genuinely unique story, but its length [635 pages] may deter readers."

Working in collaboration with Bill Fawcett, Yarbro has also produced two historical series, one involving the brother of Sherlock Holmes, Mycroft Holmes, and the other featuring Madam Vernet set in the late eighteenth century. In the Mycroft stories, Yarbro employs the usual Homes format, though in this case the narrator is Paterson Erskine Guthrie who plays Dr. Watson to Mycroft's adventures. In the series opener, *Against the Brotherhood,* peace in the Europe of 1887 depends on a secretly negotiated treaty that needs to be delivered back to England. Mycroft puts his young secretary, Guthrie, into the thick of things infiltrating the Brotherhood, an evil group that wants to topple the legitimate governments of Europe and is after the treaty. Once again, Yarbro's talent for historical detail comes through here in "fluent prose" which "captures a wealth of detail without slowing down the proceedings," according to a writer for *Publishers Weekly.* "Mystery fans will wolf down this page–turner," wrote Whitney Scott in a *Booklist* review of the same title.

A second Mycroft Holmes adventure is served up in *Embassy Row,* dealing with secret naval negotiations with the Japanese, and in his third outing, *The Flying Scotsman,* more treaties are involved, this time one involving that signed by Sweden's Prince Oscar. Once again assassination attempts and secret cabals all need to be foiled by the resourceful Mycroft, who decides that the easiest and fastest method to get the Prince out of harm's way would be aboard the famed Flying Scotsman of the title, England's fastest train. However, once on board, the passen-

gers of the train prove an interesting if not dangerous bunch. A *Publishers Weekly* reviewer felt the "appealingly grave and perceptive Holmes and the eager Guthrie," in addition to the "effortless descriptions of the era, keep the novel right on track." John Rowen, writing in *Booklist,* praised the "evocative Victorian atmosphere" and "lively prose and brisk storytelling" evident in this third outing. And with *The Scottish Ploy* "International intrigue, phrenology, and the theater" all serve to confound Mycroft, according to a contributor in *Publishers Weekly.*

If you enjoy the works of Chelsea Quinn Yarbro, you might want to check out the following books:

Cynthia DeFelice, *The Apprenticeship of Lucas Whitaker,* 1996.
Mary Downing Hahn, *The Doll in the Garden,* 1989.
Mary Kiraly, *Mina,* 1994.
Anne Rice, *The Vampire Lestat,* 1985.

Yarbro maintains her prolific publishing schedule—three novels per year, as well as short stories and essays—by dint of hard work. She is at her desk six days a week and six hours a day. She still finds time, however, for her favorite hobby, horseback riding. She is also a composer, and has studied seven different instruments as well as voice and music theory. But writing continues to be her main passion. Yarbro once stated: "I've written since I've known how to read. I'm not trying to do anything other than entertain my reader. 'Entertain' is not a dirty word, by the way. Much of my work is quite grim, but that should not be taken as an indication that I am a grim person. Please do not confuse me with my work; it is not me and I am not it. I dislike being categorized as anything beyond writer. For me, clarity of writing is essential. The reader should not be aware of how the words are on the page, or with what pyrotechnics the language is thrown around. Language is not an end in itself, but a means, a channel that a writer must, by the nature of the art, use. Beyond that, the words should not get in the way of the reader building the story in his or her head."

■ Biographical and Critical Sources

BOOKS

D'Ammassa, Don, "Yarbro, Chelsea Quinn," *St. James Guide to Horror, Ghost and Gothic Writers,* St. James (Detroit, MI), 1998, pp. 656–657.

Magill, Frank N., editor, *Survey of Modern Fantasy Literature*, Volume III, Salem Press (Englewood Cliffs, NJ), 1983.

PERIODICALS

Analog, October, 1987.

Booklist, July, 1983; August 15, 1996, Roland Green, review of *Mansions of Darkness*, p. 1884; June 1, 1997, Sally Estes, review of *Monet's Ghost*, p. 1687; July, 1997, Roland Green, review of *Writ in Blood*, p. 1801; September 15, 1997, Whitney Scott, review of *Against the Brotherhood*, p. 213; September 15, 1998, Roland Green, review of *Blood Roses*, p. 206; October 1, 1999, Roland Green, review of *Communion Blood*, p. 347; October 15, 1999, John Rowen, review of *The Flying Scotsman*, p. 421.

Christian Science Monitor, June 5, 1987.

Fantasy Newsletter, December, 1981; October, 1982, Roger C. Schlobin, review of *Tempting Fate*; August, 1983; August, 1984.

Fantasy Review, April, 1985; April, 1986; April, 1987.

Foundation, spring, 1985.

Janus, autumn, 1979.

Kirkus Reviews, February 1, 1993; June 15, 1996; May 1, 1997.

Library Journal, November 15, 1990, p. 94; May 15, 1993, p. 98; February 15, 1994, p. 186; July, 1997, Patricia Altner, review of *Writ in Blood*, p. 128; September 15, 1998, Jackie Cassada, review of *Blood Roses*, p. 117.

Locus, November, 1993.

Magazine of Fantasy and Science Fiction, January, 1979.

Publishers Weekly, October 26, 1990, Sybil Steinberg, review of *Out of the House of Life*, p. 55; August 23, 1991, p. 44; March 1, 1993, review of *Darker Jewels*, p. 44; July 5, 1993, p. 67; November 29, 1993, review of *Better in the Dark*, p. 58; November 28, 1994, p. 48; July 22, 1996, review of *Mansions of Darkness*, p. 230; June 16, 1997, review of *Writ in Blood*, p. 48; August 11, 1997, review of *Against the Brotherhood*, p. 389; August 3, 1998, p. 78; September 21, 1998, review of *Blood Roses*, p. 79; September 13, 1999, review of *The Flying Scotsman*, p. 64; September 20, 1999, review of *Communion Blood*, p. 79; May 22, 2000, review of *Magnificat*, pp. 46, 48; October 2, 2000, review of *Come Twilight*, p. 63; November 27, 2000, review of *The Scottish Ploy*, p. 58.

School Library Journal, November, 1984, pp. 140–141; November, 1986, p. 110; March, 2001, Christine C. Menefee, review of *Come Twilight*, p. 282.

Science Fiction Review, January–February, 1979; spring, 1982; fall, 1983; summer, 1985, Paul McGuire, review of *A Mortal Glamour*.

Voice of Youth Advocates, February, 2001, John Charles, review of *Come Twilight*, pp. 437–438.

Washington Post, February 8, 1985, Parke Godwin, review of *A Mortal Glamour*.

Washington Post Book World, March 28, 1982, Susan M. Shwartz, review of *Tempting Fate*.

Wilson Library Bulletin, October, 1993, pp. 124–125.

ONLINE

Amazon.com, "Amazon.com Talks to Chelsea Quinn Yarbro," http://www.amazon.com/ (April 30, 2001).

Amazon.com, "From Dracula to Saint–Germain," http://www.amazon.com/ (April 30, 2001).

The Saint–Germain Tribute Page, http://www.velvetspyder.f2s.com (April 23, 2001).

Yarbro Web site, http://www.chelseaquinnyarbro.com (March 26, 2001).*

—Sketch by J. Sydney Jones

Author/Artist Index

The following index gives the number of the volume in
which an author/artist's biographical sketch appears: